T. O. 1F-86E-1

North American F-86 Sabre
Pilot's Flight Operating Instructions

This manual is sold for historic research purposes only, as an entertainment. It is not intended to be used as part of an actual flight training program. No book can substitute for flight training by an authorized instructor. The licensing of pilots is overseen by organizations and authorities such as the FAA and CAA. Operating an aircraft without the proper license is a federal crime.

©2007-2010 Periscope Film LLC
All Rights Reserved
ISBN #978-1-935700-39-5
www.PeriscopeFilm.com

26 NOVEMBER 1956

T.O. 1F-86E-1

FLIGHT HANDBOOK
USAF SERIES
F-86E
AIRCRAFT

Commanders are responsible for bringing this handbook to the attention of all personnel cleared for operation of affected aircraft.

Published under authority of the Secretary of the Air Force.

This reissue replaces T. O. 1F-86E-1 dated 5 November 1954, and Safety of Flight Supplements -1R through -1CP. See Weekly Index, T. O. 0-1-1A, for current status of Safety of Flight Supplements.

26 NOVEMBER 1956

T. O. 1F-86E-1

Reproduction for non-military use of the information or illustrations contained in this publication is not permitted without specific approval of the issuing service (BuAer or USAF). The policy for use of Classified Publications is established for the Air Force in AFR 205-1 and for the Navy in Navy Regulations, Article 1509.

LIST OF EFFECTIVE PAGES

INSERT LATEST REVISED PAGES. DESTROY SUPERSEDED PAGES.

NOTE: The portion of the text affected by the current revision is indicated by a vertical line in the outer margin of the page.

TOTAL NUMBER OF PAGES IN THIS PUBLICATION IS 249 CONSISTING OF THE FOLLOWING:

Page No.	Issue
Title	Original
A	Original
i thru iv	Original
1-1 thru 1-56	Original
2-1 thru 2-34	Original
3-1 thru 3-24	Original
4-1 thru 4-36	Original
5-1 thru 5-8	Original
6-1 thru 6-16	Original
7-1 thru 7-8	Original
9-1 thru 9-20	Original
A-1 thru A-34	Original
X-1 thru X-7	Original

This manual is sold for historic research purposes only, as an entertainment. It is not intended to be used as part of an actual flight training program. No book can substitute for flight training by an authorized instructor. The licensing of pilots is overseen by organizations and authorities such as the FAA and CAA. Operating an aircraft without the proper license is a federal crime.

*The asterisk indicates pages revised, added or deleted by the current revision.

ADDITIONAL COPIES OF THIS PUBLICATION MAY BE OBTAINED AS FOLLOWS:

USAF ACTIVITIES.—In accordance with Technical Order No. 00-5-2.
NAVY ACTIVITIES.—Submit request to nearest supply point listed below, using form NavAer-140; NASD, Philadelphia, Pa.; NAS, Alameda, Calif.; NAS, Jacksonville, Fla.; NAS, Norfolk, Va.; NAS, San Diego, Calif.; NAS, Seattle, Wash.; ASD, NSC, Guam.
For listing of available material and details of distribution, see Naval Aeronautics Publications Index NavAer 00-500.

table of contents

Section I	DESCRIPTION	1-1
Section II	NORMAL PROCEDURES	2-1
Section III	EMERGENCY PROCEDURES	3-1
Section IV	Description and Operation of AUXILIARY EQUIPMENT	4-1
Section V	OPERATING LIMITATIONS	5-1
Section VI	FLIGHT CHARACTERISTICS	6-1
Section VII	SYSTEMS OPERATION	7-1
Section VIII	CREW DUTIES	(Not Applicable)
Section IX	ALL-WEATHER OPERATION	9-1
Appendix I	PERFORMANCE DATA	A-1
Alphabetical Index		X-1

"Major... I think we'd better issue these boys their PERSONAL copies of the Flight Handbook."

The intent of Air Force Regulation 5-13, dated 11 August 1953, is to entitle each pilot (except those attached to an administrative base) to his own copy of the Flight Handbook for his airplane. However, since the Flight Handbook is Government property and subject to specific controls, distribution responsibility rests with the Base Commander.

Scope. This handbook contains all the information necessary for safe and efficient operation of the F-86E Airplane. These instructions do not teach basic flight principles, but are designed to provide you with a general knowledge of the airplane, its flight characteristics and specific normal and emergency operating procedures. Your flying experience is recognized and elementary instructions have been avoided.

Sound Judgment. The instructions in this handbook are designed to provide for the needs of a pilot inexperienced in the operation of this airplane. This book provides the best possible operating instructions under most circumstances, but it is a poor substitute for sound judgment. Multiple emergencies, adverse weather, terrain, etc, may require modification of the procedures contained herein.

Permissible Operations. The Flight Handbook takes a "positive approach" and normally tells you only what you can do. Any unusual operation or configuration (such as asymmetrical loading) is prohibited unless specifically covered in the Flight Handbook. Clearance must be obtained from ARDC before any questionable operation is attempted which is not specifically covered in the Flight Handbook.

Standardization. Once you have learned to use one Flight Handbook, you will know how to use them all—closely guarded standardization assures that the scope and arrangement of all Flight Handbooks is identical.

Arrangement. The handbook has been divided into 10 sections, each with its own table of contents. The objective of this subdivision is to make it easy to read the book straight through when it is first received and thereafter to use it as a reference manual. The independence of these sections also makes it possible for the user to rearrange the book to satisfy his personal taste and requirements. The first three sections cover the minimum information required to safely get the airplane into the air and back down again. Before flying any new airplane, these three sections must be read thoroughly and fully understood. Section IV covers all equipment not essential to flight, but which permits the airplane to perform special functions. Sections V and VI are obvious. Section VII covers lengthy discussions on any technique or theory of operation which may be applicable to the particular aircraft in question. The experienced pilot will probably not need to read this section, but he should check it for any possible new information. The contents of the remaining sections are fairly obvious.

Your Responsibility. These Flight Handbooks are constantly maintained current through an extremely active revision program. Frequent conferences with operating personnel and constant review of UR's, accident reports, flight test reports, etc, assure inclusion of the latest data in these handbooks. In this regard, it is essential that you do your part! If you find anything you don't like about the book, let us know right away. We cannot correct an error that is unknown to us.

Binders and Tabs. Flexible binders and loose leaf tabs have been provided to hold your personal copy of the Flight Handbook. These good-looking, simulated-leather binders will make it much easier for you to revise your handbook, as well as to keep it in good shape. These tabs and binders are secured through your local contracting officer.

How to Get Copies. If you want to be sure of getting your handbooks on time, order them before you need them. Early ordering will assure that enough copies are printed to cover your requirements. Technical Order 0-5-2 explains how to order Flight Handbooks so that you automatically will get all revisions, reissues, and Safety of Flight Supplements. Basically, all you have to do is order the required quantities in the Publication Requirements Table (T. O. 0-3-1). Talk to your base supply officer—it is his job to fulfill your Technical Order requests. Establish some system that will rapidly get the books and Safety of Flight Supplements to pilots once the books are received on the base.

Safety of Flight Supplements. Safety of Flight Supplements are used to get information to you in a hurry. Safety of Flight Supplements use the same number as your Flight Handbook, except for the addition of a suffix letter. Supplements covering loss of life will get to you in 48 hours; those concerning serious damage to equipment will make it in 10 days. You can determine the status of Safety of Flight Supplements by referring to the Index of Technical Publications (T. O. 0-1-1) and the Weekly Supplemental Index (T. O. 0-1-1A). The title page of the Flight Handbook and title block of each Safety of Flight Supplement should also be checked to determine the effect that these publications may have on existing Safety of Flight Supplements. If you have ordered your Flight Handbook on the Publications Requirements Table, you automatically will receive all supplements pertaining to your airplane. Technical Order 0-5-1 covers some additional information regarding these supplements.

Warnings, Cautions, and Notes. For your information, the following definitions apply to the warnings, cautions, and notes found throughout the handbook.

Operating procedures, practices, etc, which will result in personal injury or loss of life if not carefully followed.

Operating procedures, practices, etc, which if not strictly observed will result in damage to equipment.

Note	An operating procedure, condition, etc, which is essential to emphasize.

Maintenance Handbooks. One more thing. If you desire more detailed information on the various airplane systems and components than that provided within the scope of the Flight Handbook, refer to the Maintenance Handbook (T. O. 1F-86E-2) for your airplane.

Comments and Questions. Comments and questions regarding any phase of the Flight Handbook program are invited and should be addressed to Detachment #1, HQ Air Research and Development Command, Wright-Patterson AF Base, Ohio, Attn: RDZSTH.

T. O. 1F-86E-1

F-86E
SABRE

SECTION I

DESCRIPTION

TABLE OF CONTENTS

	PAGE
Airplane	1-1
Engine	1-2
Oil System	1-19
Airplane Fuel System	1-19
Electrical Power Supply System	1-21
Hydraulic Power Supply Systems	1-26
Flight Control System	1-27
Wing Flap System	1-36
Wing Leading Edge	1-37
Speed Brake System	1-37
Landing Gear System	1-37
Nose Wheel Steering System	1-40
Wheel Brake System	1-41
Instruments	1-41
Emergency Equipment	1-43
Canopy	1-43
Ejection Seat	1-46
Auxiliary Equipment	1-56

AIRPLANE.

The North American F-86E Sabre, typified by its swept-back wing and empennage, is powered by a General Electric axial-flow, turbojet engine. Development features include combining the action of the elevator and horizontal stabilizer into one unit, known as the controllable "flying tail;" a hydraulically actuated, irreversible control system for flight control surface operation; an artificial feel system incorporated in the flight control system to provide normal stick forces throughout all flight conditions; leading edge wing slats to reduce stalling speeds; and fuselage speed brakes to provide effective and quick deceleration. Some airplanes have a fixed-contour extended leading edge on the wings, to provide an increase in performance and to improve maneuverability, particularly at high altitudes. This single-place, high-altitude fighter, designed primarily for operation in the sonic and subsonic speed regions, is also effective in ground support or attacking naval objectives with gunfire, bombs, rockets, or chemicals.

AIRPLANE DIMENSIONS.

Over-all dimensions of the airplane (airplane on landing gear at normal weight and with tires inflated and gear struts extended as specified) are as follows:

Wing span	37.1 feet
Length	37.5 feet
Height	14.7 feet

AIRPLANE GROSS WEIGHT.

The approximate take-off gross weight of the airplane, including full fuel load (JP-4), 300 rounds of ammunition per gun, and the pilot (230 pounds), is as follows:

Clean airplane	14,850 pounds
With two 120 US gallon drop tanks	16,625 pounds
F-86E-15 Airplanes with two 200 US gallon drop tanks	17,800 pounds

1-1

ARMAMENT.

The airplane is armed with six .50-caliber machine guns. The addition of removable racks permits the airplane to carry bombs, rockets, or chemical tanks on the lower surface of the wing. (Refer to "Armament Equipment," Section IV, for detailed information.)

ENGINE.

The engine (figure 1-10) is a General Electric axial-flow, turbojet unit, Model J47-GE-13, having a rated sea-level static thrust of approximately 5200 pounds. During engine operation, air enters the intake duct in the nose of the airplane, is routed through an internal duct (which runs under the cockpit), and is passed through to an axial-flow compressor where the air is compressed progressively in 12 stages. The compressed air then flows to eight cannular combustion chambers, where atomized fuel is injected and combustion occurs continuously once ignition is obtained during starting. From the combustion chambers, the hot exhaust gases pass through a single-stage turbine and on out the tail pipe in gradually expanding form to provide the high-velocity jet and reaction thrust. The turbine, which is rotated by the exhaust gases passing through it, is directly connected to, and drives, the compressor and engine accessory section. A bulkhead, which serves as a fire wall, separates the engine compartment from the cockpit and the forward fuel tank. The engine compartment is divided into two compartments by a fire wall; the forward compartment contains the relatively cool compressor and accessory sections of the engine, and the aft compartment contains the engine combustion chamber and turbine section and the tail pipe.

ENGINE AIR INTAKE SCREENS.

Fixed air intake screens are installed on the engines of airplanes changed by T. O. 2J-J47-537, to prevent foreign objects from entering the engine.

WARNING

Engines with air intake screens are more susceptible to icing than engines without intake screens.

ENGINE FUEL CONTROL SYSTEMS.

Fuel flow to the engine is regulated by a fuel system consisting of a main system and an emergency system.

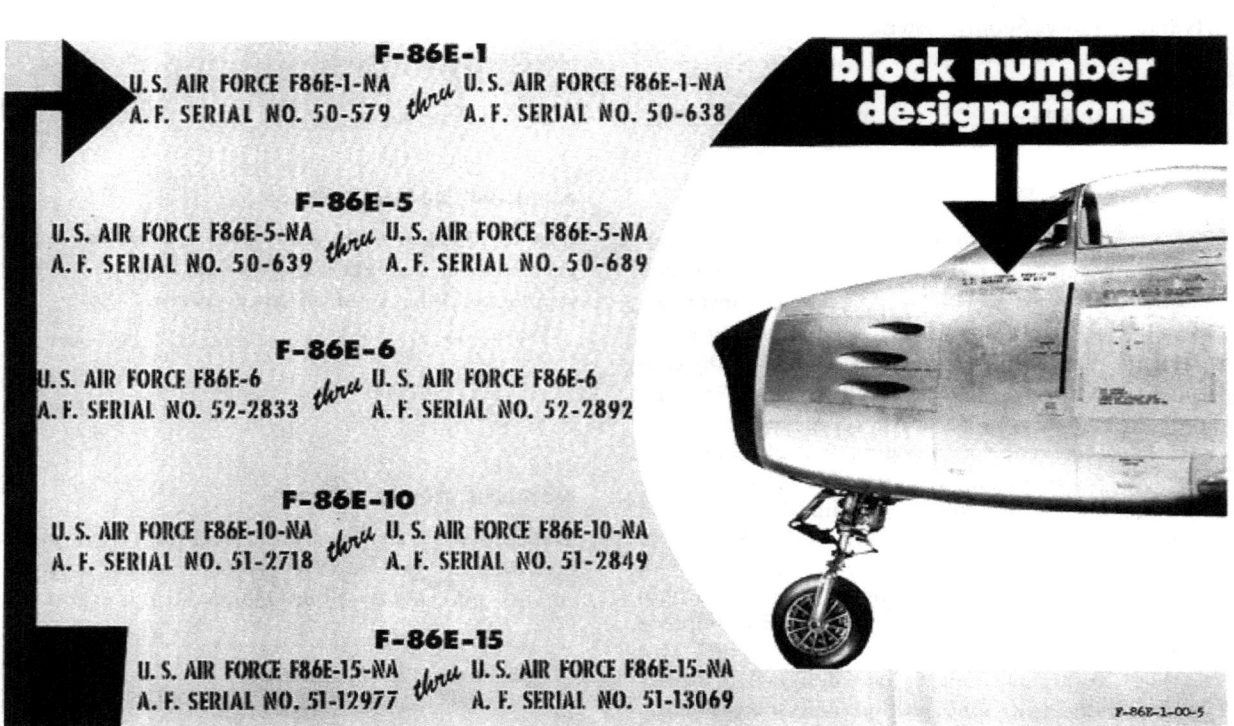

Figure 1-1

main differences table

F-86 SERIES

ITEM	A (F-86A)	D and K (F-86D and F-86K)	E (F-86E)	F (F-86F)	H (F-86H)
Engine	J47-GE-7 or -13	J47-GE-17, -17B, or -33 with afterburner	J47-GE-13	J47-GE-27	J73-GE-3 Series
Engine Control	Mechanical	Electronic	Mechanical	Mechanical	Hydromechanical
Automatic Pilot	No	Yes	No	No	No
Horizontal Tail	Conventional	Single, controllable surface	Controllable stabilizer and elevator	Controllable stabilizer and elevator	Controllable stabilizer and elevator
Aileron & Horizontal Tail Control	Conventional and hydraulic boost	Full-power hydraulic irreversible control	Full-power hydraulic irreversible control	Full-power hydraulic irreversible control	Full-power hydraulic irreversible control
Aileron & Horizontal Tail Artificial Feel System	No	Yes	Yes	Yes	Yes
Armament	Machine guns, bombs, rockets, or chemical tanks	F-86D: Rockets in fuselage package F-86K: 20mm guns	Machine guns, bombs, rockets, or chemical tanks	Machine guns, bombs, rockets, or special external store	Machine guns, bombs, rockets, or special external store
Windshield	Curved or "V"	Flat	"V" or flat	Flat	Flat
Canopy Ejection Control	Handle on pedestal Right handgrip on seat	Right handgrip on seat Either handgrip (some airplanes)	Right handgrip on seat Either handgrip (some airplanes)	Right handgrip on seat Either handgrip (some airplanes)	Either handgrip on seat
Canopy	Sliding	Clamshell	Sliding	Sliding	Clamshell
Oxygen Regulator	A-14	D-1, D-2, or D-2A	A-14 or D-2	D-1, D-2, or D-2A	D-2

Figure 1-2

Section I   T. O. 1F-86E-1

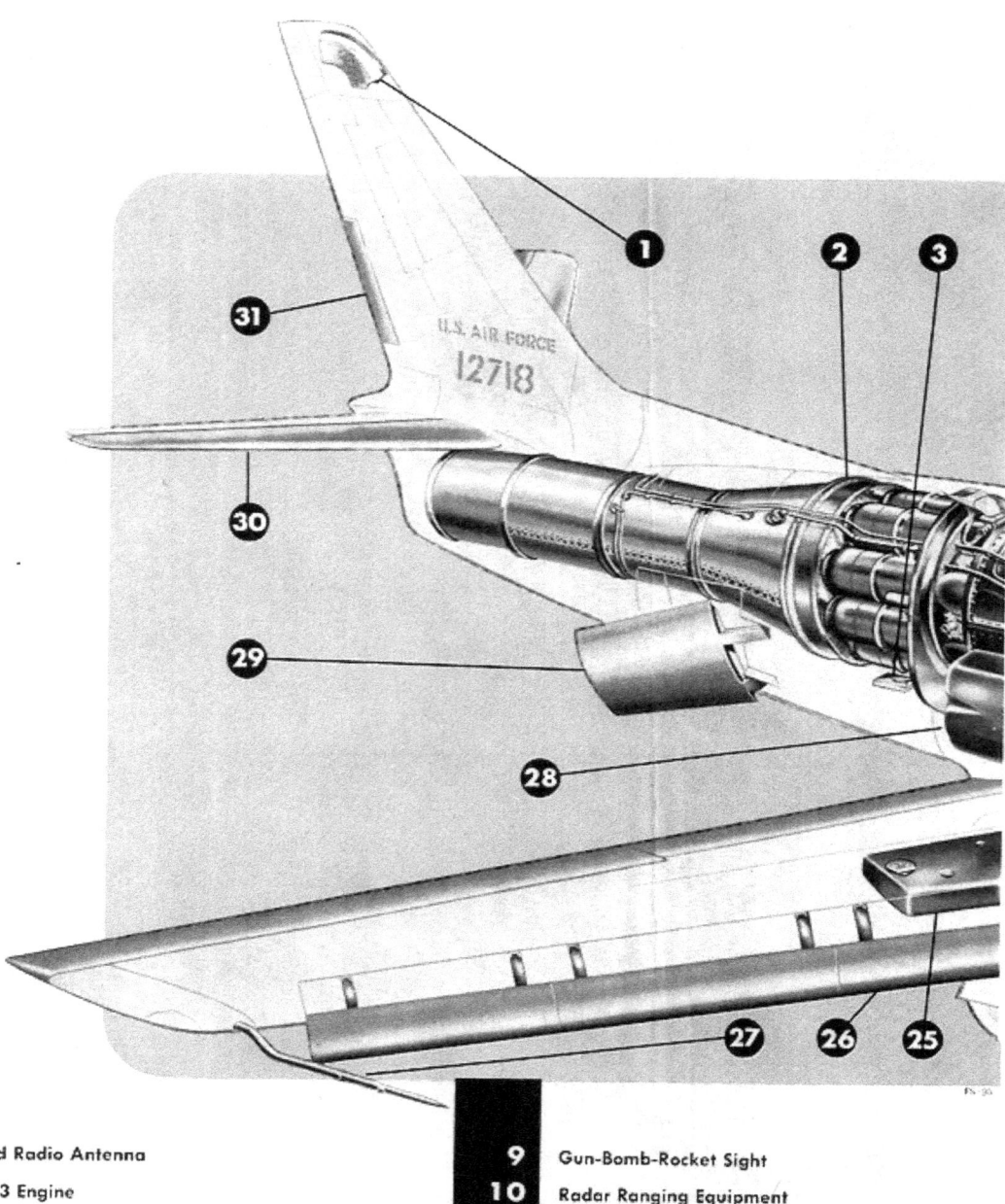

1	Command Radio Antenna		9	Gun-Bomb-Rocket Sight
2	J47-GE-13 Engine		10	Radar Ranging Equipment
3	Data Case		11	Battery
4	Radio Compass Sense Antenna		12	Radar Antenna
5	Radio Compass Loop Antenna		13	Gun Camera
6	Directional Indicator Transmitter		14	Retractable Landing and Taxi Light
7	Ejection Seat		15	Retractable Landing Light
8	Rear-vision Mirror		16	Oxygen Cylinders

Figure 1-3

general arrangement

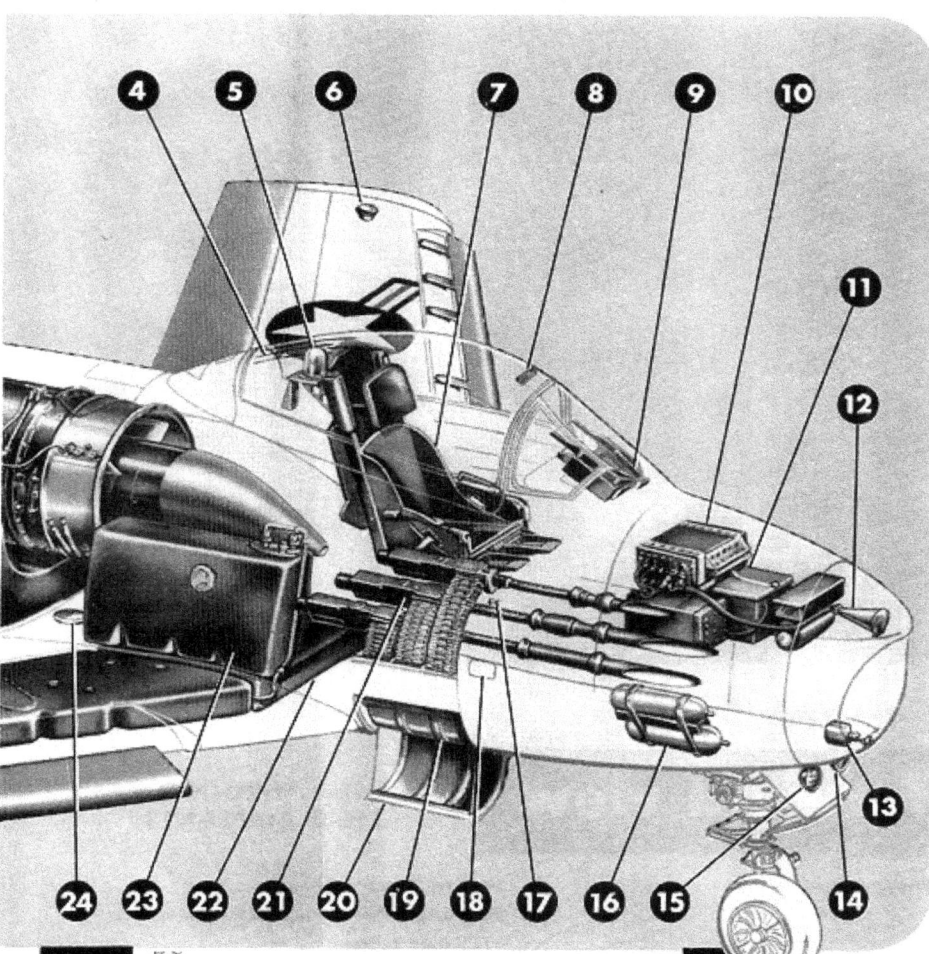

17	Canopy External Control Buttons
18	Kick Step
19	Ammunition Compartment
20	Ammunition Compartment Access Door
21	Gun Compartment
22	Forward Fuselage Fuel Tank (Lower Cell)
23	Forward Fuselage Fuel Tank (Upper Cell)
24	IFF Antenna
25	Outer Wing Fuel Tank
26	Automatic Wing Slats (Some Airplanes)
27	Pitot-Static Head
28	Aft Fuselage Fuel Tank
29	Speed Brake
30	Controllable Horizontal Tail (Elevator and Controllable Stabilizer)
31	Rudder Trim Tab

Section I T. O. 1F-86E-1

cockpit forward view

F-86E-1 THROUGH F-86E-6 AIRPLANES

1. Fuel Filter Icing Warning Light
2. A-1CM Sight
3. Accelerometer
4. Instrument Power Warning Light*
5. Hydraulic Pressure Gage and Selector Switch
6. Alternate-on Warning Light (Flight Control Alternate Hydraulic System)
7. Oil Pressure Gage
8. Take-off (Trim) Position Indicator Light
9. Exhaust Temperature Gage
10. Fuel Pressure Gage*
11. Fire-warning Lights
12. Stand-by Compass
13. Fire-warning Light Test Button
14. Stand-by Compass Light Switch
15. Engine Tachometer
16. Attitude Indicator
17. Fuel Flowmeter
18. Cabin Pressure Altimeter*
19. Fuel Quantity Gage
20. Vertical Velocity Indicator (Rate-of-Climb)
21. Center Pedestal
22. Turn-and-Slip Indicator
23. Clock
24. Loadmeter
25. Generator Warning Light
26. Voltmeter
27. Altimeter
28. Machmeter
29. Directional Indicator (Slaved)
30. Landing Gear Emergency-up Button
31. Radio Compass
32. Airspeed Indicator
33. Fuel Filter Deicer Button
34. Emergency Fuel Switch*

*Some airplanes. (Refer to applicable text.)

F-86E-1-00-16C

Figure 1-4

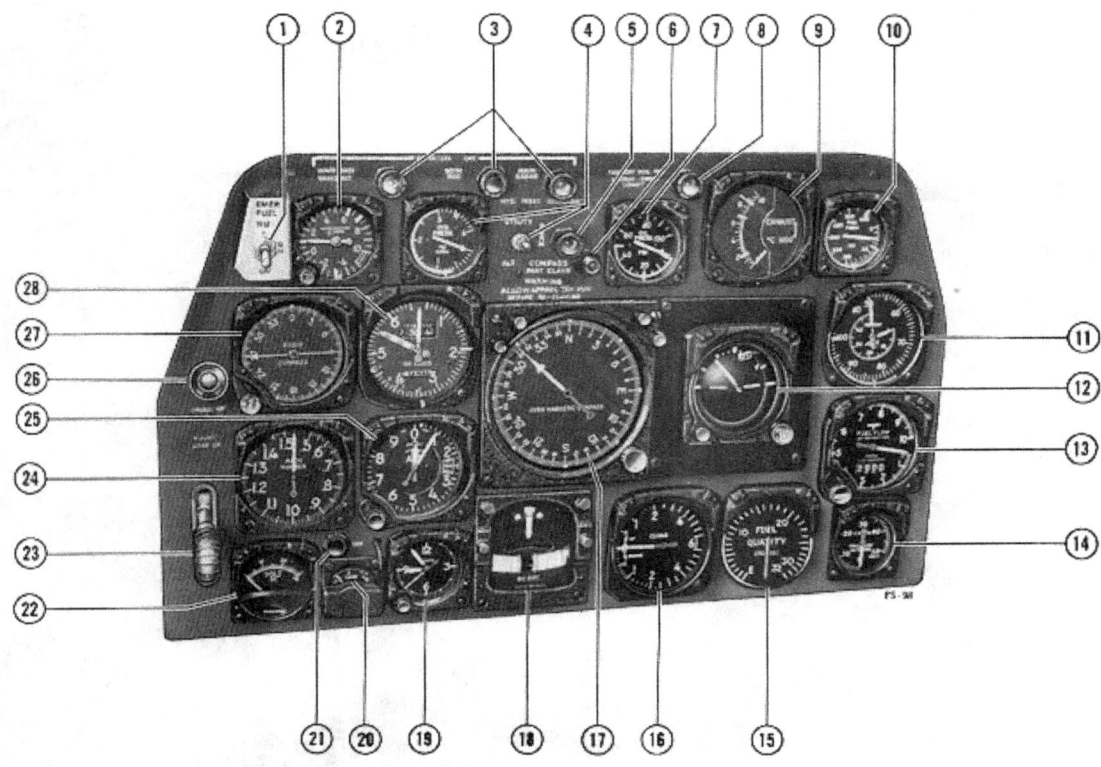

F-86E-10 AND F-86E-15 AIRPLANES

instrument panel

1. Emergency Fuel Switch*
2. Accelerometer
3. Inverter Warning Lights
4. Hydraulic Pressure Gage and Selector Switch
5. Alternate-on Warning Light
   (Flight Control Alternate Hydraulic System)
6. Directional Indicator (Slaved) Fast Slaving Switch*
7. Oil Pressure Gage
8. Take-off (Trim) Position Indicator Light
9. Exhaust Temperature Gage
10. Fuel Pressure Gage
11. Tachometer
12. Attitude Indicator
13. Fuel Flowmeter and Totalizer
14. Cabin Pressure Altimeter

15. Fuel Quantity Gage
16. Vertical Velocity Indicator (Rate-of-Climb)
17. Directional Indicator (Slaved)
18. Turn-and-Slip Indicator
19. Clock
20. Loadmeter
21. Generator Warning Light
22. Voltmeter
23. Landing Gear Handle
24. Machmeter
25. Altimeter
26. Landing Gear Emergency-up Button
27. Radio Compass
28. Airspeed Indicator

*Some airplanes. (Refer to applicable text.)

Figure 1-5

Section I T. O. 1F-86E-1

cockpit-left side

F-86E-1, F-86E-5, AND F-86E-6 AIRPLANES

1. Circuit-breaker Panel
2. Ammunition Compartment Heat Emergency Shutoff Handle
3. Ammunition Compartment Overheat Warning Light
4. Console Floodlight
5. Side Air Outlet
6. Windshield Anti-icing Lever
7. Floodlight Control Rheostat
8. Rocket Intervalometer
9. Canopy Auxiliary Defrost Lever
10. Speed Brake Emergency Lever
11. Emergency Fuel Switch*
12. Instrument Panel Floodlight
13. Longitudinal Alternate Trim Switch
14. Left Forward Console
15. Parking Brake Handle
16. Canopy Switch
17. Landing Gear Emergency-up Button
18. Landing Gear Handle
19. Emergency Jettison Handle
20. Type D-2 Oxygen Regulator Panel
21. Throttle Friction Wheel
22. Wing Flap Lever
23. Throttle
24. Flight Control Switch
25. Rudder Trim Switch
26. Lateral Alternate Trim Switch
27. Cockpit Air Temperature Control Rheostat
28. Cabin Pressure Control Lever
29. Air Outlet Selector Lever
30. Cockpit Air Temperature Control Switch
31. Drop Tank Pressure Shutoff Valve
32. Anti-G Suit Pressure-regulating Valve

*Some airplanes. (Refer to applicable text.)

Figure 1-6

T. O. 1F-86E-1

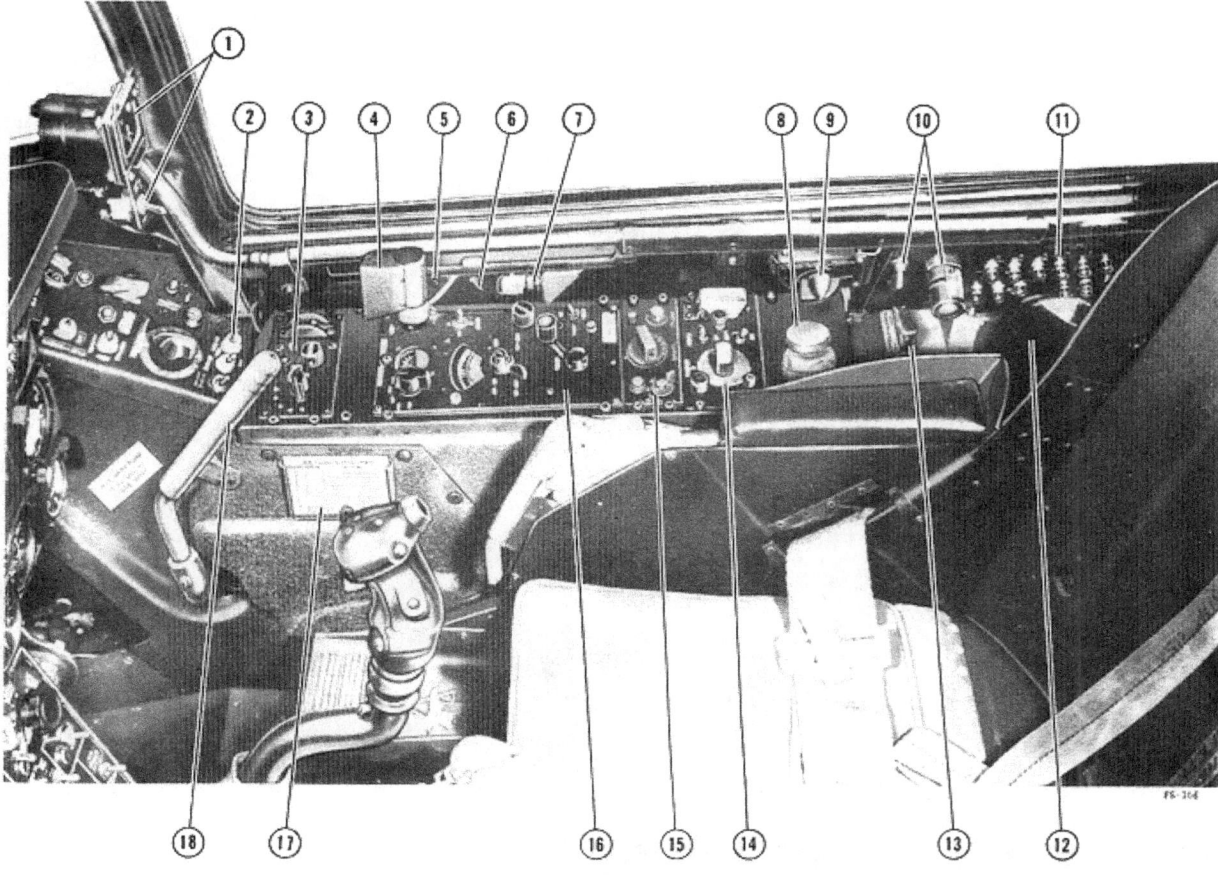

F-86E-1 THROUGH F-86E-6 AIRPLANES

cockpit-right side

1. Stand-by Compass and Compass Light Switch
2. Right Forward Console
3. VHF Command Radio Control Panel*
4. Instrument Panel Floodlight
5. Side Air Outlet
6. Air Outlet Control Valve
7. Console Floodlight
8. Gun Sight Test Plug†
9. Instrument Ring Light Rheostat
10. Extension Light and Light Switch
11. Circuit-breaker Panel
12. Map Case
13. Densitometer Selector Valve
14. IFF Control Panel
15. UHF Command Radio Control Panel*
16. Radio Compass Control Panel
17. Radio Frequency Card
18. Emergency Hydraulic Hand-pump*

*Some airplanes. (Refer to applicable text.)
†F-86E-6 Airplanes

Figure 1-7

Section I
T. O. 1F-86E-1

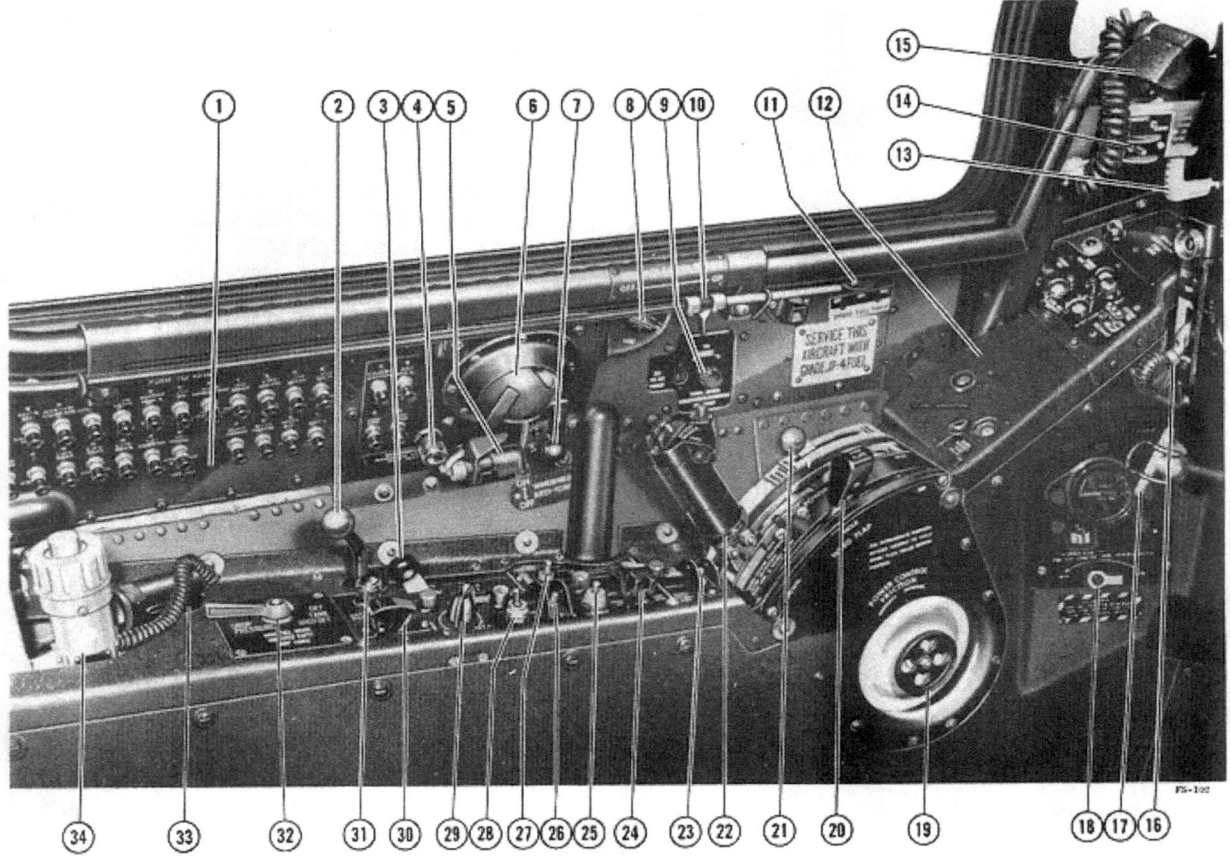

cockpit—left side

F-86E-10 AND F-86E-15 AIRPLANES

1. Circuit-breaker Panel
2. Ammunition Compartment Heat Emergency Shutoff
3. Air Outlet Selector Lever
4. Windshield Anti-ice Overheat Warning Light
5. Console Floodlight
6. Side Air Outlet
7. Windshield Anti-icing Lever
8. Floodlight Control Rheostat*
9. Rocket Intervalometer
10. Canopy Auxiliary Defrost Lever
11. Emergency Fuel Switch*
12. Left Forward Console
13. Parking Brake Handle
14. Canopy Switch
15. Instrument Panel Floodlight
16. Landing Gear Handle
17. Emergency Jettison Handle
18. Type D-2 Oxygen Regulator Panel
19. Throttle Friction Wheel
20. Wing Flap Lever
21. Speed Brake Emergency Lever
22. Throttle
23. Flight Control Switch
24. Longitudinal Alternate Trim Switch
25. Rudder Trim Switch
26. Cockpit Pressure Control Switch
27. Lateral Alternate Trim Switch
28. Cockpit Pressure Selector Switch
29. Cockpit Air Temperature Control Rheostat
30. Cockpit Air Temperature Control Switch
31. Ammunition Compartment Overheat Warning Light
32. Drop Tank Pressure Shutoff
33. Extension Light†
34. Anti-G Suit Valve

*Some airplanes. (Refer to applicable text.)
†F-86E-15 Airplanes

Figure 1-8

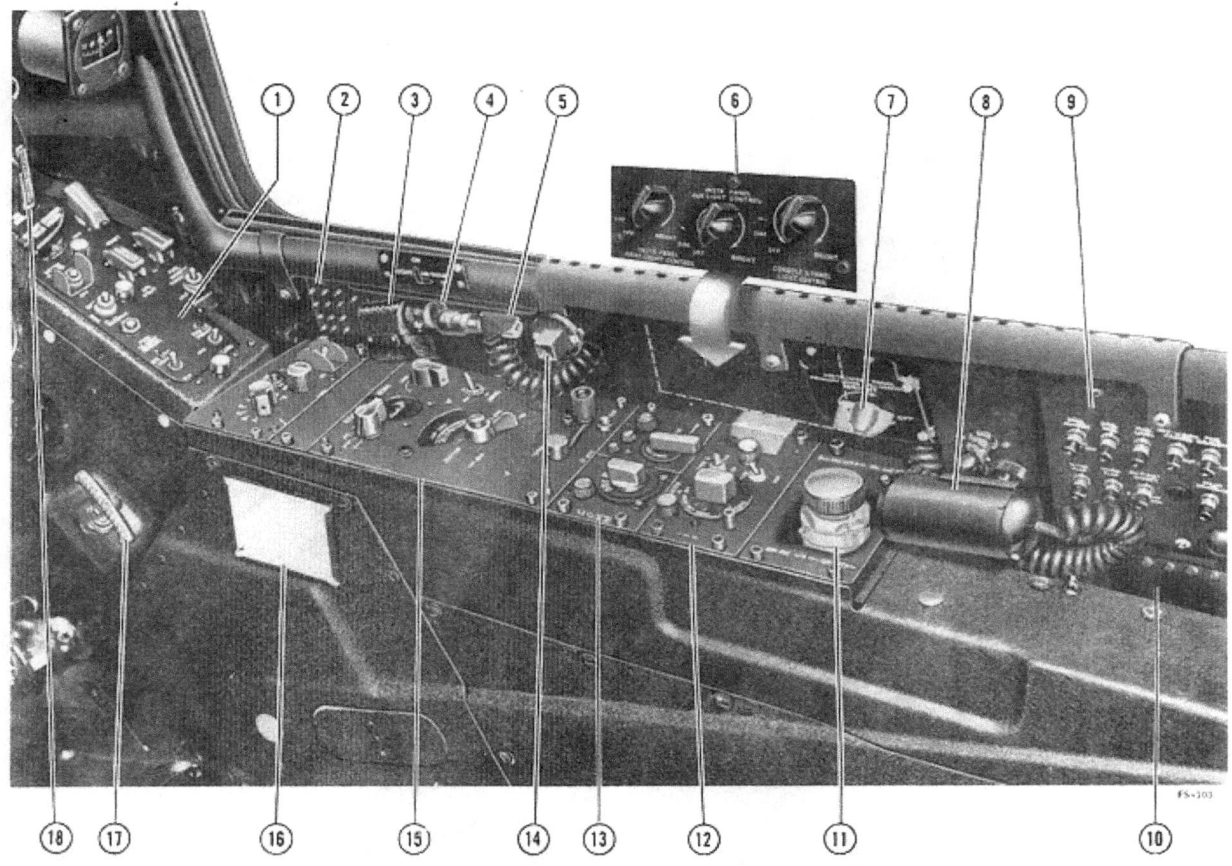

F-86E-10 AND F-86E-15 AIRPLANES

cockpit—right side

1. Right Forward Console
2. Spare Lamp Storage
3. Instrument Panel Floodlight
4. Air Outlet Control Valve
5. Console Floodlight
6. Instrument Panel and Console Panel Light Rheostats*
7. Instrument Panel Light Rheostat*
8. Extension Light*
9. Circuit-breaker Panel
10. Map Case
11. Gun Sight Test Plug
12. IFF Control Panel
13. UHF Command Radio Control Panel*
14. Side Air Outlet
15. Radio Compass Control Panel
16. Radio Frequency Card
17. Emergency Override Handle (Flight Control Alternate Hydraulic System)
18. Canopy Alternate Emergency Jettison Handle*

*Some airplanes. (Refer to applicable text.)

Figure 1-9

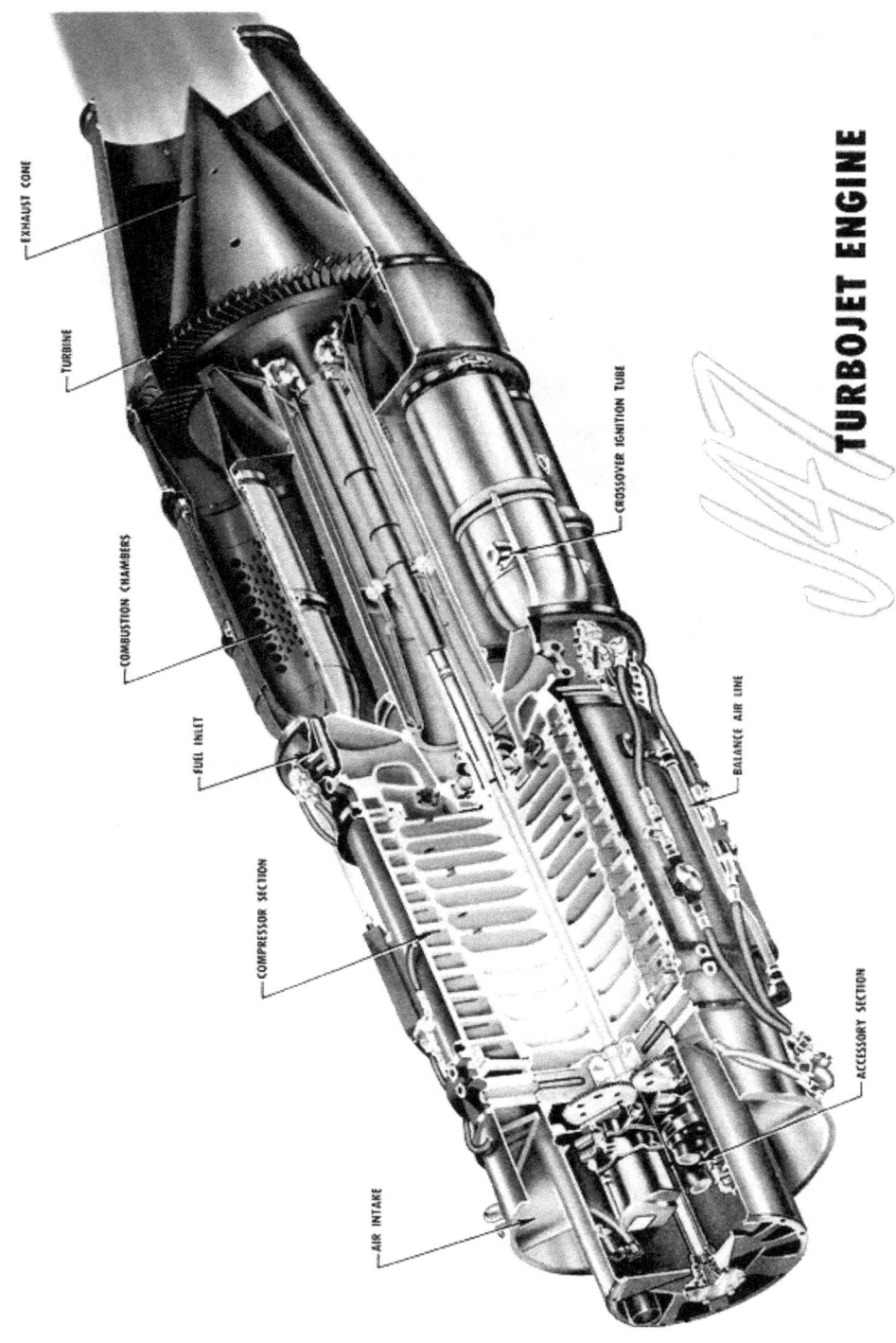

Figure 1-10

The major units of the main system are duplicated in the emergency system, which is used to maintain fuel flow to the engine if the main system fails.

Main Fuel Control System.

The main fuel control system (figure 1-11) is controlled by the throttle, and includes an engine-driven, constant-output fuel pump, a main fuel regulator, and a fuel control valve. Because pump output is constant for any given rpm, it is the function of the main fuel regulator to determine the amount of fuel the engine receives for varied operating conditions and to maintain the selected rpm regardless of altitude and/or airspeed changes. The regulator, operated by mechanical linkage from the throttle, regulates fuel flow to the engine according to throttle setting, engine rpm, and altitude by adjusting the fuel control valve by-pass position. (No fuel passes through the regulator.) The fuel control valve is basically a variable by-pass valve that responds to regulator control by varying the amount of fuel directed to the engine. It by-passes the fuel not needed for the particular operating condition back to the main fuel pump. A constant-speed governor, effective in the range between about 30% to 100% engine rpm at sea level, is included in the regulator. Within its range, the governor maintains constant engine speed for the selected throttle setting and prevents overspeed during rapid altitude and attitude changes.

WARNING

When outside air temperature is less than 50°F, rapid throttle movement during operation on the main fuel system below 10,000 feet, when engine speed is below 70% rpm, may produce compressor stall or total loss of power.

For information on main fuel regulator characteristics, as well as details of compressor surge and stall and acceleration flame-outs, refer to Section VII.

Emergency Fuel Control System.

The emergency fuel control system (figure 1-11), consisting of the emergency element of the engine-driven, dual fuel pump and an emergency fuel regulator, may be used to maintain engine operation if the main fuel control system fails. On some airplanes, the emergency fuel system includes a stand-by provision. These airplanes can be identified by a three-position emergency fuel switch in the cockpit. On other airplanes, the stand-by provision has been removed. These airplanes can be identified by a two-position emergency fuel switch in the cockpit. During normal operation, the emergency system is not engaged, since electrical (dc) power holds the emergency regulator inoperative so that it continuously by-passes the total output of the emergency segment of the fuel pump. On airplanes with the three-position emergency fuel switch, when the emergency system is engaged it is set in a stand-by condition. The emergency regulator is then free to maintain a fuel pressure schedule slightly below that of the main system, and to sense main system pressure. If main system pressure drops below emergency system pressure, the emergency regulator assumes control of fuel flow to the engine. This flow is varied according to operating conditions, with the emergency regulator by-passing any fuel not required by the engine. On airplanes with the two-position emergency fuel switch, when the emergency fuel system is engaged it assumes control of fuel flow to the engine, and the main fuel system regulator is electrically (dc) disabled, so that the total output of the main system element of the fuel pump is continuously by-passed. On all airplanes, the emergency regulator, which is mechanically actuated by the throttle, compensates for altitude changes to maintain the approximate rpm selected by the throttle setting. However, this regulator is not provided with a governor as is the main fuel regulator and, consequently, provides neither precise speed regulation nor overspeed protection.

Note

The emergency fuel regulator is set to give a maximum of 99% rpm on a 100°F day, and therefore will provide somewhat less than 99% at lower ambient temperatures. (See figure 2-4.)

Engine Fuel System Stopcock.

Located downstream of the main and emergency fuel control systems, the fuel stopcock (figure 1-11) is a positive, high-pressure fuel shutoff valve actuated through mechanical linkage by throttle movement. Initial movement of the throttle from OFF to IDLE partially opens the stopcock, which acts as a metering valve up to about 15 degrees of throttle movement. The stopcock is fully opened by additional throttle movement past the IDLE position.

Fuel System Flow Divider.

The engine fuel system flow divider (figure 1-11) is downstream of the stopcock. The flow divider directs fuel to one or both engine fuel manifolds, depending on engine operating conditions. (The small-slot manifold is used during starting and is also used in conjunction with the large-slot manifold for normal operation.) To facilitate starting, the flow divider directs fuel through only the small-slot manifold when fuel pressure is approximately 50 psi or less. At pressures above

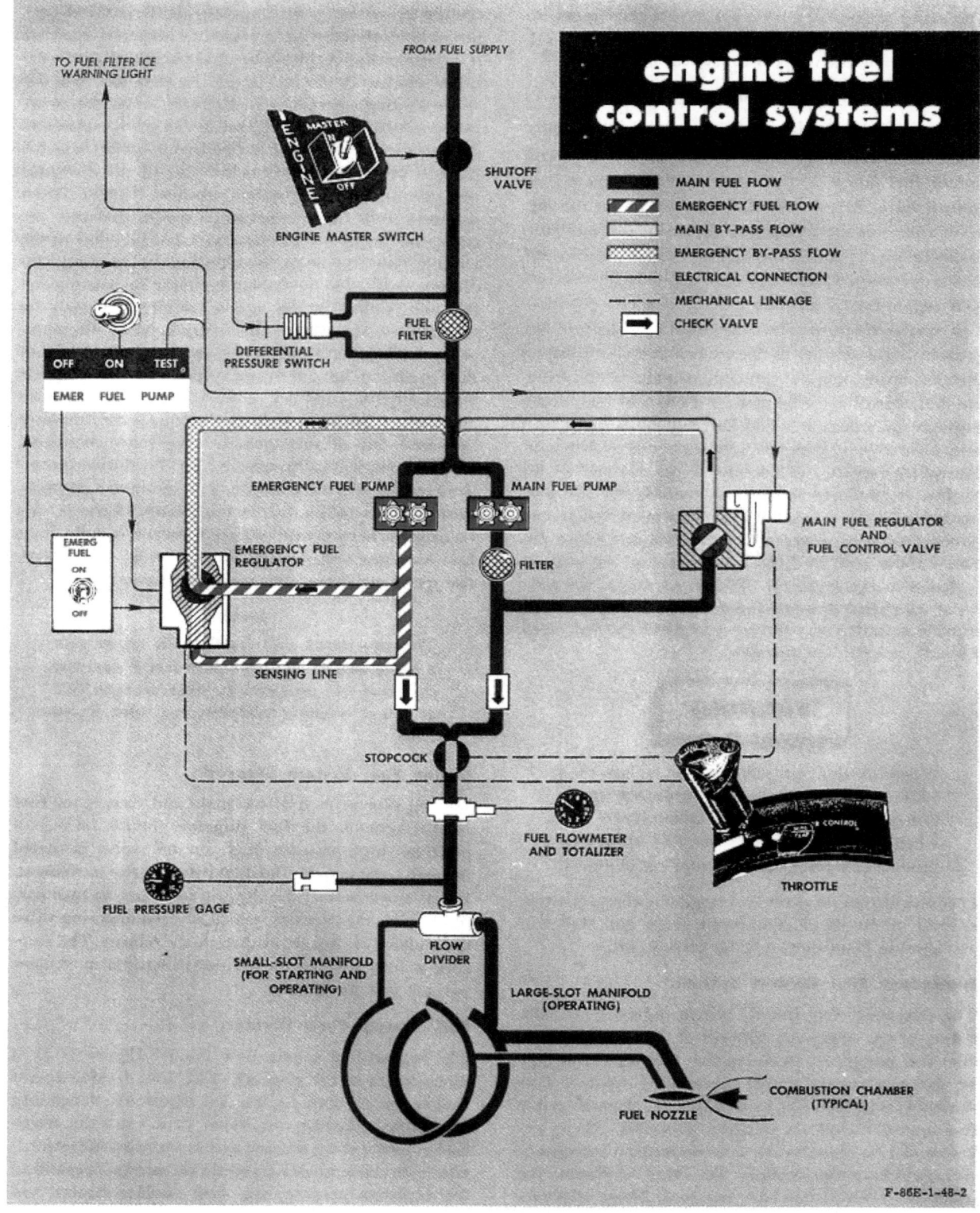

Figure 1-11

this, the flow divider routes fuel through the large-slot manifold and the small-slot manifold, for normal operations. The flow divider is controlled by fuel pressure. Its operation is completely automatic.

ENGINE CONTROLS.

Throttle (Power Control).

Engine power is controlled by the throttle (23, figure 1-6; 22, figure 1-8), which is in a quadrant on the left side of the cockpit. The throttle is spring-loaded inboard and mechanically actuates the main and emergency fuel regulators and the fuel stopcock. When the engine master switch is ON, initial outboard movement of the throttle from OFF starts the fuel booster pumps and completes the ignition circuit when the starter is energized; subsequent movement of the throttle to IDLE opens the fuel stopcock. (Ignition is automatically cut off when engine speed reaches about 23% rpm.) When the engine is running, additional throttle advancement produces increasing engine rpm. To prevent inadvertent shutting off of the fuel supply when the throttle is retarded, a stop is provided on the throttle quadrant between the IDLE and OFF positions. Outboard movement of the throttle allows the stop to be by-passed when the engine is being started or stopped. Clockwise rotation of the throttle grip provides manual ranging for the sight; the grip is spring-loaded to the full counterclockwise (maximum range) position. The throttle grip (figure 1-12) contains a sight electrical caging button, a microphone button, and the speed brake switch. Rotation of the wheel (21, figure 1-6; 19, figure 1-8) on the inboard face of the throttle quadrant adjusts the throttle friction.

Engine Master Switch.

The guarded engine master switch (figure 1-16), on the right forward console, supplies primary bus power for controlling various engine and fuel system units. Moving the switch to ON opens the main fuel shutoff valve and completes the electrical circuits to the throttle-actuated microswitch to start the fuel booster pumps and to provide ignition during starting. Ignition is supplied when the engine master switch is ON, the battery-starter switch is held momentarily at STARTER, and the throttle is moved outboard from OFF. When the engine master switch is moved to OFF, the fuel booster pumps are de-energized, and the fuel shutoff valve is closed.

Emergency Fuel Switch (Three-Position).

The three-position emergency fuel switch (1, figure 1-5; 11, figure 1-6; and 11, figure 1-8), powered by the primary bus, is located either on the left side of the cockpit,

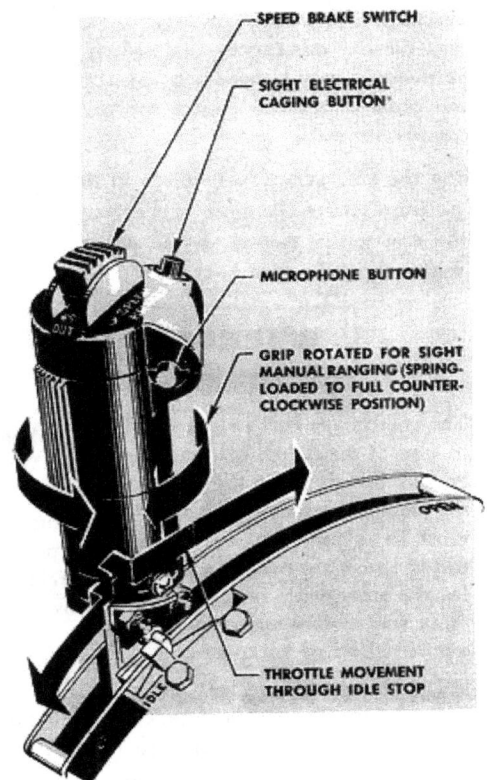

Figure 1-12

above the throttle quadrant, or on the upper left corner of the instrument panel. When the switch is ON, the emergency fuel system acts as a stand-by for the main fuel system and will govern fuel supply to the engine in case of main system failure. When the switch is OFF, an electrical solenoid mechanically positions the emergency fuel regulator to the full by-pass position, making the emergency system inoperative and preventing it from overriding the main system during normal engine operation.

During engine operation, if primary bus failure occurs, if the battery-starter switch is moved to OFF upon generator failure, or if the generator switch is OFF when the battery-starter switch is OFF, the emergency fuel system will be in the stand-by condition automatically, regardless of emergency fuel switch position. Subsequent rapid movement of the throttle can cause dangerous engine overspeeding or compressor stall.

Holding the emergency fuel switch in the momentary TEST position makes the main fuel system inoperative, and the emergency system should automatically take over with very little drop in rpm.

WARNING

The emergency fuel switch should be ON only in case of main fuel system failure; it should be OFF for all other flight conditions. When the emergency fuel switch is ON, extreme care must be taken when advancing the throttle. Rapid throttle advancement makes it possible for the emergency fuel system to override the main fuel system and cause dangerous engine overspeeding or compressor stall.

Emergency Fuel Switch (Two-Position).

The two-position emergency fuel switch (34, figure 1-4) is on the upper left corner of the instrument panel. With the emergency fuel switch OFF, primary bus electrical power is directed to a solenoid which mechanically holds the emergency fuel regulator in the full by-pass position. This makes the emergency system inoperative, because the total output of the emergency element of the fuel pump is by-passed. Thus, the emergency system is prevented from overriding the main system during normal operation.

WARNING

If, during engine operation, primary bus power failure occurs or the battery-starter switch is moved to OFF when generator output is not available, the emergency fuel system operates automatically, regardless of emergency fuel switch position. Subsequent rapid throttle advancement can cause the emergency system to override the main system, resulting in complete power failure as a result of engine overspeeding or compressor stall.

The emergency fuel switch should be kept at OFF for all flight conditions, except in case of actual main fuel control system failure. When the emergency fuel switch is at ON, the holding circuit to the emergency regulator is broken, and the main fuel system regulator is electrically (dc) disabled, allowing the emergency system to assume control of fuel flow to the engine.

WARNING

- The emergency fuel switch should be at OFF for take-off, approach, landing, or go-around. The emergency fuel system should be used only when actual failure of the main fuel system occurs. With the emergency fuel switch ON, rapid throttle advancement can cause compressor stall or flame-out, resulting in complete loss of power.

- If rpm is below 80% when the main fuel system fails, do not turn on emergency fuel switch without first retarding throttle to IDLE. To do so may cause dangerous engine overheating or compressor stall.

ENGINE INDICATORS.

Exhaust Temperature Gage.

The exhaust temperature gage (9, figure 1-4; 9, figure 1-5), on the instrument panel, indicates engine exhaust temperature in degrees centigrade. The gage is a self-generating electrical unit, not requiring power from the airplane electrical system. Gage indications are received from bayonet-type thermocouples mounted in the forward section of the tail pipe.

Tachometer.

The tachometer (15, figure 1-4; 11, figure 1-5), on the instrument panel, registers engine speed in percentage of maximum rated rpm (7950). This indication, when used in conjunction with that of the exhaust temperature gage, permits engine power to be accurately set without exceeding engine limitations. The tachometer receives its power from the tachometer generator, which is geared to the engine rotor shaft and, therefore, does not depend on the airplane electrical system.

Oil Pressure Gage.

The oil pressure gage (7, figure 1-4; 7, figure 1-5), on the upper center of the instrument panel, registers engine oil pressure in pounds per square inch. The gage receives power from the three-phase ac electrical system.

Fuel Pressure Gage.

The fuel pressure gage (10, figure 1-4; 10, figure 1-5; and figure 5-1) is in the upper right corner of the instrument panel. The gage is powered by the three-phase ac electrical system. Fuel pressure is recorded in pounds per square inch. Some airplanes have a fuel gage with an expanded scale which facilitates reading of slight fuel pressure fluctuations at the lower end of the scale. This will assist in making successful air starts.

Fuel Flowmeter and Totalizer.

The fuel flowmeter (17, figure 1-4; 13, figure 1-5), on the instrument panel, shows the rate of fuel flow in pounds per hour and includes a totalizer dial which indicates the number of pounds of fuel remaining. The flowmeter is electrically powered by the single-phase electrical system. A knob on the flowmeter is used to preset the totalizer to correspond to the total pounds of fuel in the tanks before take-off. The totalizer is preset to agree with the quantity gage. However, the uncompensated totalizer indication will not continuously coincide with the density-corrected fuel quantity gage when fuel is consumed. On some airplanes, the fuel flowmeter does not have a totalizer dial.

Note

The totalizer dial of the fuel flowmeter should not be relied upon for accurate fuel-remaining indications. Large errors are inherent in the instrument because of uncompensated fuel density, unmetered fuel passing around the instrument, and instrument inaccuracy; therefore, it should be used for rough estimates only. Accurate fuel-remaining data can be obtained only from the fuel quantity gage.

ENGINE IGNITION SYSTEM.

The ignition system provides ignition through two spark plugs. The system works only during starting. With the engine master switch at ON and the battery-starter switch momentarily held at STARTER, ignition will occur automatically when the throttle is moved from OFF. For ignition, dc power is routed through the ignition vibrators, which supply high-tension voltage to the spark plugs in combustion chambers 2 and 7. The ignition circuit is opened automatically when the starter disengages as engine speed reaches about 23% rpm. A manually controlled emergency ignition system is provided for supplying ignition during an air start.

Engine Master Switch.

Refer to "Engine Controls" in this section.

Emergency Ignition Switch.

The guarded emergency ignition switch (figure 1-16), on the right forward console, receives power from the primary bus to permit manual operation of the ignition system for engine restart in flight. When the switch is ON, advancing the throttle from OFF energizes the emergency ignition circuit. The emergency ignition will remain on until the emergency ignition switch is turned OFF.

CAUTION

- Continuous operation of the emergency ignition circuit is limited to a maximum of 3 minutes per start. Longer periods of use, or too frequent use, will damage the ignition vibrator units.
- The emergency ignition should be used for air starts only. An external supply provides ignition for ground starts.

STARTER-GENERATOR.

The combination starter-generator, mounted on the front of the engine, functions as a starter until engine speed reaches approximately 23% rpm. Above this speed, the unit serves as a generator. However, normal generator output of 28.5 volts is not obtained until engine rpm is approximately 45%. If the engine fails to start, the starter can be de-energized by a manually operated switch to permit another starting attempt. The starter can be energized only when an external power source is connected to the airplane electrical system.

CAUTION

A 28.25-volt (nominal) dc power source, capable of supplying a minimum of 500 amperes continuous power and 1200 amperes surge power, must be connected to both external power receptacles to provide adequate electrical power for starting.

Battery-Starter Switch.

The three-position battery-starter switch (figure 1-16) is on the right forward console. The switch is spring-loaded to the OFF position from the STARTER position. The OFF and BATTERY positions are maintained. When the switch is held momentarily at STARTER, the starter is actuated and continues to be energized through an

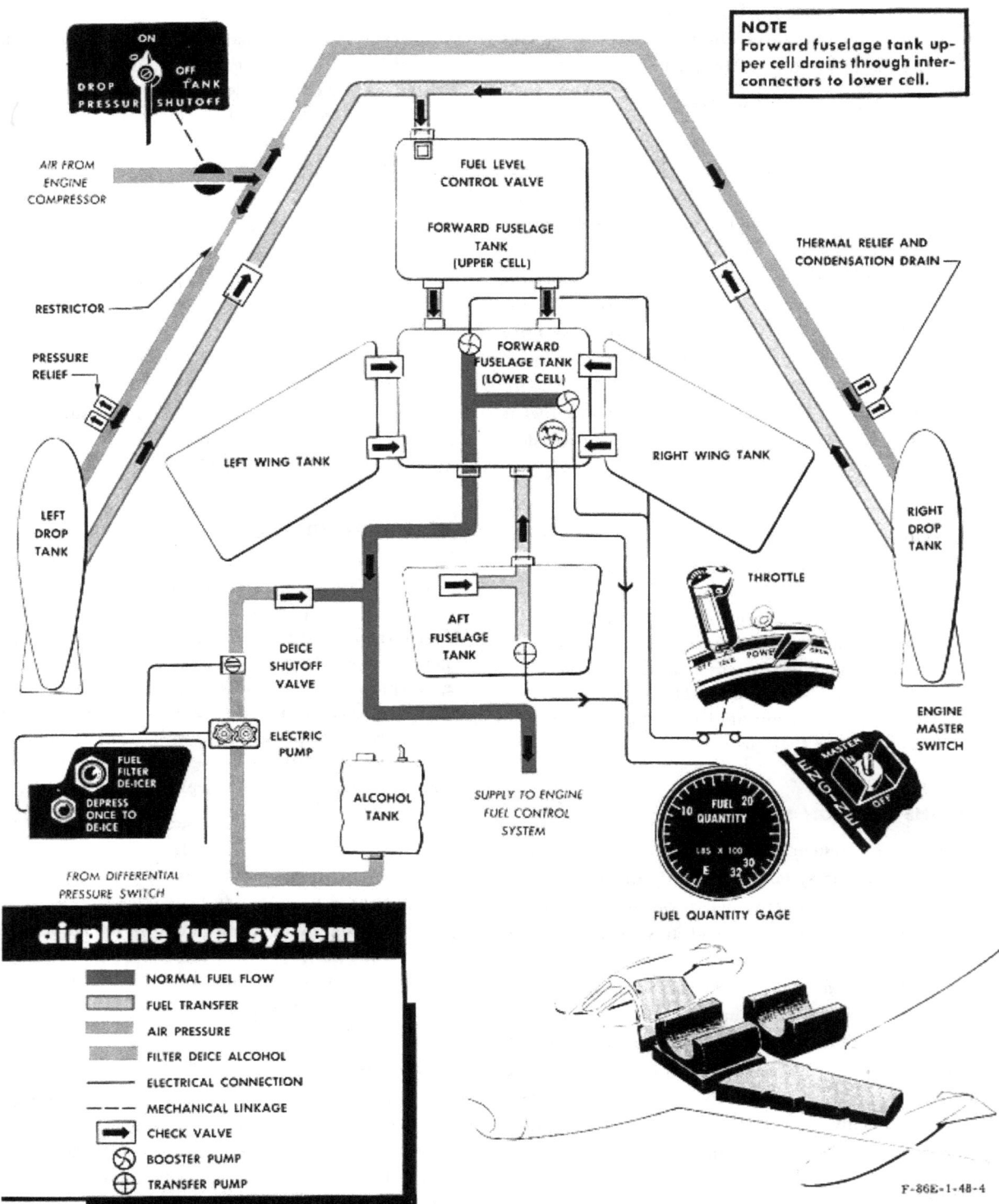

Figure 1-13

electrical relay until the engine rpm reaches about 23%. The starter is then automatically disconnected. When released, the switch will return to OFF from the STARTER position and should be set at BATTERY for all normal operation. With the switch at BATTERY, the primary bus is powered by the battery. When the battery-starter switch is OFF, battery power will be supplied only to those units powered directly from the battery bus. (See figure 1-15.)

Stop-Starter Button.

The stop-starter button (figure 1-16), located outboard of the battery-starter switch on the right forward console, receives power from the primary bus. The button is used to de-energize the starter if the engine fails to start or a malfunction occurs. Depressing the button cuts off primary bus (dc) current to the starter and to the ignition system. The button should not be used to disengage the starter after normal starts, because the starter cuts out automatically at 23% rpm.

Use of the stop-starter button after normal starts will cause rapid deterioration of the starter control relay and may also cut out the starter too soon, slowing the rate of engine acceleration.

OIL SYSTEM.

The oil system is completely automatic. The engine is lubricated by a gear-type pressure oil pump that includes lubricating and scavenging elements. Early airplanes* are equipped with a 5.7 US gallon tank, and later airplanes† are equipped with a 3.5 US gallon tank. Oil is supplied by gravity feed from the tank to the pump, which supplies oil pressure to all engine parts requiring it. The scavenging unit on the oil pump returns oil from the gear case sump to the oil tank. Oil is returned through an oil cooler to the tank from the mid-, aft-, and damper-bearing sump by a mid-frame (aft) oil scavenging pump (driven by the compressor shaft). To ensure that the main fuel regulator receives internal cooling and control oil, a portion of the oil discharged by the pump is directed to the main fuel regulator. See figure 1-35 for oil specifications and grade.

*F-86E-1 through F-86E-6 Airplanes
†F-86E-10 and F-86E-15 Airplanes

AIRPLANE FUEL SYSTEM.

The airplane fuel system (figure 1-13) includes four self-sealing tanks: two in the fuselage, and one in each wing outer panel. The forward fuselage tank consists of two cells. The lower cell, located in the wing center section, receives fuel from the upper cell and from all the internal tanks by gravity feed. Fuel is supplied to the engine from the forward fuselage tank under pressure by means of two electrical booster pumps. The main fuel supply can be augmented by installation of a 120 US gallon drop tank under each wing. On F-86E-15 Airplanes, either two 120-gallon or two 200-gallon drop tanks can be carried. Compressed air from the engine compressor forces fuel from the drop tanks to the forward fuselage tank through a fuel level control valve. Drop tank fuel should be used before fuel in the internal tanks. The fuel filler access doors at the tank filler points cannot be closed unless the tank caps are secured in the locked position. During normal refueling operations, the forward fuselage tank must be filled first, to utilize full tank capacity; if the aft fuselage tank or the wing tanks are filled first, fuel from these tanks will slowly drain into the forward fuselage tank lower cell while the forward fuselage tank is being serviced. Fuel tank capacities are shown in figure 1-14; for fuel specifications, see figure 1-35.

fuel quantity data — POUNDS AND US GALLONS

NOTE: Multiply gallons by 6.5 to convert JP-4 fuel to pounds (Standard Day only).

TANK	NO.	USABLE FUEL IN LEVEL FLIGHT (EACH)		FULLY SERVICED (EACH)	
		POUNDS	GALLONS	POUNDS	GALLONS
FORWARD FUSELAGE TANK	1	1274	196	1306	201
AFT FUSELAGE TANK	1	682	105	689	106
OUTER WING TANKS	2	435	67	442	68
DROP TANKS	2	780	120	780	120
DROP TANKS*	2	1300	200	1306	201

- Total usable internal fuel, 2828 pounds or 435 gallons.
- Total usable fuel with 120-gallon drop tanks, 4387 pounds or 675 gallons.
- Total usable fuel with 200-gallon drop tanks, 5427 pounds or 835 gallons.

*F-86E-15 Airplanes

Figure 1-14

Drop Tanks.

Four types of drop tanks can be carried externally on this airplane. Types I and II are of knockdown construction and are designed so that final assembly can be accomplished in the field by maintenance personnel. Types III and IV are completely assembled for installation, and no provision for disassembly is required. Only Types II and IV tanks will have identifying stencils, visible from the cockpit. (See figure 5-2 and refer to "Drop Tank Release Airspeeds" in Section V for flight and dropping restrictions for all types of tanks.) Each type tank may be of 120- or 200-gallon capacity. All F-86E Airplanes can carry 120-gallon drop tanks. Only F-86E-15 Airplanes can carry 200-gallon drop tanks. Fuel in the drop tanks should be used before that in the internal tanks. Pressurized air for the drop tanks is controlled by a two-position drop tank pressure shutoff valve. When the drop tank system is turned on, compressed air from the engine compressor section forces fuel from the drop tanks through a fuel level control valve into the upper cell of the forward fuselage tank. The fuel level control valve automatically controls fuel flow from the drop tanks to the upper cell.

Fuel Booster Pumps.

Two electric booster pumps (figure 1-13), in the lower cell of the forward fuselage tank, are energized when the engine master switch is ON and the throttle is moved outboard from the OFF position to pass the IDLE stop. The forward booster pump is powered by the secondary bus, and the aft booster pump is powered by the primary bus.

Note
The booster pumps and aft fuselage tank transfer pump may be tested on the ground by means of switches accessible in the left and right wheel wells.

Fuel Shutoff Valve.

The fuel shutoff valve (figure 1-11), upstream of the low-pressure filter, is electrically controlled by the engine master switch. When the switch is ON, primary bus power opens the valve, allowing fuel to feed to the fuel pumps.

Fuel Filter Deicing System.

Refer to "Anti-icing and Defrosting Systems" in Section IV.

AIRPLANE FUEL SYSTEM CONTROLS AND INDICATOR.

Drop Tank Pressure Shutoff Valve.

The mechanical two-position drop tank pressure shutoff valve (31, figure 1-6; 32, figure 1-8) is on the left aft console. When the valve is ON, both tanks are pressurized by air from the engine compressor section, so that fuel from the drop tanks is forced into the upper cell of the forward fuselage tank. As there is no fuel quantity gage to indicate when the drop tanks are empty, the pressure shutoff valve should be ON at all times in flight when drop tanks are installed, to ensure that all drop tank fuel is consumed and to prevent drop tank collapse during rapid descent from altitude.

CAUTION
The drop tank pressure shutoff valve should be OFF whenever the airplane is on the ground and the engine is not running. If the valve is left ON when engine is not running, expansion of fuel in drop tanks may cause fuel to enter engine compressor section and create a fire hazard.

Drop Tank Release.

The drop tanks may be released by means of the normal bomb release system, or both tanks can be jettisoned simultaneously by means of the battery-bus-powered bomb-rocket-tank salvo button, on the left forward console. (See figure 1-16.) An emergency jettison handle (19, figure 1-6; 17, figure 1-8), may be used to release both drop tanks simultaneously. This release is independent of the electrical system.

WARNING
To prevent accidental explosion of drop tanks, they must not be installed, removed, or given an operational drop test (either manually or electrically) unless the airplane and drop tanks are electrostatically grounded.

Densitometer Selector Switch.

A guarded densitometer selector switch, on the right aft console (13, figure 1-7) on early airplanes* and on the right forward console (figure 1-16) on later airplanes,† controls selection of the compensating fuel quantity indicator system. When the guard is down, the switch is at IN (normal position) and the fuel quantity gage will show the total fuel supply in pounds, corrected for any variations in fuel density. When the guard is raised and the switch is moved to OUT, the system is

---

*F-86E-1 through F-86E-6 Airplanes
†F-86E-10 and later airplanes

adjusted so that the quantity gage indicates pounds of fuel as determined by volume. This condition is used when a standard indication of quantity, such as a full condition after refueling, is desired.

Fuel Quantity Gage.

The fuel quantity gage (19, figure 1-4; 15, figure 1-5), on the instrument panel, indicates the total internal fuel supply in pounds, as determined by a densitometer-type indicator system. The gage receives its power supply from the primary bus. This system automatically compensates for changes in fuel density, so that the quantity gage will register the actual number of pounds of fuel, regardless of the type of fuel used or of fuel expansion or contraction caused by temperature changes. The densitometer system includes a selector switch to permit uncompensated gage indications when desired. No indication of drop tank fuel supply is provided; therefore, the fuel quantity gage will not indicate a decrease in fuel supply until the drop tank fuel has been used and the engine is using internal fuel.

ELECTRICAL POWER SUPPLY SYSTEM.

The airplane is equipped with ac and dc electrical power systems. The 28-volt dc system is powered by a 400-ampere, engine-driven starter-generator. A 24-volt, 34-ampere-hour battery serves as a stand-by for dc power. Direct current can also be supplied to the airplane through two receptacles by an external power source. On early airplanes* not changed by T. O. 1F-86E-47 or T. O. 1F-86E-507, power for the alternating-current system is supplied by a single-phase inverter, with a three-phase inverter as a stand-by. On late airplanes† and early airplanes* changed by T. O. 1F-86E-47 or T. O. 1F-86E-507, the alternating-current system is powered by a single-phase inverter and two three-phase inverters.

DC Electrical Power Distribution.

Direct-current power is distributed from three electrical busses: battery, primary, and secondary. (See figure 1-15.) The battery bus is "hot" at all times, so that the essential equipment, powered by the battery, is operable regardless of the position of the battery-starter switch. When the battery-starter switch is at BATTERY, the battery bus can be energized by generator output or by an external power source applied to the No. 1 receptacle. The primary bus is energized by the battery bus when the battery-starter switch is at the BATTERY position and is energized directly when the generator is functioning or an external power supply is used. The secondary bus, which receives power through the primary bus, is energized, in addition to the primary and battery busses, whenever the generator is operating or an external power source is connected to the No. 1 receptacle.

AC Electrical Power Distribution (Early Airplanes*).

On early airplanes* not changed by T. O. 1F-86E-47 or T. O. 1F-86E-507, alternating-current power is supplied by a single-phase inverter, combined with a phase adapter, and a stand-by three-phase inverter. The single-phase inverter, which serves as the normal source of ac power, is powered by the primary bus, but controlled by the secondary bus; therefore, it is energized only when the generator is operating or when an external power source is plugged in. This inverter furnishes single-phase ac power to the A-1CM sight, IFF radar, fuel flowmeter and totalizer, and the cockpit air conditioning control systems. The phase adapter transforms a portion of the single-phase inverter output to three-phase power for the attitude indicator, the directional indicator, and the fuel, oil, and hydraulic pressure indicating systems. The alternate three-phase inverter, energized by the primary bus, operates only in case of single-phase inverter failure. If the generator fails, causing loss of single-phase inverter power, the three-phase instruments normally powered by the single-phase system (through the phase adapter) are automatically transferred to the alternate three-phase inverter. The units requiring single-phase power will be inoperative. If the single-phase inverter fails, the transfer to the three-phase inverter must be made by means of a manually operated transfer switch on the center pedestal. (See figures 4-12 and 4-13.) This switch is also used if the automatic transfer does not function when the generator fails. Warning lights indicate generator or inverter failure.

AC Electrical Power Distribution (Late Airplanes†).

On late airplanes† and early airplanes* changed by T. O. 1F-86E-47 or T. O. 1F-86E-507, alternating-current power is supplied by a single-phase and a three-phase inverter. An additional three-phase inverter

---

*F-86E-1 through F-86E-6 Airplanes, and F-86E-10 Airplanes AF51-2718 through -2747
†F-86E-10 Airplane AF51-2748 and all later airplanes

electrical power distribution

FUNCTIONAL FLOW DIAGRAM

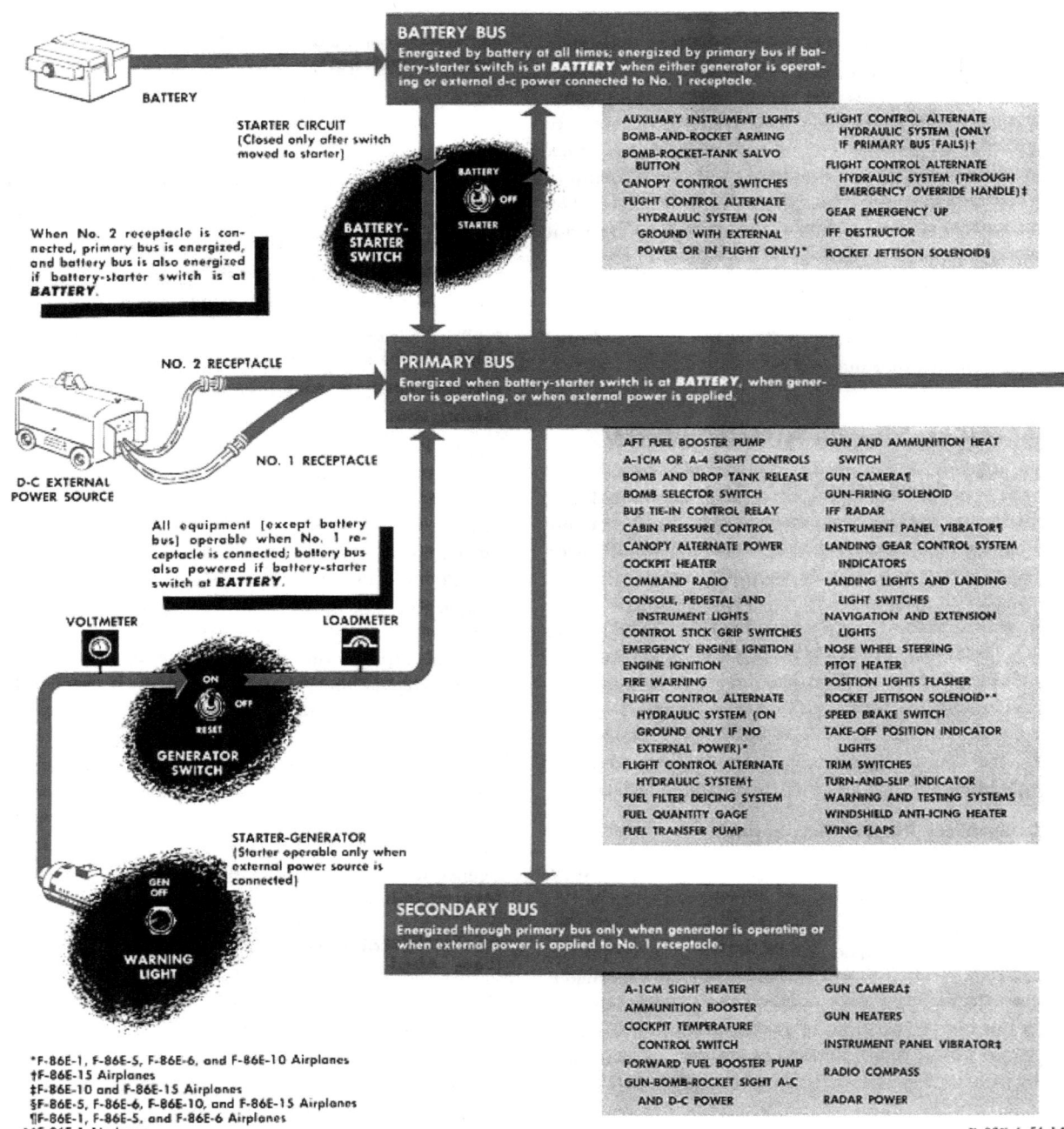

Figure 1-15

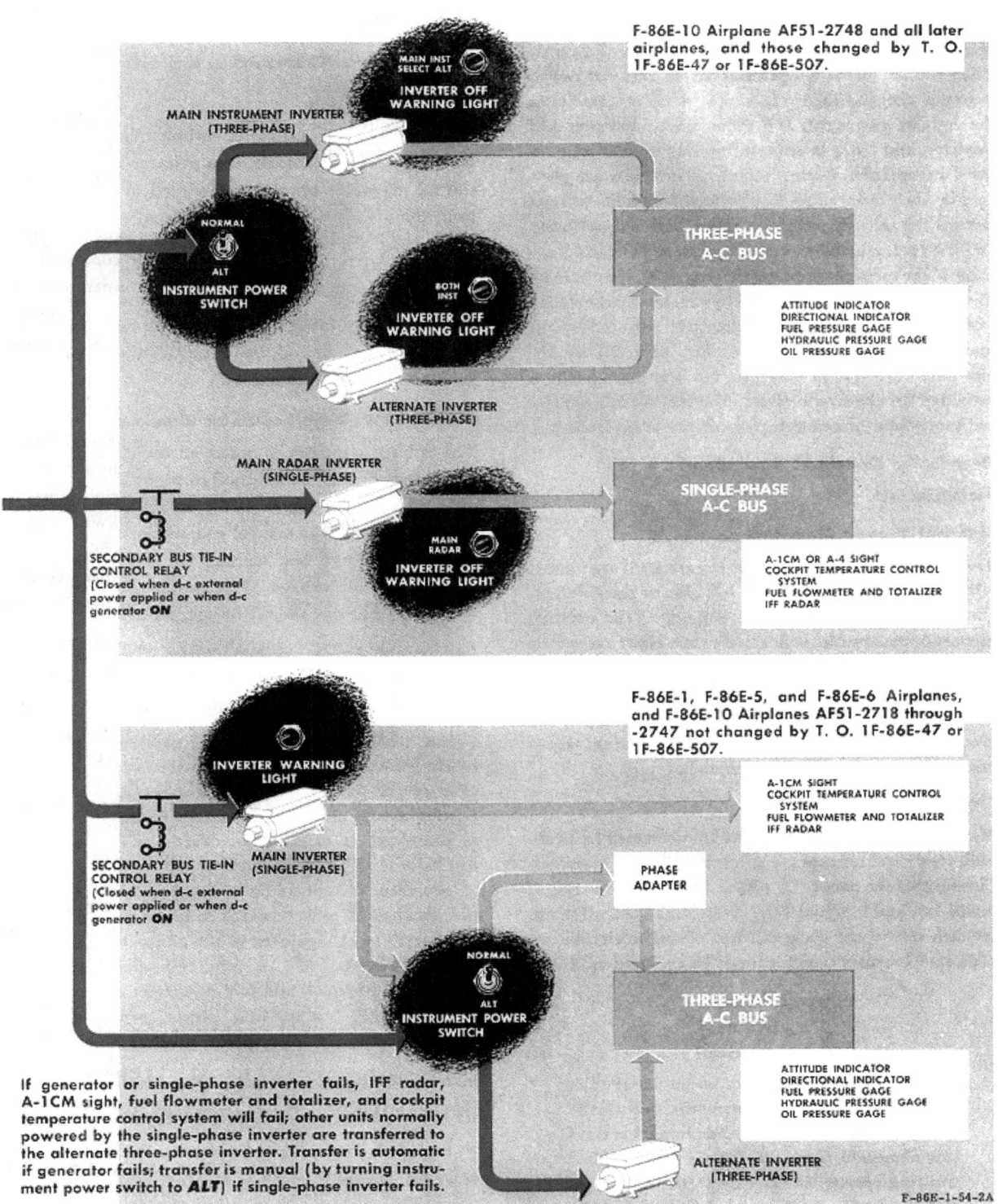

Section I   T. O. 1F-86E-1

serves as an alternate power source if the main three-phase inverter fails. The single-phase inverter is controlled by the secondary bus, but is powered by the primary bus and, consequently, will be energized only when the generator is operating or an external power source is plugged in. If the single-phase inverter fails, the A-1CM gun sight, IFF radar, fuel flowmeter and totalizer, and cockpit air conditioning system will become inoperative. Both three-phase inverters are powered by the primary bus. The main three-phase inverter powers the attitude indicator, the directional indicator, and the fuel, oil, and hydraulic pressure indicating systems. If the main three-phase inverter fails, the alternate three-phase inverter is engaged by a manually controlled transfer switch. Instruments normally powered by the main three-phase inverter are then powered by the alternate three-phase inverter. No transfer system is provided for the single-phase inverter. Warning lights indicate when the generator or individual inverters fail.

Electrically Operated Equipment.

See figure 1-15.

External Power Receptacles.

Two external power receptacles (figure 1-35) are located within an access panel on the left side of the fuselage, above and aft of the wing trailing edge. The external power source must be connected to the No. 1 receptacle to supply power to both the primary and secondary busses. If No. 2 receptacle is connected, power is supplied only to the primary bus. To provide adequate electrical power for starting the engine, external power must be connected to both receptacles.

Circuit Breakers.

Most of the dc electrical circuits are protected by push-pull type circuit breakers or circuit-breaker switches. Circuit-breaker panels (1, figure 1-6; 11, figure 1-7; 1, figure 1-8; and 9, figure 1-9), accessible to the pilot, are on each side of the cockpit. Most of the ac circuits are protected by fuses which cannot be replaced in flight.

CAUTION

Circuit breakers should not be pulled or reset without a thorough understanding of all the effects and results. Use of the circuit breakers can eliminate from the system some related warning system, interlocking circuit, or cancelling signal, which could result in an undesirable reaction.

ELECTRICAL POWER SUPPLY SYSTEM CONTROLS.

Battery-Starter Switch.

Refer to "Starter-Generator" in this section.

Generator Switch.

The three-position generator switch (figure 1-16), on the right forward console, uses primary bus power to control generator operation. Guarded in the ON position, the switch is spring-loaded from RESET to OFF. When the generator switch is OFF, the generator is out of the power circuit. If an overvoltage condition cuts out the generator, as indicated by illumination of the generator-off warning light, the switch can be momentarily held at RESET and then returned to ON, to restore generator operation to normal.

Generator Voltage Regulator Rheostat.

The voltage regulator is preset on the ground, but in an emergency may be adjusted in flight by means of a guarded rheostat (figure 1-16), on the right forward console. Turning the control counterclockwise will decrease the voltage, and turning the control clockwise will increase the voltage. With engine rpm above 45%, voltmeter readings should be approximately 28 volts.

Instrument Power Switch (Early Airplanes*).

On early airplanes* not changed by T. O. 1F-86E-47 or T. O. 1F-86E-507, the instrument power switch (figure 4-12), on the lower center pedestal, is powered by the primary bus and is positioned to select the source of ac power. When the switch is at NORMAL, ac power is supplied by the single-phase inverter, and transfer to the alternate three-phase inverter will occur automatically if single-phase inverter output ceases because of generator failure. If the single-phase inverter fails, the instrument power switch must be moved to ALT (alternate) to change over to the alternate three-phase inverter. The A-1CM gun sight, IFF radar, cockpit air conditioning system, and fuel flowmeter and totalizer, which require single-phase power, are inoperative when the alternate three-phase inverter is energized.

Instrument Power Switch (Late Airplanes†).

On late airplanes† and early airplanes* changed by T. O.

---

*F-86E-1 through F-86E-6 Airplanes and F-86E-10 Airplanes AF51-2718 through -2747
†F-86E-10 Airplane AF51-2748 and all later airplanes

1-24

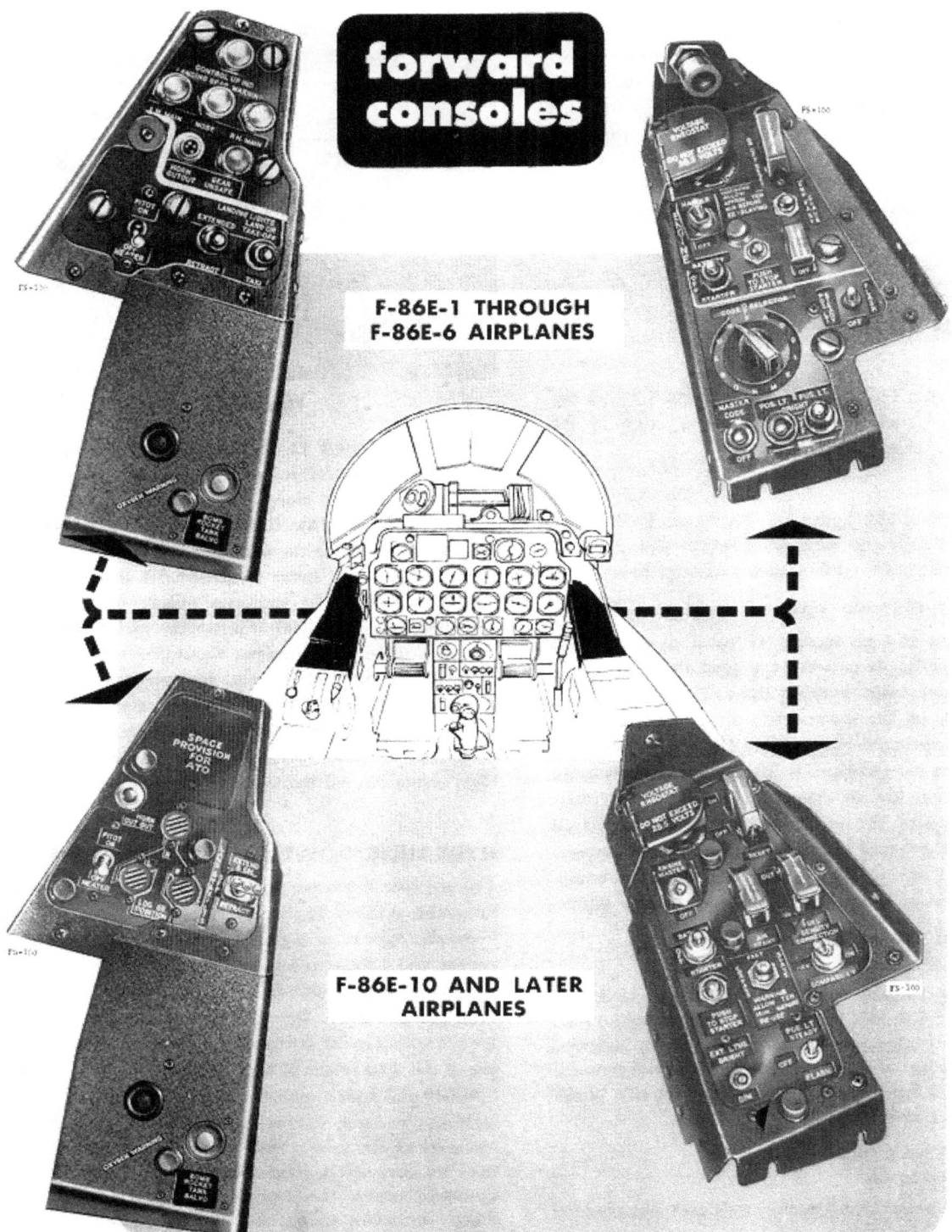

Figure 1-16

1F-86E-47 or T. O. 1F-86E-507, the instrument power switch (figures 4-12 and 4-13), on the lower center pedestal, controls the source of three-phase ac power. With the switch at NORMAL, the ac power is being supplied by the main three-phase inverter. Transfer to the alternate three-phase inverter will occur when the switch is moved to ALTERNATE. The main instrument (three-phase) inverter warning light is illuminated when the instrument power switch is at the ALTERNATE (ALT) position.

ELECTRICAL SYSTEM INDICATORS.

Voltmeter.

The voltmeter (26, figure 1-4; 22, figure 1-5), on the instrument panel, provides direct indication of the generator voltage output.

Loadmeter.

The loadmeter (24, figure 1-4; 20, figure 1-5), on the instrument panel, is marked "LOAD" and indicates the percentage of total dc system amperage being used.

Generator Warning Light.

If generator voltage exceeds 31 volts, an overvoltage relay automatically cuts out the generator and illuminates the generator warning light (25, figure 1-4; 21, figure 1-5), on the lower left side of the instrument panel. The primary-bus-powered light will also come on any time the generator is inoperative or the voltage output is too low to close the reverse-current relay. Illumination of the warning light indicates that all equipment powered by the secondary bus is inoperative; therefore, all other nonessential electrical equipment should be turned off to conserve battery power.

Instrument Power Warning Light (Early Airplanes*).

On early airplanes* not changed by T. O. 1F-86E-47 or T. O. 1F-86E-507, failure of the operating inverter (either the single-phase or the three-phase) is indicated by illumination of a primary-bus-powered amber warning light (4, figure 1-4), on the upper left side of the instrument panel.

Inverter Failure Warning Lights (Late Airplanes†).

On late airplanes† and early airplanes* changed by

---

*F-86E-1 through F-86E-6 Airplanes and F-86E-10 Airplanes AF51-2718 through -2747
†F-86E-10 Airplane AF51-2748 and all later airplanes

Figure 1-17

T. O. 1F-86E-47 or T. O. 1F-86E-507, three primary-bus-powered inverter failure warning lights (figure 1-17) are set horizontally along the upper left edge of the instrument panel. One light is provided for each of the three inverters in the system. An amber light comes on when the main radar (single-phase) inverter fails. Another amber light indicates failure of the main instrument (three-phase) inverter, at which time the alternate three-phase inverter should be selected. The main instrument (three-phase) inverter warning light will come on whenever the alternate three-phase inverter is selected. When both instrument inverters (main and alternate three-phase) fail, the red warning light comes on. All lights are of the push-to-test type.

HYDRAULIC POWER SUPPLY SYSTEMS.

The airplane has three separate constant-pressure type hydraulic systems (figures 1-18 and 1-21); a utility hydraulic system, a flight control normal hydraulic system, and a flight control alternate hydraulic system. F-86E-1 through F-86E-6 Airplanes, which have not been changed by T. O. incorporate an emergency hydraulic system in the utility system for emergency lowering of the nose wheel in flight and for ground testing. F-86E-10 and later airplanes and those changed by T. O. include a pressure storage accumulator for emergency lowering of the nose wheel. The utility hydraulic systems are completely independent of the flight control hydraulic systems. Each system has it own supply reservoir, hydraulic pump, and separate hydraulic lines. Pressure in any individual system (except the emergency utility system) can be selectively read on a single hydraulic pressure gage, by positioning of the pressure gage selector switch. See figure 1-35 for hydraulic fluid specification.

UTILITY HYDRAULIC SYSTEM.

The utility hydraulic system (figure 1-18) is a constant-pressure (3000 psi) type system which supplies hydraulic pressure for normal operation of the landing gear, wheel brakes, nose wheel steering, and speed brakes. Fluid is supplied to the system from a reservoir (figure 1-35) in the side of the fuselage. System pressure is maintained by an engine-driven, variable-volume pump. Output of the pump depends on the demands of the hydraulic system. If the system pressure decreases because of unit operation, the pump will automatically increase the output to restore the pressure. If system pressure remains constant or builds up to 3000 psi (normal pressure), the pump output decreases automatically to zero output until demands are again made on the system.

FLIGHT CONTROL HYDRAULIC SYSTEM.

Refer to "Flight Control Systems" in this section.

EMERGENCY HYDRAULIC SYSTEM.

The emergency hydraulic system (figure 1-18) consists of an emergency reservoir, an emergency hydraulic selector, and an emergency hydraulic hand-pump. This system, incorporated on F-86E-1 through F-86E-6 Airplanes not changed by T. O., provides a means for lowering the nose wheel in case of failure of the utility hydraulic system during flight, and for supplying pressure to the utility hydraulic system units for ground testing purposes only.

Emergency Hydraulic Selector.

The emergency hydraulic selector (figure 1-24), located at the bottom of the center pedestal, has three positions: GND TEST (ground test), NOSE GR, and OFF. The GND TEST position is selected for ground-checking any utility hydraulic system unit by operation of the emergency hydraulic hand-pump; the NOSE GR position is selected when the nose wheel is to be lowered by operation of the emergency hydraulic hand-pump; the OFF position is selected for normal operation. (The emergency hydraulic selector is included only on airplanes which have the emergency hydraulic system.)

CAUTION

- To ensure proper system operation, the emergency hydraulic selector must engage detent at the selected position.
- The GND TEST position is to be used for ground testing only, as its use during flight could cause all hydraulic fluid of both normal and emergency utility systems to be pumped overboard through a damaged unit or line.

Emergency Hydraulic Hand-pump.

The emergency hydraulic hand-pump (18, figure 1-7) is located on the right forward side of the cockpit. The pump supplies hydraulic pressure to the utility system for ground testing when the engine is not running and for extending the nose wheel in flight in an emergency. The extension-type handle is spring-loaded in the stowed position. (The emergency hydraulic hand-pump is incorporated only on airplanes which have the emergency hydraulic system.)

HYDRAULIC PRESSURE GAGE AND SELECTOR SWITCH.

The hydraulic pressure gage and selector switch (5, figure 1-4; 4, figure 1-5), powered by the three-phase ac bus, are on the upper portion of the instrument panel. When the three-position pressure gage selector switch is at UTILITY, NORMAL (flight control normal hydraulic system), or ALTERNATE (flight control alternate hydraulic system), the pressure of the respective system is indicated on the pressure gage. The switch may be maintained at any position desired on late airplanes;* however, on early airplanes,† the switch is spring-loaded to the UTILITY position and will return to that position upon release.

Note

On some early airplanes, the pressure gage selector switch setting for the flight control alternate hydraulic system is marked "EMERG."

FLIGHT CONTROL SYSTEM.

Four unique features are incorporated in surface control action. (See figure 1-19.) First, ailerons and horizontal tail are completely hydraulically operated; movement of the control stick mechanically positions hydraulic control valves. This action directs pressure to the respective control surface actuating cylinder. Second, action of the horizontal stabilizer and the elevators is combined. The two surfaces are known as the controllable horizontal tail and are jointly operated for longitudinal control through normal stick action; elevator movement is obtained at low speeds only by virtue of the

---

*F-86E-10 and later airplanes
†F-86E-1 through F-86E-6 Airplanes

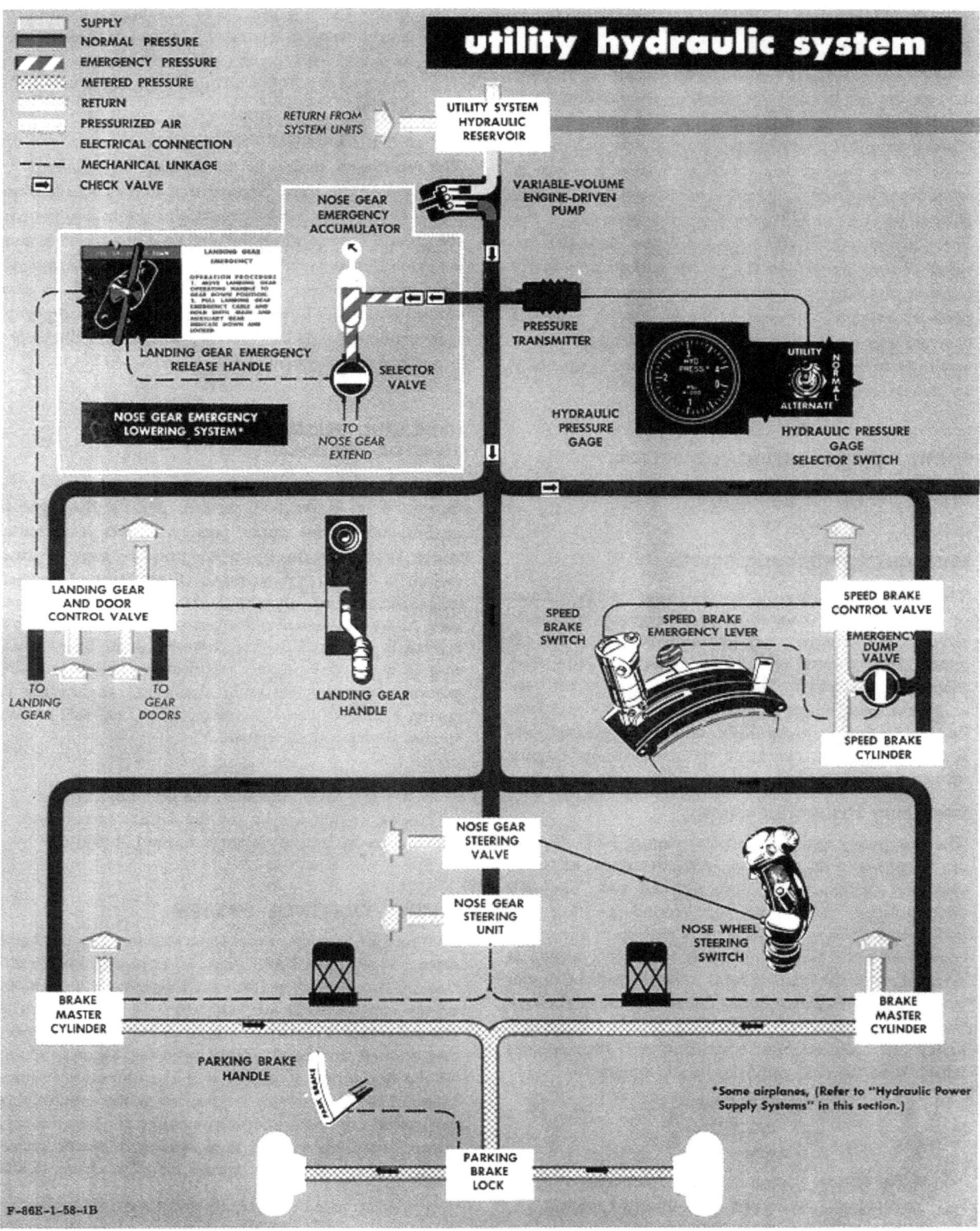

Figure 1-18

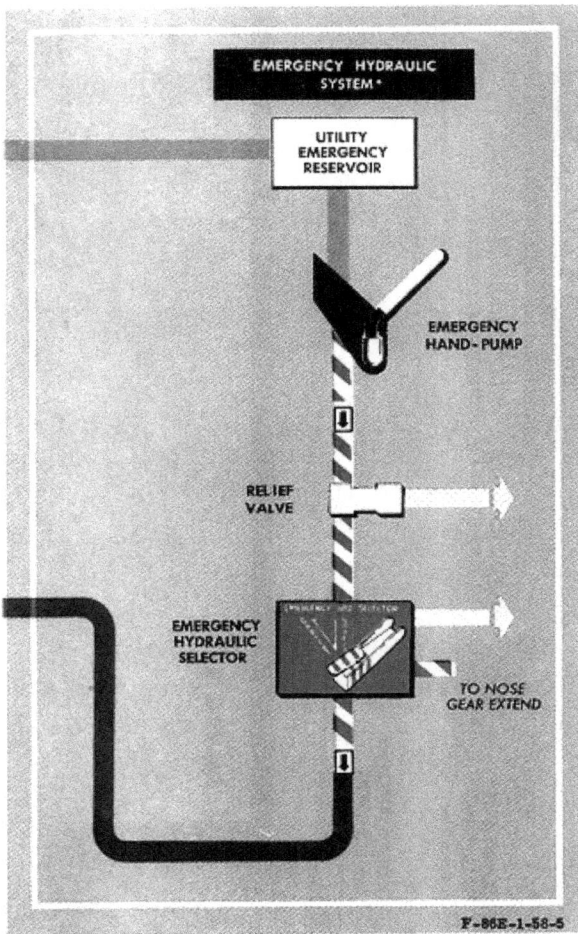

Controllable Horizontal Tail.

The elevators and horizontal stabilizer are controlled and operated as one unit, known as the controllable horizontal tail. The horizontal stabilizer is pivoted at its rear spar, so that the leading edge is moved up or down by normal control stick action. The elevator is connected to the stabilizer by mechanical linkage, and it moves in a definite relationship to stabilizer movement. Elevator travel is slightly greater than stabilizer travel. This type control surface eliminates many of the undesirable effects of compressibility, such as loss of control effectiveness at high Mach numbers. It also affords more positive action and greater control effectiveness with less control surface movement than a conventional control system.

Artificial Feel System.

Because of the irreversible characteristics of the aileron and horizontal tail hydraulic control system, air loads are not transmitted to the stick; as a result, no conventional stick feel is present. Therefore, an artificial feel bungee system is installed to supply the desired stick feel under all flight conditions. Control surface air loads are simulated by spring bungees connected into the control system, and the additional stick forces normally resulting from G-loads are provided through a bobweight. The bungees apply loads to the stick in proportion to the degree of stick deflection from the trim (or neutral) position. To hold the ailerons and horizontal tail in the desired position, the neutral (no-load) position of the stick is changed by actuation of the normal or alternate trim switches. (Refer to "Normal Trim Switch" in this section.)

FLIGHT CONTROLS AND INDICATOR.

Control Stick.

The control stick is of conventional design and is mechanically connected to hydraulic control valves at the control surfaces. Movement of the stick positions the control valves so that pressure from the flight control hydraulic system is directed to the control surface actuating cylinder. The stick mounts a pistol-type grip. (See figure 1-20.) The grip includes the following switches: radar target selector button, horizontal stabilizer and aileron trim switch, bomb-rocket release button, gun trigger, and nose wheel steering button.

Rudder Pedals.

The rudder is controlled by a cable system from conventional hanging-type rudder pedals. The pedals are adjustable fore and aft. Exact alignment of the pedals is facilitated by position indicators on the outboard side of each pedal. Each indicator consists of a numbered

gearing between stabilizer and elevator. Third, to provide normal stick feel, an artificial feel system is built into the aileron and horizontal tail control systems. Fourth, no aileron or horizontal tail trim tabs are required; trimming is accomplished by changing the neutral (no-load) position of the stick. The rudder is conventionally operated by a cable control system and has an electrically actuated trim tab. The aileron and horizontal tail control system holds the control surfaces against any forces that do not originate from control stick action and prevents these forces from being transmitted back to the stick. This irreversible feature of the hydraulic control system prevents aerodynamic loads of any kind from reaching the pilot through the controls. To help the pilot avoid overcontrol, centering springs are installed in the horizontal tail actuator to resist too-rapid fore and aft stick movements by applying a resisting force which increases proportionally to the rate of surface control movement.

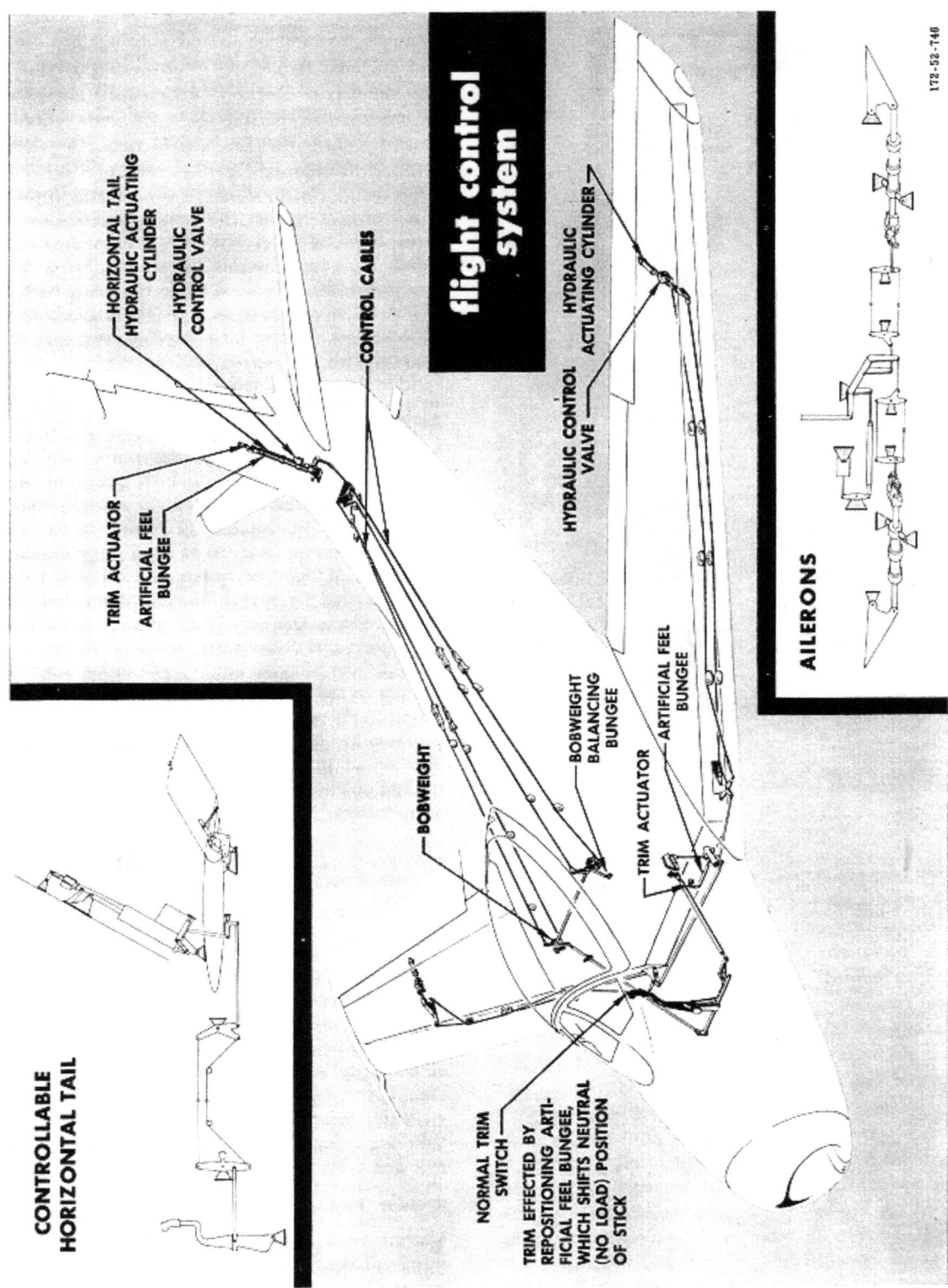

Figure 1-19

dial; when the visible dial numbers correspond, the pedals are adjusted evenly. Toe action on the pedals operates the wheel brakes.

Rudder Gust Lock.

The rudder gust lock (figures 4-12 and 4-13) is permanently installed and consists of an extendible tube located beneath the instrument panel at the top of the center pedestal. Pulling the tube aft engages the rudder lock when the rudder pedals are neutralized. On some airplanes,* to reduce the probability of a take-off being made with the rudder locked, the nose wheel steering system is also locked when the rudder gust lock is engaged. (No gust locks are provided for the ailerons and horizontal tail, because these units are locked against externally applied loads at all times because of the irreversible characteristics of the flight control hydraulic system.)

Normal Trim Switch.

Normal trim control for the ailerons and horizontal tail is accomplished electrically (by primary bus power) by means of a five-position, thumb-actuated switch (figure 1-20), on top of the control stick grip. Trim is effected by positioning the stick for the desired flight attitude, and then operating the trim switch to remove stick loads. When the lateral alternate trim switch is at NORMAL and the longitudinal alternate trim switch is at NORMAL GRIP CONT, holding the normal trim switch to either side causes the electric trim actuator to reposition the artificial feel bungee. This shifts the neutral (no-load) position of the stick and effects a new trim position of the ailerons. When the longitudinal alternate trim switch is at NORMAL GRIP CONT, holding the normal trim switch forward or aft causes the controllable horizontal tail trim actuator to reposition the artificial feel bungee (to relieve the pilot-applied push or pull forces) and allows the stick to assume a new neutral (no-load) position.

CAUTION

The lateral alternate trim switch must be at NORMAL, and the longitudinal alternate trim switch must be at NORMAL GRIP CONT for the normal trim switch to be effective for lateral trim. For the normal trim switch to be operable for longitudinal trim, the longitudinal alternate trim switch must be at NORMAL GRIP CONT.

*F-86E-15 Airplanes
†F-86E-1 through F-86E-6 Airplanes

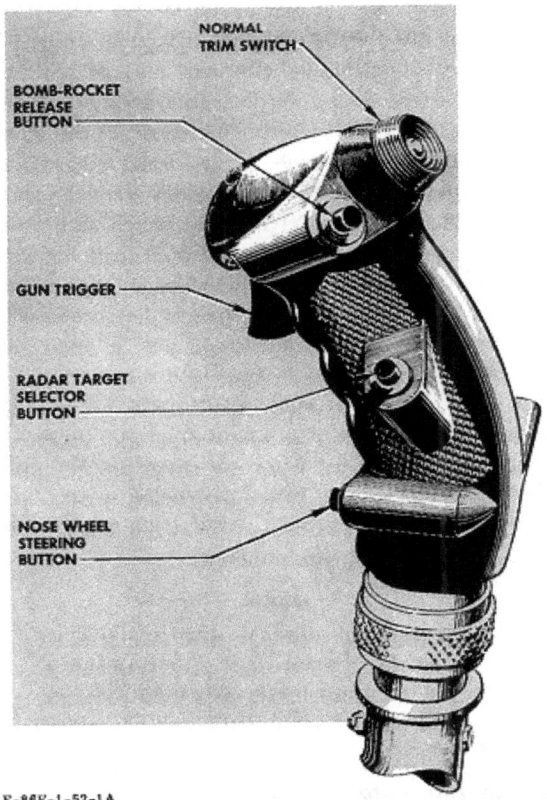

F-86E-1-52-1A

stick grip

Figure 1-20

The normal trim switch is spring-loaded to the center (OFF) position; when released, it automatically returns to this position and trim action stops.

WARNING

The normal trim switch is subject to sticking in any or all of the actuated positions, resulting in application of extreme trim. If this occurs in flight, the switch must be returned manually to the center (OFF) position after the desired amount of trim is obtained. If the switch sticks in any actuated position during ground check, enter this fact with a red cross in the DD Form 781 *and do not fly the airplane*.

Longitudinal Alternate Trim Switch.

An alternate trim circuit (primary-bus-powered) is provided for the horizontal tail. On early airplanes,† a four-position longitudinal alternate trim switch (13, figure 1-6) is on the left side of the cockpit, above and outboard of the throttle. On late airplanes,* a guarded four-position longitudinal alternate trim switch (24, figure 1-8) is on the left aft console. Operation of this switch accomplishes longitudinal trim in the same manner and at the same speed as the normal trim switch. The longitudinal alternate trim switch is usually kept at the NORMAL GRIP CONT position, which allows use of the normal trim switch on the stick grip for trim control. Holding the longitudinal alternate trim switch at NOSE UP or NOSE DOWN disconnects the normal trim circuits for ailerons and horizontal tail. It also trims the artificial feel bungee to reposition the neutral (no-load) position of the stick accordingly through the alternate trim circuit. The longitudinal alternate trim switch is spring-loaded from the NOSE UP and NOSE DOWN positions to OFF. When the switch is OFF, both of the normal trim circuits, as well as the longitudinal alternate trim circuit, are inoperative.

Note

The longitudinal alternate trim switch must be kept at the NORMAL GRIP CONT position in order for the normal trim switch on the stick grip to be operable for aileron and horizontal tail trim.

Lateral Alternate Trim Switch.

A four-position, primary-bus-powered switch (26, figure 1-6; 27, figure 1-8), on the left aft console, controls an alternate circuit for controlling lateral trim. The lateral alternate trim switch is ordinarily kept at NORMAL, which permits use of the normal trim switch on the stick grip. When the lateral alternate trim switch is held at either LEFT or RIGHT, the normal aileron trim circuit is disconnected, and the artificial feel bungee is trimmed to reposition the neutral (no-load) position of the stick, allowing the ailerons to assume a new trim position. The switch is spring-loaded from the LEFT and RIGHT positions to OFF. The normal and the alternate aileron trim circuits are inoperative when the lateral alternate trim switch is OFF.

CAUTION

The lateral alternate trim switch must be at the NORMAL position for the normal trim switch to be operable for lateral trim.

Rudder Trim Switch.

The rudder trim tab is actuated by primary bus power and is controlled by a three-position switch (25, figure 1-6; 25, figure 1-8), on the left aft console. The switch is held at LEFT or RIGHT for corresponding rudder trim and is spring-loaded from these positions to the center (OFF) position.

Take-off (Trim) Position Indicator Light.

A primary-bus-powered amber light (8, figure 1-4; 8, figure 1-5), on the instrument panel, indicates take-off trim position of the ailerons, horizontal tail, and rudder. On F-86E-1 through F-86E-10 Airplanes and on F-86E-15 Airplanes changed by T. O. 1F-86F-216, the light comes on whenever any one of these control surfaces is trimmed to its take-off position. The light will go out when the respective trim switch is released, and it comes on again as each subsequent control is trimmed for take-off. On F-86E-15 Airplanes not changed by T. O. 1F-86F-216, the light comes on whenever the ailerons and rudder are trimmed to take-off position and when the horizontal tail is trimmed to position the control stick grip full aft. The proper horizontal tail take-off trim is reached on these airplanes when the control stick grip is trimmed full aft (indicator light glows), then 2 inches forward.

Note

On F-86E-1 through F-86E-10 Airplanes, the take-off trim indicator light comes on when either the normal trim switch or the longitudinal alternate trim switch is used. On F-86E-15 Airplanes, however, only the normal trim switch can be used to obtain an indication of proper take-off trim.

The take-off trim position for the ailerons and rudder is neutral; horizontal tail take-off trim position is set for an airplane nose-up condition.

FLIGHT CONTROL HYDRAULIC SYSTEMS.

Two complete, independent hydraulic systems (figure 1-21) are provided to actuate the ailerons and controllable horizontal tail. A constant-pressure hydraulic system, powered by an engine-driven, variable-volume pump, serves as the flight control normal hydraulic system. An alternate constant-pressure hydraulic system, pressurized by an electrically powered (dc) pump, operates the controls if the normal system fails or does not work properly. The transfer from the normal to the alternate system is made automatically, or the alternate system can be selected by the pilot. Automatic change-over to the alternate system is done electrically

*F-86E-10 and later airplanes

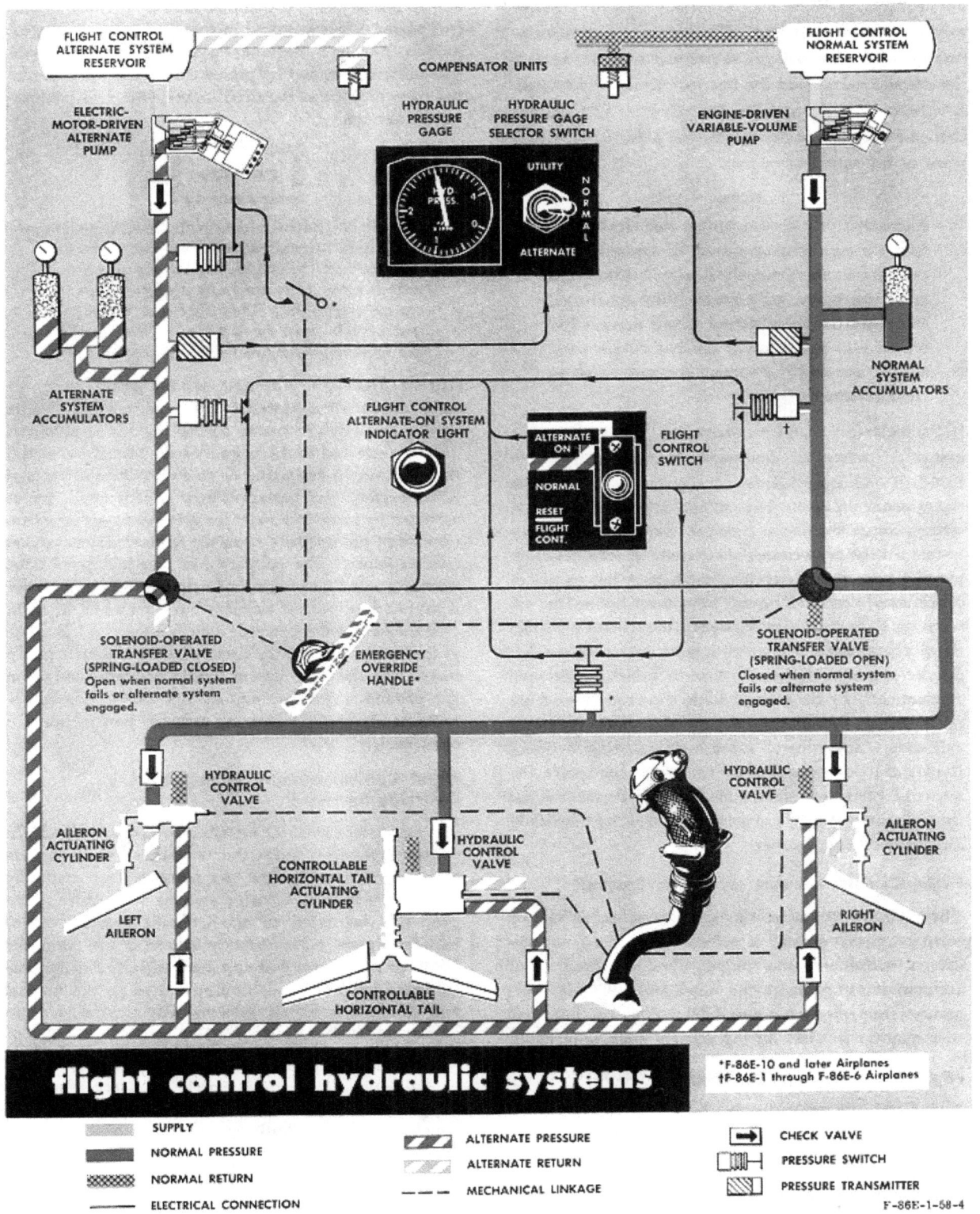

Figure 1-21

by pressure switches and solenoid-operated transfer valves within the systems. When normal system pressure drops below 650 psi, the pressure switches actuate the transfer valves, and the alternate system is engaged. A selector switch permits the pilot to initiate the change-over from one system to the other for test purposes or for actual operation.

Note

Automatic or pilot-controlled electrical transfer to the alternate system is prevented if pressure in the alternate system is below the minimum operating pressure. Pilot-controlled transfer from the alternate to the normal system is also prevented if normal system pressure is low and if adequate pressure exists in the alternate system.

If the electrical transfer systems fail, actuation of the manually controlled emergency transfer system (in F-86E-10 and later airplanes) mechanically positions the transfer valves to engage the alternate hydraulic system, regardless of the pressure available within this system. At the same time, the alternate hydraulic system pump is connected directly to the battery bus to ensure continuous electrical power for pump operation. (A warning light on the instrument panel comes on when the flight controls are operating on the alternate hydraulic system.) Hydraulic control valves, positioned mechanically by the control stick, direct pressure from the engaged system to the control surface actuating cylinders. Each control valve and actuating cylinder is of the dual-segment type (one segment serves the normal hydraulic system, and the other segment is for the alternate system), and each segment is hydraulically independent of the other.

Flight Control Normal Hydraulic System.

The flight control normal hydraulic system has its own separate reservoir and is pressurized by an engine-driven, variable-volume pump. Fluid is stored in an accumulator to meet sudden, high-rate demands. Normal system pressure is about 2700 to 3000 psi, but pressure may be reduced during control stick movement.

Flight Control Alternate Hydraulic System.

The flight control alternate hydraulic system has a separate reservoir, an electrically driven pump, and two accumulators to provide an alternate source of control power. Fluid is stored in the accumulators to meet sudden, high-rate demands. System pressure is automatically maintained by pressure switches that operate the pump motor as required to keep the two accumulators charged.

The flight control alternate hydraulic system is engaged automatically when external power is connected for engine start, because normal system pressure is not built up until after the engine is running. Therefore, the flight control switch must be held at RESET to effect change-over to the normal system before flight.

During flight, the alternate system pump motor of early airplanes* is powered by the battery bus. While on the ground, the motor control circuit is automatically transferred to the primary bus. Therefore, unless the generator is operating or an external power source is connected, the battery-starter switch must be at BATTERY to provide power for alternate system operation when the airplane is on the ground. However, on late airplanes,† the primary bus provides power for normal ground and flight operation. Battery bus power is supplied only if the primary bus fails while in flight or if the emergency override handle is actuated. Because of the heavy drain on the battery by the alternate pump motor, the alternate system should not be operated on the ground unless the engine is running (above approximately 45% rpm) or an external power source is connected.

Flight Control Manual Emergency Override System.‡

The emergency override system is used to transfer flight control operation from the normal to the alternate hydraulic system in case the automatic or manually operated electrical transfer systems do not function properly. Actuation of the override system control handle (figure 1-22) directly connects the alternate pump to the battery bus and mechanically engages the alternate system by positioning valves in the normal and alternate hydraulic systems. The change-over can be accomplished by the override system, regardless of the position of pressure switches within the flight control hydraulic systems or the setting of the manually operated electric transfer switch. An alternate-on warning light (6, figure 1-4; 5, figure 1-5), on the instrument panel, is illuminated when the alternate system is operating.

Note

When actuating the emergency override handle, make sure that it locks in the full extended

---

*F-86E-1 through F-86E-10 Airplanes
†F-86E-15 Airplanes
‡F-86E-10 and later airplanes

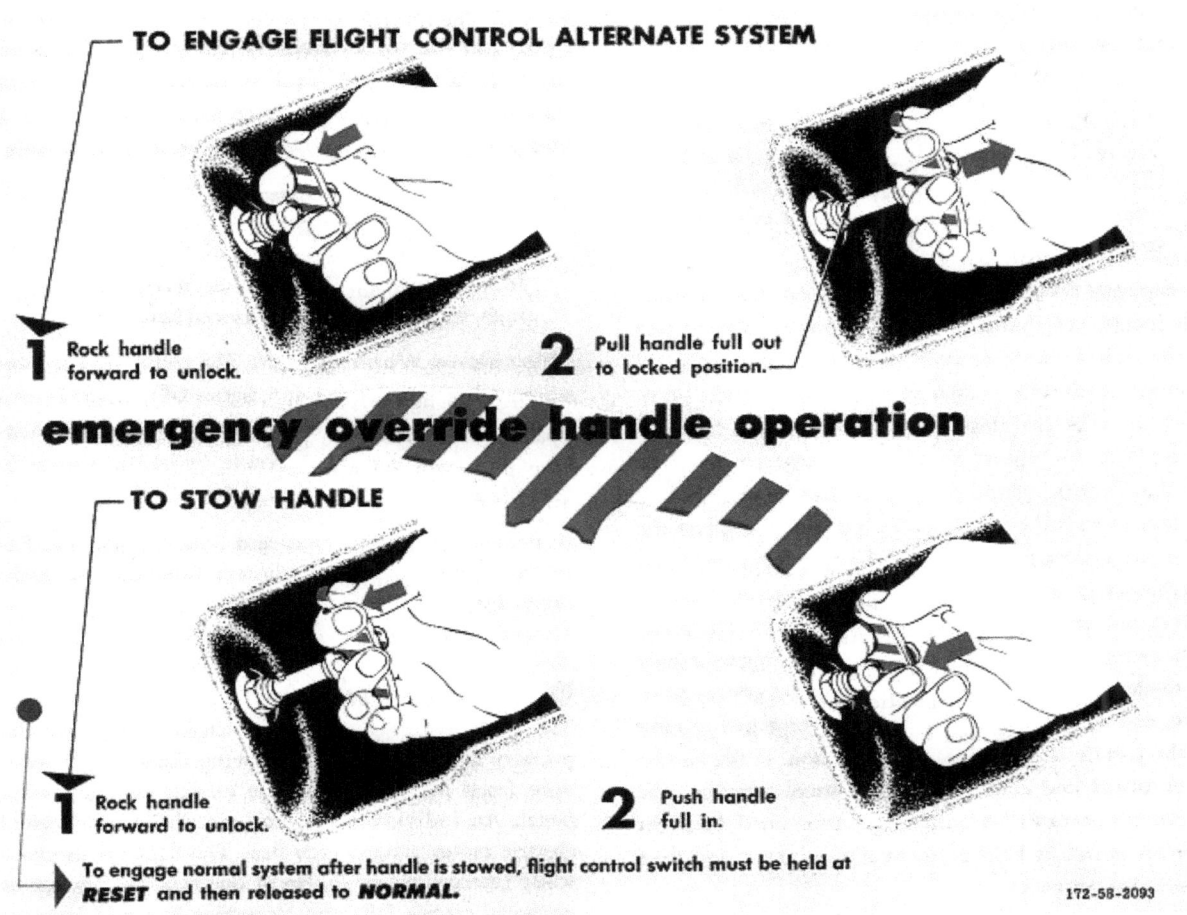

Figure 1-22

position to prevent it from returning to the stowed (inoperative) position.

Flight Control Hydraulic System Controls.

Flight Control Switch. The three-position flight control switch (24, figure 1-6; 23, figure 1-8), on the left aft console, provides a means of manually selecting either the normal or the alternate flight control hydraulic systems. The switch is normally primary-bus-powered. (If primary bus power is not available, battery bus power is supplied to the switch.) When the switch is at NORMAL (engine running), the normal system supplies hydraulic pressure to the flight controls, and the alternate system will cut in automatically if the normal system does not work properly. When the switch is moved to ALTERNATE ON, a transfer valve in the normal system is actuated to block normal system pressure, and a transfer valve in the alternate system is opened, permitting alternate system pressure to power the flight controls. (This transfer cannot be completed unless adequate pressure is available in the alternate system.) The RESET position, which is spring-loaded to NORMAL, de-energizes both the normal and alternate system transfer valves, allowing them to return to their normal positions (normal system operating). The RESET position of the flight control switch must be used whenever a transfer from the alternate to the normal system is desired. However, the engine must be running or a hydraulic test stand must be connected whenever this transfer is to be effected.

Note

On some early airplanes, this switch is marked "POWER CONTROLS" and has an ON EMERG. position instead of the ALTERNATE ON position.

If the alternate system fails after a normal system failure, the flight control system will automatically return to the normal system, whether the normal system will work or not. This is called the "automatic-return-to-normal" system.

> **Note**
>
> If the flight control alternate system has been selected by the emergency override handle and the alternate system fails, the system will not return to normal until the handle is returned to the stowed position.

Emergency Override Handle.* The emergency override handle (17, figure 1-9), recessed in the inboard face of the right forward console, permits the flight control alternate hydraulic system to be engaged if the automatic or selective electrical transfer systems fail. See figure 1-22 for operation of the emergency override handle. Unlocking and pulling the handle aft (about 3 inches) to its full out and locked position energizes the alternate system pump through battery bus power and mechanically actuates two solenoid-operated transfer valves to transfer flight control operation to the alternate system. The manual emergency change-over may be made regardless of normal or alternate system pressure, and the alternate system will be engaged as long as the handle is in the extended position. If the handle is unlocked and returned to its normal position, the alternate system will remain in operation until the flight control switch is held momentarily at RESET and then released to NORMAL.

> **CAUTION**
>
> Since the alternate system pump will operate continuously as long as the handle is extended, this override should be used only in case of emergency. The life of the pump may be shortened by excessive periods of operation. Also, drain on the battery in case of generator failure will appreciably shorten battery life.

Flight Control Hydraulic System Indicators.

Flight Control Hydraulic Fluid Level Indicator. Fluid level of the flight control hydraulic systems is indicated by a compensator shaft that extends down from each of the two hydraulic system compensator units. The white indicator shafts are checked visually through small access doors aft of the speed brakes. (See figure 1-35.) The normal system compensator is on the right side, and the alternate system compensator is on the left. When fluid level is correct (with system purged), the shaft will be extended at least 1/4 to 1 1/4 inches from the bottom of the compensator unit housing.

> **CAUTION**
>
> If the shaft does not protrude more than 1/4 inch, the system must be serviced before flight.

Alternate-on Warning Light. The amber alternate-on warning light (6, figure 1-4; 5, figure 1-5), on the instrument panel, is illuminated by primary bus power whenever the flight control alternate hydraulic system is operating.

Hydraulic Pressure Gage and Selector Switch. Refer to "Utility Hydraulic System Controls and Indicator" in this section.

WING FLAP SYSTEM.

The wing flaps are controlled and operated by the primary bus. The slotted-type wing flaps extend spanwise from the fuselage to the aileron on each wing panel. An individual electrical circuit and individual electric motor actuate each flap. The flaps are mechanically interconnected so that if one actuating motor or electrical circuit fails, the respective flap will be actuated through mechanical interconnection with the opposite flap. This mechanical interconnection also prevents individual or uneven flap operation, and a brake coil within each actuator prevents air loads from moving the flaps. Flap up-travel is limited by mechanical stops; flap down-travel is limited by electrical limit switches. No emergency system is provided, because enough protection is afforded in the normal system by the mechanical interconnection, the individual actuator motors, and the individual actuator motor circuits. There is no flap position indicator.

WING FLAP LEVER.

The wing flap lever (22, figure 1-6; 20, figure 1-8) moves in a quadrant inboard of the throttle. To position the flaps full up or down, the flap lever is moved to the UP or DOWN detent position. It is not necessary to return the flap lever to the HOLD detent position. To obtain intermediate flap positions in flight, the lever, which actuates a primary-bus-powered microswitch, is held at

---

*F-86E-10 and later airplanes

UP or DOWN and then is moved to HOLD when the desired flap setting is obtained. When the flaps are full up in flight, the flap lever should be at HOLD, to prevent damage to the flap actuating mechanism. Air loads cause the flaps to creep down slightly in flight. If the flap lever is not at HOLD, the flaps will continuously cycle up. On some airplanes, the flap lever must be moved outboard while on others it must be moved inboard to clear the detent.

WING LEADING EDGE.

Some airplanes are equipped with wing slats which extend along the leading edge of each wing from just outboard of the fuselage to the wing tip. (See 26, figure 1-3.) Aerodynamic forces acting upon the slats cause them to open and close automatically, depending upon the airspeed and attitude of the airplane. Upon opening, the slats move forward along a curved track to create a slot in the wing leading edge. This slot formation smoothes airflow over the upper surface of the wing and increases lift, resulting in lower stalling speeds. At higher airspeeds in unaccelerated flight, the slats close automatically to offer minimum drag for maximum flight performance. Other airplanes have a fixed-contour extended leading edge assembly, providing an increase in performance and improved maneuverability. On airplanes without slats, the chord of the extended leading edge is 6 inches greater at the root and 3 inches greater at the tip. Favorable low-speed characteristics have been retained on airplanes without slats by addition of a wing fence on the upper surface of each wing. For detailed comparison of the flight characteristics afforded by either leading edge configuration, refer to applicable paragraphs in Section VI.

SPEED BRAKE SYSTEM.

A hydraulically operated speed brake (29, figure 1-3) is located on each side of the fuselage, below the dorsal fin. Each brake consists of a hinged panel which, when open, extends down and forward into the air stream. Pressure for normal operation of the speed brakes is supplied by the utility hydraulic system. Emergency control for closing the speed brakes is also provided. With the engine at high rpm, the speed brakes will open in about 2 seconds. The brakes will close in about 2½ seconds at 435 knots in flight and in about 5 seconds at high rpm on the ground. There is no speed brake position indicator.

SPEED BRAKE SWITCH.

A serrated, sliding switch (figure 1-12), on top of the throttle, controls the speed brake operation. The switch, powered by the primary bus, has three fixed positions: IN, OUT, and a neutral (HOLD) position which is indicated by a white mark on the switch guide. The speed brakes can be stopped at any position by moving the switch to the neutral (HOLD) position. After the brakes have been opened or closed, the switch should be returned to the neutral (HOLD) position.

WARNING

Since the hydraulic lines to the speed brake actuating cylinders are routed near the engine, it is extremely important that the speed brake switch be kept in the neutral position to minimize the fire hazard if a line is damaged.

CAUTION

If the speed brakes are actuated while taxiing, hydraulic boost pressure will not be available for applying the wheel brakes until speed brake operation is completed and system pressure is restored. However, conventional hydraulic braking action will be available in direct proportion to pilot pressure on the brake pedals.

SPEED BRAKE EMERGENCY LEVER.

To provide a means of closing the speed brakes when normal operation fails, an emergency lever (10, figure 1-6; 21, figure 1-8) is installed just outboard of the throttle. Normally, the control is safety-wired at its aft, NORMAL, position. When pushed forward to EMERG. CLOSED, the control mechanically opens a dump valve, relieving hydraulic pressure from the speed brake actuating cylinders and permitting air loads to close the brakes. No emergency method of opening the speed brakes is provided.

LANDING GEAR SYSTEM.

The fully retractable tricycle landing gear, as well as the gear and wheel fairing doors, are hydraulically actuated and electrically (dc) controlled and sequenced. The main gear retracts inboard into the lower surface of the wing and fuselage; the nose gear retracts aft into the fuselage. The nose-gear strut and wheel are rotated 90 degrees, so that the nose wheel is horizontal when retracted. After the gear is down and locked, the wheel fairing doors are retracted to the closed position to prevent mud, dirt, etc, from entering the wheel wells during landing, taxiing, and take-off. Landing gear and wheel fairing door extension time is approximately 10 seconds, while retraction time is 8 seconds. A hydraulic steering unit is built into the nose gear assembly and serves as a conventional shimmy damper when the steering mechanism is not engaged. The main wheels are equipped with hydraulically operated, disk-type brakes. A brake lock, consisting of a parking brake valve and compensator, is provided for parking. The valve is operated when pressure is applied to the brake pedal and the parking brake handle (15, figure 1-6; 13, figure 1-8) in the cockpit is pulled. The parking brake valve also includes a compensator, which affords a small storage space for locked fluid under pressure when brakes are in the parked condition. The compensator also provides relief from thermal expansion.

Nose Gear Ground Safety Lock.

A ground safety lock may be inserted in the nose gear assembly to prevent collapsing of the nose gear on the ground. (See figure 1-23.) The lock has a conventional warning streamer which must be removed before flight. No ground safety locks are provided for the main gear, because weight of the airplane on the main gear prevents accidental release while the airplane is motionless.

LANDING GEAR HANDLE.

The landing gear handle (23, figure 1-5; 18, figure 1-6; and 16, figure 1-8), through primary bus power, electrically controls the gear and gear door hydraulic selector valves. Moving the handle to UP or DOWN causes utility hydraulic system pressure to position the gear correspondingly. On some airplanes, the handle has three marked positions: UP, COMBAT (neutral), and DOWN. On other airplanes, the handle has only two marked positions: UP and DOWN. When the gear is down and locked and the weight of the airplane is on the gear, a ground safety switch prevents gear retraction if the gear handle is inadvertently moved to UP. The wheel fairing doors on airplanes with the two-position landing gear handle are not controlled by this switch and will follow their normal sequence, opening when the handle is moved to UP, thereby providing warning to the ground crew that the gear control is in the wrong position for ground operation.

Note

To facilitate ground handling on airplanes with the two-position landing gear handle, the gear doors may be opened (without moving the gear handle) by means of a switch in the left gear strut well. If the switch has been used, it must be reset before flight; otherwise, the doors will not close when the gear is extended for landing.

The ground safety switch can be intentionally overridden by use of a landing gear emergency-up button.

LANDING GEAR EMERGENCY RELEASE HANDLE.

If the utility hydraulic system or electrical system fails, the gear can be lowered mechanically by use of the landing gear emergency release handle (figure 1-24), at the bottom of the center pedestal.

The emergency release handle must be pulled to full extension (approximately 20 inches) with a force of about 60 pounds to release all

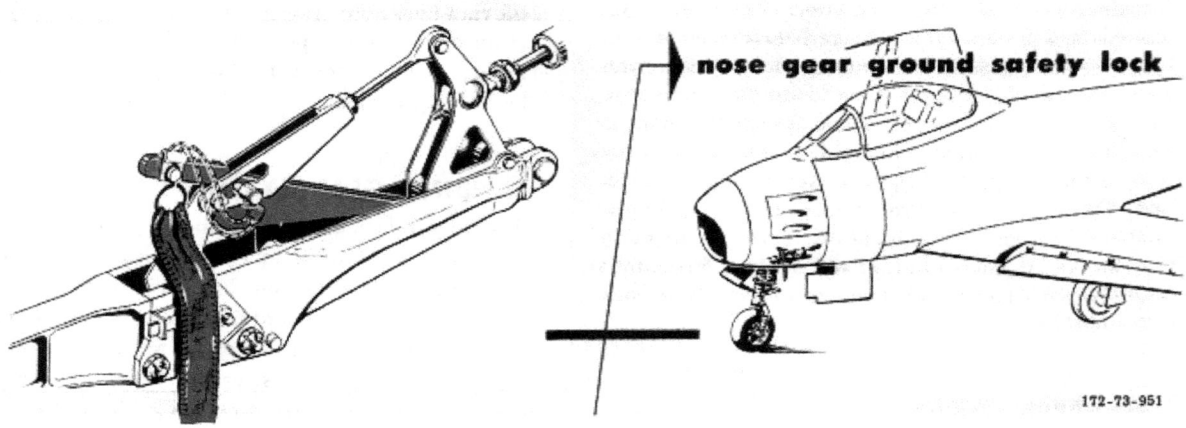

Figure 1-23

gear uplocks and properly position the hydraulic selector valves.

When the release handle is pulled, the main gear and all gear doors are mechanically unlocked. As long as the handle is held extended, the landing gear hydraulic valves are held in position to lower the landing gear. If hydraulic pressure is available and the emergency release handle is held fully extended until a safe gear indication has been obtained for at least 11 seconds, all three gears will extend and lock down.

If the gear must be lowered in this manner, the landing gear handle must first be placed in the DOWN position; otherwise, the main gear may retract when the emergency release handle is released.

If hydraulic pressure is not available, the main gear will fall free when the release handle is pulled. However, the emergency hydraulic selector on airplanes so equipped must be placed at NOSE GEAR and pressure supplied with the hand-pump to unlock the nose gear uplocks and force the nose gear down. On airplanes without the emergency hydraulic selector, pulling the release handle also opens a control valve, which allows pressure from the nose gear emergency accumulator to extend the nose gear. This pressure is sufficient for one extension only, and the control valve must be reset on the ground.

After being lowered by means of the emergency release handle, the nose gear cannot be retracted in flight on airplanes without the emergency hydraulic selector. Therefore, to restore normal operation, the nose gear selector valve must be reset before the next flight if the gear has been lowered by use of the landing gear emergency release handle.

LANDING GEAR EMERGENCY-UP BUTTON.

Do not use the landing gear emergency-up button in flight to raise the gear, because damage to gear doors and the gear lowering mechanism may result.

If it is necessary to collapse the gear on the ground (because of insufficient runway in which to stop the air-

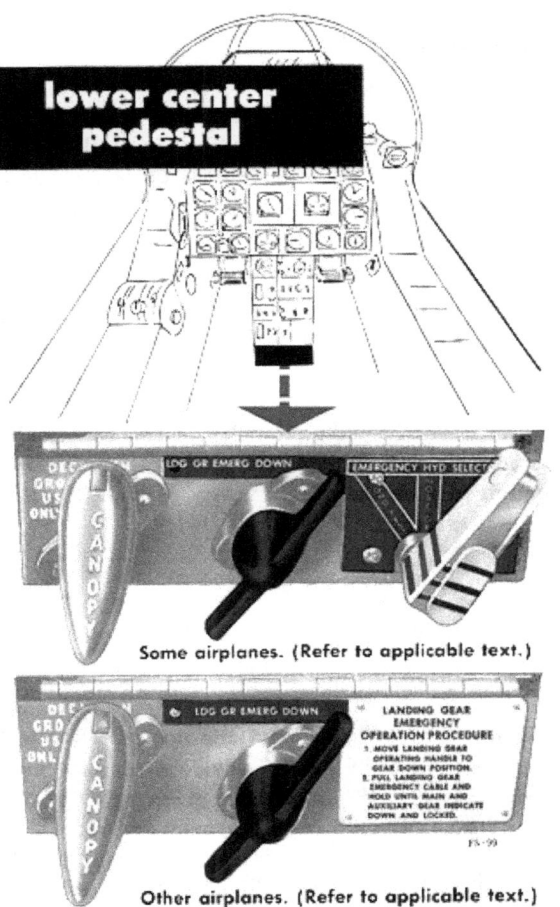

Figure 1-24

plane), the landing gear ground safety switch can be overridden by use of a guarded emergency-up button switch (17, figure 1-6), powered by the battery bus and located above the gear control handle. When the emergency-up button is depressed and the landing gear handle is up, the ground safety switch is by-passed, and the gear is retracted hydraulically in the normal manner, except that the gear fairing doors may not have sufficient time to fully open. The button must be held depressed until the gear retracts completely (about 5 seconds). The button is effective only if hydraulic pressure and battery power are available.

Note

To accelerate gear retraction by the emergency-up button, alternately pump the brake pedals or engage the nose wheel steering, and give alternate rudder applications. These actions will relieve the pressure on the main gear downlock pins and result in faster retraction.

LANDING GEAR HANDLE-UP INDICATOR LIGHT.

On airplanes with the three-position landing gear handle, a primary-bus-powered amber light (figure 1-16), located on the left forward console, illuminates whenever the gear handle is in the UP position to remind the pilot that the handle should be returned to COMBAT. (The gear handle-up indicator light can be turned to dim when desired.) In flight, if the handle is left at UP, negative G acceleration may actuate the gear sequence switch and cause the gear doors to open and close, which, at high speeds, would damage the doors. On the ground, if the handle is inadvertently moved to UP, the ground safety switch will prevent gear retraction; however, if the airplane is subsequently taxied on rough ground, the gear struts may extend enough to open the ground safety switch and permit the gear to retract.

LANDING GEAR POSITION INDICATORS.

On early airplanes,* landing gear position indicator lights, powered by the primary bus, are on the left forward console (figure 1-16). Three green lights (one for each corresponding gear) and one red light (connected to the three gears) provide a constant visual indication of gear position. Each green light comes on when the corresponding gear is down and locked. The red light comes on when any gear is in an unlocked position. It will also come on if the gear is up and locked and the throttle is retarded below minimum cruising rpm or if gear is up and locked and any door is not completely closed. On late airplanes,† the position of the landing gear is shown by three primary-bus-powered indicators on the left forward console (figure 1-16). One indicator is provided for each gear and will display parallel red and yellow diagonal lines if its respective gear is unlocked. The word "UP" appears if the gear is up and locked, and a miniature wheel shows when the gear is down and locked.

CAUTION

If the switch assembly in the landing gear handle should fail, the landing gear unsafe warning light and landing gear warning horn may not operate, and the landing gear cannot be raised or lowered. For this reason, the landing gear position indicators must be used as the primary indication of gear position.

Note

Since the indicators are actuated by primary bus power, diagonal lines also appear when the battery-starter switch is not at BATTERY or when the primary bus is not energized.

LANDING GEAR UNSAFE WARNING LIGHT.

On airplanes with the two-position landing gear handle, a red warning light within the wheel of the landing gear handle is illuminated by power from the primary bus when any gear is unlocked. It also comes on if the gear is up and locked when the throttle is retarded below minimum cruising rpm or if the gear is up and locked and any gear door is not completely closed. On some of these airplanes, the light dims automatically when the instrument ring lights are turned on.

LANDING GEAR WARNING HORN.

A warning horn (powered by the primary bus), in the cockpit, sounds steadily if the gear is not down and locked when the throttle is retarded below cruising power. A horn cutout button (figure 1-16) is provided to silence the horn. Advancing the throttle resets the horn circuit.

NOSE WHEEL STEERING SYSTEM.

Nose wheel steering is electrically engaged (by primary bus power) and hydraulically powered, and is controlled by rudder pedal action. The steering system is engaged when the steering button, on the control stick grip, is depressed and the rudder pedals are operated to control a hydraulically operated nose wheel steering unit. (The flight control lock must be disengaged—full in.) This unit allows the wheel to be turned about 21 degrees each side of center by pressure on the respective rudder pedal. When not engaged for steering, the unit serves as a conventional hydraulic shimmy damper. A safety switch, on the nose wheel strut scissors, prevents engagement of the steering unit whenever the weight of the airplane is off the nose gear.

NOSE WHEEL TOWING RELEASE PIN.

The nose wheel towing release pin is on the left side of the nose gear strut, just above the wheel fork. For towing the airplane, the pin is disengaged by removing the safety cap and inserting the tow pin wedge in the tow

---

*F-86E-1 through F-86E-6 Airplanes
†F-86E-10 and later airplanes

pin. This disconnects the steering unit damper, allowing the wheel to swivel.

CAUTION

The safety cap should be on and tight before flight; this will ensure that the pin is engaged and that the nose wheel will retract properly. Also make sure that the tow pin wedge is securely stowed on the tow lug.

NOSE WHEEL STEERING BUTTON.

A finger-operated, push-button type nose wheel steering button, on the control stick grip (figure 1-20), actuates a shutoff valve by means of primary bus power to supply hydraulic pressure to the nose gear steering unit. In order to engage the steering unit, the button must be depressed, and the rudder pedals must be aligned in the direction the nose wheel is turned. When the nose wheel and rudder pedals are coordinated in this manner, the nose wheel steering unit is automatically engaged.

Note

The nose wheel steering unit will not engage if the nose wheel is more than 21 degrees either side of center. If the nose wheel is turned more than this, it must be brought into the steering range by use of the wheel brakes.

WHEEL BRAKE SYSTEM.

The wheel brakes are operated by toe action on the rudder pedals. Brake pressure is supplied from two brake master cylinders supplemented by pressure from the utility hydraulic system. However, in the event that no pressure is available from the utility hydraulic system, the brakes function through conventional action of the brake master cylinders when toe pressure is applied to the rudder pedals.

PARKING BRAKE HANDLE.

The parking brake handle (15, figure 1-6; 13, figure 1-8) is on the left side of the cockpit, above and outboard of the landing gear handle. To set the parking brakes, it is necessary to press hard on the toe brakes, pull the parking brake handle all the way out (approximately 2 inches), release toe brake pressure, and then release the parking brake handle, making sure it remains extended. Parking brakes are released when pressure is exerted on the toe brakes. If brakes do not release easily, the toe brakes should be pressed hard, and the parking brake handle should be pushed all the way in. If the parking brake handle is not full in, the brakes will be inoperative.

INSTRUMENTS.

Most of the instruments are of the electrical type and are located on the instrument panel. (See figures 1-4 and 1-5.) Power for these instruments is received from the ac and/or dc electrical systems. A secondary-bus-powered automatic vibrator is mounted on the forward side of the instrument panel to prevent instrument lag or sticky pointer indications. (Refer to system involved for information concerning instruments associated with specific systems.)

AIRSPEED INDICATOR.

The airspeed indicator (32, figure 1-4; 28, figure 1-5) is conventional, with the addition of a red and yellow limiting hand. This hand has two adjustments. The first permits setting the hand to indicate the airspeed corresponding to a limit Mach number. This adjustment is indicated by the position of a small index marker on the Mach scale on the circumference of the dial. The second prevents clockwise movement of the limiting hand beyond a limit airspeed. The limiting hand will indicate the airspeed corresponding to a limit Mach number or limit airspeed, whichever is less, for a given external loading configuration. (Refer to "Airspeed Limitations" in Section V.) If there is no airspeed or Mach number limit for the airplane, the hand will be set to show, at any altitude, the airspeed corresponding to Mach 1.0, which is the design limit of the instrument.

On some airplanes, the indicator is also equipped with a vernier drum, which allows the pilot to read airspeed to the nearest knot. The pitot-static head is installed on a boom on the right wing tip. Airspeed indications do not have to be corrected for installation error.

ALTIMETER.

Some airplanes have a conventional-type altimeter. Other airplanes are equipped with a modified altimeter (figure 1-25), which in addition to the standard 1,000 and 100 foot pointers, includes a new 10,000 foot pointer (notched disc with an extension pointer), which serves a second function as a warning indicator. The warning indicator is a striped section which appears through the notched disc at altitudes below 16,000 feet. This altimeter offers improved readability and gives warning when an altitude of less than 16,000 feet is entered.

modified altimeter

Figure 1-25

MACHMETER.

A Machmeter (28, figure 1-4; 24, figure 1-5) is provided as a flight instrument for indicating speed. (Refer to "Mach Number" in Section VI.) The Machmeter is valuable to you, especially at high altitudes, because its reading is more closely related to true airspeed than is indicated airspeed. For example, at 45,000 feet an indicated airspeed of 240 knots is actually a true airspeed of 510 knots. This true airspeed is indicated on the Machmeter as Mach .89 at 45,000 feet or Mach .77 at sea level. Thus, there is a difference of only about one-tenth Mach number between 45,000 feet and sea level, while indicated airspeed varies 270 knots.

ACCELEROMETER.

Some airplanes are equipped with a two-pointer type accelerometer with one pointer indicating the current positive accelerations and the other pointer recording and remaining set at the maximum positive acceleration encountered. The remaining airplanes have a three-pointer accelerometer (3, figure 1-4; 2, figure 1-5) that indicates positive and negative accelerations. In addition to the normal indicator pointer, two movable recording pointers (one for positive G and one for negative G) follow the indicator pointer to its maximum travel. The recording pointers remain at the respective maximum travel positions, thus providing a record of maximum accelerations encountered. To return the recording pointers to the normal (1G) position, it is necessary to press the knob on the lower left corner of the instrument ring.

STAND-BY COMPASS.

A conventional magnetic compass (12, figure 1-4), on the windshield bow, to the right of the instrument panel, is furnished for navigation in the event of instrument or electrical system failure. On early airplanes,* the illumination is controlled by a switch (primary-bus-powered) just below the compass; on later airplanes,† illumination is controlled by a switch (primary-bus-powered) on the right forward console, and brilliancy of illumination is controlled by the console lighting rheostat (primary-bus-powered).

DIRECTIONAL INDICATOR (SLAVED).

Refer to "Navigation Equipment" in Section IV.

ATTITUDE INDICATOR.

A visual indication of the flight attitude of the airplane in pitch and roll is provided by the gyro-controlled J-8 attitude indicator (16, figure 1-4; 12, figure 1-5) on the instrument panel. The unit is electrically operated (three-phase ac) and has an "OFF" indicator flag, which appears in the upper right arc of the dial whenever power is not being supplied or if the indicator is not up to speed. Within a range of 27 degrees in a climb or dive, the pitch attitude of the airplane is indicated by displacement of the horizon bar in relation to the miniature indicator airplane. When the pitch attitude of the airplane exceeds 27 degrees, the horizon bar remains in the extreme position, and the sphere then serves as the reference. If the climb or dive angle is further increased with the airplane approaching a vertical position, the attitude is indicated by graduations on the sphere. After certain maneuvers, the attitude indicator will "lag" approximately 5 degrees upon return to straight and level flight. The unit begins to correct these errors immediately. The gyro may be manually caged by use of the caging knob on the lower right side of the bezel. Caging is accomplished by smoothly pulling the knob away from the instrument and releasing it quickly, as soon as it reaches the limit of travel. The manual caging feature permits fast gyro

---

*F-86E-1 through F-86E-6 Airplanes
†F-86E-10 and later airplanes

erection for scramble take-offs or for erecting the gyro to correct in-flight errors caused by turns or aerobatics. For scramble take-offs, 30 seconds should be allowed after the power is applied to bring the gyro up to speed; it should then be caged immediately. The gyro should be caged to correct in-flight errors only when the airplane is in straight and level flight as determined by visual reference to a true horizon, since the indicator cages to the attitude of the airplane. A knob on the lower left side of the bezel permits the miniature indicator airplane to be adjusted to compensate for longitudinal trim changes.

TURN-AND-SLIP INDICATOR.

An electrically driven (primary-bus-powered) turn-and-slip indicator (22, figure 1-4; 18, figure 1-5) is on the instrument panel. The instrument is calibrated so that one standard needle-width turn will accomplish a 360-degree turn in 4 minutes (1½-degree-per-second rate of turn).

EMERGENCY EQUIPMENT.
ENGINE FIRE DETECTOR SYSTEM.

Two fire detector systems are provided to detect and indicate fire in the forward and aft engine compartments. (The forward engine compartment, which includes the compressor and accessory section, and the aft compartment, which includes the combustion chambers and the tail pipe, are divided by a fire wall at the engine mid-frame.) The system consists of fire detector units, mounted throughout the engine and engine compartments, and warning lights in the cockpit. No fire extinguishing system is installed. An abnormal rise of temperature within either engine compartment is indicated by red warning lights (11, figure 1-4), mounted on the shroud, above the right side of the instrument panel. The two lights (powered by the primary bus), one for the forward and one for the aft compartment, come on to show an excessive temperature condition of fire in the respective engine section. Operation of the system and lights can be checked by means of a test button (13, figure 1-4) below the lights; the lights are push-to-test type, permitting check of bulb illumination independent of system operation.

CANOPY.

The sliding canopy can be controlled from either inside or outside of the airplane. The canopy actuator is powered by the primary bus when the secondary bus is energized. If secondary bus power is not available, the actuator circuit is transferred to the battery bus or an external power source, and the battery-starter switch

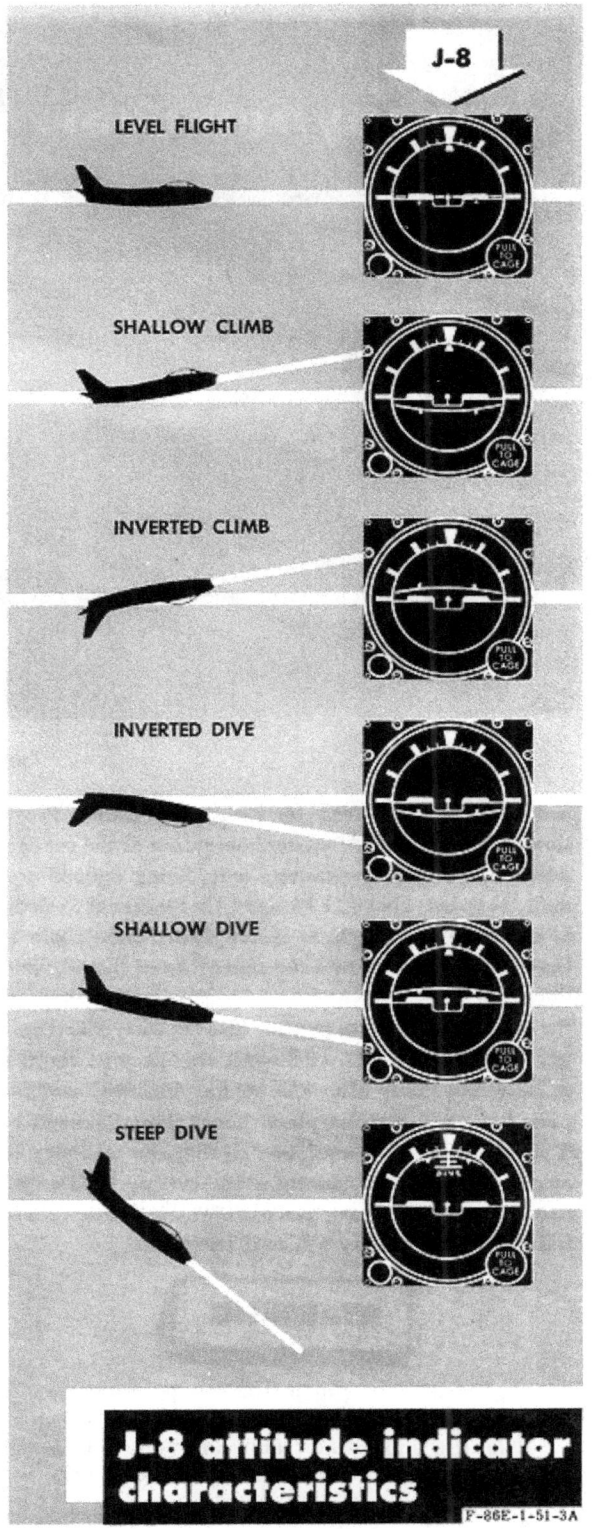

Figure 1-26

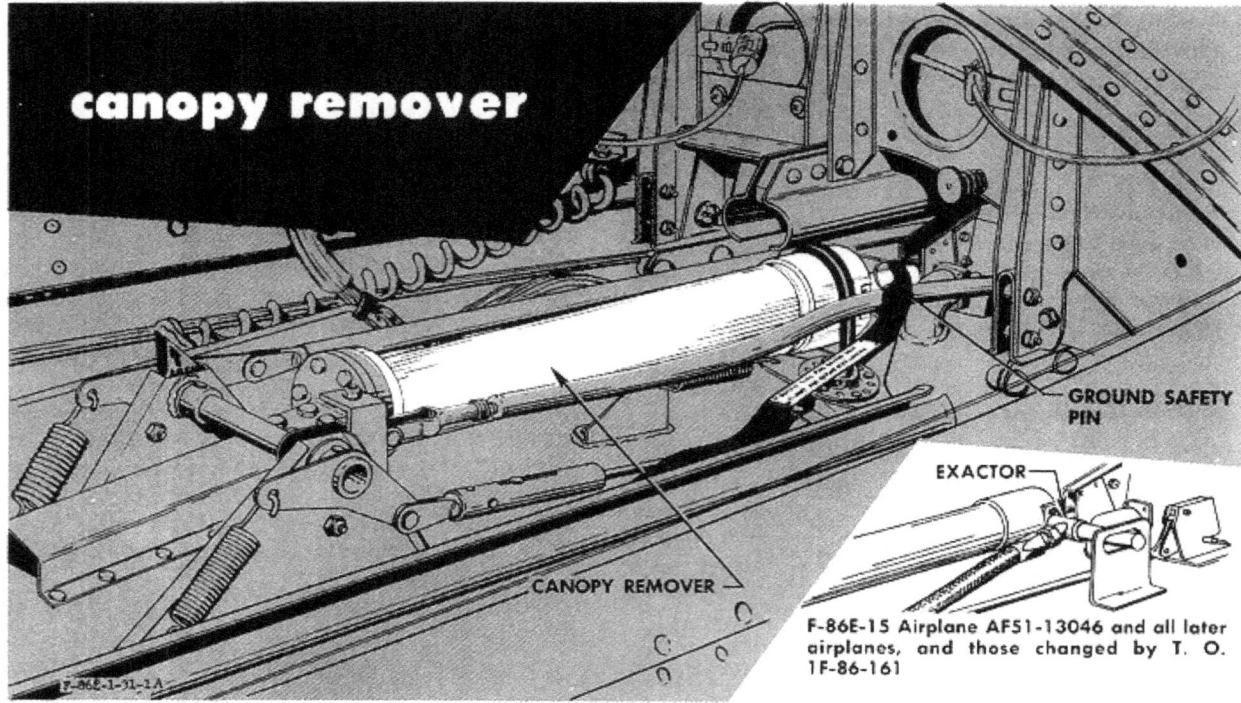

Figure 1-27

need not be at BATTERY for canopy operation. Provisions are also made for manual operation of the canopy. Air loads prevent the canopy from being opened normally at speeds above 215 knots IAS. Emergency release of the canopy in flight is accomplished by a remover (figure 1-27), which fires the canopy from the airplane. When the canopy is ejected, it pulls a safety pin from the seat catapult firing mechanism. On early airplanes* not changed by T. O. 1F-86-161, this permits the seat to be ejected only after the canopy has fired and has pulled the pin. Late airplanes† and those changed by T. O. 1F-86-161 are equipped so that the seat may be ejected through the canopy if the canopy fails to jettison; or the seat may be ejected normally if the canopy fails to pull the safety pin as it jettisons.

WARNING

A ground safety pin in the canopy remover on early airplanes* not changed by T. O. 1F-86-161, and in the canopy initiator on late airplanes† and those changed by T. O.

1F-86-161 prevents the remover from being fired accidentally while the airplane is on the ground. This safety pin must be removed before flight and stowed in the map case, and must be reinstalled after flight.

Canopy Seal.

Pressure for inflation of the seal, which seals the canopy in the closed position, is provided by air from the engine compressor section and is automatically controlled by a pressure regulator. The seal is inflated whenever the canopy is fully closed and the engine is operating. When the canopy switch is actuated, the seal is automatically deflated to allow the canopy to move. The seal is also automatically deflated before canopy ejection.

Note

If the canopy switch is moved to CLOSE during flight, the canopy seal will be deflated. This action at altitude will result in loss of cockpit pressurization. However, when the switch is released, the seal will be inflated and the cockpit will become pressurized again.

---

*F-86E-1 through F-86E-10 Airplanes and F-86E-15 Airplanes AF51-12977 through -13045
†F-86E-15 Airplane AF51-13046 and all later airplanes

CANOPY CONTROLS.

Canopy External Control Buttons.

The canopy is electrically operated and externally controlled by two battery-bus-powered, spring-loaded push buttons (17, figure 1-3), located on each side of the fuselage about 2 feet below and in line with the windshield bow. One button is marked "OPEN," the other "CLOSED." Depressing either button results in corresponding operation of the canopy.

Note

Operation of any external button overrides the setting of the canopy switch in the cockpit; however, if the canopy switch is left at OPEN and an external button is used for closing, the canopy will open as soon as the external button is released.

Canopy Switch.

The canopy is controlled from within the cockpit by a three-position toggle switch (16, figure 1-6; 14, figure 1-8) above the left forward console. To close the canopy, the battery-bus-powered switch must be held at the spring-loaded CLOSE position. Moving the switch to OPEN will open the canopy. When the canopy reaches the full open position, power to the canopy actuator is automatically cut off. When the switch is at its center (OFF) position, the canopy is locked, whether fully open, partially open, or closed.

Canopy Declutch Handle.

The canopy declutch handle (figure 1-24), at the bottom of the center pedestal, is intended for emergency use on the ground only. Pulling the declutch handle to its full extension (about 2 inches) disengages the canopy from the drag latches, so that the canopy can be moved manually. On most airplanes,* when the handle is released the canopy is automatically re-engaged, unless the canopy has been moved aft from the drag latches after release. On late airplanes,† when the handle is released the canopy can re-engage only by releasing the lock mechanism located just aft of the seat. The declutch handle may be used in flight, but only if the canopy cannot be jettisoned by the right handgrip on the seat.

Canopy Manual Operating Handle.

A manual operating handle is on the inside of the canopy, on the right side of the canopy bow. It is used for pulling the canopy open on the ground, in the event that it cannot be opened electrically, or in flight only if the canopy must be declutched for removal. The handle must be held out while the canopy is being pulled open manually.

Canopy Emergency Jettison Release.

When the hinged right handgrip on airplanes not changed by T. O. 1F-86-227 or either handgrip on airplanes changed by T. O. 1F-86-227 is pulled full up in preparation for seat ejection, the canopy remover is fired, jettisoning the canopy rearward to permit emergency ejection. The canopy can be jettisoned at any airspeed or airplane attitude. On early airplanes* not changed by T. O. 1F-86-161, mechanical linkage from the right handgrip releases the sear pin in the canopy remover, thus firing the cartridge. On late airplanes† and those changed by T. O. 1F-86-161, the mechanical linkage assembly for firing the canopy has been replaced by an initiator-exactor system. Raising the right handgrip fires a cartridge within the initiator. On airplanes changed by T. O. 1F-86-227, raising either handgrip fires the cartridge. The gases produced move a piston in the exactor. Movement of the piston pulls the sear pin from the canopy remover, causing the remover to fire.

WARNING

A ground safety pin in the canopy remover, on early airplanes* not changed by T. O. 1F-86-161 and in the canopy initiator on late airplanes† and those changed by T. O. 1F-86-161, prevents the remover from being fired accidentally while the airplane is on the ground. This safety pin must be removed before flight and stowed in the map case. It must be reinstalled after flight.

Canopy Alternate Emergency Jettison Handle.

Some airplanes have been changed to include a canopy alternate emergency jettison handle (18, figure 1-9) whereby the canopy may be jettisoned without arming the seat catapult. The handle, labeled "ALT CANOPY JET" is mounted on the frame just to the right of the instrument panel. When this handle is pulled to its full extended position (approximately 2 inches), a mechanical linkage withdraws the initiator sear pin, firing a cartridge within the canopy initiator. This actuates the exactor and fires the canopy remover.

Note

This handle is provided as an alternate means of removing the canopy and is designed to be

---

*F-86E-1 through F-86E-10 Airplanes and F-86E-15 Airplanes AF51-12977 through -13045
†F-86E-15 Airplane AF51-13046 and all later airplanes

Section I
T. O. 1F-86E-1

used when it is desired to jettison the canopy without arming the seat catapult. It should not be used in place of the seat handgrip sequence when ejection from the airplane is intended.

Canopy External Emergency Release Handle.

The canopy external emergency release handle (figure 1-28) can be reached through an access door on the left side of the fuselage, below the canopy frame. Pulling this handle to its full extension (approximately 2 inches) disengages the canopy and allows it to be moved manually by means of hinged handles on each side of the canopy. The canopy external emergency release handle does not fire the canopy remover.

EJECTION SEAT.

The ejection seat (figures 1-29, 1-30, and 1-31) permits emergency ejection at any speed or flight attitude. An explosive cartridge-type catapult is mounted vertically behind the seat and, when fired, supplies the necessary propulsion force to eject the seat and pilot from the airplane. The seat has either a manual opening or automatic opening safety belt. The seat accommodates a back-type parachute. A one-man life raft or survival kit may be used in place of the seat cushion. If additional height is needed when raft or survival kit is carried, use a solid filler block, provided combined thickness does not exceed 5 inches.

WARNING

Do not use the A-5 seat cushion, or any similar sponge rubber cushion, when equipped with a one-man life raft or survival kit. If ejection is necessary, serious spinal injuries can result when the ejection force compresses the cushion and enables the seat to gain considerable momentum before exerting a direct force on the pilot. In addition, where a crash landing is made, the combined compressiveness of the two items will permit the pilot to sink far enough to loosen the shoulder harness, allowing him to slump forward. In this forward position, the back may be severely injured on impact.

The seat may be adjusted vertically, and the headrest has provisions for fore and aft horizontal adjustment. The armrests and footrests are fixed; however, handgrips at the forward end of the armrests are hinged to actuate the ejection sequence. Airplanes not changed by T. O. 1F-86-227 have a mechanical linkage assembly which operates the firing lever in the seat catapult. Airplanes changed by T. O. 1F-86-227 have mechanical

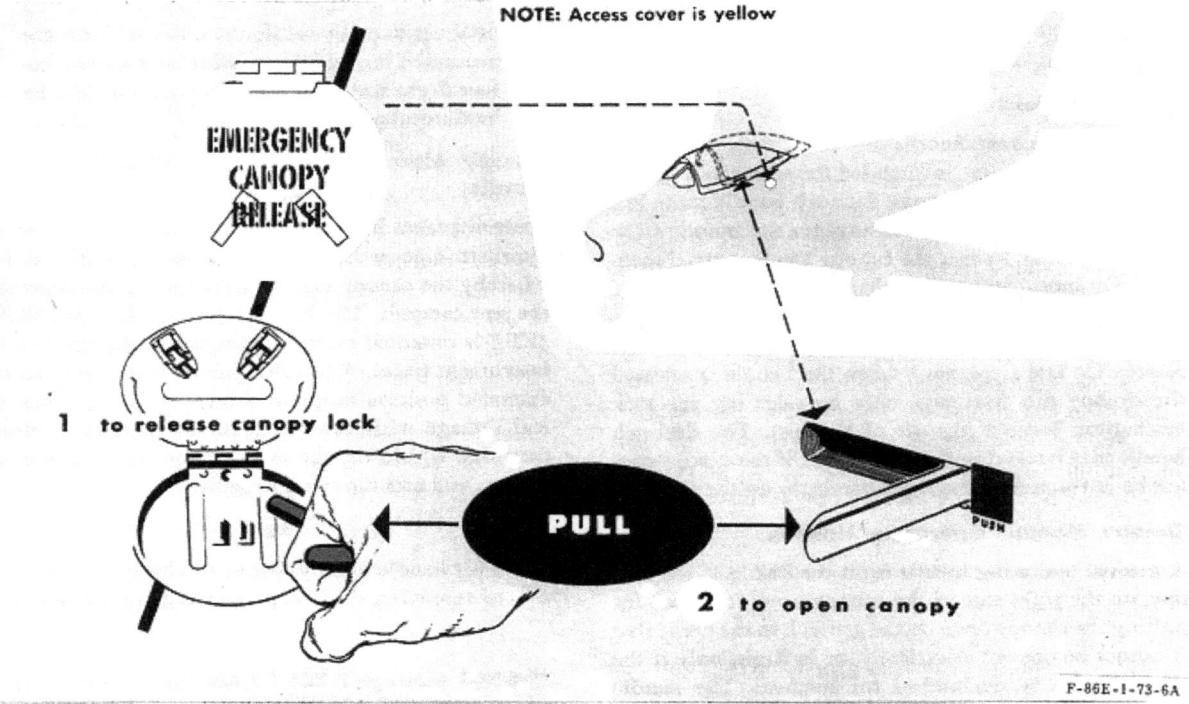

Figure 1-28

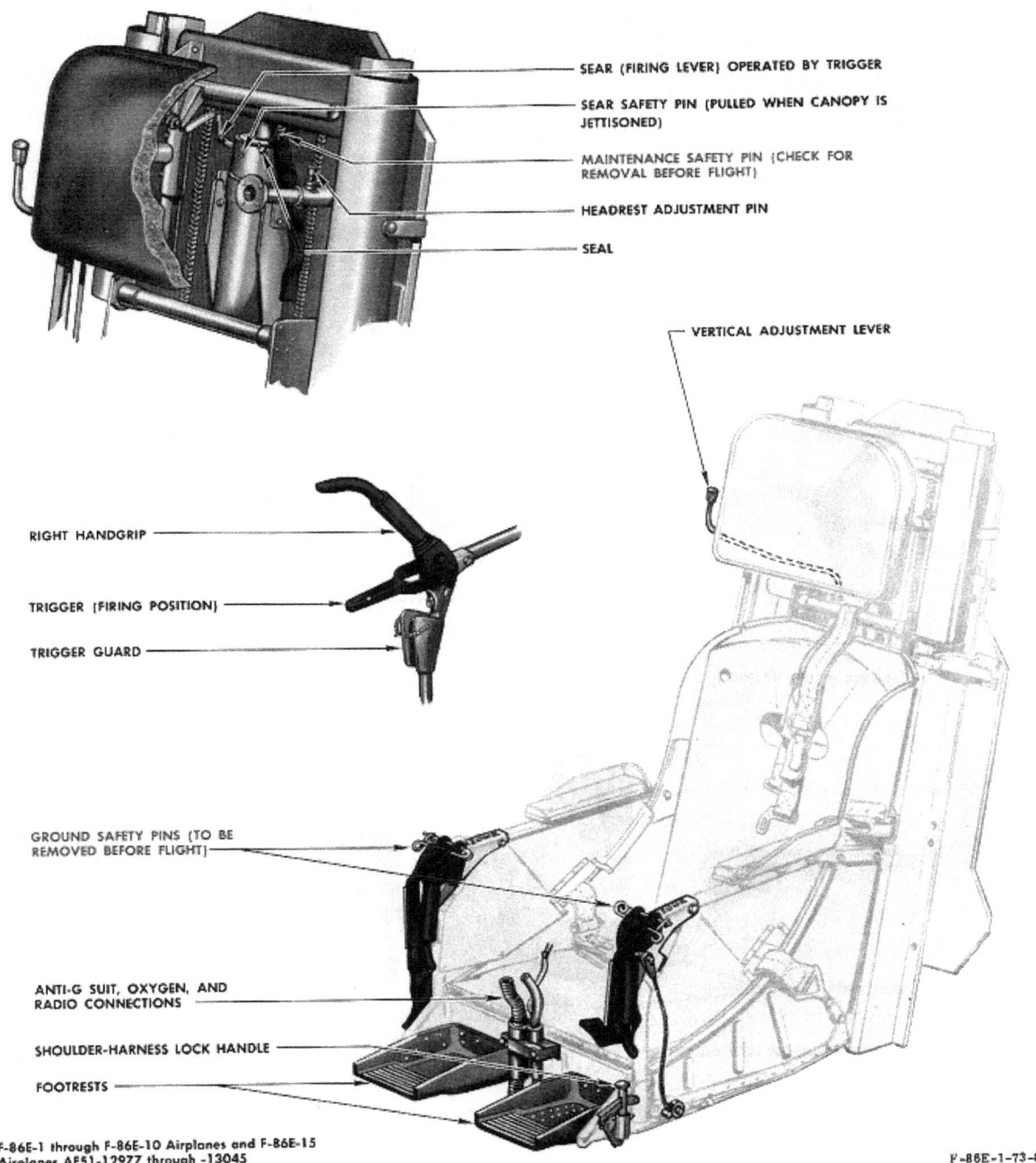

Figure 1-29

Section I
T. O. 1F-86E-1

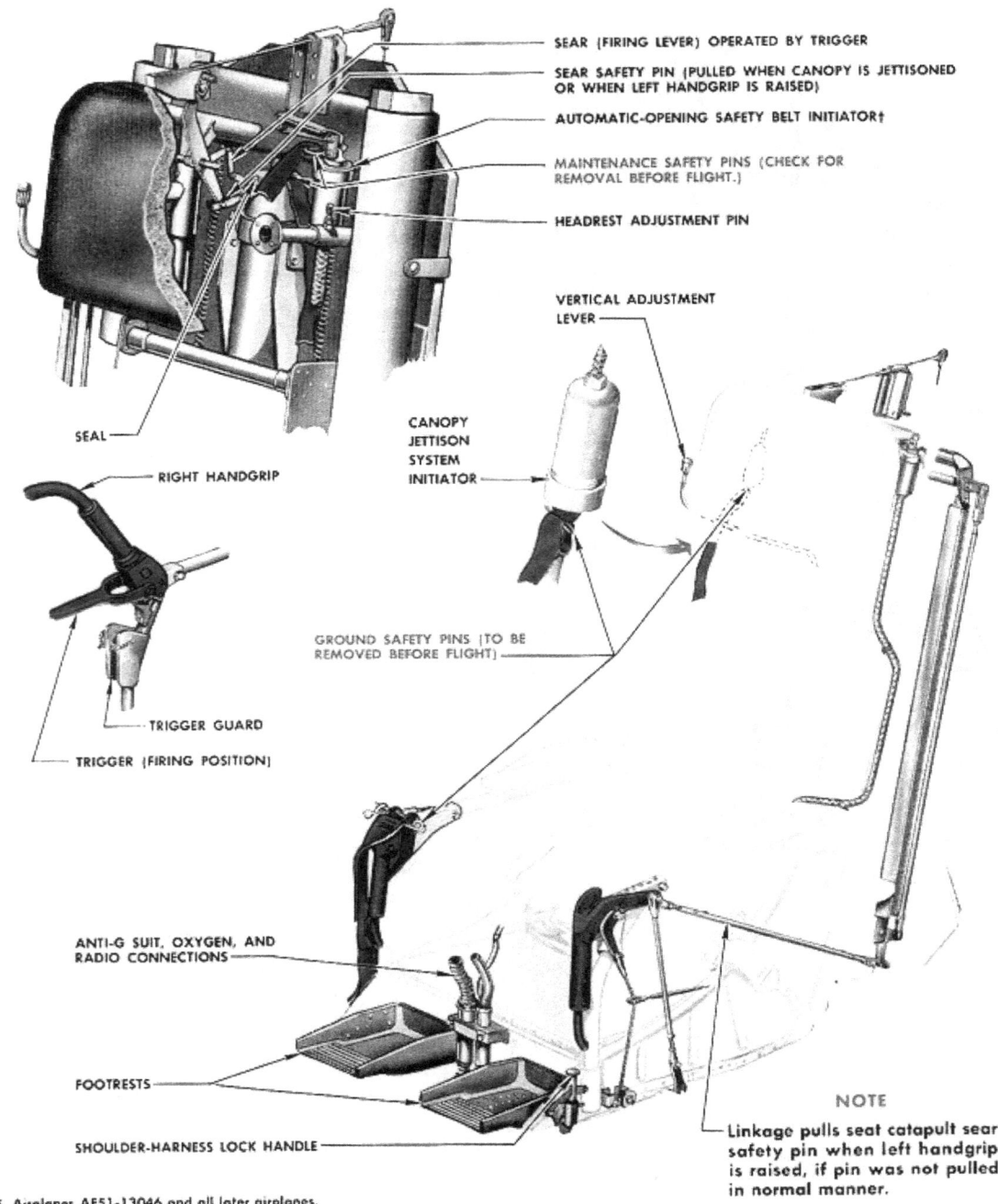

ejection seat LATE AIRPLANES*
NOT CHANGED BY T. O. 1F-86-227

- SEAR (FIRING LEVER) OPERATED BY TRIGGER
- SEAR SAFETY PIN (PULLED WHEN CANOPY IS JETTISONED OR WHEN LEFT HANDGRIP IS RAISED)
- AUTOMATIC-OPENING SAFETY BELT INITIATOR†
- MAINTENANCE SAFETY PINS (CHECK FOR REMOVAL BEFORE FLIGHT.)
- HEADREST ADJUSTMENT PIN
- VERTICAL ADJUSTMENT LEVER
- CANOPY JETTISON SYSTEM INITIATOR
- SEAL
- RIGHT HANDGRIP
- TRIGGER GUARD
- TRIGGER (FIRING POSITION)
- GROUND SAFETY PINS (TO BE REMOVED BEFORE FLIGHT)
- ANTI-G SUIT, OXYGEN, AND RADIO CONNECTIONS
- FOOTRESTS
- SHOULDER-HARNESS LOCK HANDLE

NOTE
Linkage pulls seat catapult sear safety pin when left handgrip is raised, if pin was not pulled in normal manner.

*F-86E-15 Airplanes AF51-13046 and all later airplanes, and those changed by T. O. 1F-86-161

†Some airplanes. (Refer to applicable text.)

Figure 1-30

ejection seat
AIRPLANES CHANGED BY T. O. 1F-86-227

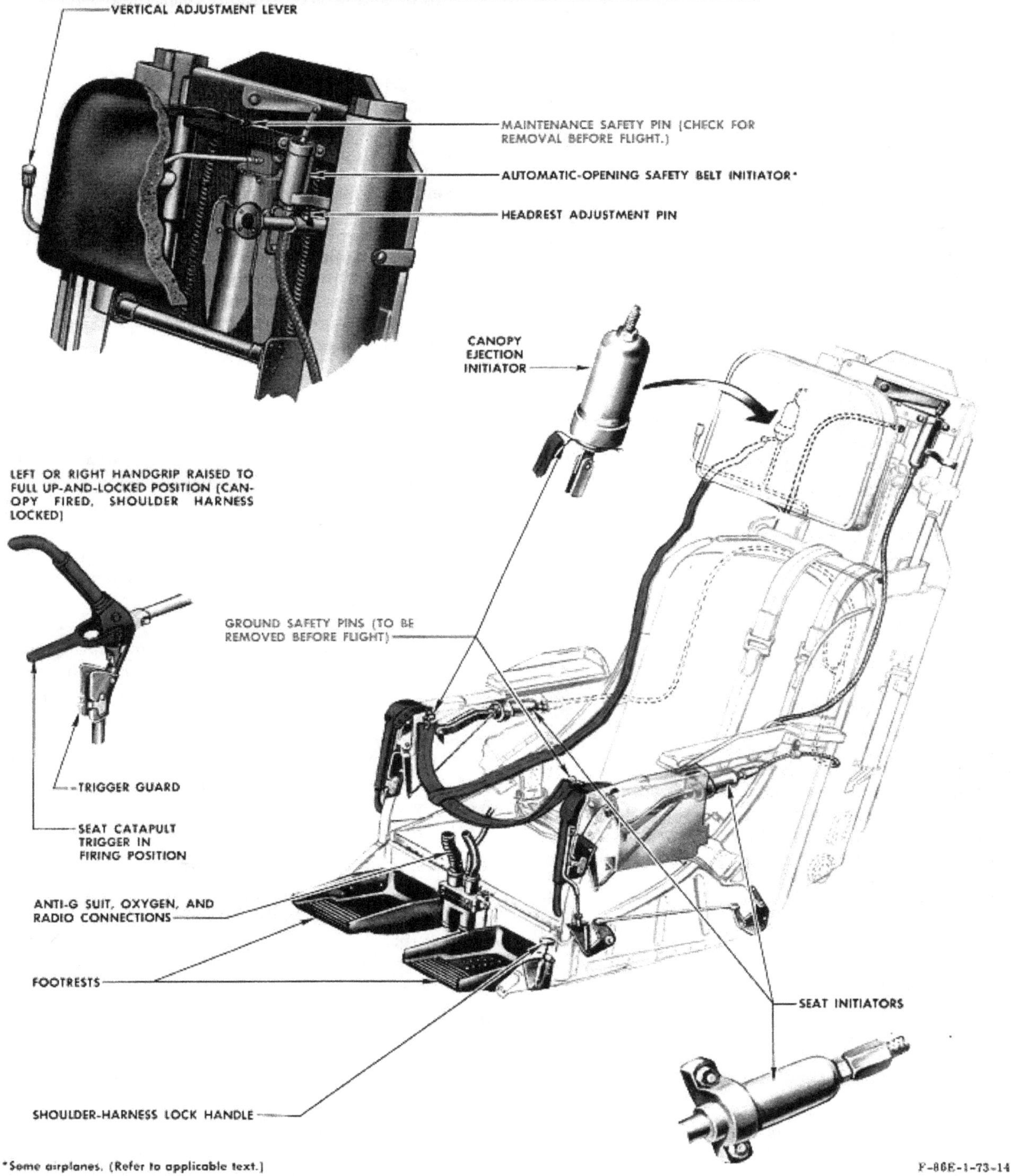

- VERTICAL ADJUSTMENT LEVER
- MAINTENANCE SAFETY PIN (CHECK FOR REMOVAL BEFORE FLIGHT.)
- AUTOMATIC-OPENING SAFETY BELT INITIATOR*
- HEADREST ADJUSTMENT PIN
- CANOPY EJECTION INITIATOR
- LEFT OR RIGHT HANDGRIP RAISED TO FULL UP-AND-LOCKED POSITION (CANOPY FIRED, SHOULDER HARNESS LOCKED)
- GROUND SAFETY PINS (TO BE REMOVED BEFORE FLIGHT)
- TRIGGER GUARD
- SEAT CATAPULT TRIGGER IN FIRING POSITION
- ANTI-G SUIT, OXYGEN, AND RADIO CONNECTIONS
- FOOTRESTS
- SEAT INITIATORS
- SHOULDER-HARNESS LOCK HANDLE

*Some airplanes. (Refer to applicable text.)

Figure 1-31

Section I   T. O. 1F-86E-1

linkage assemblies which fire the seat initiators. On early airplanes* not changed by T. O. 1F-86-161, ground safety pins are inserted through both handgrips and in the seat catapult to prevent inadvertent firing on the ground. They must be removed before flight. On late airplanes† and those changed by T. O. 1F-86-161, ground safety pins inserted through the right handgrip and in the seat catapult must be removed before flight. On airplanes changed by T. O. 1F-86-227, ground safety pins inserted in the seat initiators must be removed before flight. The radio lead and the anti-G suit and oxygen hoses are fitted into a single disconnect assembly on the forward edge of the seat, between the footrests. On airplanes changed by T. O. 1F-86-530, the radio headset plug-in is just above the left seat armrest. When the seat is ejected, these connections are severed automatically at the disconnect assembly.

EJECTION SEAT CONTROLS.

Right Handgrip.

When the hinged right handgrip, at the forward end of the right armrest, is raised to its full up position, the canopy is fired from the airplane, and the handgrip is locked. Raising the grip also lifts the seat catapult trigger from its guard. On late airplanes† and those changed by T. O. 1F-86-161, raising the handgrip also locks the shoulder harness.

Seat Catapult Trigger.

The seat catapult trigger, located beneath the right handgrip or either handgrip (airplanes changed by T. O. 1F-86-227) is protected by a guard and a safety wire or clip. As the handgrip is raised, the safety wire is broken or the clip is opened, and the trigger is raised out of its guard into the firing position. The handgrip locks into the full up position, and the trigger is within reach of the fingers. Squeezing (rotating) the trigger against the full up and locked handgrip fires the seat catapult. On airplanes changed by T. O. 1F-86-227, the seat catapult is fired through either of two initiator systems. One initiator is connected to each trigger, and each initiator operates independently of the other. Squeezing either trigger fires a cartridge in its respective initiator. The gases thus produced move a piston-type firing pin in the seat catapult, causing the catapult to fire.

WARNING

On airplanes not changed by T. O. 1F-86-227, before the trigger is squeezed to fire the seat, the seat handgrip must be raised to the full up and locked position to fire the canopy and pull the seat catapult safety pin. If handgrip and trigger are raised and squeezed simultaneously on these airplanes, the firing mechanism may not work properly. On airplanes changed by T. O. 1F-86-227, the handgrip must be in the full up and locked position before the trigger can be squeezed.

Note

On early airplanes* not changed by T. O. 1F-86-161, a safety pin in the seat catapult firing mechanism (released when the canopy is jettisoned) prevents the trigger from firing the seat until after the canopy has been jettisoned. On late airplanes† and those changed by T. O. 1F-86-161, if the canopy fails to jettison and release the seat catapult sear safety pin or if the canopy jettisons and fails to release the pin, the pin can be withdrawn by raising the left handgrip, and the seat can then be ejected (even through the canopy if it has not jettisoned) when the trigger is squeezed.

Left Handgrip.

Raising the hinged left handgrip to the full up position automatically locks the shoulder harness for ejection. In addition to locking the shoulder harness, actuation of the left handgrip, on late airplanes† and those changed by T. O. 1F-86-161, pulls the safety pin from the seat catapult. Thus, if the pin is not removed because the canopy fails to jettison, or if the canopy in jettisoning fails to pull the safety pin, emergency ejection still can be accomplished (even through the canopy if it has not jettisoned). To prevent inadvertent use of the left handgrip and to maintain the correct sequence during the ejection procedure on late airplanes† and those changed by T. O. 1F-86-161, the left handgrip cannot be raised until the right handgrip has been pulled up and locked in the canopy firing position. On airplanes changed by T. O. 1F-86-227, raising the left handgrip fires the canopy and locks the shoulder harness. Raising the left handgrip on these airplanes also lifts the seat catapult trigger from its guard.

Seat Vertical Adjustment Lever.

The seat is mechanically adjusted by a handle at the right of the headrest. Pulling the handle down releases the seat for adjustment, and it can be raised when the pilot lifts his weight from the seat. After adjustment is made, check that the seat is locked in position.

Headrest Adjustment Pins.

The seat headrest may be adjusted fore and aft on the ground. Pulling up the spring-loaded pin in each of the

---

*F-86E-1 through F-86E-10 Airplanes and F-86E-15 Airplanes AF51-12977 through -13045
†F-86E-15 Airplane AF51-13046 and all later airplanes

1-50

two tubes aft of the headrest releases the headrest for manual adjustment.

Shoulder Harness Lock Handle.

The shoulder harness inertia reel lock handle, on the left side of the seat, outboard of the left footrest, is operated for manually locking and unlocking the shoulder harness. The shoulder harness inertia reel is actuated mechanically when the top of the handle is moved fore and aft. Forward is the locked position; aft is unlocked. It is recommended that the shoulder harness be locked manually during maneuvers and flight in rough air, or as a safety precaution in event of a forced landing. On airplanes not changed by T. O. 1F-86-227, the shoulder harness is locked automatically when the left handgrip on the seat is raised during seat ejection. On airplanes changed by T. O. 1F-86-227, the shoulder harness is locked automatically when either handgrip is raised.

Note

Because of the design characteristics of the shoulder harness inertia reel, no preflight operational check can be made. The shoulder harness inertia reel will lock automatically under a 2 to 3 G forward deceleration, as in a crash landing. Pulling on the shoulder harness straps by hand will not check the inertia reel.

If the harness is manually locked while the pilot is leaning forward the harness will retract with him as he straightens up, moving into successive locked positions as he moves back against the seat and tension is released from the harness.

CAUTION

Before a forced landing, cut the engine master, generator, and battery-starter switches (in that order), because these controls are hard to reach with the shoulder harness locked.

To unlock the harness, the pilot must be able to lean back enough to relieve the tension on the lock. Therefore, if the harness is locked while the pilot is leaning back hard against the seat, he may not be able to unlock the harness without first releasing it momentarily at the safety belt or releasing the harness buckles. After automatic locking, the harness will remain locked until the lock handle is moved to the locked position and then back to unlocked.

SAFETY BELT.

The airplane is equipped with a B-18 manual-opening type safety belt, or an MA-1, MA-3 or MA-4 or an MA-5 or MA-6 automatic-opening type safety belt.

Automatic-Opening Safety Belt.

The primary purpose of the automatic belt is to raise the maximum and lower the minimum altitudes at which escape may be successfully accomplished with the ejection seat. In high-altitude ejections (above 15,000 feet), use of the automatic belt, *in conjunction with the automatic-opening parachute,* avoids parachute deployment at an altitude where sufficient oxygen would not be available to permit safe parachute descent. In a low-altitude ejection, use of the automatic belt greatly reduces the time required for separation from the seat. If an automatic parachute is used in conjunction with the automatic belt, the time for full parachute deployment also is reduced. Consequently, use of the automatic belt and automatic parachute would lower the minimum altitude required for safe ejection. Until you have become thoroughly familiar with the automatic belt and have been convinced that the automatic belt has been designed to save your life, you may have a tendency to distrust the automatic feature and feel that you can only be sure of its operation by manually operating it. However, the automatic belt has been thoroughly tested and is completely reliable. *Under no circumstances should the automatic belt be manually opened before ejection, regardless of altitude.* No matter how fast your reactions are, you cannot beat the automatic operation. Before the use of automatic belts, instructions were issued that when ejection was necessary at less than 2000 feet above the terrain the conventional safety belt should be opened manually before ejection. However, manual release of automatic belts is not only undesirable but dangerous. The escape operation using the automatic feature is not only faster, since the belt automatically opens 2 seconds after ejection, but it also protects the pilot from severe injury at high speeds. (If the airplane is equipped with an M-12 automatic belt initiator, the belt opens one second after ejection.) Since the drag-to-weight ratio of the seat is considerably greater than that of the pilot, immediate separation would result if the belt were opened manually before ejection. This could result in accidental opening of the parachute due to the pack being blown open, and the high opening shock of the parachute could cause serious or fatal injuries. So remember, *the automatic operation can't be beaten.*

MA-1, MA-3, and MA-4 Automatic Safety Belts.

The Type MA-1, MA-3, or MA-4 automatic safety belt is a cartridge-operated device designed for use with the same webbing and fittings as used with the standard B-18 (manual) safety belt, but differs in the center section or release portion of the belt. Release of the MA-1, MA-3 or MA-4 belt is accomplished either by manual operation by the pilot, or by gas pressure from a separate

Section I T. O. 1F-86E-1

MA-1 automatic-opening safety belt

LOCKED

1. Belt locking key (attached to automatic parachute arming lanyard) inserted in belt locking mechanism.

   WARNING
   - This key must be used when an automatic parachute is worn, in order for the parachute to function automatically if ejection is necessary.
   - Lanyard must be outside parachute harness and not fouled on any equipment, to permit clean separation from seat.

2. Belt locking key (attached to belt). Used to close belt only when automatic parachute is *not* worn.

3. Initiator hose.

4. Manual release lever closed. (shown with NAA type handle extension).

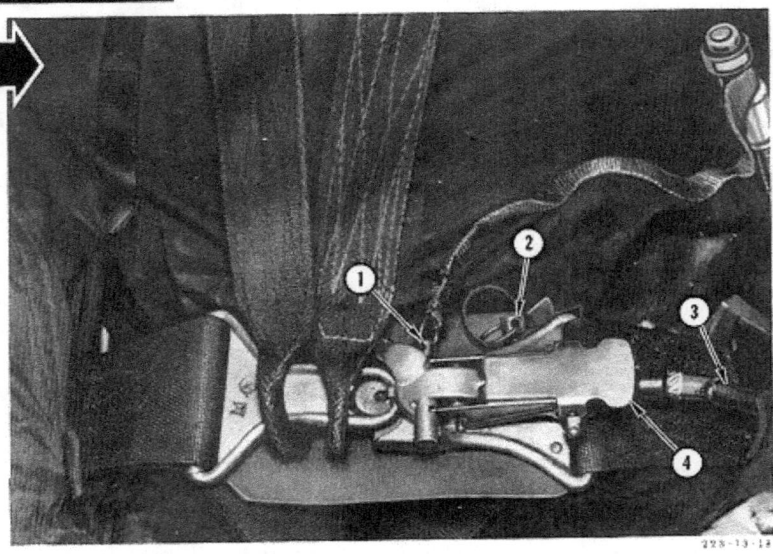

AUTOMATICALLY OPENED

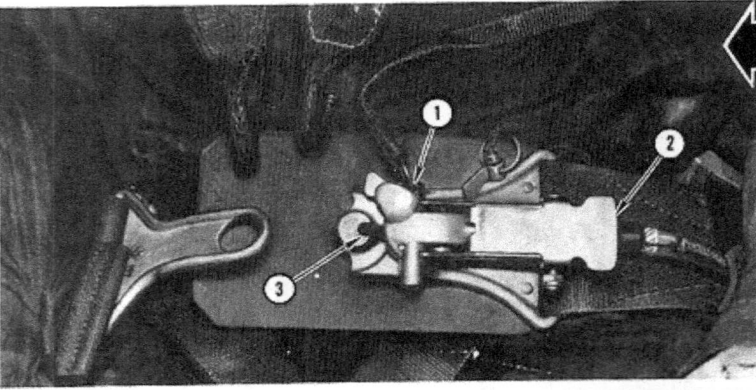

1. Belt locking key (from automatic parachute arming lanyard) retained in belt locking mechanism.

2. Manual release lever closed.

3. Belt latch opened by gas pressure from initiator.

MANUALLY OPENED

1. Belt locking key ejected from locking mechanism when manual release lever is opened.

   WARNING
   If automatic parachute is worn and belt is manually opened during ejection, parachute will not open automatically upon separation from seat.

2. Manual release lever opened.

3. Belt latch opened by manual release lever.

   NOTE
   Manual release lever can be used to unlock belt at any time, even if automatic-opening sequence already has been initiated.

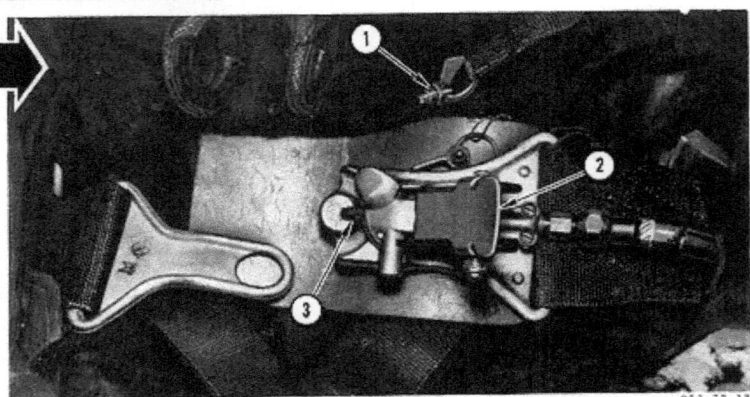

Figure 1-32

MA-3 and -4 automatic-opening safety belt

LOCKED

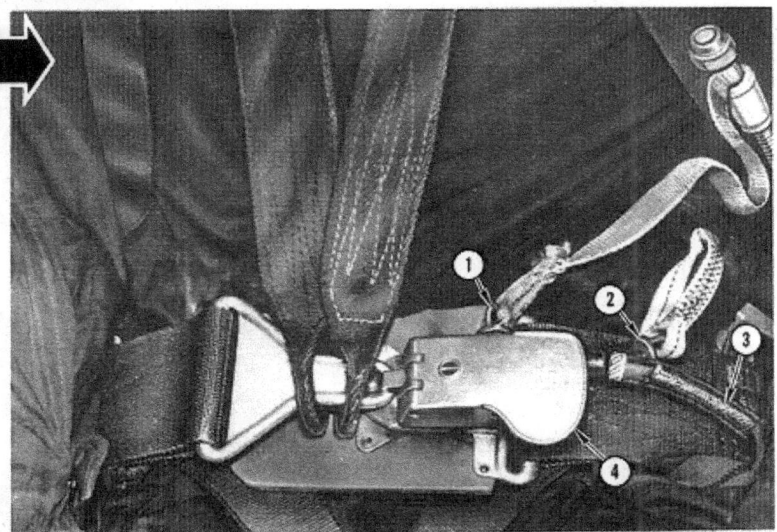

1. Belt locking key (attached to automatic parachute arming lanyard) inserted in belt locking mechanism.

   WARNING
   - This key must be used when an automatic parachute is worn, in order for the parachute to function automatically if ejection is necessary.
   - Lanyard must be outside parachute harness and not fouled on any equipment, to permit clean separation from seat.

2. Belt locking key (attached to belt). Used to close belt only when automatic parachute is *not* worn.
3. Initiator hose.
4. Manual release lever closed.

AUTOMATICALLY OPENED

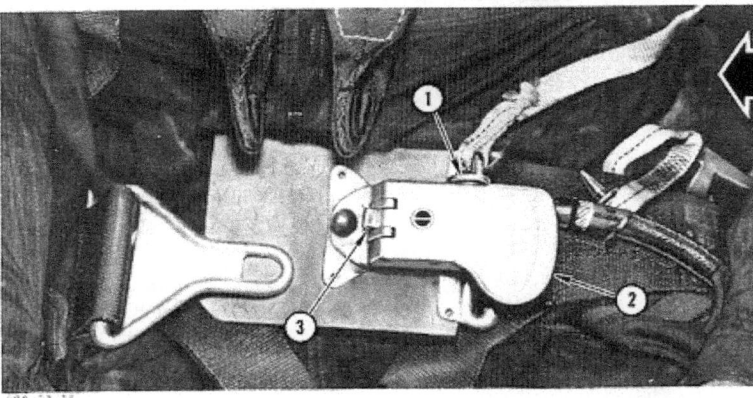

1. Belt locking key (from automatic parachute arming lanyard) retained in belt locking mechanism.
2. Manual release lever closed.
3. Belt latch opened by gas pressure from initiator.

MANUALLY OPENED

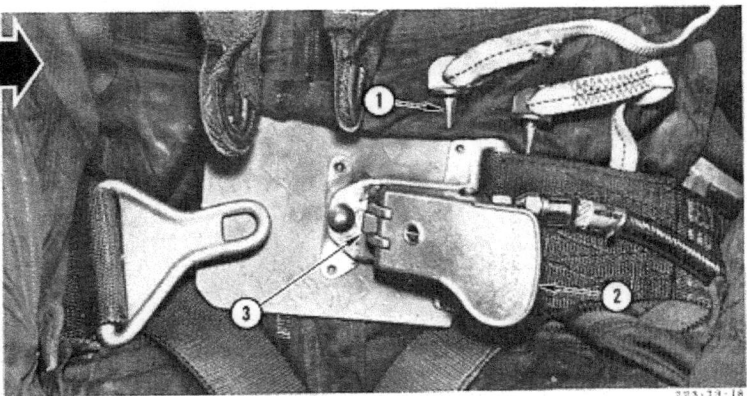

1. Belt locking key ejected from locking mechanism when manual release lever is opened.

   WARNING
   If automatic parachute is worn and belt is manually opened during ejection, parachute will *not* open automatically upon separation from seat.

2. Manual release lever opened.
3. Belt latch opened by manual release lever.

   NOTE
   Manual release lever can be used to unlock belt at any time, even if automatic-opening sequence already has been initiated.

Figure 1-33

MA-5 and -6 automatic-opening safety belt

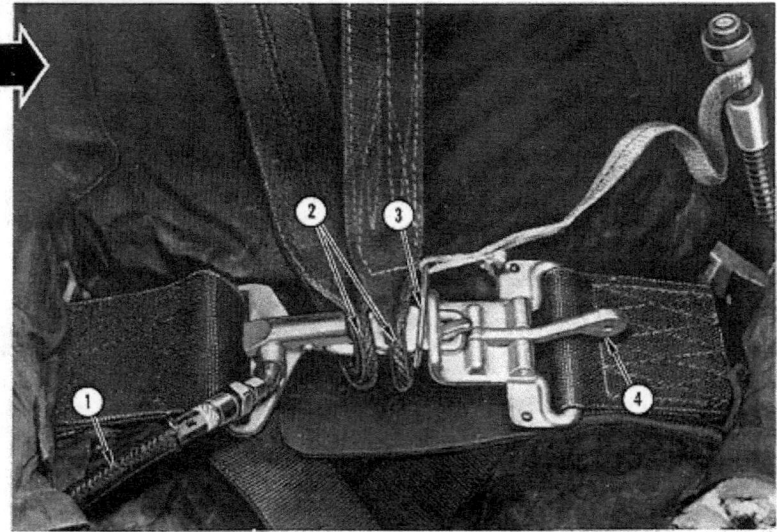

LOCKED

1. Initiator hose to automatic release mechanism.
2. Shoulder harness loops over swivel link.
3. Anchor (from automatic parachute arming lanyard) slipped over swivel link.

WARNING
- Although not necessary to close belt, anchor must be installed, when automatic parachute is worn, so that parachute will function automatically if ejection is necessary.
- Lanyard must be outside parachute harness and not fouled on any equipment, to permit clean separation from seat.

4. Manual release lever closed.

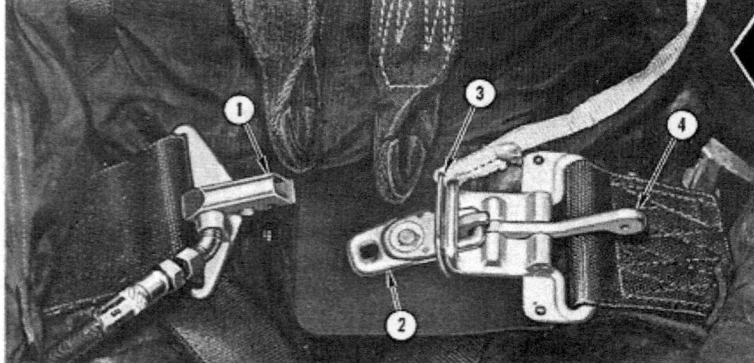

AUTOMATICALLY OPENED

1. Automatic release mechanism actuated by gas pressure from initiator, detaching swivel link on automatic release side.
2. Swivel link retained by manual release lever.
3. Anchor (from automatic parachute arming lanyard) retained by swivel link.
4. Manual release lever closed.

MANUALLY OPENED

1. Swivel link released by manual release lever (automatic release mechanism not actuated).
2. Anchor (from automatic parachute arming lanyard) freed from swivel link.

WARNING
If automatic parachute is worn and belt is manually opened during ejection, parachute will not open automatically upon separation from seat.

3. Manual release lever opened.

NOTE
Manual release lever can be used to unlock belt at any time, even if automatic-opening sequence has been initiated.

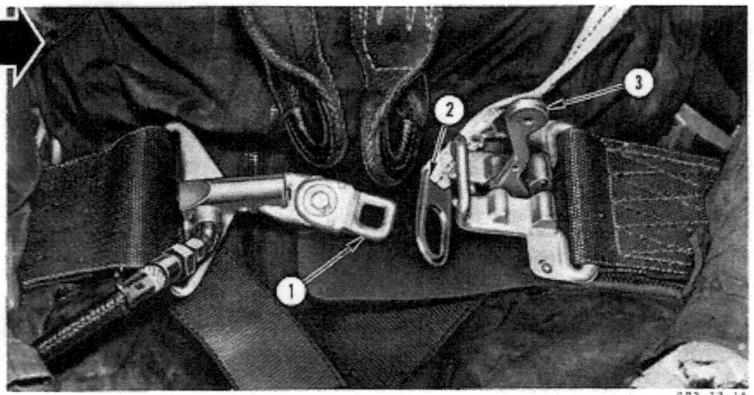

Figure 1-34

T. O. 1F-86E-1

1. Flight Control Normal Hydraulic System Fluid Level Indicator Access Door
2. Flight Control Alternate Hydraulic System Accumulators* (Accumulator†)
3. Engine Oil Tank
4. Cooling-air Turbine Oil Reservoir
5. Utility Hydraulic System Reservoir
6. Battery
7. Oxygen Filler Valve*
8. Nose Gear Emergency Extension System Accumulator ‡
9. Forward Fuselage Fuel Tank—Lower Cell
10. Forward Fuselage Fuel Tank—Upper Cell (Filled First To Utilize Full Tank Capacity)
11. Right Wing Fuel Tank

servicing diagram

SPECIFICATIONS

FUEL — JP-4 (MIL-F-5624)
Alternate—Gasoline (MIL-F-5572)

OIL — MIL-O-6081, Grade 1010
Alternate—MIL-O-6081, Grade 1005
Below −29°C, use Grade 1005.

HYDRAULIC FLUID — MIL-O-5606
ALCOHOL — MIL-A-6091
OXYGEN—BB-O-925

12. Oxygen Filler Valve†
13. Fuel Filter Deicer Alcohol Tank
14. Flight Control Normal and Alternate Hydraulic System Filler Point†
15. External DC Power Receptacles
16. Aft Fuselage Fuel Tank
17. Flight Control Alternate Hydraulic System Accumulator†
18. Flight Control Alternate Hydraulic System Fluid Level Indicator Access Door
19. Flight Control Normal and Alternate Hydraulic System Filler Points* (Bottom of Aft Fuselage)
20. Left Wing Tank
21. Flight Control Normal Hydraulic System Accumulator

*F-86E-10 and later airplanes
†F-86E-1 through F-86E-6 Airplanes
‡Some airplanes. (Refer to applicable text.)

Figure 1-35

automatically controlled source, the M-4 (or M-12) initiator on the back of the seat. The initiator supplies about 1500 psi pressure through a high-pressure hose which actuates a piston inside the belt, retracting the latch tongue and releasing the link. The release incorporates a key which is attached to a lanyard leading to the automatic rip cord release. The key provides an anchor for the static line to the timer of the automatic parachute. The release is designed so that the belt cannot be locked until the key is first inserted into the belt locking mechanism. This is a feature of the design so that the pilot will not neglect to tie the automatic parachute into the system. The key is necessary for proper operation of the automatic belt. If the automatic parachute is used, the key attached to the parachute lanyard is inserted into the belt locking mechanism. If the automatic parachute is not used, a spare key which is attached to the automatic belt must be inserted into the belt locking mechanism. (This spare key must not be removed from the belt.) When the belt is manually opened, the key is ejected automatically so that inadvertent actuation of the automatic parachute will not occur. During automatic operation of the safety belt, the key remains firmly locked in the belt release, thereby arming the automatic parachute aneroid timer as the pilot separates from the seat. Manual operation of the automatic belt can override the automatic function at any time. For example, it is possible to manually open the belt even though initiator action has started. The parachute automatic feature may likewise be overridden by manually pulling the "D" ring, even though the automatic parachute rip cord release has been actuated.

WARNING

If the safety belt is opened manually, the parachute must be opened manually. (For automatic-opening parachutes, the aneroid-timer arming lanyard should be pulled to open parachute, if above 14,000 feet.)

Figure 1-32 shows the MA-1 automatic belt closed with the shoulder harness attached, automatically opened, and manually opened. Figure 1-33 shows the MA-3 and MA-4 automatic belts in the same conditions.

MA-5 and MA-6 Automatic Safety Belts. The MA-5 and MA-6 automatic safety belts are similar in design and function to the MA-1, MA-3 and MA-4 belts. However, the MA-5 and MA-6 belts have a swivel link. When the belt is fully locked, the swivel is attached on one end to the manual release lever and on the other end to the automatic release. The swivel link is detached from the automatic release by actuation of the automatic release initiator. In addition, the MA-5 and MA-6 belts are designed to retain a ring-type anchor for actuating the automatic parachute, in place of a key. It is not mechanically necessary that the anchor, which slips over the manual release end of the swivel link, be used to close the belt. However, when the MA-5 or MA-6 belt is used in conjunction with an automatic parachute, the ring-type anchor *must* be attached to the parachute arming lanyard and then slipped over the swivel link in order for the parachute to work automatically when ejection is necessary. Figure 1-34 shows the MA-5 and MA-6 belts closed with shoulder harness and automatic parachute anchor attached, automatically opened, and manually opened. Manual operation of the automatic belt can override the automatic function at any time. For example, it is possible to manually open the belt even though initiator action has started. The parachute automatic feature may likewise be overridden by manually pulling the "D" ring, even though the automatic parachute rip cord release has been actuated.

WARNING

If the safety belt is opened manually, the parachute *must* be opened manually. (For automatic-opening parachutes, the aneroid arming lanyard should be pulled to open parachute, if above 14,000 feet.)

AUXILIARY EQUIPMENT.

Information concerning the following auxiliary equipment is supplied in Section IV: cockpit air conditioning and pressurization, anti-ice and defrosting, communication and associated electronics, lighting, oxygen, armament, and miscellaneous equipment.

NORMAL PROCEDURES

TABLE OF CONTENTS

	PAGE
Status of the Airplane	2-1
Preflight Check	2-2
Starting Engine	2-6
Engine Ground Operation	2-8
Ground Tests	2-9
Taxiing	2-10
Before Take-off	2-10
Take-off	2-13
After Take-off	2-15
Climb	2-16
Flight Characteristics	2-16
Systems Operation	2-16
Descent	2-16
Pre-traffic-pattern Check	2-17
Traffic-pattern Check	2-17
Landing	2-17
Go-around	2-21
After Landing	2-21
Stopping Engine	2-21
Before Leaving Airplane	2-21
Condensed Check Lists	2-23

STATUS OF THE AIRPLANE.

FLIGHT RESTRICTIONS.

Refer to Section V for flight restrictions and engine operating limitations.

FLIGHT PLANNING.

The operating data in Appendix I is provided to determine fuel consumption and correct airspeed, power setting, and altitude for the intended flight and mission.

WEIGHT AND BALANCE.

Refer to Section V for weight and balance limitations. Refer to Handbook of Weight and Balance Data, T. O. 1-1B-40, for loading information. Before each mission, make the following checks:

1. Gross weight—Check.

Check take-off and anticipated landing gross weight and balance, and check that weight and balance clearance DD Form 365 F is satisfactory. If guns and/or ammunition is not installed, check for proper ballast installation.

CAUTION

- The airplane should be loaded with full ammunition or equivalent ballast for take-off, to produce more stable take-off, flight, and landing characteristics.
- When flying gunnery training missions, pilot should retain one-third of the full ammunition load to produce more stable flight and landing characteristics.

2. Airplane serviced—Check.

Make sure fuel, oil, armament, oxygen, and special equipment carried are sufficient to accomplish mission.

ENTRANCE.

The cockpit can be entered from either side of the airplane. The lower ammunition access door on either side of the fuselage hinges down to serve as a step. A kick-in step and recessed handle are above the access door. (See figure 2-1.)

CAUTION

Don't use handle on fuselage side for a step, since it could break and cause injury to personnel, and be careful not to step on the canopy seal or track when entering cockpit.

Note

The ammunition compartment access door cannot be closed from the cockpit; it must be closed by the ground crew.

PREFLIGHT CHECK.

BEFORE EXTERIOR INSPECTION.

1. DD Form 781—Check.

Check DD Form 781 for engineering status, and make

Figure 2-1

sure the airplane has been properly serviced. See figure 1-35 for complete servicing data.

EXTERIOR INSPECTION.

The exterior inspection should be accomplished as shown in figure 2-2.

CANOPY AND EJECTION SEAT CHECK.

Before entering cockpit, open canopy fully, and check canopy remover and ejection seat as follows:

1. Handgrips and triggers—Check.

Visually check connections from seat handgrips and triggers to canopy remover, seat catapult, and canopy

exterior inspection...

- While making exterior inspection, check all surfaces for cracks, distortion, loose rivets, and indications of damage; check for signs of hydraulic fluid, fuel, and oil leaks; check tires for general condition, slippage, and proper inflation; check all access doors, panels, and filler caps secured; and check position of gear doors, gear strut extension, and condition of wheels.
- Accumulator gage pressures (given on placard next to gage) are for 70°F; pressure will be higher on hotter days.

Starting at nose of airplane, make the following checks:

1 NOSE
Nose wheel chock removed.
Nose gear ground safety lock removed.
Tow pin safety cap tight.
Nose gear emergency extension accumulator* (in nose wheel well).
Landing and taxi lights retracted.
Intake duct clear, except nose screen installed, if required by base policy.
Gun port plugs installed.

2 FORWARD FUSELAGE AND RIGHT WING LEADING EDGE
Emergency nose gear selector valve† reset.
Slats† for freedom of movement.
Main gear wheel chocked.
External load installation and mounting.
Position light and wing tip.
Pitot head uncovered.

*You may rely on your crew chief to check these items if you desire. However, if preflight inspection or servicing was performed at a base where ground personnel are not completely familiar with your airplane, then you should check these items yourself.

†Some airplanes. (Refer to applicable text.)

3 RIGHT WING TRAILING EDGE AND AFT FUSELAGE
Aileron and flap.
Speed brake.
Flight control alternate hydraulic system accumulators* (in speed brake well‡).
Flight control normal hydraulic system fluid level compensator shaft extension 1/4 to 1-1/4 inches.

4 EMPENNAGE
Tail-pipe cover removed.
Tail cone and position lights.
Aspirator fuel drain for freedom of movement.

5 AFT FUSELAGE AND LEFT WING TRAILING EDGE
Speed brake.
Aileron and flap.
Flight control alternate hydraulic system fluid level compensator shaft extension 1/4 to 1-1/4 inches.
Flight control alternate hydraulic system accumulator* (in speed brake well§).
Flight control normal hydraulic system accumulator* (in left wheel well).

6 LEFT WING LEADING EDGE AND FORWARD FUSELAGE
Position light and wing tip.
External load installation and mounting.
Main gear wheel chocked.
Landing gear door ground control switch (in left gear strut well) at **CLOSE**.
Slats† for freedom of movement.

‡F-86E-10 and later airplanes
§F-86E-1 through F-86E-6 Airplanes

Figure 2-2

Section II T. O. 1F-86E-1

initiators, according to whichever modification of seat and canopy ejection systems is installed in the airplane.

2. Safety pins—Check.

Check that seat catapult sear safety pin is connected and that safety pins are in both seat handgrips or right handgrip as applicable to the seat modification for the airplane you are flying. (See figures 1-29, 1-30, and 1-31.)

Note

On airplanes changed by T. O. 1F-86-227, remove safety pin from left seat handgrip only.

Check that all other safety pins which have red streamers attached have been removed, except for the canopy initiator safety pin on airplanes changed by T. O. 1F-86-227.

3. Seat quick-disconnects—Check.

Check that seat quick-disconnects for oxygen, radio, and anti-G suit are properly mated. Check bail-out bottle on seat.

4. Lead seals—Check.

Check that neither lead seal on seat catapult (airplanes not changed by T. O. 1F-86-227) nor lead seal on canopy remover is broken.

INTERIOR CHECK.

Note

A pilot's check list is on a sliding board under the right side of the instrument panel.

1. Stick grip—Check.

Check stick grip for firmness of attachment.

2. Safety belt and shoulder harness—Check.

If the airplane has an automatic-opening safety belt, the belt must be properly fastened to ensure safe operation if ejection is necessary. (See figures 1-32, 1-33, and 1-34 for proper methods to secure the type of automatic belt and automatic parachute you may be wearing.)

3. Seat—Adjust.

4. Rudder pedals—Unlock and adjust.

5. Armament switches—Off.

CAUTION

Armament switches must be off before starting and during ground operation, because low voltages will cause damage to the sight electronic inverter with the switches on.

6. Throttle—OFF (adjust friction).

7. Landing gear handle—DOWN.

Make sure gear position indicators are showing gear down and locked. Test operation of landing gear unsafe warning light by depressing horn cutout button while throttle is at OFF; light should come on.

8. Speed brake switch—Neutral (HOLD).

9. Engine master, emergency ignition, and battery-starter switches—OFF.

10. External power—Connected.

11. Circuit breakers—In.

Note

- The flight control alternate hydraulic system will become operative when external power is connected. The flight control normal hydraulic system must be manually engaged after the engine has started.

- An external 28.25-volt (nominal) dc power source, capable of supplying a minimum of 500 amperes continuous power and 1200 amperes surge power, must be connected to both external receptacles for starting. External power units suitable for use on this airplane (provided they have been properly maintained to produce their rated output) are the A-3, A-4, C-22, C-26, and V-1.

12. Oxygen regulator—Check.

- A-14 oxygen regulator: Oxygen regulator diluter handle NORMAL OXYGEN. Oxygen system checked for operation. [Refer to "Oxygen System Preflight Check (A-14 Regulator)" in Section IV.]

- D-2 oxygen regulator: Oxygen regulator diluter lever NORMAL OXYGEN, emergency toggle lever at CENTER position. Oxygen system checked for operation. [Refer to "Oxygen System Preflight Check (D-2 Regulator)" in Section IV.]

WARNING

If the airplane is to be operated on the ground under possible conditions of carbon monoxide contamination, such as directly behind another operating jet airplane or during operation with tail into the wind, use oxygen with diluter lever at 100% OXYGEN.

13. Anti-G suit regulator valve—Check.

Anti-G suit regulator valve HI or LO, as desired.

14. Drop tank pressure shutoff valve—OFF.

15. Ammunition compartment heat emergency shutoff handle—NORMAL.

16. Cockpit air temperature control switch—AUTO.

17. Cabin pressure control lever (cockpit pressure control switch—As desired.

18. Air outlet selector lever—FLOOR.

19. Windshield anti-icing lever—OFF.

20. Rudder trim switch—OFF.

21. Lateral alternate trim switch—NORMAL.

22. Longitudinal alternate trim switch—NORMAL GRIP CONT.

23. Flight control switch—NORMAL.

24. Speed brake emergency lever—NORMAL.

25. Wing flap lever—UP.

26. Emergency fuel switch—OFF.

27. Emergency jettison handle—In.

28. Pitot heater switch—ON, then OFF.

Check operation of pitot heater with crew chief while switch is ON.

29. Landing and taxi light switches—Off. (Check lights retracted.)

30. Parking brake handle—In.

Note

If handle is not full in, brakes will be inoperative.

31. Clock, accelerometer, and altimeter—Set.

Note error against field elevation for consideration when resetting altimeter during flight.

Note

If error exceeds 75 feet, do not accept airplane for IFR operation.

32. Generator switch—ON.

33. Position and fuselage light switches—Off.

34. Communication equipment switches—As desired.

35. Cockpit light switches—OFF.

36. Flight control emergency override handle*—In.

37. Canopy alternate emergency jettison handle (on airplanes so equipped)—In.

38. Fuel quantity—Check; totalizer dial—Set.

Note

Move densitometer switch to OUT, to check that fuel tanks are full. Then return switch to IN, to provide a continuous gage indication of actual fuel quantity based on fuel density.

39. Warning lights and indicators and test warning systems—Check.

40. Attitude indicator—Check.

Check erection and retraction of warning "off flag." For quick erection during scramble operation, cage and uncage gyro 30 seconds after power has been turned on.

41. Directional indicator against stand-by compass—Check.

Check for stabilization of needle and for 180-degree ambiguity.

42. Vertical velocity indicator—Set.

43. Operation of sight—Check.

Allow approximately 5 to 15 minutes for A-1 sight to warm up and at least 5 minutes for A-4 sight to warm up. Mechanically cage sight.

44. Instrument power switch—NORMAL, then ALTERNATE (ALT).

Check operation of main and alternate inverters.

45. Emergency utility hydraulic system selector valve—OFF (some airplanes).

46. Landing gear emergency release—In.

47. Canopy declutch handle—In.

48. Rudder gust lock handle—In.

49. Flight controls—Check.

Operate trim and flight controls through complete cycle, checking for proper response to control action.

50. Normal trim switch—Check.

Operate normal trim switch on stick grip in all actuated positions, and note that it automatically returns to the neutral (CENTER) position when released.

CAUTION

The normal trim switch is subject to sticking in any or all of the actuated positions, resulting in application of extreme trim. If the switch sticks in any actuated position during ground check, enter this fact with a red cross on the DD Form 781, and do not fly the airplane.

*F-86E-10 and later airplanes

Section II   T. O. 1F-86E-1

Note

The flight control alternate hydraulic system will become operative automatically when external power is connected. The flight control normal hydraulic system must be manually engaged after the engine has started.

51. Radio compass—Check.

Check frequency alignment, antenna reception, manual loop rotation, and ADF operation. Tune in low-frequency range or homer that serves field of departure. Identify station, and turn function selector switch to COMP and check compass indicator for correct bearing reading. (Canopy must be closed.)

52. Interior and exterior lights—Check.

Check operation of all interior and exterior lighting (night flights).

53. Flashlight—Check.

Check that a properly operating flashlight is included in personal gear (night flights).

STARTING ENGINE.

CAUTION

Start engine with airplane headed into, or at right angles to, the wind whenever possible, as exhaust temperatures may be increased or an engine fire during starting will be aggravated by a tail wind.

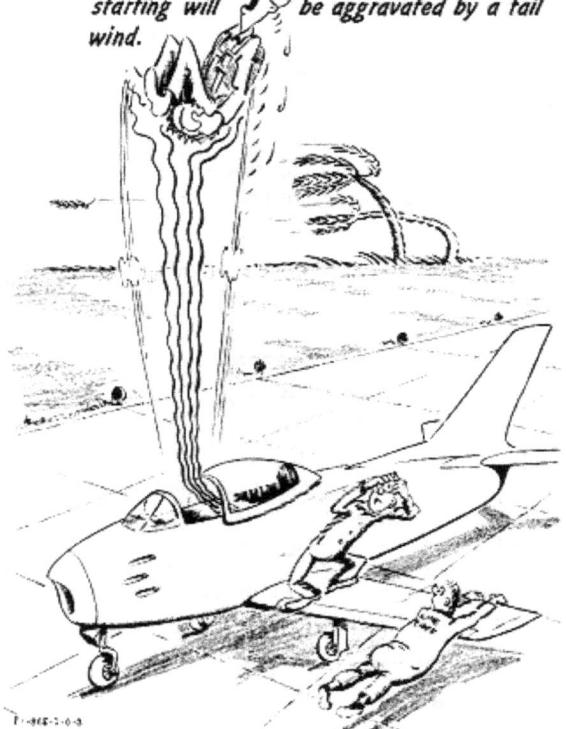

Note

The flight control alternate hydraulic system will operate before engine start; the flight control normal hydraulic system must be manually selected after the engine is started.

Intake duct suction can draw personnel into or against duct, causing death or serious injury. High exhaust temperatures and blast create danger aft of airplane.

WARNING

- Before starting the engine, make sure that main gear wheels are chocked and that danger areas fore and aft of the airplane are clear of personnel, aircraft, and vehicles. (See figure 2-3.) Danger aft of the airplane is created by high exhaust temperatures and blast from the tail pipe.

- Whenever possible, start and run up engine on a concrete surface to minimize the opportunities for dirt and foreign objects to be drawn into the compressor and damage the engine.

- When operating within the jet blast of another F-86E airplane, maintain a minimum of 80 feet distance, to prevent damage to the canopy.

External power must be supplied through both receptacles for starting, because the battery does not supply

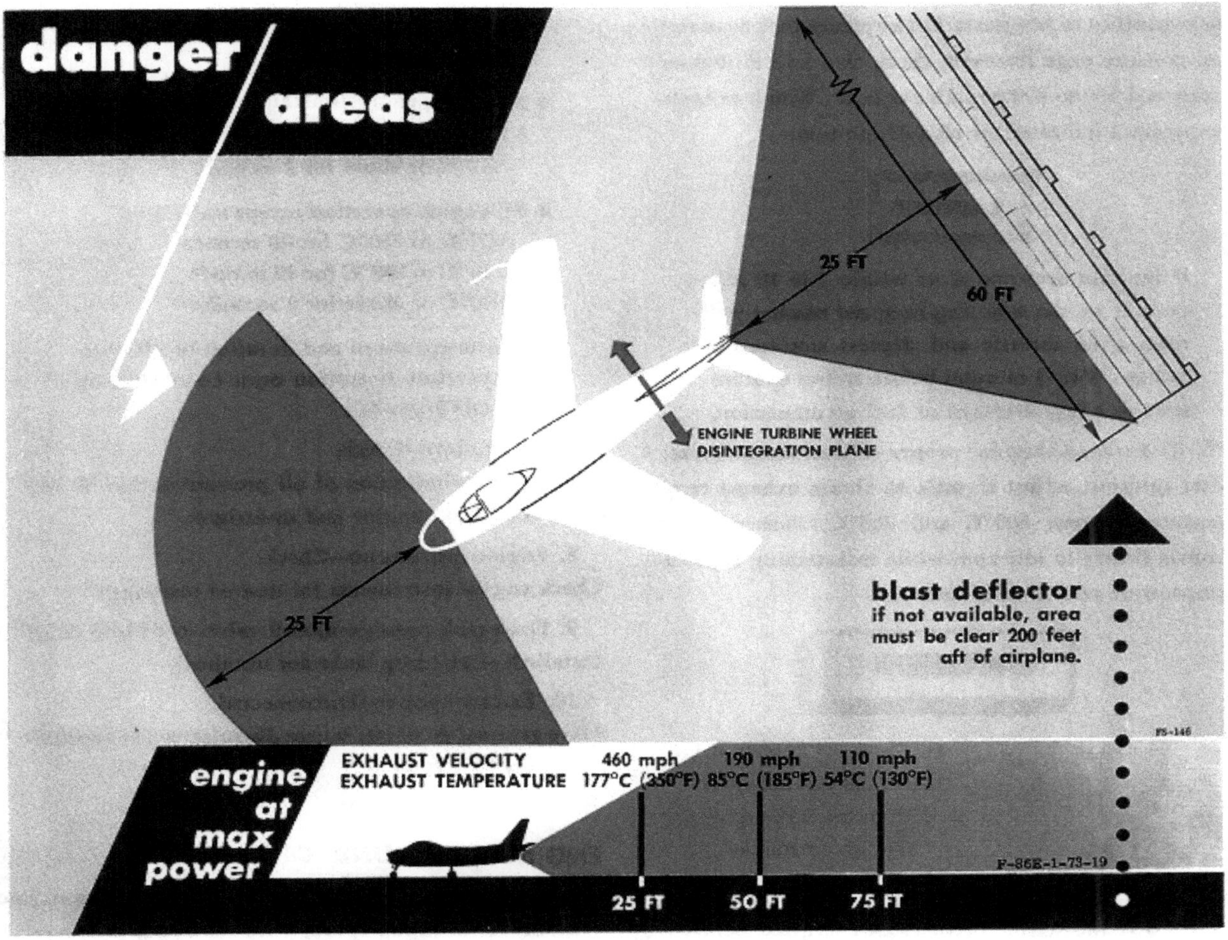

Figure 2-3

power to the starter. Start engine as follows:

1. Throttle—OFF.
2. Engine master switch—ON.
3. Battery-starter switch—STARTER (momentarily), then BATTERY.

CAUTION

- The high current required for starting will burn out the starter within a few seconds if the turbine does not begin to turn as soon as the starter is engaged. If there is no audible indication of engine rotation or if tachometer fails to register within a few seconds, depress the stop-starter button immediately.

- The starter is limited to three starts of one minute duration any 30-minute period; if more than three starts are required, allow starter to cool 30 minutes before using again.

Note

It is not necessary to position battery-starter switch to OFF during engine start, because battery is automatically cut out when starter is in operation.

4. 3% rpm—Throttle outboard.
At 3% rpm, move throttle outboard to engage fuel booster pumps and energize ignition system.

5. 6% rpm—Throttle halfway between IDLE and OFF.
At 6% rpm, open throttle slowly to a position approximately halfway between IDLE and OFF positions. Check that fuel pressure does not exceed 40 psi, to minimize

2-7

the possibility of hot starts. On airplanes that have the fuel pressure gage removed, check that fuel flow does not exceed 500 to 800 pounds per hour. Watch exhaust temperature indicator for sign of ignition.

CAUTION

If ignition does not occur within 5 to 10 seconds or by the time engine speed reaches 9% rpm, close throttle and depress stop-starter button. Wait 3 minutes before trying another start to allow drainage of fuel accumulation.

6. Throttle—Adjust for proper exhaust temperature. After ignition, adjust throttle to obtain exhaust temperature between 600°C and 700°C; then advance throttle slowly to idle rpm while maintaining exhaust temperature within these limits.

WARNING

- If engine speed does not reach 23% rpm in one minute, shut down engine and investigate. Excessive operation below 23% rpm can cause extensive damage to starter and engine.
- If the starter becomes de-energized before the engine reaches approximately 20% rpm, shut down engine immediately. No attempt should be made to accelerate the engine.

CAUTION

Do not use stop-starter button to disengage the starter after normal starts, because this will cause rapid deterioration of the starter control relay and may also cut out the starter too soon, slowing rate of acceleration. The starter is designed to cut out automatically at approximately 23% rpm.

WARNING

- The engine must be shut down and inspected when any overtemperature condition occurs during ground operation. The following conditions constitute overtemperature operation.

- During engine start up to idle rpm (within 2 minutes):
  950°C or above for 2 seconds.

- All engine operation except starting:
  690°C to 750°C for 40 seconds
  750°C to 800°C for 10 seconds
  800°C or above for 2 seconds

- The temperature and duration of all overtemperature operation must be entered on the DD Form 781.

7. Oil pressure—Check.

If there is no indication of oil pressure within 30 seconds, shut down engine and investigate.

8. Engine instruments—Check.

Check engine instruments for desired readings.

9. Drop tank pressure shutoff valve—ON (drop tanks installed)—OFF (drop tanks not installed).

10. External power—Disconnected.

Have external dc power source disconnected at approximately 25% rpm.

ENGINE GROUND OPERATION.

No engine warm-up is necessary. As soon as the engine stabilizes at idling speed, with normal gage readings, the throttle may be slowly opened to full power. Idle rpm should be between 34% and 38% rpm, but will vary with altitude and outside air temperature. The idle rpm also depends somewhat on the manner in which the throttle is retarded, that is, whether it is eased back to IDLE or pulled back abruptly.

Note

The engine has poor acceleration characteristics between IDLE and 63% rpm.

CAUTION

- Rapid acceleration to 100% rpm on a cold engine may result in the exhaust temperature exceeding the limits.

- If a full-power run-up is made during ground operation or ground test, be sure that wheels are chocked, and hold wheel brakes on.

GROUND TESTS.

Note

- The flight control alternate hydraulic system will become operative automatically when external power is applied. It will continue to function until the flight control normal hydraulic system is manually engaged.

- The following checks of the flight control and utility hydraulic systems are necessary to ensure proper operation of the system.

1. Throttle—IDLE.
2. Hydraulic pressure gage selector switch—NORMAL.
3. Flight control switch—RESET.

Engage the flight control normal hydraulic system on early airplanes,* by holding flight control switch at RESET for 2 seconds or until pressure reaches at least 850 psi. On late airplanes,† the switch must be held at RESET only momentarily. Check that switch returns to NORMAL. Check that alternate-on warning light is out.

CAUTION

When checking control surface movement on both normal and alternate systems, check rate of travel of control stick by rapid, full-throw movements of the stick. If rate is slower than normal, as determined by experience, have ground personnel check systems to determine what is wrong. Refer to "Hydraulic Systems," Section VII.

4. Flight control normal hydraulic system—Check.

   a. Flight control switch—NORMAL.

   b. Control stick—Move, and visually check for proper control surface movement.

   c. Pressure—After 5 seconds, 2900 to 3200 psi (control stick not in motion).

5. Flight control alternate hydraulic system—Check.

   a. Flight control switch—ALTERNATE (ON EMERG).

   b. Alternate-on warning light—On.

   c. Control stick—Move and visually check for proper control surface movement.

   d. Hydraulic pressure gage selector switch—ALTERNATE.

   e. Pressure—2550 to 3200 psi (control stick not in motion).

Note

The alternate system pressure should slowly fluctuate between the maximum limits of 2550 and 3200 psi because the designed leakage in the flight control actuators causes the alternate system hydraulic pump to cycle on and off.

   f. Flight control switch—RESET.

Momentarily hold flight control switch at RESET and then release. Check that alternate-on warning light is out.

6. Flight control manual emergency override system† —Check.

   a. Hydraulic pressure gage selector switch—ALTERNATE.

   b. Flight control switch—Hold at RESET.

   c. Emergency change-over handle—Pull to full extension.

Holding flight control switch at the RESET position opens the electrical circuit to the flight control system transfer valves. This ensures that the normal system transfer valve is held in the closed position and the alternate system transfer valve is held in the open position by the mechanical emergency change-over handle only. The alternate-on warning light should not be on.

   d. Control stick—Move and visually check for proper control surface movement.

   e. Flight control switch—NORMAL.

   f. Alternate-on warning light—On (indicating electrical circuit complete).

   g. Pressure—3050 to 4000 psi.

Pressure should remain constant (except for momentary surges) at a value between the maximum limits of 3050 and 4000 psi (control stick not in motion).

7. Emergency change-over handle—In.
8. Pressure—2550 to 3200 psi.

Note

Because of the tolerances of the alternate system relief valves and the pressure indicating system, the pressure may exceed the red limit value (3200 psi) and may even reach 4000 psi when the emergency change-over handle is actuated. These pressures are considered normal for this portion of the alternate system operation.

9. Automatic return to flight control normal system—Check.

   a. Flight control switch—NORMAL.

---

*F-86E-1, F-86E-5 and F-86E-6 Airplanes
†F-86E-10 and later airplanes

b. Control stick—Move rapidly.

c. Alternate-on warning light—Out.

Check that light goes out within range of 575 to 775 psi, indicating that normal system is again in control.

d. Hydraulic pressure gage selector switch—NORMAL.

e. Pressure—2900 to 3200 psi.

10. Utility hydraulic system—Check.

a. Hydraulic pressure gage selector switch—UTILITY.

b. Speed brake switch—OUT, IN, then neutral (HOLD).

Operate speed brakes through one complete cycle.

c. Pressure—Approximately 3000 psi.

Warning

Before operating speed brakes, be sure aft fuselage area is clear, as the speed brakes move rapidly and forcefully and could injure any personnel in their path.

11. Loadmeter and voltmeter—Check.

At 45% engine rpm, check loadmeter reading; check voltmeter for approximately 28.5 volts (generator will not produce operating voltage below this rpm).

TAXIING.

1. Gun sight caging lever—CAGE (CAGED).
2. Main gear wheel chocks—Removed.

Note

The airplane has excellent ground handling characteristics.

3. Throttle—Advance, then return to IDLE.

To obtain initial taxi roll, open throttle to approximately 60% rpm; then retard throttle immediately. Once the airplane is rolling, it can be taxied at idling rpm on hard surface.

CAUTION

- As initial taxi roll is started, test wheel brakes to ensure proper braking action.
- Care should be used when taxiing (and turning sharply) while carrying 200-gallon drop tanks, because the ground clearance of the tanks in the normal attitude is only 7-½ inches.
- While taxiing, do not operate speed brakes, because hydraulic pressure is inadequate for wheel brakes and nose wheel steering during speed brake operation.

4. Nose wheel steering switch—Depress (for directional control).

With the nose wheel steering switch constantly depressed, maintain directional control through use of the rudder pedals. (Nose wheel and rudder pedals must be coordinated before steering mechanism will engage.)

Note

- Avoid excessive or rapid jockeying of throttle during taxiing.
- Minimize taxi time, because airplane range is considerably decreased by high fuel consumption during ground operation. Fuel consumption with engine operating at 35% to 40% rpm is approximately 20 pounds per minute.

5. Gyro instruments—Check.

BEFORE TAKE-OFF.

PREFLIGHT AIRPLANE CHECK.

After taxiing to take-off position, complete the following checks:

1. Nose screen—Removed.

WARNING

Nose screen must be removed before preflight engine check and with engine at idle rpm. Ground personnel removing screen must not wear articles of loose clothing or carry equipment likely to be drawn into intake duct.

2. Safety belt—Tighten; shoulder harness—Adjust.
3. Shoulder-harness lock handle—UNLOCKED.
4. Safety pins—Remove.

Remove safety pins from both seat handgrips (or right seat handgrip) and, on airplanes changed by T. O. 1F-86-227, from canopy initiator. Stow in an accessible place.

5. Armament switches—Off.

If external loads have to be jettisoned on take-off, they may be jettisoned unarmed by means of the bomb-rocket jettison button or by the emergency jettison handle.

Note

On F-86E-6 Airplanes, the rockets cannot be jettisoned by means of the emergency jettison handle.

6. Trim for take-off—Check.

On F-86E-1 through F-86E-10 Airplanes, horizontal tail, rudder, and ailerons trimmed individually until take-off trim indicator light glows; on F-86E-15 Airplanes not changed by T. O. 1F-86F-216, rudder and ailerons trimmed individually until take-off trim indicator light glows, and horizontal tail trimmed for control stick full aft (take-off trim indicator light glows) and then control stick grip 2 inches forward.

7. Wing flap lever—DOWN.
8. Canopy switch—CLOSED.
9. Oxygen regulator diluter lever—NORMAL OXYGEN (100% OXYGEN if carbon monoxide suspected).

If carbon monoxide contamination is suspected, use 100 percent oxygen as long as considered necessary.

WARNING

Oxygen diluter lever should be returned to NORMAL OXYGEN as soon as possible, because use of 100 percent oxygen will deplete the oxygen supply enough to be hazardous.

10. Take-off position—Check.

Make sure airplane is headed straight down runway with nose wheel centered.

11. Toe brakes—Hold.

PREFLIGHT ENGINE CHECK.

The emergency fuel system check is to be made only before the first flight of the day. Perform check in take-off position, making sure airplane does not move forward and cause the nose wheel to cant.

Emergency Fuel System Check (Three-position Switch)

1. Throttle—80% rpm.
2. Emergency fuel switch—ON.
3. Throttle—Full OPEN; rpm—Check.

Allow to stabilize at 100%.

CAUTION

Advance throttle slowly and cautiously to prevent compressor stall in the event the emergency system overrides the main system.

4. Emergency fuel switch—OFF.
5. Emergency fuel switch—TEST; rpm—Check.

Move the emergency fuel switch to TEST without hesitating in the ON position, and allow engine rpm to stabilize at its new value. This stabilized value should conform to the limits shown graphically in figure 2-4. If the rpm momentarily drops more than 2% rpm below the stabilized value and the time required for the rpm to stabilize exceeds 3 seconds, do not fly the airplane. The emergency fuel regulator will require adjustment. If the rpm momentarily drops less than 2% rpm below the stabilized value and the time required for the rpm to stabilize exceeds 5 seconds, do not fly the airplane. The emergency fuel regulator will require adjustment.

Note

The time limits for rpm stabilization are applicable only when engine rpm falls momentarily below the stabilized value. If the rpm does not go below the stabilized value when the emergency fuel switch is moved to TEST, the emergency fuel regulator is working satisfactorily.

WARNING

Be prepared to retard throttle immediately to prevent engine overspeeding in case the emergency fuel regulator is defective. If the engine overspeeds more than 104% rpm, with or without an overtemperature condition, the engine must be removed for overhaul.

6. Emergency fuel switch—OFF.

Return the emergency fuel switch to OFF, without hesitating in the ON position, for take-off.

2-11

emergency fuel system test — maximum rpm available

Chart shows variation (due to temperature change) in engine rpm when operating on emergency fuel system with throttle in full **OPEN** position.

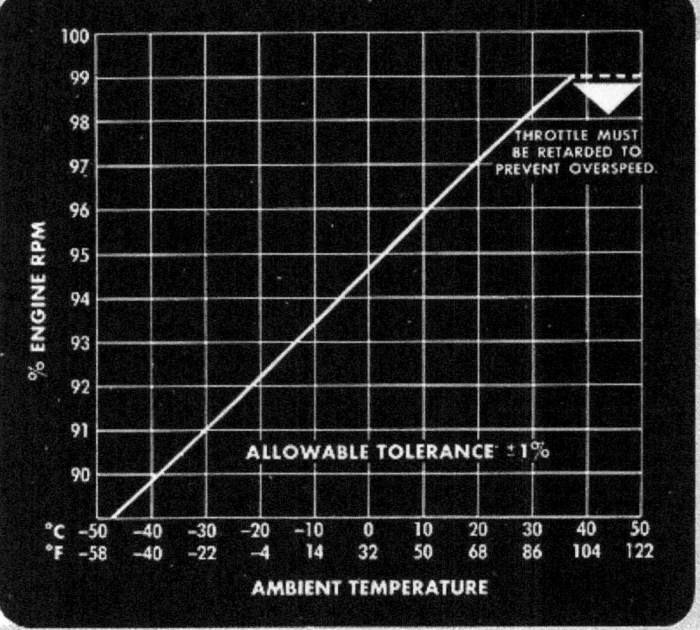

Figure 2-4

- If the throttle is advanced with the emergency fuel switch ON, the emergency system may override the main fuel system and cause complete power failure resulting from compressor stall or flame-out.

- Engine rpm should drop off (it may drop to as low as 80% rpm) when the emergency fuel switch is moved from TEST to OFF, without hesitating in the ON position, because of the time required for the main fuel regulator to recover from the disabled condition. This drop-off is normal and does not indicate main regulator malfunction. If engine rpm drop does not occur, you should suspect that the emergency fuel system has not been disabled and not fly the airplane until the system has been checked; otherwise, compressor stall may occur during rapid throttle advancement, resulting in over-temperature operation and possible complete loss of power.

Note

Repeated checks of the emergency fuel system on the same engine run-up should result in the same stabilized rpm within 1%. If this tolerance cannot be maintained, the emergency fuel regulator must be replaced.

Emergency Fuel System Check (Two-position Switch).

1. Throttle—80% rpm.
2. Emergency fuel switch—ON.

If engine rpm drops to less than 70%, advance throttle slowly and cautiously to prevent compressor stall if the emergency system overrides the main system.

3. Throttle—full OPEN; rpm—Check.

Advance throttle to full OPEN and allow engine rpm to stabilize. This rpm value should conform to the limits shown in figure 2-4.

4. Emergency fuel switch—OFF.

5. Emergency fuel switch—ON; rpm—Check.

With engine rpm at 100%, move the emergency fuel switch to ON. Observe the minimum rpm obtained, elapsed time between movement of the switch to ON and stabilization of rpm, and the stabilized rpm value. The stabilized rpm should conform to the limits shown in figure 2-4. If the rpm momentarily drops more than 2% rpm below the stabilized value and the time required for the rpm to stabilize exceeds 3 seconds, do not fly the airplane. The emergency fuel regulator will require adjustment. If the rpm momentarily drops less than 2% rpm below the stabilized value and the time required for the rpm to stabilize exceeds 5 seconds, do not fly the airplane. The emergency fuel regulator will require adjustment.

6. Emergency fuel switch—OFF.

Return the emergency fuel switch to OFF for take-off.

Note

Repeated checks of the emergency fuel system on the same engine run-up should result in the same stabilized rpm within 1%. If this tolerance cannot be maintained, the emergency fuel regulator must be replaced.

CAUTION

- The emergency fuel switch should be OFF at all times, except in case of main fuel system failure.

- Engine rpm should drop off (it may drop to as low as 80% rpm) when the emergency fuel switch is moved from ON to OFF, because of the time required for the main fuel regulator to recover from the disabled condition. This drop-off is normal and does not indicate main regulator malfunction. If engine rpm drop does not occur, you should suspect that the emergency fuel system has not been disabled and not fly the airplane until the system has been checked; otherwise, compressor stall may occur during rapid throttle advancement, resulting in overtemperature operation and possible complete loss of power.

Engine Instrument Check.

1. Throttle—Full OPEN.
2. Engine Instruments—Check.

Tachometer—not less than 98% rpm nor greater than 100% rpm.

Exhaust temperature—between 675°C and 690°C.

Oil pressure—between 10 and 22 psi.

WARNING

Do not take off if exhaust temperature is below 675°C.

TAKE-OFF.

NORMAL TAKE-OFF.

Note

The following procedures will produce the results tabulated in the Appendix.

For normal take-off, with or without external load, proceed as follows:

1. Throttle—Take-off rpm.
2. Wheel brakes—Release.
3. Maintain directional control.

Maintain directional control during first part of take-off run by use of nose wheel steering. Rudder control becomes effective at approximately 50 knots IAS.

Note

Use of brakes to maintain directional control on take-off will increase take-off run.

4. Maintain near-level attitude until take-off speed is attained.

During take-off, the airplane should be held in a near-level attitude at nose wheel lift-off. In this attitude, the nose wheel will be just slightly off the runway. This attitude should be held until the recommended take-off speed is attained and the airplane lifts off.

WARNING

Do not assume a nose-high attitude before reaching the recommended take-off speed. Any attempt to take off at lower than recommended speeds can bring about a stalled condition. This could be disastrous because of the resultant excessively long take-off run. If a ground stall does occur, indicated by failure of the airplane to lift off and loss of acceleration, the nose must be lowered to a three-point attitude to eliminate the stalled condition of the wings.

Section II · T.O. 1F-86E-1

The recommended nose wheel lift-off and take-off speeds for airplanes without slats are distinctly different from those for airplanes with slats, and you must learn them for each type of wing leading edge configuration. Because of the lower speeds for airplanes with slats, the control stick must be pulled back further in order to pull the nose wheel off the runway. Nose wheel lift-off and take-off speeds (with flaps full down) are:

AIRPLANES WITH SLATS

GROSS WEIGHT	NOSE WHEEL LIFT-OFF	TAKE-OFF SPEED
13,000 lb	90 knots IAS	105 knots IAS
15,000 lb	100 knots IAS	115 knots IAS
18,000 lb	110 knots IAS	125 knots IAS

AIRPLANES WITHOUT SLATS

GROSS WEIGHT	NOSE WHEEL LIFT-OFF	TAKE-OFF SPEED
13,000 lb	100 knots IAS	115 knots IAS
15,000 lb	110 knots IAS	125 knots IAS
18,000 lb	120 knots IAS	135 knots IAS

Airplanes without slats are noticeably more adversely affected when taking off with external stores than airplanes with slats.

5. Assume nose-high attitude when take-off speed is attained.

At take-off speed nose-high attitude must be maintained for take-off. (After take-off, the airplane will assume a more normal attitude as airspeed increases and the flaps are raised.)

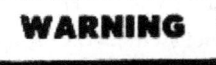

Abrupt or steep pull-ups immediately after take-off must be avoided.

See figures A-3 and A-4 for required take-off distances.

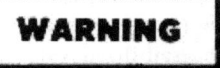

When outside air temperature is less than 50°F, rapid throttle movement during operation on the main fuel system below 10,000 feet, when engine speed is below 70% rpm, may produce compressor stall or total loss of power.

TAKE-OFF WITH HIGH OUTSIDE AIR AND RUNWAY TEMPERATURES.

Caution must be used to prevent premature nose wheel and airplane lift-off during take-off with high outside air and runway temperatures. Since take-off roll distance is increased under these conditions, it is imperative that the recommended take-off speed be followed. See figures A-3 and A-4 for required take-off distances.

MINIMUM-RUN TAKE-OFF.

A minimum-run take-off is a maximum performance maneuver with the airplane lifted off near stalling speed. It is closely related to slow flying with the airplane in a high-angle-of-attack attitude; consequently, you should be familiar with the characteristics of this maneuver in order to be able to maintain the necessary

Figure 2-5

safe margin above the stall. In addition to the complete "before take-off" check, trim the controllable horizontal tail to airplane full nose up and wing flaps full down. The initial take-off run is the same as for a normal take-off. In the clean configuration, with the stick held in the full aft position, nose wheel lift-off should occur as indicated in figure 2-5. It is necessary to pull approximately 20 pounds stick force before lift-off when full nose-up trim is used. This force is reduced to 0 pounds to maintain the proper attitude when the airplane breaks ground. Therefore, as the airplane lifts off, reduce back pressure sufficiently to maintain minimum airspeed build-up and maximum climb angle to effect the shortest air run that will clear all obstacles. After all obstacles are cleared, retrim the airplane to reduce stick forces, and accelerate to best climb speed.

CROSS-WIND TAKE-OFF.

In addition to the procedures used in a normal take-off, be prepared to counteract airplane drift at lift-off by lowering upwind wing or crabbing into the wind. Also, increase nose wheel lift-off speed approximately 10 to 15 knots IAS by holding nose wheel down a little longer during ground run.

Note

Increased speed is necessary to counteract reduced controllability caused by loss of lift on the downwind wing at normal speeds.

AFTER TAKE-OFF.

When airplane is definitely air-borne:

1. Landing gear handle—UP.

Landing gear handle UP below gear-down limit speed.

Check gear position indicators.

WARNING

Do not retract landing gear until the airplane accelerates to normal take-off speed, which is approximately 5 knots higher than the minimum-run take-off speed for the particular weight and external loading. If the gear is retracted very close to stall speed, the nose may pitch up enough to cause a stall. Delaying gear retraction until normal take-off speed is reached will eliminate this hazard.

CAUTION

- Do not retract landing gear while airplane is yawing or slipping, because the gear doors may be damaged.

- If landing gear unsafe warning light remains on, have tower check gear on a fly-by, or have a formation member check it before handle is moved.

2. Wing flap lever—UP, then HOLD.

Wing flap lever UP at 160 knots IAS. Rapid acceleration will prevent any tendency for the airplane to sink. When flaps are full up, move wing flap lever to HOLD.

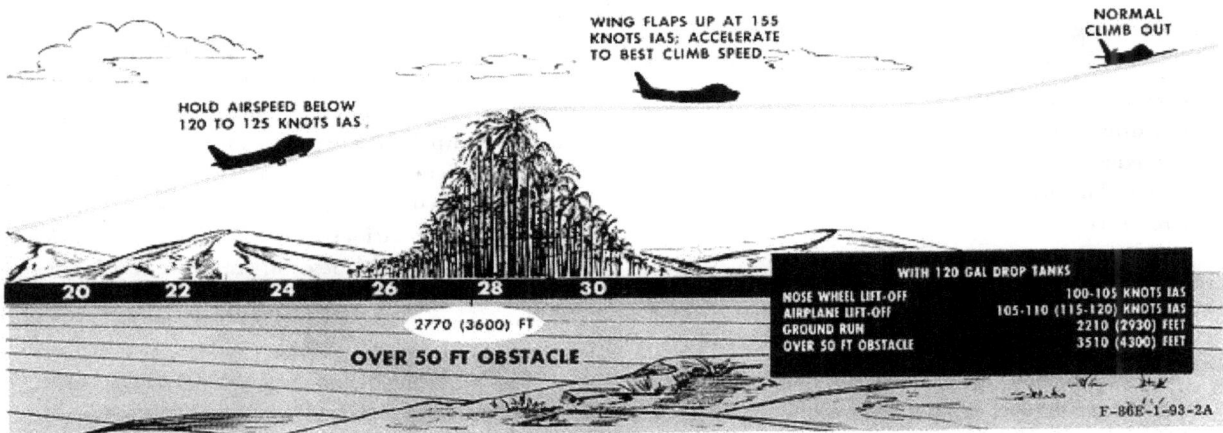

> **CAUTION**
>
> - Raise gear and flaps below gear- and flaps-down limit airspeed; otherwise excessive air loads may damage gear or flap operating mechanism and prevent subsequent operation.
> - If flaps do not fully retract, avoid high-speed pull-up. The flap actuating mechanism may fail if the flaps are not supported against the up-stop (fully retracted) during accelerated maneuvers at high speed.
> - During flight, do not move wing flap lever from UP position unless airspeed is below gear- and flaps-down limit airspeed.

3. Horizontal tail—Trim as required.

After take-off, use a slight push or pull stick force, as necessary, to maintain take-off attitude. It is recommended that stick forces be trimmed out after the airplane is safely air-borne.

4. Level off and accelerate to best climb speed. See figures A-5 through A-7 for climb data.

> **Note**
>
> - Slats will become fully closed at approximately 180 knots IAS, with or without external load.
> - During flight, do not move canopy switch to CLOSE when the canopy is already fully closed, because the canopy seal will deflate and cockpit pressure will be lost as long as the switch is actuated.

5. Oxygen regulator diluter lever—NORMAL OXYGEN (100% OXYGEN if carbon monoxide suspected).

If 100% OXYGEN was used for take-off, return oxygen regulator diluter lever to NORMAL OXYGEN, unless carbon monoxide contamination is suspected. If such is the case, continue use of 100 percent oxygen as long as considered necessary.

> **WARNING**
>
> Oxygen diluter lever must be returned to NORMAL OXYGEN as soon as possible, because use of 100 percent oxygen will deplete the oxygen supply enough to be hazardous.

CLIMB.

Climb at take-off rpm (time limit 30 minutes). Refer to climb charts (figures A-5 and A-6) for recommended indicated airspeeds to be used during climb and for estimated rates of climb and fuel consumption. Initial climb speed after accelerating from take-off should be approximately 430 knots IAS at sea level for a clean airplane. Airspeed should decrease approximately 50 knots IAS for every 10,000 feet increase of altitude.

> **CAUTION**
>
> During extended climbs to high altitude wherein an extreme nose-high attitude is maintained, level off for at least one minute between 18,000 and 20,000 feet, to permit adequate scavenging of engine oil. If you do not level off in this manner, severe engine surging may occur because of inadequate engine oil supply for main fuel regulator control. (Refer to "Engine Surge" in Section VII.)

FLIGHT CHARACTERISTICS.

Refer to Section VI for information regarding flight characteristics.

SYSTEMS OPERATION.

Refer to Section VII for information regarding systems operation.

DESCENT.

Circumstances may arise which require a descent from high altitude in the shortest possible time. The maximum rate of descent can be obtained when dive angle is increased until limit airspeed and/or Mach number is reached. Refer to "Cockpit Air Conditioning and Pressurization Systems" in Section IV for minimum throttle settings at various altitudes to maintain cockpit pressurization during descent. See figure A-8 for descent information.

> **Note**
>
> The windshield and canopy defrosting system provides sufficient heating of the transparent surfaces to effectively eliminate formation of frost or fog during descent.

PRE-TRAFFIC-PATTERN CHECK.

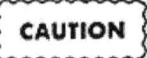

During landing, the emergency fuel system should never be on unless the main fuel regulator has failed; otherwise, any rapid throttle advancement would cause the emergency fuel system to override the main fuel system and cause a complete power failure as a result of a flame-out or compressor stall.

During approach to field, perform the following checks:

1. Safety belt and shoulder harness—Tighten.
2. Shoulder harness lock handle—UNLOCKED.
3. Gun sight caging lever—CAGE (CAGED).
4. Armament switches—Off.
5. Hydraulic pressure—Normal.
6. Oxygen diluter lever—NORMAL OXYGEN.
7. Windshield anti-icing lever*—ON (if vision impaired by rain).

Note

Sufficient anti-icing airflow is available over the windshield to effectively improve vision if a minimum of 75% engine rpm is maintained. If rain still is encountered as power is reduced for landing, it may be necessary to look through the windshield side panels.

CAUTION

- If windshield overheat light comes on, attempt to extinguish it by reducing power if possible, or move cockpit pressure switch to RAM. Anti-icing system may be left on, if necessary, to improve forward vision, even though windshield overheat light comes on.
- If warning light is on after landing, leave anti-icing lever ON. Reduced power on ground will allow gradual cooling of windshield and prevent cracking of glass by sudden temperature changes.

Note

The windshield anti-icing system cannot be used for rain removal on F-86E-1, F-86E-5, and F-86E-6 Airplanes.

*F-86E-10 and later airplanes

TRAFFIC-PATTERN CHECK.

See figure 2-6 for complete approach and landing procedures. Rapid increases in thrust are possible only above approximately 63% rpm; therefore, to ensure adequate acceleration in an emergency, it is desirable to use full flaps and speed brakes, and to hold a minimum of 60% to 70% rpm on final approach.

WARNING

Since very little stall warning exists under landing pattern flight conditions for airplanes without slats, and G-loads imposed by an abrupt flare-out at touchdown may cause wing drop, the landing pattern should be widened and speed increased with respect to airplanes with slats, as shown in figure 2-6. Also note increased stall speeds as shown in figure 6-2.

CAUTION

Do not lower landing gear in turns or pull-ups, above gear-and flaps-down limit airspeed, or while airplane is yawing or slipping, because the gear doors may be damaged.

LANDING.

NORMAL LANDING.

Note

- See figure 2-6 for landing pattern procedure. When properly followed, these procedures will produce the results tabulated in the Appendix. (See figures A-9 and A-10.)
- The full length of the runway should be used during the landing roll so that the brakes can be used as little and as lightly as possible when bringing the airplane to a stop.

CAUTION

- Do not attempt a full-stall landing, because the angle of attack would be so high that the aft section of the fuselage would drag.
- Do not apply brakes hard before nose wheel has touched down and speed has diminished enough for effective braking.

2-17

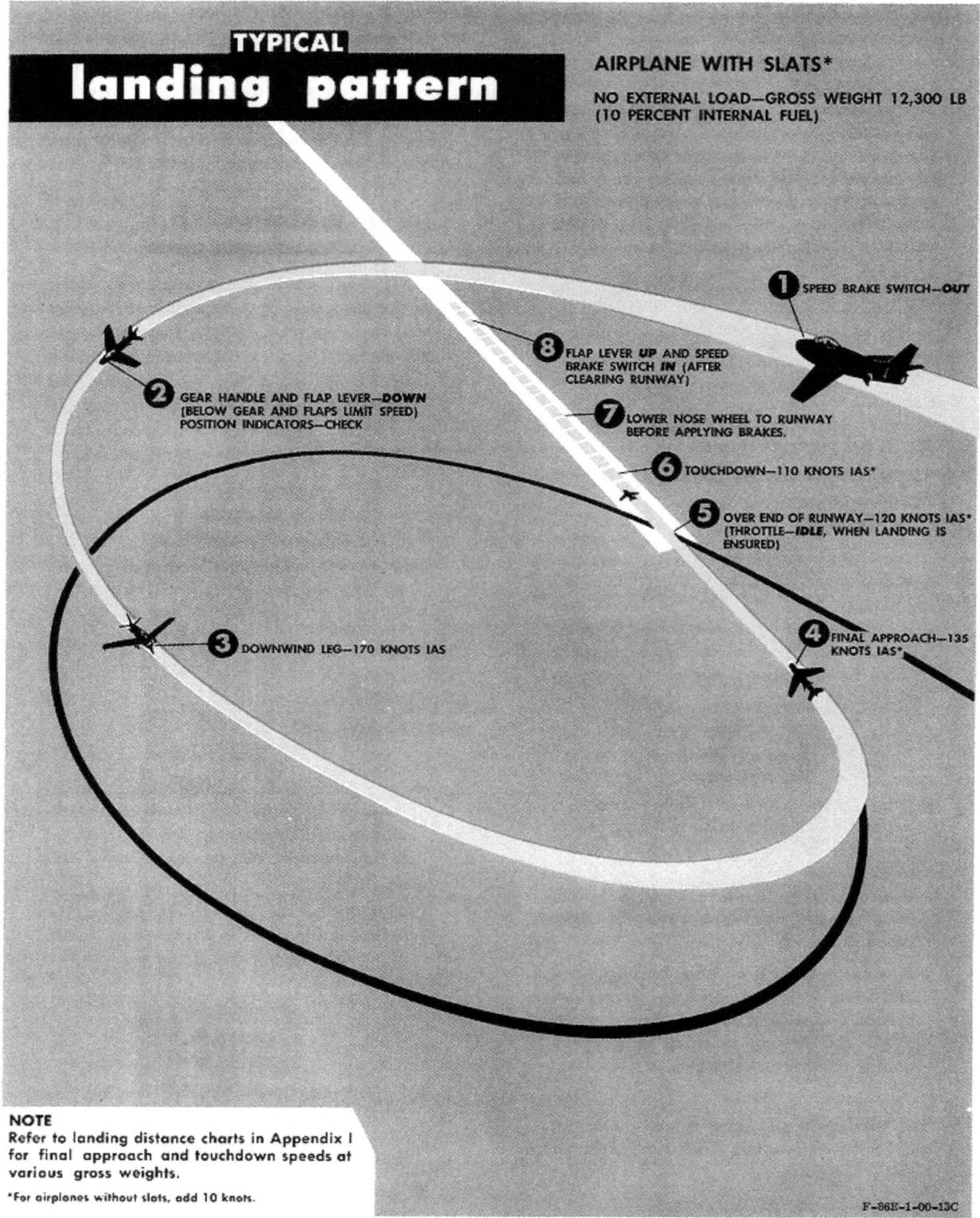

Figure 2-6

After rudder control loses effectiveness, use differential braking to maintain directional control.

HEAVY-WEIGHT LANDING.

The same technique for normal landing applies for heavy-weight landing, except for necessary increases in power settings. As gross weight increases, approach and touchdown speeds should be increased accordingly. A stall landing should be avoided, if at all possible, in an attempt to keep the G to a minimum at point of touchdown.

Note

If a hard heavy-weight landing is made, the airplane should be checked before the next flight for signs of overstress.

CROSS-WIND LANDING.

Adequate control is available for landing in a direct cross-wind with a velocity of 25 knots. However it is recommended that if the cross-wind component is above that of a direct 25 knot cross-wind, another runway be used. If that is not available, and fuel permits, a landing should be made at an airfield with more favorable wind conditions. In addition to the procedure used in a normal landing, the following procedure should be accomplished:

Maintain 160 knots IAS in turn onto final approach. On final approach, crab or drop wing to keep lined up with runway, maintaining 135 to 160 knots IAS.

CAUTION

Touchdown speed should be increased about 5 knots for every 10 knots of direct cross-wind component.

Slow to 110-130 knots IAS for touchdown. If crabbing, align airplane with runway before touchdown; if using wing-down approach, lift wing before touchdown. At touchdown, lower nose wheel to runway as quickly and smoothly as possible.

MINIMUM-RUN LANDING.

WARNING

Since a minimum-run landing is a maximum performance maneuver, and final approach speeds will be nearer to stall than in a normal landing, use a straight-in final approach; otherwise, stall will be more likely to occur when G-loads are imposed during shallow turns.

Final approach speed, for a minimum-run landing should be about 20 percent above stall speed for the particular weight and wing leading edge configuration you are flying. (Final approach speeds for airplanes without slats would vary from approximately 125 knots IAS at 12,600 pounds to 150 knots IAS at 17,800 pounds. Final approach speeds for airplanes with slats would vary from approximately 115 knots IAS at 12,600 pounds to 140 knots IAS at 17,800 pounds.) When sure of making the field, close the throttle. Set the nose wheel down quickly and smoothly after touchdown to allow for braking. Apply brakes smoothly and steadily to the point just short of locking wheels; then release and apply brakes intermittently and forcefully at one-second intervals, holding for approximately 2 to 3 seconds, but avoid sliding the wheels.

CAUTION

If brakes are applied above 100 knots IAS, be alert to prevent locking wheels.

Note

Opening the canopy will help decrease the roll, especially with a landing speed of 120 knots.

WET-RUNWAY LANDING.

When landing on a wet runway, care must be taken during braking action to prevent the locking of wheel brakes, causing skidding and loss of directional control. Braking effectiveness is greatly reduced, and landing roll is increased when the runway is wet.

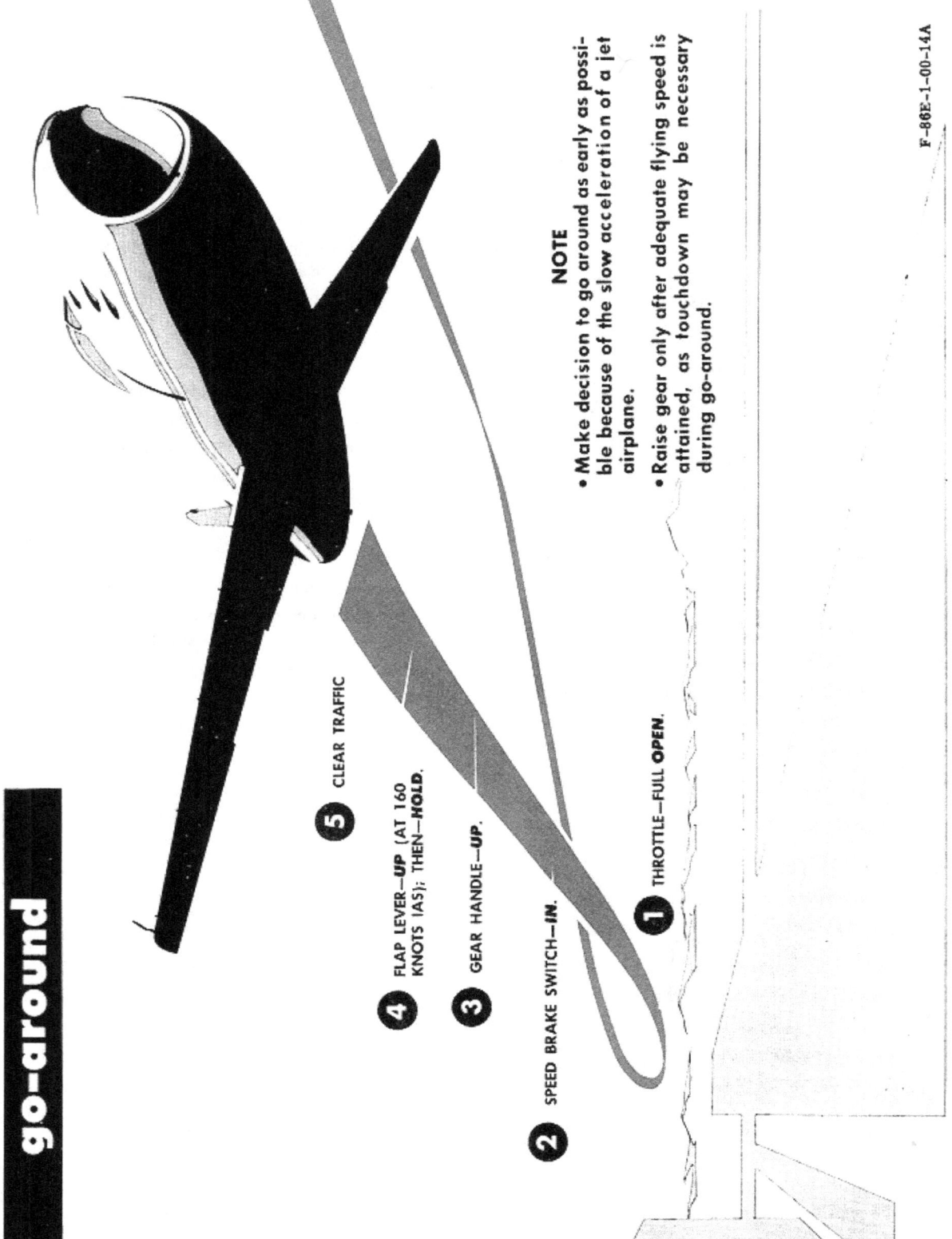

Figure 2-7

GO-AROUND.

See figure 2-7 for complete go-around procedure.

WARNING

- The emergency fuel switch should be OFF for a go-around.

- On a go-around procedure, the emergency fuel system will automatically be in stand-by condition (on airplanes with the two-position emergency fuel switch, the emergency fuel system would be operating as though in stand-by condition) if any of the following situations is present: emergency fuel switch ON, primary bus fails, battery-starter switch is moved to OFF upon generator failure, or generator switch is OFF when battery-starter switch is OFF. Therefore, under such conditions, rapid throttle advancement must be avoided to avert complete power failure caused by engine overspeeding or compressor stall.

- When outside air temperature is less than 50°F, rapid throttle movement during operation on the main fuel system below 10,000 feet, when engine speed is below 70% rpm, may cause compressor stall or total loss of power.

AFTER LANDING.

1. Maintain directional control.

Maintain directional control by differential braking on the landing roll. Engage nose wheel steering after clearing the runway and when slow taxiing becomes necessary.

2. Speed brake switch—Neutral.
3. Nose screen—Installed.

WARNING

If required by base procedure, nose screen must be installed before taxiing and with engine at idle rpm. Ground personnel installing screen must not wear articles of loose clothing or carry equipment likely to be drawn into the intake duct.

STOPPING ENGINE.

To stop the engine, proceed as follows:

1. Toe brakes—Hold.
2. Engine—65% to 70% rpm for 2 minutes.

Note

This permits engine stabilization at the lowest temperature which minimizes the possibility of shroud ring rub. If required by emergency, engine may be shut down immediately.

3. Throttle —OFF.

Note

If operation at idling speed is performed for more than 3 minutes, operate engine at 100% rpm for 30 seconds, to reduce carbon accumulation on spark plugs. Then operate engine at 65% to 70% rpm for 2 minutes and shut down engine.

4. Engine master switch—OFF.

Turn engine master switch to OFF below 10% rpm.

5. Speed brake switch—OUT.

Dump utility hydraulic system pressure by operating speed brakes.

If speed brakes are to be extended to dump hydraulic pressure, be sure aft fuselage area is clear. The speed brakes move rapidly and can injure any personnel in their path.

6. Battery-starter switch—OFF.
7. All switches except generator switch—OFF.

WARNING

Keep clear of tail pipe and do not move airplane into hangar for at least 15 minutes after shutdown, because of the possibility of explosion due to the accumulation of fuel vapors.

BEFORE LEAVING AIRPLANE.

Make the following checks before leaving the airplane:

1. Safety pins—Installed.

Canopy remover and seat catapult systems safetied, as applicable to the seat modification for the airplane you are flying. (See figures 1-29, 1-30, and 1-31.) On airplanes with seat initiators, if ground personnel are not available to obtain seat initiator pins, be sure not to foul gear on ejection mechanism when leaving seat. Insert safety pins in initiators after leaving seat.

CAUTION

If the airplane is equipped with an automatic-opening safety belt and you are wearing an automatic-opening parachute that has a key or a ring-type anchor attached to the aneroid arming lanyard, make sure key or anchor and lanyard are not fouled in any equipment before leaving seat, to prevent chute from opening accidentally.

2. Drop tank pressure shutoff valve—OFF.
3. Rudder gust lock handle—Engaged.
4. DD Form 781—Complete.
5. Main gear wheels—Chocked.
6. Parking brake handle—In.

Note

If parking brake handle is not full in, brakes will be inoperative.

CONDENSED CHECK LISTS.

Refer to pages 2-23 through 2-33 for the condensed check lists.

CUT ON SOLID LINE

F-86E CONDENSED CHECK LIST

NOTE

The following check lists are condensed versions of the procedures presented in Section II. These condensed check lists are arranged so that you may remove them from your Flight Handbook and insert them into a flip pad for convenient use. They are arranged so that each action is in sequence with the expanded procedure given in Section II. Presentation of these condensed check lists does not imply that you need not read and thoroughly understand the expanded versions. To fly the airplane safely and efficiently, you *must* know the reason why each step is performed and why the steps occur in certain sequence.

T.O 1F-86E-1
26 November 1956

Section II T. O. 1F-86E-1

CUT ON SOLID LINE

T. O. 1F-86E-1
26 November 1956

2

STATUS OF THE AIRPLANE

WEIGHT AND BALANCE.

1. Gross weight—Check.
2. Airplane serviced—Check.

PREFLIGHT CHECK.

BEFORE EXTERIOR INSPECTION.

1. DD Form 781—Check.

EXTERIOR INSPECTION.

Check all surfaces for cracks, distortion, loose rivets, and indications of damage; check for signs of hydraulic fluid, fuel, and oil leaks; check tires for general condition, slippage, and proper inflation; check all access doors and panels, and all filler caps secured; check position of gear doors, gear strut extension, and condition of wheels.

1. **Nose:**

   Nose wheel chock—Removed.
   Nose gear ground safety lock—Removed.
   Tow pin safety cap—Tight.
   Nose gear emergency extension accumulator air pressure—Check.
   Landing and taxi lights—Retracted.
   Intake duct—Clear (except nose screen installed).
   Gun port plugs—Installed.

2. **Forward Fuselage and Right Wing Leading Edge:**

   Emergency nose gear selector valve—Reset.
   Slats*—Check.
   Main gear wheel—Chocked.
   External load—Installation and mounting.
   Position light and wing tip—Check.
   Pitot head—Uncovered.

   *Some airplanes

2-24

CUT ON SOLID LINE

3. Right Wing Trailing Edge and Aft Fuselage:

Aileron and flap—Check.

Speed brake—Check.

Flight control alternate hydraulic system accumulators*
air pressure—Check.

Flight control normal hydraulic system fluid level compensator
shaft extension—Check.

4. Empennage:

Tail-pipe cover—Removed.

Tail cone and position lights—Check.

Aspirator fuel drain for freedom of movement—Check.

5. Aft Fuselage and Left Wing Trailing Edge:

Speed brake—Check.

Aileron and flap—Check.

Flight control alternate hydraulic system fluid level compensator
shaft extension—Check.

Flight control alternate hydraulic system accumulator*
air pressure—Check.

Flight control normal hydraulic system accumulator
air pressure—Check.

6. Left Wing Leading Edge and Forward Fuselage:

Position light and wing tip—Check.

External load—Installation and mounting.

Main gear wheel—Chocked.

Landing gear door ground control switch—CLOSE.

Slats*—Check.

*Some airplanes

Section II   T. O. 1F-86E-1

CUT ON SOLID LINE

T. O. 1F-86E-1
26 November 1956   4

CANOPY AND EJECTION SEAT CHECK.

1. Handgrips and triggers—Check.
2. Safety pins—Check.
3. Seat quick-disconnects—Check.
4. Lead seals—Check.

INTERIOR CHECK.

1. Stick grip—Check.
2. Safety belt and shoulder harness—Check.
3. Seat—Adjust.
4. Rudder pedals—Unlock and adjust.
5. Armament switches—Off.
6. Throttle—OFF (adjust friction).
7. Landing gear handle—DOWN.
8. Speed brake switch—Neutral (HOLD).
9. Engine master, emergency ignition, and battery-starter switches—OFF.
10. External power—Connected.
11. Circuit breakers—In.
12. Oxygen regulator—Check.
13. Anti-G suit regulator valve—Check.
14. Drop tank pressure shutoff valve—OFF.
15. Ammunition compartment heat emergency shutoff handle—NORMAL.
16. Cockpit air temperature control switch—AUTO.
17. Cabin pressure control lever (cockpit pressure control switch)—As desired.
18. Air outlet selector lever—FLOOR.
19. Windshield anti-icing lever—OFF.
20. Rudder trim switch—OFF.
21. Lateral alternate trim switch—NORMAL.
22. Longitudinal alternate trim switch—NORMAL GRIP CONT.
23. Flight control switch—NORMAL.
24. Speed brake emergency lever—NORMAL.
25. Wing flap lever—UP.
26. Emergency fuel switch—OFF.
27. Emergency jettison handle—In.
28. Pitot heater switch—ON then OFF.

2-26

CUT ON SOLID LINE

29. Landing and taxi light switches—Off (check lights retracted).
30. Parking brake handle—In.
31. Clock, accelerometer, and altimeter—Set.
32. Generator switch—ON.
33. Position and fuselage light switches—Off.
34. Communication equipment switches—As desired.
35. Cockpit light switches—OFF.
36. Flight control emergency override handle*—In.
37. Canopy alternate emergency jettison handle*—In.
38. Fuel quantity—Check; totalizer dial—Set.
39. Warning lights and indicators and test warning systems—Check.
40. Attitude indicator—Check.
41. Directional indicator against stand-by compass—Check.
42. Vertical velocity indicator—Set.
43. Operation of sight—Check.
44. Instrument power switch—NORMAL, then ALTERNATE (ALT).
45. Emergency utility hydraulic system selector valve—OFF (some airplanes).
46. Landing gear emergency release—In.
47. Canopy declutch handle—In.
48. Rudder gust lock handle—In.
49. Flight controls—Check.
50. Normal trim switch—Check.
51. Radio compass—Check.
52. Interior and exterior lights—Check.
53. Flashlight—Check.

*Some airplanes

CUT ON SOLID LINE

STARTING ENGINE.

1. Throttle—OFF.
2. Engine master switch—ON.
3. Battery-starter switch—STARTER (momentarily), then BATTERY.
4. 3% rpm—Throttle outboard.
5. 6% rpm—Throttle halfway between IDLE and OFF.
6. Throttle—Adjust for proper exhaust temperature.
7. Oil pressure—Check.
8. Engine instruments—Check.
9. Drop tank pressure shutoff valve—ON (drop tanks installed)—OFF (drop tanks not installed).
10. External power—Disconnected.

GROUND TESTS.

1. Throttle—IDLE.
2. Hydraulic pressure gage selector switch—NORMAL.
3. Flight control switch—RESET.
4. Flight control normal hydraulic system—Check.
   a. Flight control switch—NORMAL.
   b. Control stick—Move and visually check for proper control surface movement.
   c. Pressure—After 5 seconds, 2900 to 3200 psi (control stick not in motion).
5. Flight control alternate hydraulic system—Check.
   a. Flight control switch—ALTERNATE (ON EMERG).
   b. Alternate-on warning light—On.
   c. Control stick—Move and visually check for proper control surface movement.
   d. Hydraulic pressure gage selector switch—ALTERNATE.
   e. Pressure—2550 to 3200 psi (control stick not in motion).
   f. Flight control switch—RESET.

T. O. 1F-86E-1
26 November 1956

6

CUT ON SOLID LINE

6. Flight control manual emergency override system*—Check.
    a. Hydraulic pressure gage selector switch—ALTERNATE.
    b. Flight control switch—Hold at RESET.
    c. Emergency change-over handle—Pull to full extension.
    d. Control stick—Move and visually check for proper control surface movement.
    e. Flight control switch—NORMAL.
    f. Alternate-on warning light—On.
    g. Pressure—3050 to 4000 psi.
7. Emergency change-over handle—In.
8. Pressure—2550 to 3200 psi.
9. Automatic return to flight control normal system—Check.
    a. Flight control switch—NORMAL.
    b. Control stick—Move rapidly.
    c. Alternate-on warning light—Out.
    d. Hydraulic pressure gage selector switch—NORMAL.
    e. Pressure—2900 to 3200 psi.
10. Utility hydraulic system—Check.
    a. Hydraulic pressure gage selector switch—UTILITY.
    b. Speed brake switch—OUT, IN, then Neutral (HOLD).
    c. Pressure—Approximately 3000 psi.
11. Loadmeter and voltmeter—Check.

TAXIING.

1. Gun sight caging lever—CAGE (CAGED).
2. Main gear wheel chocks—Removed.
3. Throttle—Advance, then return to IDLE.
4. Nose wheel steering switch—Depress (for directional control).
5. Gyro instruments—Check.

*Some airplanes

CUT ON SOLID LINE

T. O. 1F-86E-1
26 November 1956

BEFORE TAKE-OFF.

PREFLIGHT AIRPLANE CHECK.

1. Nose screen—Removed.
2. Safety belt—Tighten, shoulder harness—Adjust.
3. Shoulder harness lock handle—UNLOCKED.
4. Safety pins—Remove.
5. Armament switches—Off.
6. Trim for take-off—Check.
7. Wing flap lever—DOWN.
8. Canopy switch—CLOSE.
9. Oxygen regulator diluter lever—NORMAL OXYGEN (100% OXYGEN if carbon monoxide suspected).
10. Take-off position—Check.
11. Toe brakes—Hold.

PREFLIGHT ENGINE CHECK.

Emergency Fuel System Check (Three-position Switch).

1. Throttle—80% rpm.
2. Emergency fuel switch—ON.
3. Throttle—Full OPEN; rpm—Check.
4. Emergency fuel switch—OFF.
5. Emergency fuel switch—TEST; rpm—Check.
6. Emergency fuel switch—OFF.

Emergency Fuel System Check (Two-position Switch).

1. Throttle—80% rpm.
2. Emergency fuel switch—ON.
3. Throttle—Full OPEN; rpm—Check.
4. Emergency fuel switch—OFF.
5. Emergency fuel switch—ON; rpm—Check.
6. Emergency fuel switch—OFF.

Engine Instrument Check.

1. Throttle—Full OPEN.
2. Engine instruments—Check.

8

CUT ON SOLID LINE

TAKE-OFF.
NORMAL TAKE-OFF.
1. Throttle—Take-off rpm.
2. Wheel brakes—Release.
3. Maintain directional control.
4. Maintain near-level attitude until take-off speed attained.
5. Assume nose-high attitude when take-off speed attained.

AFTER TAKE-OFF.
1. Landing gear handle—UP.
2. Wing flap lever—UP, then HOLD.
3. Horizontal tail—Trim as required.
4. Level off and accelerate to best climb speed.
5. Oxygen regulator diluter lever—NORMAL OXYGEN (100% OXYGEN if carbon monoxide suspected).

PRE-TRAFFIC-PATTERN CHECK.
1. Safety belt and shoulder harness—Tighten.
2. Shoulder harness lock handle—UNLOCKED.
3. Gun sight caging lever—CAGE (CAGED).
4. Armament switches—Off.
5. Hydraulic pressure—Normal.
6. Oxygen diluter lever—NORMAL OXYGEN.
7. Windshield anti-icing lever*—ON (if vision impaired by rain).

*Some airplanes

T. O. 1F-86E-1
26 November 1956

9

T.O. 1F-86E-1
26 November 1956

10

TRAFFIC-PATTERN CHECK AND LANDING.

1. Speed brake switch—OUT.
2. Gear handle and flap lever—DOWN, position indicators—Check.
3. Downwind leg—Hold recommended speed.
4. Final approach—Hold recommended speed.
5. Throttle—IDLE (when landing ensured).
6. Touchdown—At recommended speed.
7. Lower nose wheel to runway before applying brakes.
8. Flap lever—UP; speed brake switch—IN (after clearing runway).

GO-AROUND.

1. Throttle—Full OPEN.
2. Speed brake switch—IN.
3. Gear handle—UP.
4. Flap lever—UP, (160 knots IAS); then—HOLD.
5. Clear traffic.

AFTER LANDING.

1. Maintain directional control.
2. Speed brake switch—Neutral (HOLD).
3. Nose screen—Installed.

STOPPING ENGINE.

1. Toe brakes—Hold.
2. Engine—65% to 70% rpm for 2 minutes.
3. Throttle—OFF.
4. Engine master switch—OFF.
5. Speed brake switch—OUT.
6. Battery-starter switch—OFF.
7. All switches except generator switch—OFF.

CUT ON SOLID LINE

CUT ON SOLID LINE

BEFORE LEAVING AIRPLANE.

1. Safety pins—Installed.
2. Drop tank pressure shutoff valve—OFF.
3. Rudder gust lock—Engaged.
4. DD Form 781—Complete.
5. Main gear wheels—Chocked.
6. Parking brake handle—In.

T. O. 1F-86E-1
26 November 1956

11

SECTION III

EMERGENCY PROCEDURES

TABLE OF CONTENTS

	PAGE
Engine Failure	3-1
Fire	3-7
Elimination of Smoke or Fumes	3-9
Landing Emergencies	3-9
Emergency Entrance	3-10
Ditching	3-10
Ejection	3-12
Fuel System Failure	3-18
Electrical Power System Failure	3-18
Utility Hydraulic System Failure	3-20
Flight Control Hydraulic System Failure	3-20
Flight Control Artificial Feel System Failure	3-21
Landing Gear Emergency Operation	3-21
Trim Failure	3-21
Speed Brake System Failure	3-22
Wing Flap Emergency Operation	3-23
External Load Emergency Release	3-23

ENGINE FAILURE.

The majority of jet-engine flame-outs is the result of improper fuel flow caused by fuel control system malfunction or incorrect operating techniques during certain critical flight conditions. Specific information on this type of engine failure is given in "Fuel System Failure" in this section. It should be noted that the engine instruments often provide indications of fuel control system failure before actual engine stoppage. If engine failure is due to malfunction of the main fuel control system or to improper operating technique, an air start can usually be accomplished when time and altitude permit. In the event of obvious mechanical failure within the engine, air starts should not be attempted.

ENGINE FAILURE DURING TAKE-OFF RUN.

If the engine fails, or if the take-off is aborted for any other reason before the airplane leaves the ground and there is sufficient runway for a normal stop, proceed as follows:

1. Throttle OFF.
2. Apply brakes as necessary.

If there is not sufficient runway for a normal stop and if the runway is equipped with an overrun barrier, follow the procedure given in "Engaging Runway Barrier" in this section. If the runway is not equipped with an overrun barrier, and if the landing gear must be retracted because of insufficient runway, follow this procedure:

1. If engine power loss is indicated by rpm or exhaust temperature drop, but rpm has not fallen below 80%, move emergency fuel switch to ON.

WARNING

If engine rpm has fallen below 80%, abort take-off. You would not have time to retard throttle to IDLE, switch emergency fuel switch to ON, and then readvance throttle. Therefore, proceed as outlined in steps 2 through 5.

2. Press bomb-rocket-tank salvo button or pull emergency jettison handle to drop external loads.

WARNING

- Rockets cannot be jettisoned by actuation of the jettison (salvo) button when the weight of the airplane is on the gear.
- The rockets cannot be jettisoned by use of the emergency jettison handle on F-86E-6 Airplanes.

3. If engine does not immediately recover sufficient power to continue take-off when emergency fuel switch is moved to ON, pull throttle to OFF, move landing gear handle UP, and hold landing gear emergency-up button depressed until gear completely retracts.

Note

Gear retraction can be accelerated by yawing the airplane to relieve load on main gear down lockpins through alternate application of right and left wheel brakes, or by applying rudder alternately with nose wheel steering engaged.

4. Lower head and raise right seat handgrip to jettison canopy. (On airplanes equipped with the alternate emergency jettison handle, pull handle to jettison canopy without arming the seat catapult.)

WARNING

If the canopy has not been jettisoned before the airplane stops, and if spilled fuel is in the vicinity of the airplane, use the mechanical or electrical means to open the canopy, if time permits. If these systems fail, the canopy jettison mechanism may be used.

5. Engine master and battery-starter switches OFF.

CAUTION

Turn engine master switch OFF while battery-starter switch is still at BATTERY, so that power will still be available to close the fuel shutoff valve.

6. Shoulder harness lock handle LOCKED.

ENGINE FAILURE DURING TAKE-OFF (AIRPLANE AIR-BORNE).

If the engine fails on take-off after the airplane is airborne, prepare for an emergency landing, accomplishing as much of the following as time permits:

1. If engine power loss is indicated by rpm or exhaust temperature drop, but rpm has not fallen below 80%, move emergency fuel switch to ON.

WARNING

If engine rpm has fallen below 80%, abort take-off. You would not have time to retard throttle to IDLE, switch emergency fuel switch to ON, and then readvance throttle. Therefore, proceed as outlined in steps 2 through 9.

2. Press bomb-rocket-tank salvo button or pull emergency jettison handle, to drop external loads.

3. If engine does not immediately recover sufficient power to sustain flight when the emergency fuel switch is moved to ON, pull throttle to OFF.

4. Landing gear handle DOWN if gear has already been raised.

5. Check wing flap lever DOWN.

6. Lower head and raise right seat handgrip to jettison canopy. (On airplanes equipped with the alternate emergency jettison handle, pull handle to jettison canopy without arming the seat catapult.)

7. Engine master, generator, and battery-starter switches OFF.

CAUTION

Turn engine master switch OFF while battery-starter switch is still at BATTERY, so that power will still be available to close the fuel shutoff valve.

8. Shoulder harness lock handle LOCKED.

9. Land straight ahead, changing course only enough to miss obstacles.

ENGINE FAILURE DURING FLIGHT.

Since power available from the battery is limited after engine failure, it is imperative to let down to below 20,000 feet immediately if a successful air start is to be made. This, of course, will result in a sacrifice of glide range, which may be undesirable in some cases. Therefore, the decision (to utilize altitude to obtain maximum range, or to descend to a favorable air-start altitude) will depend upon the distance from a suitable landing area and the altitude at time of engine failure. If engine failure occurs during flight, follow this procedure.

1. Throttle OFF.

2. Establish glide at 185 knots IAS with gear and flaps up and speed brakes closed for maximum glide distance. (Refer to "Maximum Glide" in this section.)

3. Turn off all nonessential electrical equipment.

WARNING

- At normal gliding speeds, engine windmilling does not provide adequate generator output, and the battery is then the only source of electrical power. With the engine master switch, radio, pitot heater, and lights turned off, the battery can supply power for only about 7 to 28 minutes. If engine damage prevents engine windmilling (causing flight control normal hydraulic system failure), the automatic operation of the flight control alternate hydraulic system imposes maximum drain on battery power and results in minimum battery output time.

4. Attempt an air start. (Refer to "Engine Air Start" in this section.)

5. If an air start is impossible, prepare for a forced landing, or eject. (Refer to "Landing With Engine Inoperative" in this section.)

ENGINE AIR START.

Engine air starts can be made with the most assurance of success below 20,000 feet. Starts at higher altitudes are possible, but unpredictable, and a failure to start will frequently prevent a successful restart at a lower, more favorable, altitude. Do not try to restart above 25,000 feet. To start engine in flight:

1. Check engine master and generator switches ON, and battery-starter switch at BATTERY.

Note

If a long glide is contemplated, turn off all nonessential electrical equipment to conserve battery power.

2. If altitude is available, hold airplane as level as possible for at least 5 seconds, to drain any fuel that may have accumulated in the combustion chambers or the turbine section.

3. If altitude, weather, and terrain permit, descend to 15,000 feet before attempting to start engine.

4. If engine failure was caused by main fuel regulator failure, as shown by a complete or partial drop in fuel flow indication, turn on emergency fuel system.

Note

Starts should be made on the main fuel system, if possible, because starting attempts using this system are likely to be more successful than those using the emergency system.

5. If necessary, reduce airspeed to obtain an engine windmilling speed of not more than 25% rpm.

6. Emergency ignition switch ON.

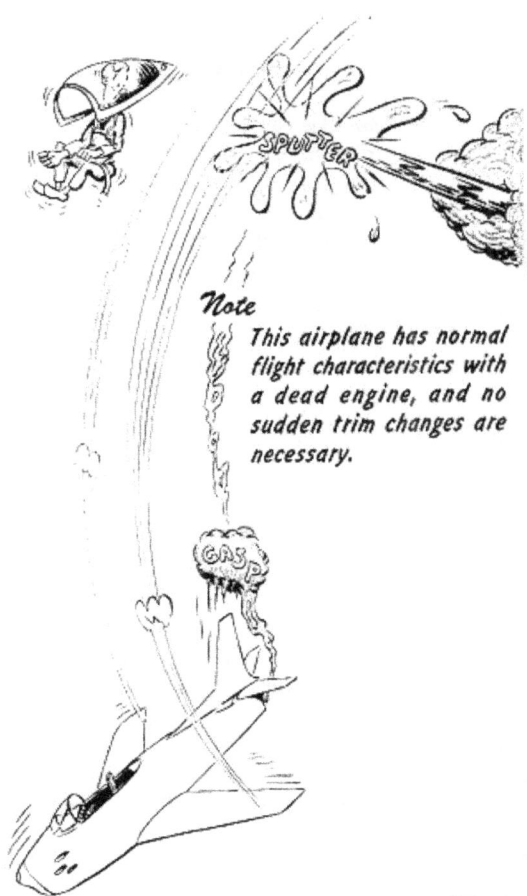

Note
This airplane has normal flight characteristics with a dead engine, and no sudden trim changes are necessary.

Section III   T. O. 1F-86E-1

7. Hold throttle outboard to energize the ignition circuit, and move it to a position slightly below the IDLE stop to obtain minimum fuel flow indication; then wait until engine starts. Ignition should occur within 45 seconds after throttle is opened. Combustion can be recognized by slowly rising exhaust temperature.

CAUTION

If ignition does not occur within 45 seconds after throttle is opened, slowly retard throttle, and then readvance it to the original position. If at the end of one minute the engine has not started, turn emergency ignition switch OFF, and retard throttle to the OFF position. Level the airplane to allow fuel drainage, and repeat starting procedure.

Note

In case you have to attempt an air start at higher altitude, it may be necessary to keep the throttle considerably below the IDLE stop to obtain ignition, because increasingly lower fuel pressures are required for ignition at the higher altitudes. Also, you should be extremely careful to regulate the throttle slowly, since very small changes in fuel pressure, due to throttle operating technique, play a major part in engine starting.

8. After ignition occurs, adjust throttle, as necessary, to avoid compressor stall and to prevent exhaust temperature from exceeding maximum allowable limits until idle rpm is reached.

CAUTION

If start is evidenced by low-temperature indication (200°C), but rpm and temperature will not increase when throttle is advanced, increase airspeed and again advance the throttle. If rpm and temperature still do not increase, shut off engine and restart. This condition indicates that all burners are not lighted, and damage to the engine may result if the condition is allowed to persist.

9. After a stable combustion is obtained, turn emergency ignition switch OFF.

CAUTION

Ignition transformers may be damaged if emergency ignition switch is left on continuously for more than 3 minutes per start.

10. Slowly bring engine up to desired rpm, adjusting the throttle, as necessary, to avoid excessive exhaust temperatures.

CAUTION

During air starts at high altitude, the engine may be on the verge of compressor stall with the throttle at IDLE, and any attempt to advance the throttle will cause a complete stall. If a stall occurs, reduce throttle setting and increase airspeed. If stall cannot be eliminated, close the throttle. Then reattempt starting, using a slightly lower throttle position to avoid repetition of stall.

11. If air start cannot be obtained, retard throttle to OFF, turn emergency ignition, engine master, and generator switches OFF, and prepare for a forced landing, or eject. (Refer to "Landing With Engine Inoperative" in this section.)

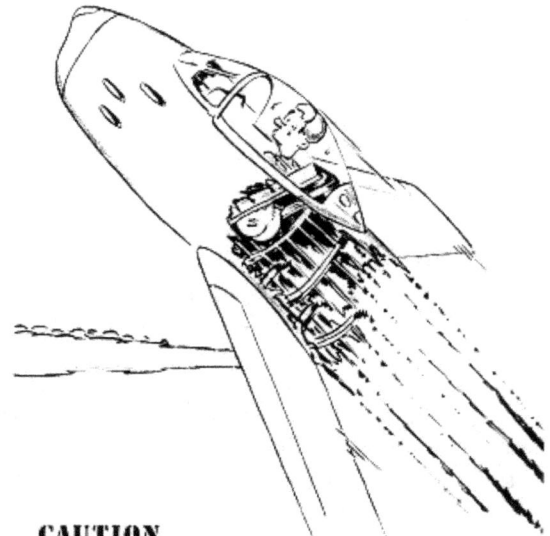

CAUTION
Air starts using rpm greater than 25% will probably result in excessive and damaging exhaust temperatures.

3-4

MAXIMUM GLIDE.

For maximum glide distance with engine windmilling or frozen, the optimum gliding speed is 185 knots IAS with gear and flaps up, speed brakes in, and no external load. (See figure 3-1.) When speed is maintained at 185 knots IAS, glide ratio and rate of descent with various airplane configurations are as follows:

	GLIDE RATIO	RATE OF DESCENT
Gear and flaps up— speed brakes in	14 to 1	2700 fpm at 40,000 ft 1500 fpm at 10,000 ft
Gear down, flaps up— speed brakes in	7.3 to 1	3000 fpm at 10,000 ft
Gear down, flaps up— speed brakes out	4.8 to 1	4500 fpm at 10,000 ft

LANDING WITH ENGINE INOPERATIVE.

If a forced landing is contemplated, maintaining the glide at 185 knots IAS (gear and flaps up, speed brakes in) will provide the maximum gliding distance. Unless the engine is damaged, it will windmill at sufficient speed to produce power for the hydraulic systems, although landing gear operation may be slower than usual.

Note

The speed brakes will not operate if utility hydraulic system has failed.

The flight control normal hydraulic system will operate normally when the engine is windmilling if recommended speeds are maintained during the forced landing. See figure 3-2 for procedure to follow in case of a forced landing.

SIMULATED FORCED LANDING.

The normal practice of retarding the throttle to idle to practice forced landing does not apply to jet airplanes. With the throttle at IDLE, the engine continues to provide thrust (about 300 pounds), whereas with complete power failure the windmilling engine creates drag. Thus, if the throttle is retarded to IDLE to simulate engine failure, the thrust still produced will cause the rate of descent to be less and the glide distance greater than during an actual flame-out forced landing. The drag of a windmilling engine can be simulated for practice forced landings by opening the speed brakes. However, the drag created by the open speed brakes is actually greater than that of the windmilling

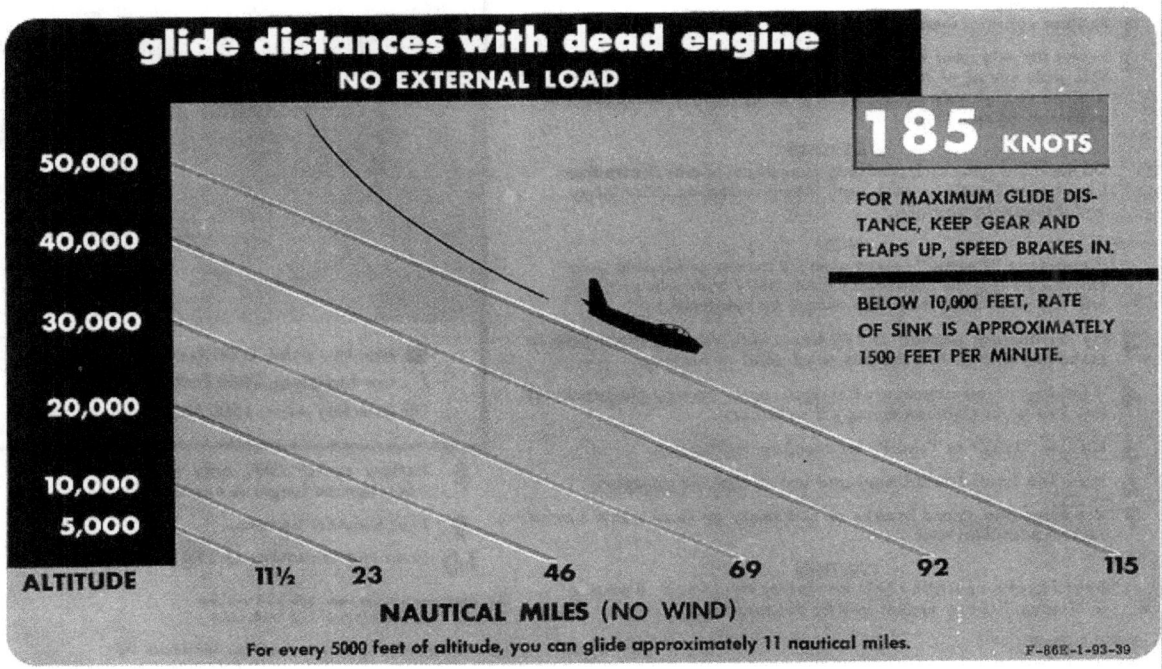

Figure 3-1

Section III T. O. 1F-86E-1

forced landing—dead engine
AIRPLANES WITH SLATS*

WARNING
IF TERRAIN IS UNKNOWN OR UNSUITABLE FOR FORCED LANDING, EJECT.

GROSS WEIGHT 12,500 LB—500 LB FUEL REMAINING

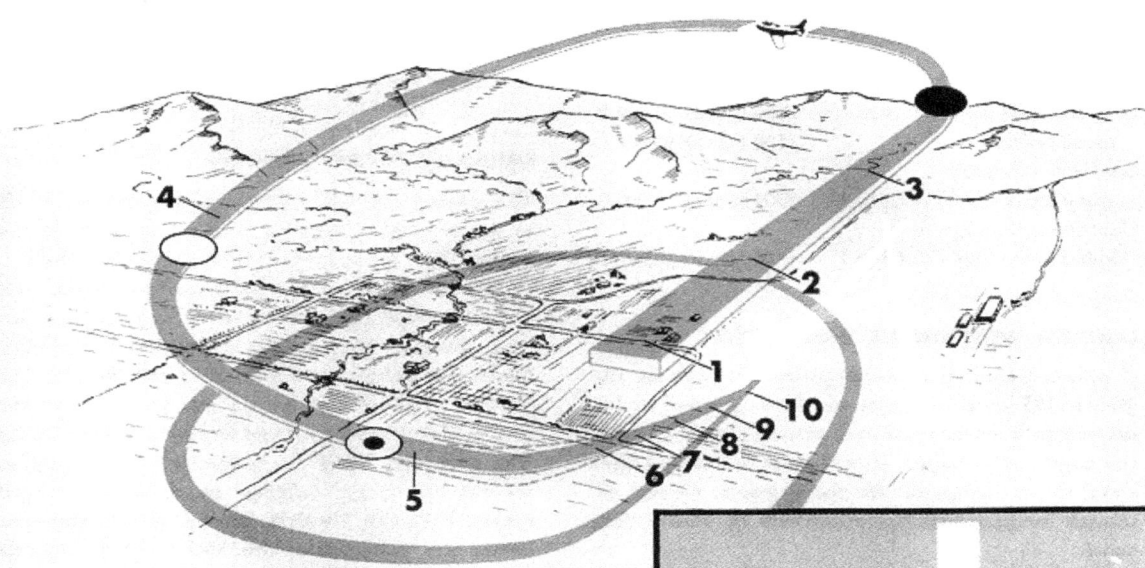

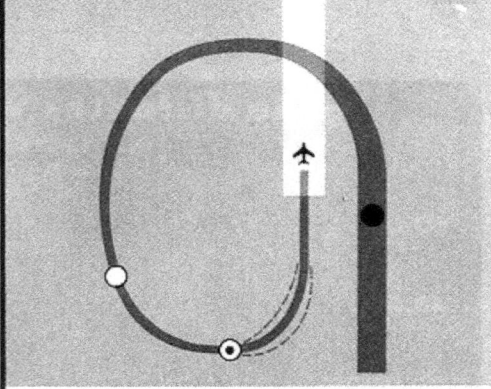

● high key point, 6000 feet above terrain.
○ low key point, 3000 feet above terrain.
◉ base key point, 1500 feet above terrain.

1. Jettison external load and maintain glide speed of 185 knots IAS.
2. Lower landing gear above 12,000 feet (field made); then establish glide speed of 170 knots IAS. If altitude is too low to enter pattern at high key point, leave gear up until a subsequent key point can be reached.

WARNING
Do not leave gear up for landing. Investigation has shown that emergency landings with gear down minimize pilot injury and damage to airplane.

NOTE
If engine is "frozen," lower gear by means of landing gear emergency release handle, because utility hydraulic pressure will not be available. (Gear cannot be retracted.)

3. Fly rectangular pattern at 170 knots IAS, varying flight path to make key points. Aim for one-third point of runway.
4. If landing on an unprepared surface, open canopy electrically at low key point (jettison canopy if necessary).
5. Fly turn "long" or "short" for accurate touchdown.
6. Hold 145 knots IAS† on final and use straight-in approach.
7. Use flaps and speed brakes as necessary on final when sure of reaching landing spot.

CAUTION
Speed brake operation will be slower than usual. If engine is "frozen," speed brakes will be inoperative.

8. Battery switch OFF, only after speed brake operation no longer is necessary.
9. Lock shoulder harness.
10. Over end of runway at 130 knots IAS.†

*For airplanes without slats, add 10 knots IAS (except for glide speeds of 185 knots IAS).

†For each additional 1000 pounds of fuel, add 5 knots IAS.

F-86E-1-93-42A

Figure 3-2

engine and a certain amount of engine power is required to offset that amount of excessive drag. Rate of descent, glide distance, and flight characteristics with the windmilling engine can be simulated above 12,000 feet by reducing the engine rpm to 72 percent, opening speed brakes, and establishing a glide speed of 185 knots IAS. Landing gear should be lowered at 12,000 feet and a glide speed of 170 knots IAS initiated. To simulate the drag of a windmilling engine at 170 knots IAS, the rpm should be reduced to 69 percent, because of decrease in drag at the lower glide speed. Familiarization with forced-landing techniques and procedures, as shown in figure 3-2, can be attained by practicing forced landings using extended speed brakes and the recommended engine power to simulate a flame-out condition. During an actual forced landing, the speed brakes may be extended as desired to prevent possible overshoot. On practice forced landings, however, the speed brakes have been opened previously; therefore, to simulate the use of speed brakes it is necessary to retard the throttle to IDLE, resulting in the already opened speed brakes becoming effective, as in an actual forced landing. It should be remembered that since the idling engine still produces some thrust, the touchdown point under practice conditions will be slightly farther down the runway than it will be when landing with a dead engine. If approach during practice forced landing is not as desired, make a normal go-around and repeat forced landing procedures until desired proficiency is attained.

FIRE.

Note

There is no fire extinguishing system on this airplane.

The fire-warning system consists of two detector circuits. Each circuit controls a red warning light in the cockpit. The forward circuit senses fire in the forward engine compartment. The aft circuit senses overheat or fire in the engine compartment aft of the engine fire wall. The aft compartment is substantially more resistant to immediate fire damage than the forward compartment. This permits less drastic action in case the aft warning light comes on, as indicated in the following procedures.

ENGINE FIRE DURING STARTING.

If there is an indication of abnormal fire, such as when a fire warning light comes on:

1. Throttle OFF.

2. Engine master switch at OFF, to close main fuel shutoff valve.

Note

With starter already locked in, moving engine master switch to OFF will not cause the starter to disengage.

3. Keep engine turning; however, if fire persists, push stop-starter button.

4. Battery-starter switch OFF.

5. Leave airplane as quickly as possible.

ENGINE FIRE DURING TAKE-OFF.

Forward Fire-warning Light.

Illumination of the forward fire-warning light during take-off indicates a fire in the forward engine section, necessitating immediate action. The exact procedure to follow will vary with each set of circumstances, and will depend upon altitude, airspeed, length of runway, overrun clearing remaining, availability of runway barrier, location of populated areas, etc. The decision you make will depend on these factors. To help you make a decision, the following procedures are presented for your consideration. If light comes on during ground roll and sufficient runway or overrun area is available to permit aborting the take-off, proceed as follows:

1. Chop throttle to OFF.

2. Jettison external load.

3. Move landing gear handle to UP, and hold landing gear emergency-up button depressed until gear completely retracts.

4. Abandon airplane immediately upon stopping, if fire is apparent.

If light comes on after airplane becomes air-borne, and if sufficient runway is not available and overrun area is congested, preventing aborting of take-off, the following is recommended if altitude is too low for a safe ejection:

1. Jettison external load.

2. Maintain power, and immediately climb to a minimum safe ejection altitude; then eject. (See figures 3-4 and 3-5 for minimum safe ejection altitude.)

Aft Fire-warning Light.

Illumination of the aft fire-warning light indicates an overheat condition or possible fire in the aft section, necessitating action as follows:

1. If light comes on during ground roll and sufficient runway and overrun area is available to abort the take-off, chop throttle to OFF, jettison external load, and

Section III T. O. 1F-86E-1

use maximum braking. If warning light is still on after stopping, abandon airplane immediately. If light is out, turn engine master switch OFF, and then turn battery-starter switch OFF.

2. If light comes on after airplane becomes air-borne and take-off cannot be aborted safely, retard throttle and continue climb-out. (Do not retard throttle below an engine rpm range where a safe climb cannot be maintained.)

　　a. If light goes out, continue flight at reduced power, landing as soon as possible.

　　b. If light remains on with reduced power, maintain climb at reduced power and check for other indications of fire, such as trailing smoke, long exhaust flame, etc.

　　c. If no fire is apparent, continue flight at reduced power, landing as soon as possible.

　　d. If positive indications of fire exist, maintain power and immediately climb to a minimum safe ejection altitude, and eject. (See figures 3-4 and 3-5 for minimum safe ejection altitude.)

ENGINE FIRE DURING FLIGHT.

Forward Fire-warning Light.

Illumination of the forward fire-warning light indicates a fire in the forward engine section, necessitating immediate action as follows:

1. Chop throttle to the CLOSED position, and place engine master switch at OFF.

2. If light goes out, and there is no other indication of continuing fire such as smoke in cockpit, engine roughness, trailing smoke, verification from another airplane, etc, make a power-off emergency landing or abandon airplane.

3. If light remains on, eject.

Aft Fire-warning Light.

Illumination of the aft fire-warning light indicates an overheat condition or possible fire in the aft section, necessitating action as follows:

1. Reduce power in attempt to extinguish light.

　　a. If light goes out, continue flight at reduced power, and land as soon as possible.

　　b. If light remains on with throttle retarded to IDLE, indicating possible fire rather than overheat, proceed to step 2.

2. Check for other indications of fire, such as trailing smoke, engine noise, verification from another airplane, etc.

　　a. If no fire is apparent, continue flight at minimum power, and land as soon as possible.

　　b. If positive indications of fire exist, proceed to step 3.

3. Chop throttle to OFF position, and place engine master switch at OFF.

　　a. If fire continues, eject.

　　b. If fire ceases, make a power-off emergency landing, or eject.

ENGINE FIRE AFTER SHUTDOWN.

If there is indication of fire in the engine or tail-pipe section after engine shutdown:

1. External power source connected to both receptacles.

2. Throttle OFF.

3. Maintain battery-starter switch at STARTER.

4. Engine master switch at ON until starter locks in; then turn engine master switch OFF to close main fuel shutoff valve.

Note

Once starter has locked in, moving engine master switch to OFF will not cause starter to disengage.

5. Allow engine to crank to approximately 6% (20 seconds maximum); then depress stop-starter button.

6. Check engine master, generator, and battery-starter switches OFF.

7. Leave airplane as quickly as possible.

ELECTRICAL FIRE.

Circuit breakers and fuses protect most of the circuits and will tend to isolate an electrical fire. However, if electrical fire occurs, turn battery-starter and generator switches OFF, and land as soon as possible.

| CAUTION |

- If engine has to be shut down or flight control normal hydraulic system fails, battery power for the flight control alternate hydraulic system will be available for only about 6 to 7 minutes with emergency override handle actuated.

- When the electrical power source is turned off, most of the electrical equipment (including fire-warning lights and some instruments will be inoperative.

WARNING

With battery-starter and generator switches OFF, the emergency fuel system is automatically put in the stand-by condition, (on airplanes with the two-position emergency fuel switch, the emergency fuel system would be operating as though in stand-by condition), regardless of emergency fuel switch setting. Use caution when moving throttle, because rapid throttle advancement with emergency fuel system in the stand-by condition can cause the emergency system to override the main fuel system, resulting in complete power failure due to engine overspeeding or compressor stall.

ELIMINATION OF SMOKE OR FUMES.

If smoke or fumes enter the cockpit, proceed as follows:

1. Move cockpit pressure control switch to RAM.
2. Oxygen regulator diluter lever 100% OXYGEN.
3. Set oxygen regulator pressure-breathing knob as required by cockpit altitude (A-14 regulators). Push oxygen regulator emergency toggle lever either way from center (D-2 regulators). (Refer to "Oxygen System" in Section IV.)

LANDING EMERGENCIES.

BELLY LANDING.

If belly landing is unavoidable, these steps should be followed:

1. Jettison external load.

Note

If landing on a prepared surface, retain empty drop tanks to reduce possible pilot injury, impact damage, and fire hazard.

2. Before final approach, canopy switch at OPEN below 215 knots IAS. Lower head, and raise right seat handgrip to jettison canopy if it fails to open. (On airplanes equipped with the alternate emergency jettison handle, pull handle to jettison canopy without arming the seat catapult.)
3. Make normal approach with flaps down, speed brakes open, and gear up.
4. When landing is ensured, throttle OFF.
5. Just before touchdown, engine master, generator, and battery-starter switches OFF. (Battery-starter switch last, so that power will be available to close fuel shutoff valve when engine master switch is turned OFF.)
6. Shoulder harness lock handle LOCKED.
7. Touchdown should be made in normal landing attitude.
8. Abandon airplane immediately after it stops.

ANY ONE GEAR UP OR UNLOCKED.

If any one gear will not extend or lock down, leave remaining gear down, and proceed as follows:

1. Salvo or jettison external load, and, if time and conditions permit, fire all ammunition and expend excess fuel to establish an aft CG condition and to minimize possible fire hazard.

Note

If landing on a prepared surface, retain empty drop tanks to reduce possible pilot injury, impact damage, and fire hazard.

Note

If nose gear is down but not locked, you can attempt to snap it down and locked by making a touch-and-go landing. Attempt this procedure only after all other emergency measures are exhausted.

2. Before final approach, canopy switch at OPEN below 215 knots IAS. Lower head, and raise right seat handgrip to jettison canopy if it fails to open. (On airplanes equipped with the alternate emergency jettison handle, pull handle to jettison canopy without arming seat catapult.)

3. Plan approach to touch down as near end of runway as possible.

4. Make normal approach with flaps down, speed brakes open.

5. Just before touchdown, close throttle and turn engine master switch OFF. Wait one second to allow fuel shutoff valve to close; then move battery-starter switch to OFF. If time permits, turn generator switch OFF.

6. Shoulder harness lock handle LOCKED.

7. After touchdown, hold unsafe gear off as long as possible, easing it down to the runway before flight controls become ineffective.

8. Do not use brakes if you can stop without them.

9. Get clear of airplane as soon as possible.

ENGAGING RUNWAY BARRIER.

In this airplane, successful engagements with the nylon net overrun barrier have been made up to 130 knots ground speed. However, minimum speeds have been established which must be exceeded to ensure successful engagement. Whenever the overrun barrier is to be engaged, you should engage it as close to the recommended minimum speeds as possible. Off-center engagements can be made successfully, but will result in the airplane swerving as a result of the webbing pulling the nose wheel unevenly. This momentary swerve is not dangerous and therefore should be disregarded. If take-off must be aborted, or if after touchdown you are unable to bring the airplane to a stop or to a safe taxiing speed before reaching the end of the runway, and if the runway is equipped with a nylon net overrun barrier, observe the following:

1. Throttle OFF.

2. Engine master, generator, and battery-starter switches OFF, in that order.

CAUTION

Do not turn battery-starter switch OFF until engine master switch has been turned OFF, so that power will be available to close fuel shutoff valve.

3. Avoid excessive braking during engagement of the barrier, to prevent tire blowouts.

4. Engage barrier at a minimum speed of 17 knots if no external loads are installed.

5. Engage barrier at a minimum speed of 40 knots if 120-gallon drop tanks are installed.

6. Jettison 200-gallon drop tanks, if installed; otherwise, main landing gear will not engage the barrier.

Note

In cases of known emergency, jettison external load before landing.

LANDING WITH FLAT TIRE.

Nose Gear Tire Flat.

When a landing is to be made with the nose gear tire flat, extend the gear in the normal manner, and proceed as follows:

1. After main gear has touched down, hold nose wheel off runway as long as possible.

2. After nose wheel touches down, use a combination of braking and nose wheel steering to maintain directional control.

Main Gear Tire Flat.

When landing with a main gear tire flat, extend the gear in the normal manner, and proceed as follows:

1. Land on side of runway away from flat tire.

Note

This is necessary to minimize the amount of differential braking required if the airplane pulls toward the flat tire.

2. Use a combination of differential braking and nose wheel steering to maintain directional control.

NO-FLAP LANDING.

This airplane requires no special technique for landing without wing flaps. Speed during turn onto final, and final approach and touchdown speeds should be increased 20 knots IAS over recommended speeds for the load and configuration.

EMERGENCY ENTRANCE.

For emergency access to the cockpit on the ground, see figure 3-3.

DITCHING.

Note

Inspect emergency equipment, life vest, and raft pack before each overwater flight.

T. O. 1F-86E-1 Section III

emergency entrance

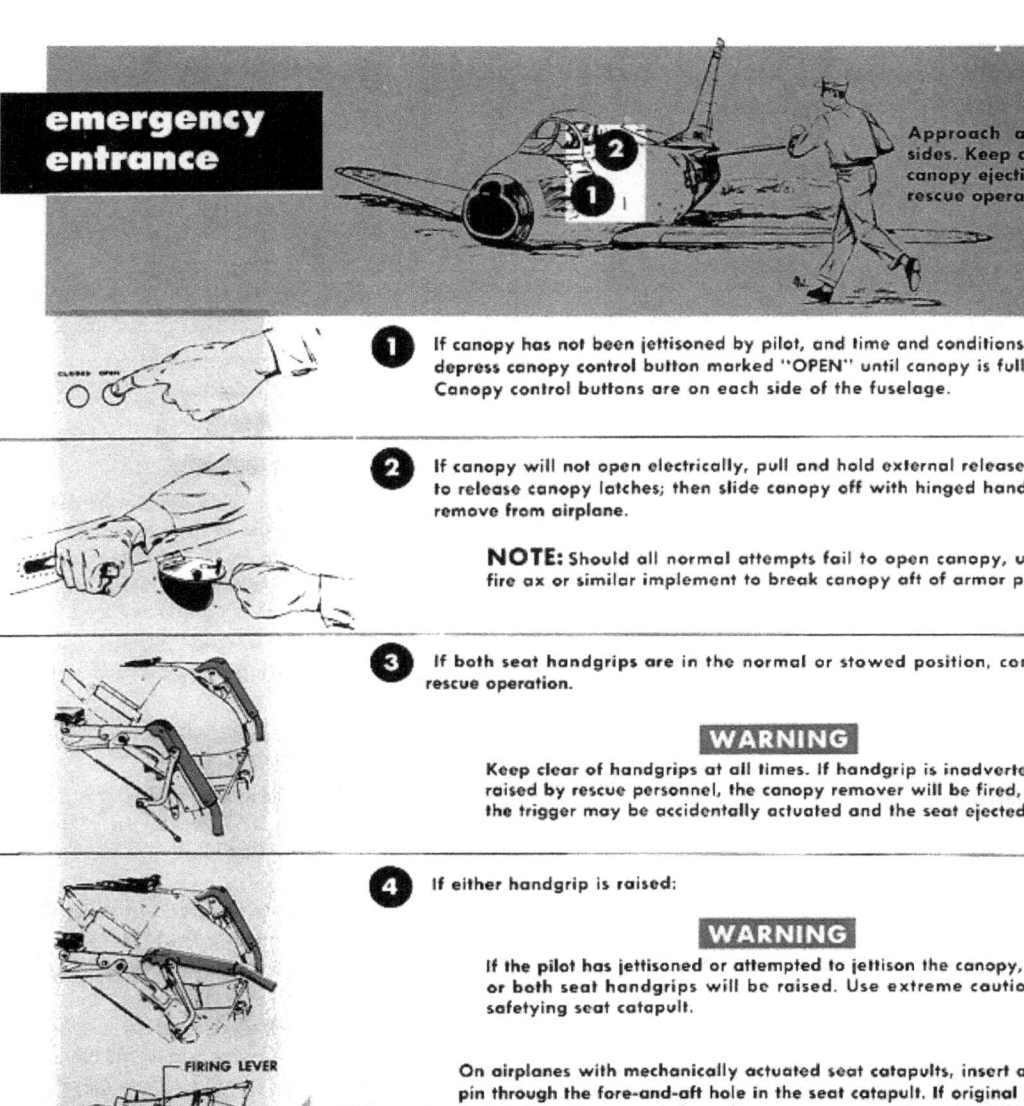

Approach airplane from sides. Keep clear of line of canopy ejection throughout rescue operation.

1 If canopy has not been jettisoned by pilot, and time and conditions permit, depress canopy control button marked "OPEN" until canopy is fully open. Canopy control buttons are on each side of the fuselage.

2 If canopy will not open electrically, pull and hold external release handle to release canopy latches; then slide canopy off with hinged handles and remove from airplane.

NOTE: Should all normal attempts fail to open canopy, use a fire ax or similar implement to break canopy aft of armor plate.

3 If both seat handgrips are in the normal or stowed position, complete rescue operation.

WARNING

Keep clear of handgrips at all times. If handgrip is inadvertently raised by rescue personnel, the canopy remover will be fired, and the trigger may be accidentally actuated and the seat ejected.

4 If either handgrip is raised:

WARNING

If the pilot has jettisoned or attempted to jettison the canopy, one or both seat handgrips will be raised. Use extreme caution in safetying seat catapult.

On airplanes with mechanically actuated seat catapults, insert a safety pin through the fore-and-aft hole in the seat catapult. If original pin has been pulled, the catapult firing lever may be moved UP slightly to allow insertion of the pin through the catapult. Then complete rescue operation.

WARNING

- If original safety pin is in seat catapult, DO NOT REMOVE IT.
- Do not move firing lever DOWN to align hole, since such movement will set off seat catapult charge and eject the seat.

On airplanes with gas-actuated seat catapults, disconnect hose* leading from "T" fitting to catapult at the catapult, or cut the hose as close to the catapult as possible; then complete rescue operation. Make sure loose hose ends are not aligned; otherwise, if seat initiators fire accidentally, expanding gases still may actuate catapult exactor and cause seat to fire.

*Use 9/16-inch open-end wrench.

F-86E-1-73-2B

Figure 3-3

3-11

Ditching is not recommended, since all emergency survival equipment is carried by the pilot; consequently, there is no advantage in riding the ship down. However, if altitude is not sufficient for bail-out, and ditching is unavoidable, proceed as follows:

1. Follow radio distress procedure.

2. Salvo (or jettison) external load.

3. See that personal equipment will not foul when you leave the cockpit. Disconnect anti-G suit. Remove oxygen mask when you leave the cockpit.

Note

If, for some reason, you are unable to escape from the cockpit of a sinking airplane after ditching, you can use the airplane oxygen equipment for temporary underwater survival until you manage to free yourself and escape. The A-14 or A-13A pressure-demand type oxygen mask and the pressure-demand or diluter demand oxygen regulators are suitable underwater breathing devices when the regulator is set at 100% OXYGEN. The mask must be in place and tightly strapped, and the regulator must be set at 100% OXYGEN. Remember, the bail-out bottle cannot be used under water.

4. Tighten safety belt and shoulder harness.

5. Check gear up and speed brakes in.

6. Canopy switch OPEN below 215 knots IAS. Lower head, and raise seat handgrip to jettison canopy if it fails to open. (On airplanes equipped with the alternate emergency jettison handle, pull handle to jettison canopy without arming the seat catapult.)

7. Throttle OFF.

8. Wing flap lever DOWN. Flaps collapse on impact and do not tend to make airplane dive.

9. Engine master, generator, and battery-starter switches OFF. (Battery-starter switch last, so that power will be available to close fuel shutoff valve when engine master switch is turned OFF.)

10. Shoulder harness lock handle LOCKED.

11. Unless wind is high or sea is rough, plan approach heading parallel to any uniform swell pattern, and try to touch down along wave crest or just after crest passes. If wind is as high as 25 knots or if surface is irregular, the best procedure is to approach into the wind and touch down on the falling side of a wave.

12. Make normal approach and flare-out, using care to keep the nose high, and attempt to touch down at minimum flying speed.

WARNING

If airplane is ditched in a near-level attitude, it will dive violently soon after contact.

EJECTION.

Escape from the airplane in flight should be made with the ejection seat. The basic seat ejection procedures for this airplane are shown in figures 3-4 and 3-5.

WARNING

- If ejection is necessary, it should not be delayed when the airplane is in a descending attitude, or cannot be leveled, because the chance of successful ejection at low altitude under these conditions is greatly reduced.

- If overwater ejection is made, remove oxygen mask before hitting water, to prevent sucking water into mask.

Study and analysis of ejection techniques by means of the ejection seat have revealed that:

a. Ejection accomplished at airspeeds ranging from stall speed to 525 knots IAS results in relatively minor forces being exerted on the body, thus reducing the injury hazard.

b. The body will undergo appreciable forces when ejection is performed at airspeeds of 525-600 knots IAS, and escape is more hazardous than at lower speeds.

c. Above 600 knots IAS, ejection is extremely hazardous because of the excessive forces on the body.

For low-altitude ejections, the technique which will result in the highest possible parachute deployment altitude is to pull the airplane nose above the horizon before ejection ("zoom-up" maneuver). Ejection seat trajectory will be closer to vertical, resulting in an increase in altitude and time for separation from the seat and for parachute deployment. Therefore, using the "zoom-up" maneuver during low-altitude ejection will help to attain maximum parachute deployment altitude, and slowing the airplane as much as possible before ejection at any altitude will reduce the forces exerted on the body.

On airplanes equipped with the automatic-opening safety belt, the belt should never be opened manually before ejection, for the following reasons:

a. If the belt is opened manually, the escape operation is prolonged.

b. Manual opening of the belt creates a hazard to survival during uncontrollable flight because the pilot cannot stay in the seat before ejection if negative G is encountered.

c. Manual opening of the belt creates a hazard to survival if the pilot decides to crash-land the airplane. He probably will not be able to fasten the belt and shoulder harness, because both hands may be needed to control the airplane.

d. Manual opening of the belt will eliminate the automatic-opening feature of the automatic-opening parachute (if worn). The pilot would have to arm the parachute manually by pulling the parachute arming lanyard.

e. If the belt is manually opened before ejection, the pilot will probably separate from the seat immediately. When this happens, tail clearance is reduced.

f. At high speeds, the peak deceleration due to air loads on the pilot and seat together approaches the limits of human tolerance. Since deceleration of the pilot alone is considerably greater than that of pilot and seat together, immediate separation at high speeds could result in severe injury.

g. Immediate separation of pilot and seat at high speeds could result in the parachute pack being accidentally blown open at the time of ejection. In this event, fatal injuries probably would be incurred because of the extremely high opening shock or because of serious damage to the parachute when it opens.

Note

- The automatic seat belt opens about 2 seconds after ejection. This is sufficient time for safe deceleration of the pilot.

- The preceding information does not imply that the pilot should not open the manual safety belt before low-altitude ejections. Opening of the manual belt before low-altitude ejections is essential because of the time element involved. If the "zoom-up" maneuver is used during low-altitude ejection, the reduced airspeed will result in lower forces on the pilot, even if he separates from the seat immediately.

FAILURE OF CANOPY TO JETTISON.

On late airplanes* and those changed by T. O. 1F-86-161, if the canopy fails to jettison when the right handgrip

---

*F-86E-15 Airplane AF51-13046 and all later airplanes
†F-86E-1 through F-86E-10 Airplanes and F-86E-15 Airplanes AF51-12977 through -13045

(either handgrip on airplanes changed by T. O. 1F-86-227) is raised, proceed as follows:

1. Slow airplane to under 215 knots IAS.

2. Move canopy aft electrically, and pull out canopy declutch handle to jettison canopy.

3. After canopy jettisons, eject.

4. If canopy cannot be moved aft electrically and canopy bow is not in the ejection path, raise left handgrip and squeeze trigger to eject through canopy.

Note

Some airplanes are equipped with the alternate emergency jettison handle. This handle should be used if canopy fails to jettison when handgrips are raised.

On early airplanes† not changed by T. O. 1F-86-161, if canopy fails to jettison when right seat handgrip is raised, proceed as follows:

1. Slow airplane to under 215 knots IAS.

2. Move canopy aft electrically, and pull out canopy declutch handle to jettison canopy.

3. After canopy jettisons, eject.

4. If canopy cannot be moved aft electrically, pull out and hold canopy declutch handle, and pull canopy aft manually. After canopy jettisons, eject.

5. If canopy fails to jettison after being pulled aft, invert airplane; then push free of airplane.

FAILURE OF SEAT TO EJECT.

If the seat does not eject when the triggers are squeezed, proceed as follows:

1. Unfasten safety belt, actuate bail-out bottle (if necessary), and disconnect personal leads (oxygen, radio, and anti-G suit).

2. If you have control of the airplane, trim nose down and pull stick back to slow airplane as much as possible; then invert airplane. Maintain positive G-load until inverted; then sharply release stick and push free of seat. If you do not have control of the airplane, slow airplane as much as possible; then bail out over the side.

3. After clearing airplane, parachute arming lanyard (automatic parachute), or "D" ring (manual parachute).

WARNING

If bail-out occurs below 14,000 feet, pull "D" ring immediately, whether parachute is automatic or manual type.

Section III T. O. 1F-86E-1

ejection procedures
AIRPLANES NOT CHANGED BY T. O. 1F-86-227

1 LOWER HEAD; THEN PULL RIGHT HANDGRIP FULL UP TO JETTISON CANOPY.

WARNING

- KEEP HEAD AS LOW AS POSSIBLE, TO PREVENT BEING HIT BY CANOPY BOW.

- DO NOT RAISE HANDGRIP AND SQUEEZE TRIGGER SIMULTANEOUSLY; OTHERWISE, SEAT EJECTION MECHANISM MAY NOT FUNCTION PROPERLY.

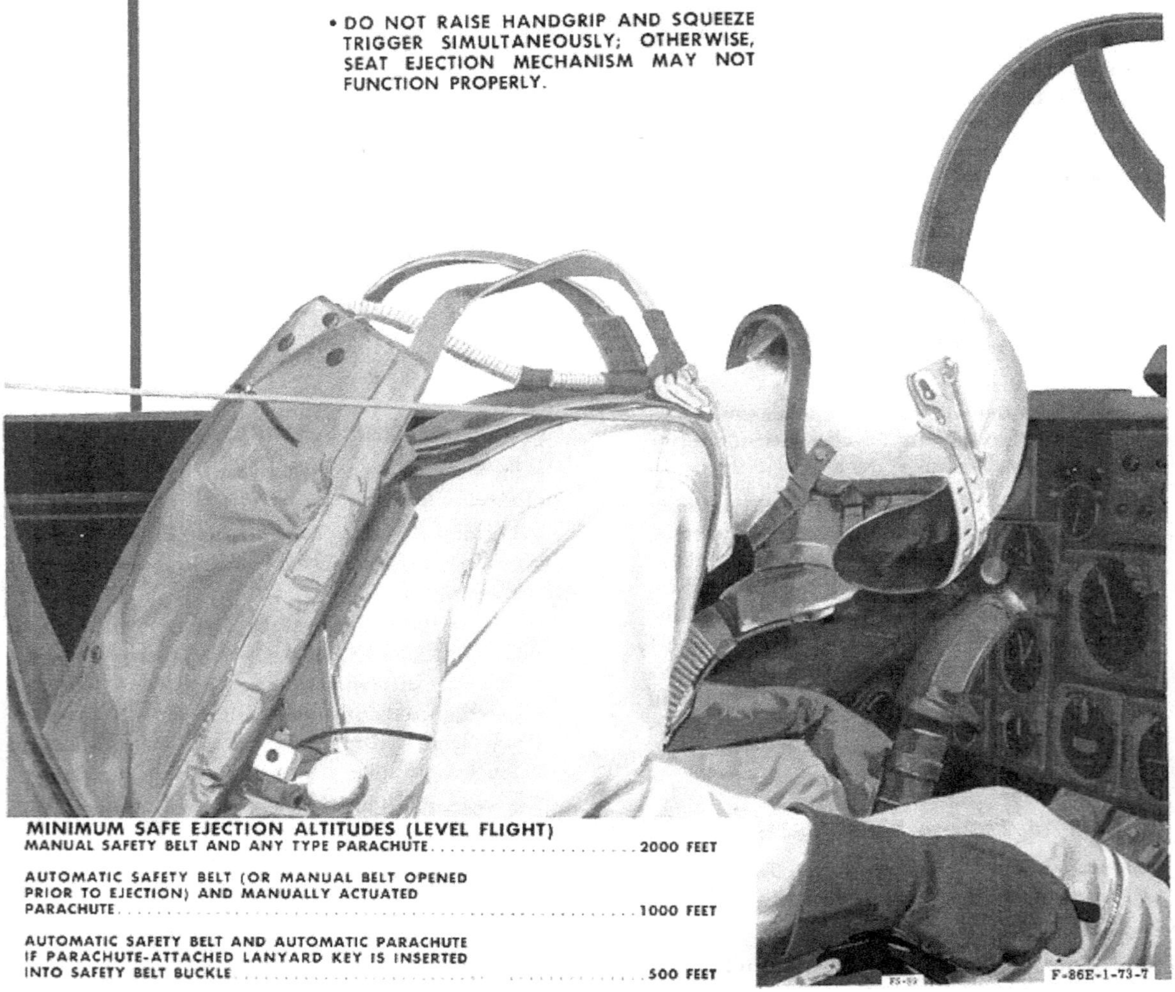

MINIMUM SAFE EJECTION ALTITUDES (LEVEL FLIGHT)
MANUAL SAFETY BELT AND ANY TYPE PARACHUTE . . . . 2000 FEET

AUTOMATIC SAFETY BELT (OR MANUAL BELT OPENED
PRIOR TO EJECTION) AND MANUALLY ACTUATED
PARACHUTE . . . . 1000 FEET

AUTOMATIC SAFETY BELT AND AUTOMATIC PARACHUTE
IF PARACHUTE-ATTACHED LANYARD KEY IS INSERTED
INTO SAFETY BELT BUCKLE . . . . 500 FEET

Figure 3-4

3-14

T. O. 1F-86E-1   Section III

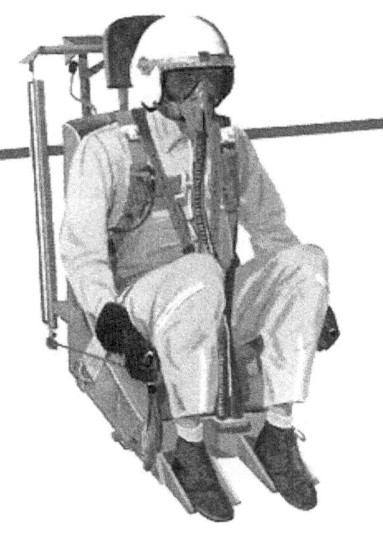

2

HOOK HEELS IN FOOTRESTS AND BRACE ARMS IN ARMRESTS. SIT ERECT, HEAD HARD BACK AGAINST HEADREST, CHIN TUCKED IN.

NOTE

TO LOCK SHOULDER HARNESS, PULL UP LEFT HANDGRIP.

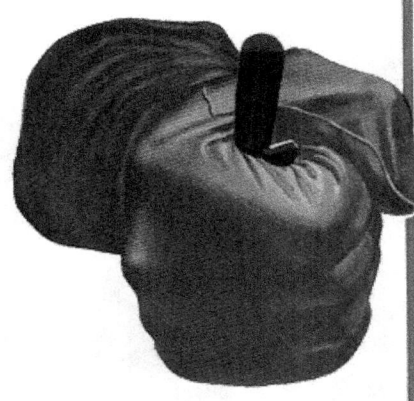

3

SQUEEZE TRIGGER TO EJECT SEAT.

NOTE

RAISING LEFT HANDGRIP ON SOME AIRPLANES* ALSO PULLS SEAT SEAR SAFETY PIN. THIS PREPARES SEAT TO BE FIRED THROUGH CANOPY IF CANOPY FAILS TO JETTISON OR TO BE FIRED IF CANOPY JETTISONS BUT DOES NOT PULL SEAT CATAPULT SEAR SAFETY PIN. (EJECT THROUGH CANOPY ONLY AS A LAST RESORT.) LEFT HANDGRIP CANNOT BE ACTUATED UNTIL RIGHT HANDGRIP HAS BEEN RAISED FULL UP.

*F-86E-15 Airplane AF51-13046 and all later airplanes, and those changed by T. O. 1F-86-161

WARNING
- During low-altitude ejections (below 2000 feet above terrain), unfasten manual belt before ejection, to aid in separating from seat. In a dive at high speeds, the manual belt should be unfastened before ejection at altitudes up to 5000 feet above the terrain, to permit rapid separation from the seat and opening of parachute. After separation from seat, pull "D" ring to open either conventional or automatic parachute.
- Do not manually open automatic-opening safety belt before ejection at any altitude or at any airspeed.

BEFORE EJECTION, IF TIME AND CONDITIONS PERMIT . . .
- Actuate bail-out oxygen bottle.
- Stow all loose equipment.

AFTER SEAT EJECTS . . .

AIRPLANES WITH MANUAL SAFETY BELT:
- Unfasten safety belt and kick free of seat.
- If wearing conventional, manually operated parachute, pull "D" ring when altitude is reached where normal breathing is possible.
- If wearing automatic parachute, pull arming lanyard manually. Parachute will open at a preset altitude. If below preset altitude, parachute will open at a preset time interval.

AIRPLANES WITH AUTOMATIC-OPENING SAFETY BELT:
- If safety belt fails to open automatically after 2 seconds, manually unfasten belt and kick free of seat. Then pull parachute arming lanyard.
- If pilot is wearing automatic parachute WITH lanyard key inserted into safety belt buckle, parachute opens at a preset altitude after pilot kicks free of seat. (Parachute opens after a preset time interval if below preset altitude.)
- If wearing automatic parachute WITHOUT lanyard key inserted into safety belt buckle, kick free of seat and pull parachute arming lanyard.
- If wearing manually operated parachute, kick free of seat; pull "D" ring at altitude where normal breathing is possible.

WARNING
After leaving seat, manually pull "D" ring for all ejections below 14,000 feet, to open parachute immediately.

Section III
T. O. 1F-86E-1

ejection procedures
AIRPLANES CHANGED BY T. O. 1F-86-227

1 LOWER HEAD; PULL EITHER RIGHT OR LEFT HANDGRIP FULL UP TO JETTISON CANOPY. (SHOULDER HARNESS LOCKS AUTOMATICALLY WHEN EITHER HANDGRIP IS RAISED.)

WARNING

- KEEP HEAD AS LOW AS POSSIBLE, TO PREVENT BEING HIT BY CANOPY BOW.

- DO NOT RAISE HANDGRIP AND SQUEEZE TRIGGER SIMULTANEOUSLY; OTHERWISE, SEAT EJECTION MECHANISM MAY NOT FUNCTION PROPERLY.

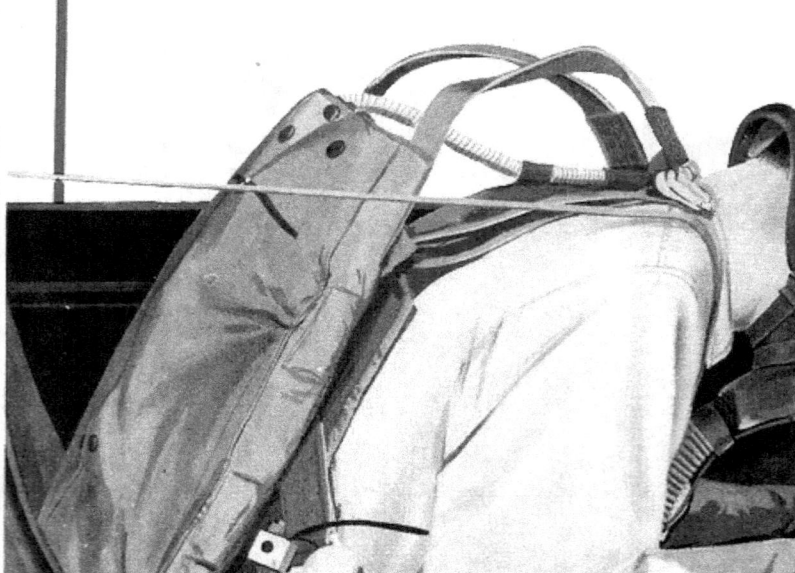

MINIMUM SAFE EJECTION ALTITUDES (LEVEL FLIGHT)
MANUAL SAFETY BELT AND ANY TYPE PARACHUTE.....................2000 FEET

AUTOMATIC SAFETY BELT (OR MANUAL BELT OPENED
PRIOR TO EJECTION) AND MANUALLY ACTUATED
PARACHUTE...1000 FEET

AUTOMATIC SAFETY BELT AND AUTOMATIC PARACHUTE
IF PARACHUTE-ATTACHED LANYARD KEY IS INSERTED
INTO SAFETY BELT BUCKLE...500 FEET

Figure 3-5

T. O. 1F-86E-1   Section III

②

HOOK HEELS IN FOOTRESTS AND BRACE ARMS IN ARMRESTS. SIT ERECT, HEAD HARD BACK AGAINST HEADREST, CHIN TUCKED IN.

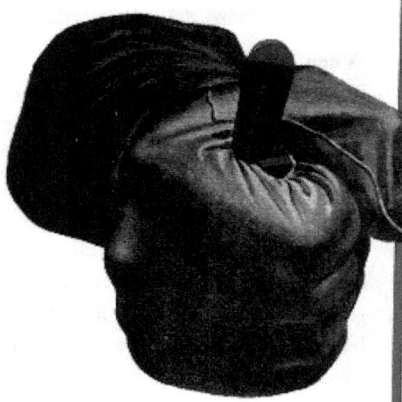

③

SQUEEZE TRIGGER UNDER RAISED HAND-GRIP TO EJECT SEAT.

WARNING

IF CANOPY FAILS TO JETTISON WHEN HANDGRIPS ARE RAISED, SEAT WILL BE EJECTED THROUGH CANOPY WHEN EITHER TRIGGER IS SQUEEZED.

WARNING

- During low-altitude ejections (below 2000 feet above terrain), unfasten manual belt before ejection, to aid in separating from seat. In a dive at high speeds, the manual belt should be unfastened before ejection at altitudes up to 5000 feet above the terrain, to permit rapid separation from the seat and opening of parachute. After separation from seat, pull "D" ring to open either conventional or automatic parachute.

- Do not manually open automatic-opening safety belt before ejection at any altitude or at any airspeed.

BEFORE EJECTION, IF TIME AND CONDITIONS PERMIT...

- Actuate bail-out oxygen bottle.
- Stow all loose equipment.

AFTER SEAT EJECTS...

AIRPLANES WITH MANUAL SAFETY BELT:

- Unfasten safety belt and kick free of seat.
- If wearing conventional, manually operated parachute, pull "D" ring when altitude is reached where normal breathing is possible.
- If wearing automatic parachute, pull arming lanyard manually. Parachute will open at a preset altitude. If below preset altitude, parachute will open at a preset time interval.

AIRPLANES WITH AUTOMATIC-OPENING SAFETY BELT:

- If safety belt fails to open automatically after 2 seconds, manually unfasten belt and kick free of seat. Then pull parachute arming lanyard.
- If pilot is wearing automatic parachute WITH lanyard key inserted into safety belt buckle, parachute opens at a preset altitude after pilot kicks free of seat. (Parachute opens after a preset time interval if below preset altitude.)
- If wearing automatic parachute WITHOUT lanyard key inserted into safety belt buckle, kick free of seat and pull parachute arming lanyard.
- If wearing manually operated parachute, kick free of seat; pull "D" ring at altitude where normal breathing is possible.

WARNING

After leaving seat, manually pull "D" ring for all ejections below 14,000 feet, to open parachute immediately.

Section III T. O. 1F-86E-1

Note

If you lose your oxygen mask and you do not have an automatic parachute, you should free-fall to 14,000 feet altitude if possible; then pull "D" ring. The length of time you can free-fall before anoxia prevents you from pulling the "D" ring depends on your physical condition and bail-out altitude.

FUEL SYSTEM FAILURE.

Erratic fluctuations of the fuel pressure gage at high altitudes, accompanied by a decrease or variations of exhaust temperature, may indicate fuel booster pump failure. A sudden loss of fuel pressure and a rapid decrease in exhaust temperature indicate a failure within the main fuel regulator. Both could result in engine flame-out, and an attempt to recover power should be made as follows:

1. Throttle IDLE and emergency fuel switch ON.

WARNING

If engine rpm is below 80%, do not turn on the emergency fuel switch until the throttle has been retarded to IDLE. This will prevent dangerous engine overheating or compressor stall.

2. Gradually advance throttle to obtain desired exhaust temperature and engine rpm.

CAUTION

When operating on the emergency system, engine speed is not governed automatically. Therefore, throttle movements must be gradual to prevent flame-out or overspeed, particularly at high altitudes.

3. If the engine does not respond, emergency fuel switch and throttle OFF. Establish a normal descent and attempt an air start. At low altitudes, booster pump failure may cause partial or complete engine flame-out, if the fuel supply is low and the airplane is subjected to negative acceleration.

If a complete flame-out occurs, attempt a normal air start. If a partial flame-out occurs, proceed as follows:

1. Throttle IDLE.

2. Emergency ignition and emergency fuel switches ON.

3. As soon as exhaust temperature and engine rpm indicate that combustion has stabilized, emergency fuel and emergency ignition switches OFF.

CAUTION

Do not leave emergency switch ON for more than 3 minutes per start. Prolonged operation will damage the ignition transformers.

4. Slowly advance throttle until engine rpm and exhaust temperature are as desired.

ELECTRICAL POWER SYSTEM FAILURE.

If a complete electrical failure should occur, or if for any reason it becomes necessary to turn off both battery and generator, remember that much of the equipment and many controls will be inoperative without electrical power. Flight under this condition will be limited, and the following precautionary remarks should be observed:

WARNING

When primary bus failure occurs, or if the battery-starter switch is OFF when generator output is not available, the emergency fuel system is automatically set in the stand-by condition, (on airplanes with the two-position emergency fuel switch, the emergency system would be operating as though in stand-by condition), regardless of emergency fuel switch setting. Use caution when moving the throttle, because rapid throttle advancement, with the emergency fuel system in the stand-by position, can cause this system to override the main fuel system, resulting in dangerous engine overspeeding or compressor stall.

1. If possible, before turning off electrical power, reduce airspeed and readjust trim, because trim is not available without electric power.

2. The fuel booster pumps will be inoperative when power is shut off; consequently, it may be necessary to reduce altitude and rpm in order to maintain satisfactory engine operation. (This condition will be aggravated by high outside air temperature and high airspeed.)

3-18

3. If reduction in rpm is necessary, airplane may have to be held in a slightly nose-high attitude to maintain altitude. If prolonged flight in this attitude is necessary, a small amount of fuel will be trapped in the aft fuselage tank. If sufficient altitude is available, nose airplane down slightly for a short period to drain some of the trapped fuel into the forward fuel tank lower cell.

4. Land as soon as possible.

Note

Use gear emergency lowering system to ensure that gear lowers and locks. (Refer to "Landing Gear Emergency Lowering" in this section.) When electrical power is not available to the primary bus, landing gear position indicators will be inoperative and will continuously show an unsafe condition.

GENERATOR IRREGULARITY.

Any generator irregularity (generator failure or a voltage rise or drop) will be indicated by illumination of the generator warning light, located on the lower left portion of the instrument panel.

Generator Failure or Undervoltage.

All equipment powered by the secondary bus will be inoperative, and equipment on the primary bus will be operated by battery power when a generator failure or lowering of output occurs. Circuits for three-phase units, normally powered by the single-phase inverter through the phase adapter, are controlled by the secondary bus and are automatically transferred to the three-phase inverter when generator output fails or is reduced on airplanes* not changed by T. O. 1F-86E-47 or T.O. 1F-86E-507. Single-phase power to the IFF radar, A-1CM sight, fuel flowmeter and totalizer, and the cockpit air conditioning control systems ceases when the generator fails. When generator output drops or fails, all nonessential equipment should be turned off to reduce load on battery. The length of time that usable battery power is available for continued operation is approximately 7 to 28 minutes. Battery output duration may be decreased, however, by a number of variable factors including low state of battery charge, excessive electrical loads, and low battery temperature. If generator output is off because of engine failure, the engine master switch should be moved to OFF to lessen battery loads.

WARNING

In case the normal flight control hydraulic system fails while generator is out, battery power for alternate hydraulic pump operation will last only 6 to 7 minutes.

For all landings where generator failure has occurred, lower the landing gear by the emergency system, to ensure that gear will extend and lock. (Refer to "Landing Gear Emergency Lowering" in this section.) Battery power may not be sufficient to position landing gear and door control valves when the normal gear lowering system is used.

CAUTION

If generator has failed and battery power is not available to primary bus or battery switch is turned off, landing gear position indicators will be inoperative and will continuously show an unsafe condition.

Generator Overvoltage.

If a generator overvoltage condition is indicated by the voltmeter and by illumination of generator warning light, try to bring the generator back into the circuit as follows:

1. Hold generator switch at RESET momentarily (generator warning light will go out); then turn switch OFF. If the voltmeter shows normal system voltage, it indicates the overvoltage was temporary; turn generator switch ON.

2. If generator overvoltage is still indicated by voltmeter, try to bring voltage down to 28 volts by adjusting the voltage regulator rheostat, with generator switch OFF. A maximum of 31 volts is allowable in an emergency if voltage cannot be decreased to 28. Again hold generator switch momentarily at RESET, and then turn switch ON. If generator warning light remains out, check voltage and readjust regulator rheostat, as necessary, to obtain normal system voltage.

3. If generator voltage cannot be brought within allowable limit, as indicated by the voltmeter, leave generator switch OFF, reduce load on battery, and land as soon as possible.

*F-86E-1 through F-86E-6 Airplanes and F-86E-10 Airplanes AF51-2718 through -2747

INVERTER FAILURE.

On airplanes* not changed by T. O. 1F-86E-47, or T. O. 1F-86E-507, if failure of the single-phase inverter is indicated by illumination of the instrument power-off warning light, move instrument power switch to ALT.

CAUTION

Failure of the single-phase inverter will cause the cockpit temperature control system, sight, IFF radar, and fuel flowmeter and totalizer to be inoperative. The fuel flowmeter and totalizer will erroneously indicate the condition existing at time of power failure, although the instrument is inoperative.

On late airplanes† and airplanes changed by T. O. 1F-86E-47 or T. O. 1F-86E-507, move the instrument power switch to ALT when the main instrument (three-phase) inverter warning light is on.

CAUTION

Loss of three-phase ac power, indicated by illumination of the instrument inverter failure warning light, results in failure of the directional indicator, attitude indicator, and the fuel, oil, and hydraulic pressure gages. However, these instruments, while inoperative, will provide erroneous indications, because the pointers continue to register the conditions that existed when power failed.

UTILITY HYDRAULIC SYSTEM FAILURE.

There are no emergency provisions in the utility hydraulic system, except the one-shot accumulator installed in the nose gear systems.

FLIGHT CONTROL HYDRAULIC SYSTEM FAILURE.

In case of failure of the normal flight control hydraulic system, the alternate system will automatically take over (provided adequate alternate system pressure is available), as indicated by illumination of the alternate-on warning light. If the alternate system fails to take over automatically, move the flight control switch to ALTERNATE ON.‡ (On later airplanes,§ unlock and pull the manual emergency override handle to its fully extended position.)

WARNING

When the emergency override handle§ is pulled out, the alternate system pump is engaged and operates continuously, regardless of system pressure. If generator output is not available, the pump will deplete battery power in approximately 6 to 7 minutes.

Note

Change-over from the normal to the alternate flight control hydraulic system is momentary and usually is not noticeable, although a slight surge or "nibble" may be felt on the stick during the change-over.

WARNING

Stick forces will become extremely high if both flight control hydraulic systems are inoperable. As a result, under such conditions, control of the airplane in cruising flight becomes very difficult, and control at high speeds or during extreme maneuvers is impossible. Therefore, if both systems fail, try to reduce airspeed to about 200 knots, and try to maintain all possible control by using rudder and varying power as necessary. Try to neutralize the ailerons and horizontal stabilizer by steady push or pull forces on the stick, allowing air loads to streamline the surfaces. If control cannot be maintained, eject immediately. If some control is available, however, and altitude permits, attempt to effect recovery and return to a suitable area. Then eject, because extended flight and a landing with these high stick forces should not be attempted under any circumstances.

On later airplanes,§ if complete failure of the flight control normal hydraulic system has been determined (i. e., system will not deliver 1000 psi), pull the manual

---

*F-86E-1 through F-86E-6 Airplanes and F-86E-10 Airplanes AF51-2718 through -2747
†F-86E-10 Airplane AF51-2748 and all later airplanes
‡F-86E-1 through F-86E-6 Airplanes
§F-86E-10 and later airplanes

emergency override handle just before entering the traffic pattern, to ensure positive, continuous engagement of the flight control alternate hydraulic system during the landing phase.

Note

This action will prevent cycling from the alternate to the "failed" normal system, possibly momentarily freezing the controls.

FLIGHT CONTROL ARTIFICIAL FEEL SYSTEM FAILURE.

Artificial feel system failure can be indicated by any combination of the following: lightening of stick forces (resulting in overcontrol); lack of trim response; and poor stick-centering characteristics. Failure of the artificial feel system leaves the pilot with no possible means of airplane recovery. Reduction of engine power may relieve the severity of oscillations of the airplane; however, when such failure occurs, ejection is recommended.

LANDING GEAR EMERGENCY OPERATION.

LANDING GEAR EMERGENCY RETRACTION.

If it is necessary to retract the landing gear while the airplane is on the ground, move landing gear handle to UP, and hold landing gear emergency-up button in until gear completely retracts. Gear retraction time, when emergency-up button is used, can be reduced by yawing the airplane with alternate application of right and left wheel brakes, or by applying rudder alternately with nose wheel steering engaged.

CAUTION

- Gear will retract only if hydraulic pressure and battery power is available.
- The nose wheel will not retract if gear has been lowered by the emergency release handle.

Landing Gear In-flight Emergency Operation.

Landing Gear In-flight Emergency Retraction. During flight, the following condition may be encountered: The landing gear unsafe warning light may remain on after the landing gear handle is placed at UP. This does not necessarily constitute an emergency condition, but under certain conditions airloads on the landing gear doors can prevent gear retraction. This would be indicated by a safe "down" condition for all three gear indicators with the landing gear handle at UP and the unsafe warning light on. If such a condition occurs, proceed as follows: Leave landing gear handle at UP. Maintain a straight flight path to minimize G-loads on the gear doors and eliminate yaw, and reduce speed to below gear-down limit speed (155 to 160 knots IAS is recommended to minimize airloads on the gear doors). If a safe indication is obtained, continue flight. If the unsafe condition still exists, extend the gear, and when a safe "down" indication is obtained, land as soon as possible. If mission is important, maintain straight flight path to minimize G-loads on the gear doors and eliminate yaw. Hold airspeed below gear-down limit speed (155 to 160 knots IAS is recommended), and cycle gear down and up. If unsafe warning light goes out, continue mission. If unsafe warning light remains on, extend gear and land as soon as possible.

CAUTION

Do not move landing gear handle when red gear unsafe warning light is on and speed is above gear-down limit speed, because gear doors may be torn off when hydraulic pressure is released from door actuating cylinders.

Landing Gear Emergency Lowering.

The landing gear emergency lowering procedure is shown in figures 3-6 and 3-7.

CAUTION

On airplanes with the two-position landing gear handle, nose gear cannot be retracted after being lowered by means of the landing gear emergency release handle.

Note

Nose gear emergency extension on airplanes equipped with the emergency hydraulic selector valve, requires about 30 to 35 seconds, and on airplanes not equipped with the emergency hydraulic selector valve, approximately 10 seconds (the same time as for normal operation); therefore, attempt to have the operation completed before entering final approach.

TRIM FAILURE.

A reasonably light pilot control force would be required to neutralize the controls if any of the trim systems

Section III
T. O. 1F-86E-1

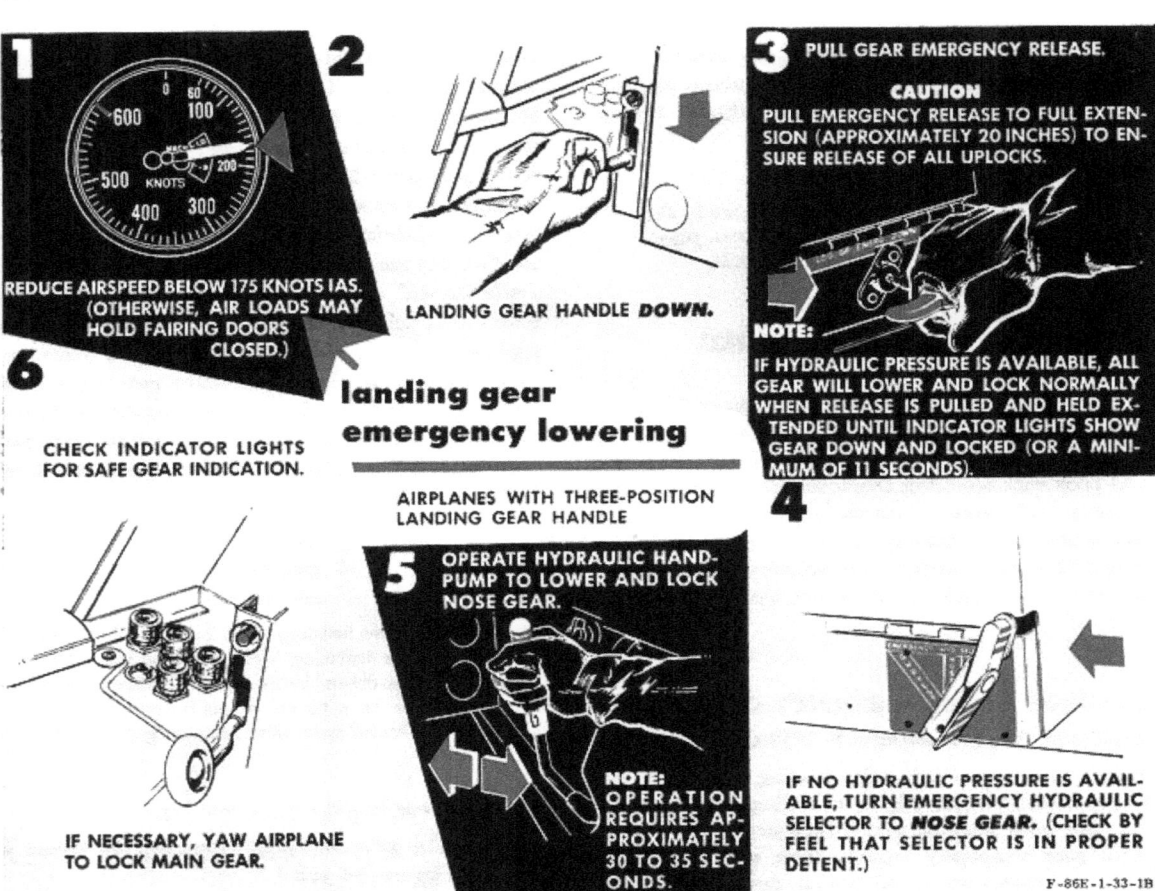

Figure 3-6

should fail in either extreme travel position, and movement of the controls to the opposite extreme of travel would not be beyond the normal physical capabilities of the pilot.

CAUTION

The normal trim switch on the stick grip is subject to sticking in an actuated position, running the trim to an extreme position. If this condition occurs in flight, the trim switch must be returned manually to the center (OFF) position after obtaining the desired amount of trim.

In the event of a failure of the normal trim switch:

1. Check circuit breakers in.
2. If normal trim switch is still inoperative, use longitudinal alternate trim switch or lateral alternate trim switch, as necessary, to obtain desired trim result.

CAUTION

The normal trim switch on the stick grip is inoperable for both lateral and longitudinal trim with the longitudinal alternate trim switch at OFF, and is inoperable for lateral trim when the lateral alternate trim switch is OFF.

SPEED BRAKE SYSTEM FAILURE.

To close speed brakes in case of electrical or hydraulic failure, move the speed brake emergency lever to EMERG. CLOSED.

Note

There is no emergency means for opening the speed brakes.

3-22

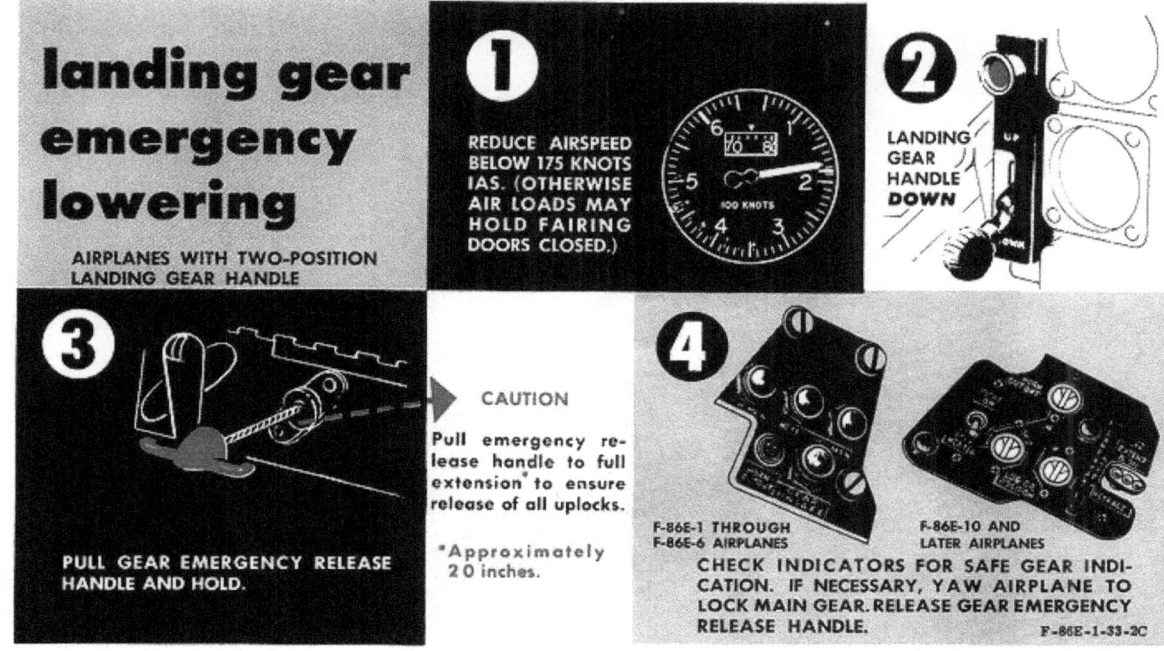

Figure 3-7

WING FLAP EMERGENCY OPERATION.

No emergency flap control system is provided. If unequal retraction or extension of the flaps occurs during normal flap operation, hold airplane level, and return flap control to original position. (Enough aileron control is available to hold wings level in this condition, or to roll against the down flap as necessary.) Land as soon as possible, without further attempt to operate flaps.

EXTERNAL LOAD EMERGENCY RELEASE.

To drop any external load during in-flight emergency:
  1. Push bomb-rocket-tank salvo button.
  2. Make sure load has released.
  3. If load fails to release, pull emergency jettison handle.

Note

On F-86E-6 Airplanes, this handle releases bombs and drop tanks only.

  4. If check reveals that load did not release, and if time permits, check circuit breakers in and demolition bomb release selector switch at MANUAL RELEASE. Place demolition bomb single-all selector switch at ALL and rocket jettison switch at JETTISON READY; then press bomb-rocket release button on the stick grip.

SECTION IV

DESCRIPTION AND OPERATION OF AUXILIARY EQUIPMENT

TABLE OF CONTENTS

	PAGE
Cockpit Air Conditioning and Pressurization Systems	4-1
Anti-icing and Defrosting Systems	4-7
Communication and Associated Electronic Equipment	4-10
Lighting Equipment	4-13
Oxygen System	4-17
Navigation Equipment	4-21
Armament Equipment	4-22
Miscellaneous Equipment	4-34

COCKPIT AIR CONDITIONING AND PRESSURIZATION SYSTEMS.

The independently controlled cockpit air conditioning and pressurization systems use compressed, heated air from the final stage of the engine compressor to maintain desired cockpit temperature and pressure. Compressor air temperature is reduced initially by means of the ram-air-cooled primary heat exchanger. (See figures 4-2 and 4-3.) The air then passes through an air mixing valve, which proportions the amount of hot and cold air furnished to the cockpit according to the positions of the temperature controls. On F-86E-10 and later airplanes, cockpit air from the primary heat exchanger is controlled by a by-pass valve. When maximum cockpit cooling is required, all incoming air is directed through a refrigeration unit consisting of an air-to-air heat exchanger combined with an expansion turbine. The air by-passes the refrigeration unit when maximum cockpit heating is needed. If additional heat is required to maintain temperatures demanded by control settings, a 4-kilowatt electric heater is energized automatically and cycled on and off, as necessary, for proper temperature control. An electronic temperature control system controls the 4-kilowatt heater, the position of the cockpit air by-pass valve, and the cooling air of the primary heat exchanger. In addition to supplying heat for the pressurized air, the 4-kilowatt heater can be used during direct ram-air operation. Cockpit pressurization is available at either of two (2.75 psi or 5 psi) pressure schedules and is automatically maintained by a pressure regulator. Air conditioning and pressurization system air is also used for canopy and windshield defrosting, windshield anti-icing, and rain removal. (Refer to "Anti-icing and Defrosting Systems" in this section.) The minimum engine rpm necessary to maintain proper air supply for the cockpit air conditioning, pressurization, and defrosting systems is as follows:

ALTITUDE—FEET	% RPM
15,000	73
20,000	75
25,000	77
30,000	80
35,000	85
40,000	92

4-1

Air Conditioning and Pressurization Air Outlets.

Air is distributed to the cockpit through side and floor outlets. The side outlets (5, figures 1-6 and 1-7) are on each side of the cockpit, above the consoles. The left side outlet is an adjustable spherical unit; the right side outlet is a fixed slot with a separate shutoff valve. The floor outlet, forward of the center pedestal, directs air down to the pilot's feet or to the windshield armor glass for defrosting. A selector control permits air to be routed to either the side or floor outlets, or to both simultaneously.

Cockpit Air Pressure Regulator.

When the pressurization system is engaged, cockpit air pressure is maintained and regulated automatically at the selected pressure schedule by the pressure regulator, mounted in the aft end of the canopy. The comparison of flight altitude to cockpit altitude for the selected pressure schedule is shown in figure 4-1. Excessive cockpit pressure is relieved by the regulator and discharged overboard.

COCKPIT AIR CONDITIONING AND PRESSURIZATION SYSTEM CONTROLS AND INDICATOR.

Cockpit Air Temperature Control Rheostat.

The temperature of air admitted to the cockpit is automatically controlled by a rheostat (27, figure 1-6; 29, figure 1-8; figure 4-4) on the left aft console. The rheostat is operated by ac power. When the cockpit air temperature control switch is at AUTOMATIC (AUTO), cockpit air is maintained at the temperature corresponding to the rheostat setting. The rheostat permits selection of cockpit temperatures. The 4-kilowatt electric heater operates automatically when additional heat is required.

Note

If cockpit air temperature exceeds the temperature for which the rheostat is set, the refrigeration unit will operate at full capacity to provide cockpit cooling. Under these conditions, turning the rheostat to a lower setting will not result in additional cockpit cooling.

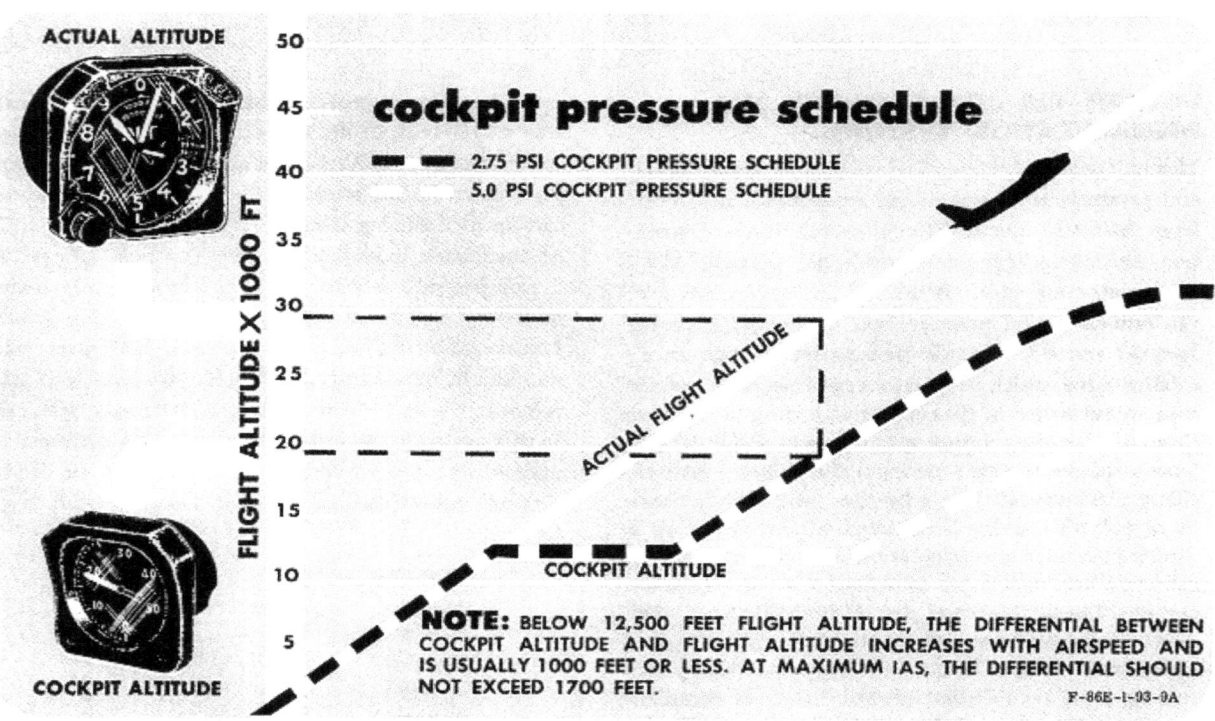

Figure 4-1

The temperature control rheostat is inoperative when the cockpit air temperature control switch is OFF; however, air will be maintained at the temperature prevailing at the time the switch was turned OFF.

Cockpit Air Temperature Control Switch.

The four-position cockpit air temperature control switch (30, figures 1-6, 1-8; figure 4-4), on the left aft console, provides normal control of cockpit air temperature. The switch is powered from the secondary bus. Temperature control is maintained automatically, in accordance with the setting of the temperature control rheostat, when the switch is in the guarded AUTOMATIC (AUTO) position. When the switch is OFF, the automatic control system is inoperative and cockpit air temperature is maintained at the temperature that prevailed when the switch was set at OFF. In case the automatic temperature control system fails or if manual control is desired, the cockpit air temperature control switch can be positioned to HOT or COLD. When the desired temperature has been obtained, the switch should be returned to OFF.

Cabin Pressure Control Lever. *

Cockpit pressurization is controlled by the cabin pressure control lever (28, figure 1-6; figure 4-4), on the left aft console. When the lever is at either ON 2.75 or ON 5.00, the system shutoff valve is open, permitting air from the engine compressor section to enter the system to maintain the selected pressure schedule. Cockpit pressure is then maintained automatically by the pressure regulator. When the cabin pressure control lever is moved to OFF-RAM AIR ON-DUMP OPEN, the system shutoff valve closes. In addition, the dump valve is opened, releasing cockpit pressure overboard, and the ram-air shutoff valve is opened, allowing ram air to enter the cockpit through the side, floor, and windshield defrost outlets.

Note

The windshield anti-icing and canopy auxiliary defrost systems are inoperative when the cabin pressure control lever is at OFF-RAM AIR ON-DUMP OPEN.

Cockpit Pressure Control Switch. †

The two-position cockpit pressure control switch (26, figure 1-8; and figure 4-4) is on the left aft console. It receives power from the primary bus. When the switch is placed at RAM, the system shutoff valve is closed and the cockpit dump valve and the ram-air shutoff valve are opened. This shuts off all incoming pressurized hot air from the engine compressor, dumps cockpit pressure,

and allows ram air to enter the cockpit. The ram air may be heated, if necessary, by turning the cockpit air temperature control rheostat to HOT & HEATER ON. To provide controlled cockpit pressures, the cockpit pressure control switch is set at PRESS. This opens the system shutoff valve and closes the ram-air valve to allow pressurized air to flow into the cockpit and thereby maintain the selected cockpit pressure schedule as determined by the pressure selector switch.

Cockpit Pressure Selector Switch. †

The cockpit pressure selector switch (28, figure 1-8; figure 4-4), on the left aft console, is positioned at either 2.75 P.S.I. or 5 P.S.I. to select the desired cockpit pressure schedule. The switch is powered from the primary bus when the cockpit pressure control switch is at PRESS.

Air Outlet Selector Lever.

Air to the windshield, side, and floor outlets is controlled by the air outlet selector lever (29, figure 1-6; 3, figure 1-8; figure 4-4), on the left aft console. Moving the lever to FLOOR or DEFROST directs air to the corresponding outlet. Air is routed to the windshield, side, and floor outlets simultaneously when the selector lever is moved to BOTH.

Side Air Outlet Controls.

The adjustable spherical side air outlet (5, figure 1-6; 6, figure 1-8), on the left side of the cockpit, can be rotated to direct air in any desired direction for air conditioning and can be turned to shut off airflow. The right outlet is fixed and controlled by an on-off shutoff valve (6, figure 1-7; 4, figure 1-9; figures 4-2 and 4-3), on the right side of the cockpit, below and outboard of the outlet.

Cabin Pressure Altimeter.

F-86E-6 Airplanes are equipped with a Type A-1 cabin pressure altimeter (18, figure 1-4), on the instrument panel. The dial of this instrument is equipped with two pointers and a scale window. Each pointer travels over a separate arc of calibrations. One pointer indicates cockpit pressure altitude, and the other indicates flight pressure altitude. The actual pressure differential between flight and cockpit pressure altitudes is shown in psi. All other airplanes are equipped with cabin pressure altimeters (14, figure 1-5) that indicate only cockpit pressure altitude in thousands of feet.

NORMAL OPERATION OF COCKPIT AIR CONDITIONING AND PRESSURIZATION SYSTEMS.

1. Cabin pressure control lever at either ON 2.75 or ON 5.00. (Cockpit pressure control switch at PRESS and

---

*F-86E-1 through F-86E-6 Airplanes
†F-86E-10 and later airplanes

Section IV

T.O. 1F-86E-1

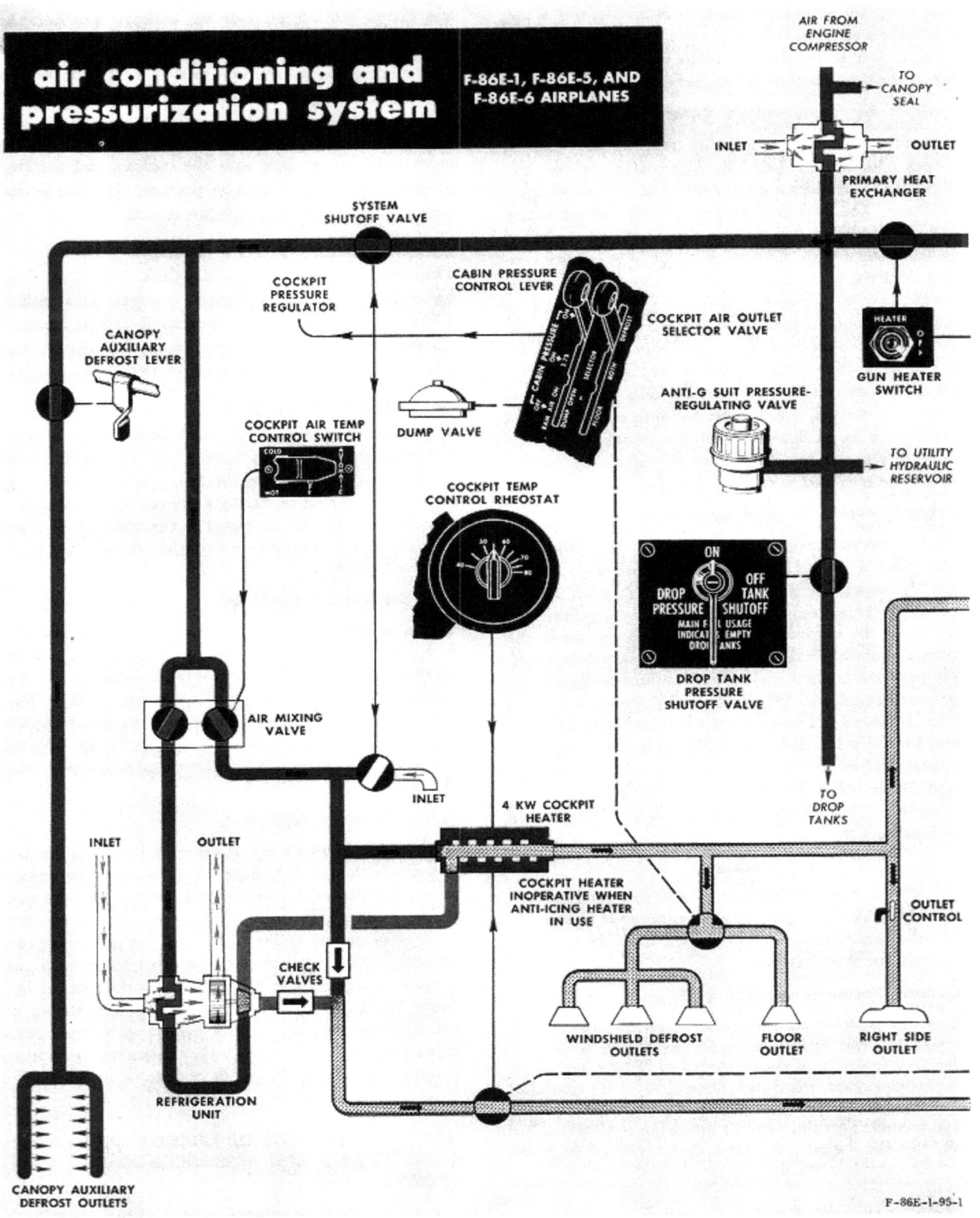

Figure 4-2

4-4

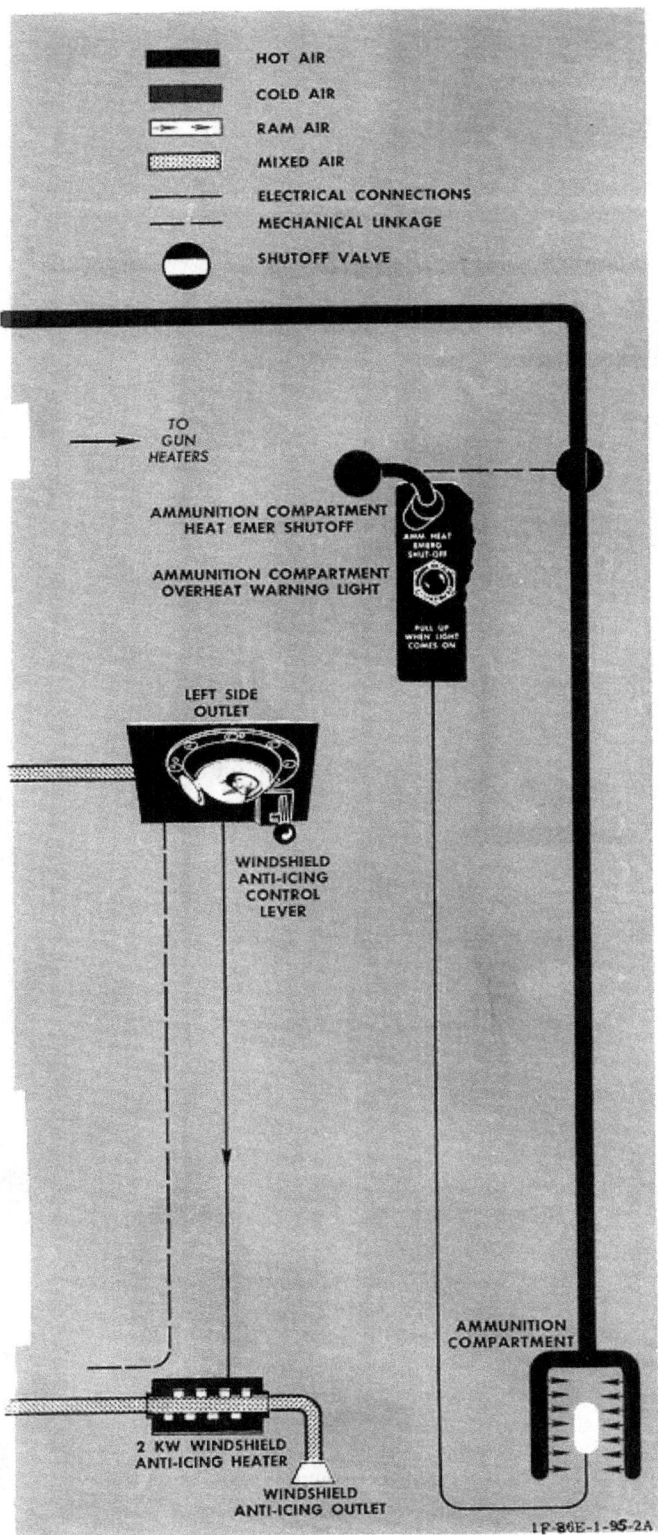

cockpit pressure selector switch at either 2.75 P.S.I. or 5 P.S.I.*)

CAUTION

On F-86E-1 through F-86E-6 Airplanes, cockpit pressure must not exceed 2.75 psi during gun firing, because a higher pressure will cause movement of windshield armor glass and subsequent line deflection.

2. Cockpit air temperature control switch AUTOMATIC (AUTO).

3. Cockpit air temperature control rheostat set for desired temperature.

4. Air outlet selector lever at FLOOR, DEFROST, or BOTH.

5. Adjust side air outlet to direct airflow as desired.

6. Turn on canopy auxiliary defrost, if necessary.

EMERGENCY OPERATION OF PRESSURIZATION SYSTEM.

If sudden depressurization of the cockpit becomes necessary:

1. Turn oxygen regulator pressure-breathing knob to ABOVE 45M on airplanes with the A-14 regulator, or diluter lever to 100% OXYGEN and push emergency toggle lever either way from center, on airplanes with the D-2 regulator. Tighten mask to hold pressure.

2. If at high altitude, immediately descend to 20,000 feet or below.

3. Move cabin pressure control lever to OFF-RAM AIR ON-DUMP OPEN. (Cockpit pressure control switch to RAM.*)

In the event of partial loss of cockpit pressurization indicated by a high-pitched noise in the cockpit and more heat than called for, do the following:

1. Descend to 20,000 feet altitude or lower.
2. Shut off pressurization system.

Note

High-pitched noise in the cockpit can be caused by either the onset of cooling turbine failure or by the cockpit side air outlets. If noise still exists after adjustment of the air outlets, it should soon stop, because the cooling turbine is designed to close tolerances and the rotating assembly will freeze before damage can be done to the remainder of the system. There is no danger of the turbine disintegrating. Therefore, leave pressurization system on at altitudes above 20,000 feet, to receive benefit of at least partial pressurization.

*F-86E-10 and later airplanes

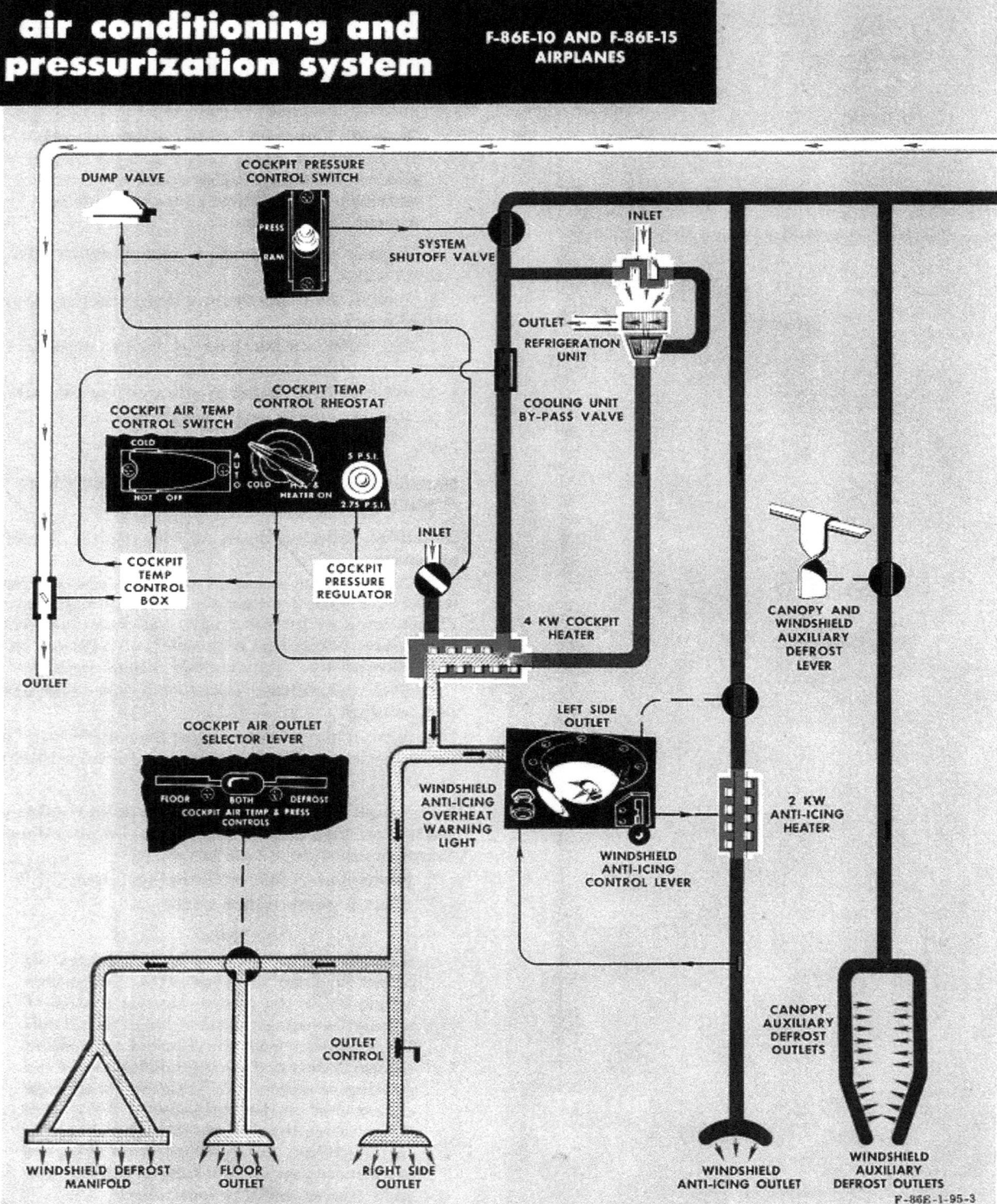

Figure 4-3

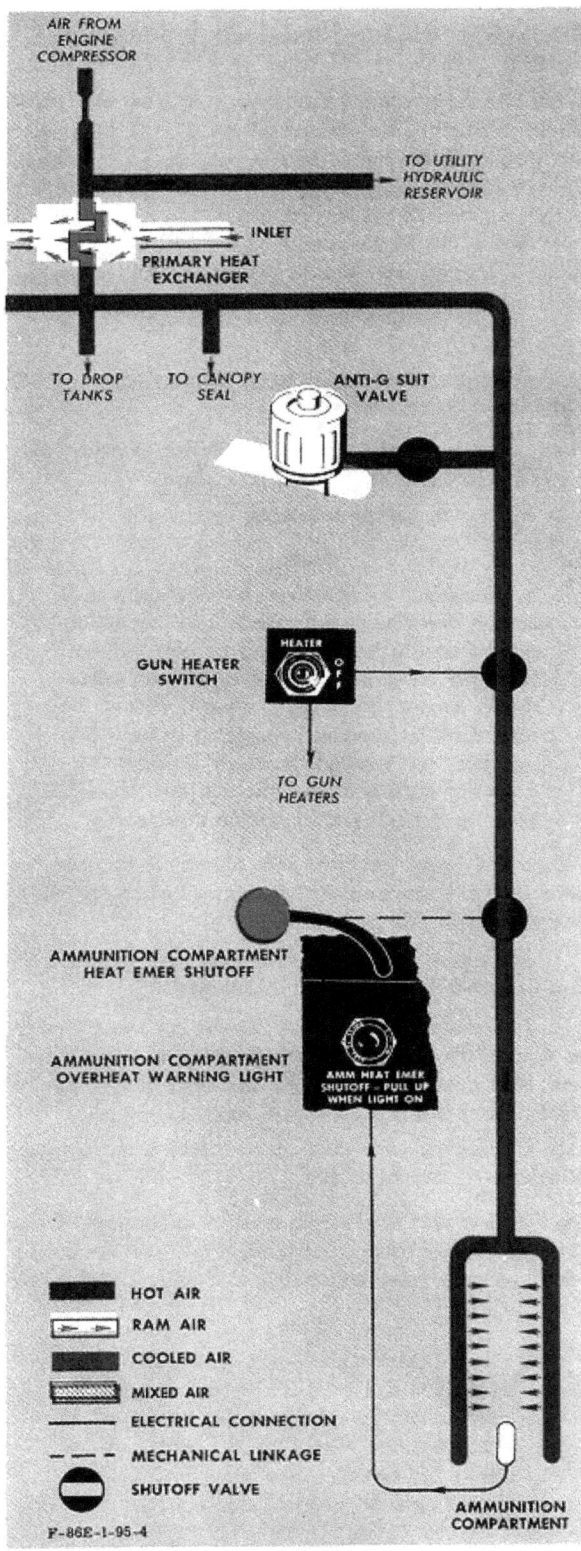

REFRIGERATION UNIT FAILURE.

Failure of the refrigeration unit in the air conditioning and pressurization systems will allow high-temperature air to enter the cockpit. If the cockpit becomes excessively hot, proceed as follows:

1. Cockpit air temperature control rheostat to COLD.
2. If temperature remains high, move cockpit air temperature control switch to COLD.
3. If temperature still remains high, move cabin pressure control lever to OFF-RAM AIR ON-DUMP OPEN (cockpit pressure control switch to RAM*), adjust oxygen pressure-breathing knob to cockpit altitude, and, if at high altitude, descend to 25,000 feet or below if circumstances permit.

ANTI-ICING AND DEFROSTING SYSTEMS.

CANOPY AND WINDSHIELD DEFROSTING AND ANTI-ICING SYSTEM.

For canopy defrosting and windshield defrosting and anti-icing, air is directed onto the inner surfaces of the canopy and windshield. For normal defrosting, air from the cockpit air conditioning and pressurization systems is directed through the cockpit side air outlets and windshield defrost outlets. An auxiliary defrosting system, having perforated tubular outlets along the canopy track and windshield, can be engaged to supplement the canopy and windshield defrosting system during severe operating conditions. The canopy and windshield auxiliary defrost system receives engine compressor air that has passed through the primary heat exchanger. For windshield anti-icing on F-86E-1 through F-86E-6 Airplanes, air from the windshield anti-icing outlet circulates between the armor glass and the inner surface of the windshield. For windshield anti-icing and rain removal on F-86E-10 and later airplanes, a layer of heated air is directed over the outside of the windshield (armor glass only) from an external outlet. A 2-kilowatt electric heater automatically furnishes additional heat for windshield anti-icing, if necessary. The defrosting and anti-icing systems are shown in figures 4-2 and 4-3. The pitot head has a conventional resistance-type electrical heater to prevent the formation of ice within the unit. The fuel system has a deicing system which will remove ice from the fuel filter.

CANOPY AND WINDSHIELD DEFROSTING AND ANTI-ICING CONTROLS AND INDICATOR.

Air Outlet Selector Lever (Windshield Defrosting).

Refer to "Cockpit Air Conditioning and Pressurization System Controls and Indicator" in this section.

*F-86E-10 and later airplanes

Cabin Pressure Control Lever.

Refer to "Cockpit Air Conditioning and Pressurization System Controls and Indicator" in this section.

Cockpit Pressure Control Switch.

Refer to "Cockpit Air Conditioning and Pressurization System Controls and Indicator" in this section.

Canopy (and Windshield*) Auxiliary Defrost Lever.

The canopy (and windshield*) auxiliary defrost lever (9, figure 1-6; 10, figure 1-8) is on the left side of the cockpit. For desired airflow, the lever is moved forward from the aft OFF position to ON or to any unmarked intermediate position. Airflow is directed to both the canopy and windshield when the lever is moved forward.

Note

The windshield and canopy defrosting system provides sufficient heating of the transparent surfaces to effectively eliminate frost or fog during descent.

Do not operate the canopy auxiliary defrost system on the ground at engine rpm above 60% if outside air temperature is 90°F or above, because there is no temperature protection in the system.

Side Air Outlet Controls.

Refer to "Cockpit Air Conditioning and Pressurization System Controls and Indicator" in this section.

Windshield Anti-icing Lever.

Windshield anti-icing is turned on or off by the windshield anti-icing lever (6, figure 1-6; 7, figure 1-8), on the left side of the cockpit above the left aft console. The windshield anti-icing air heater (2-kilowatt), powered by the primary bus, will operate only when the anti-icing lever is at ON and the engine is running. On F-86E-1 through F-86E-6 Airplanes, the pressurization system must also be on to provide windshield anti-icing.

CAUTION

To prevent possible cracking of the windshield armor glass, windshield anti-icing should be used only when necessary and should be turned off as soon as conditions permit, particularly at low altitudes.

Note

The 4-kilowatt cockpit heater is inoperative when the windshield anti-icing lever is ON.

Windshield Anti-icing Overheat Warning Light.*

When the temperature of anti-icing air from the windshield anti-icing heater rises above 275°F, an amber warning light (4, figure 1-8) comes on. The warning light, on the left side of the cockpit, aft of the side air outlet, is powered by the primary bus and is controlled by a thermostat in the anti-icing air outlet. The windshield anti-icing lever should be moved to OFF when the light comes on.

OPERATION OF WINDSHIELD DEFROSTING AND ANTI-ICING SYSTEM.

If any portion of the windshield or armor glass becomes fogged or frosted, follow this procedure:

1. Move windshield anti-icing lever to ON.

Note

If windshield icing is frequently encountered during letdowns, the windshield anti-icing system should be turned on before letdown. However, to prevent cracking of the windshield armor glass, the system should be turned off as soon as conditions permit. Remember, on F-86E-1 through F-86E-6 Airplanes, windshield anti-icing is not possible with the cockpit pressurization system off.

2. If the inner (cockpit) face of the armor glass becomes fogged, move air outlet selector lever to DEFROST, and close both side air outlets.

3. If fogging persists, move canopy (and windshield) auxiliary defrost lever to ON to dissipate fog.

4. If atmospheric or flight conditions cause fog to be emitted from windshield defrosting or side air outlets, turn cockpit air temperature control rheostat to the full HOT & HEATER ON position.

5. If fogging continues, move cockpit air temperature control switch to HOT.

On F-86E-10 and later airplanes, if rain obscures vision through the forward windshield while you are in the traffic pattern, move windshield anti-icing lever to ON.

Note

● The windshield anti-icing system will effectively remove rain from the windshield only at engine speeds above 75% rpm. If rain obscures visibility as power is reduced for landing, you may have to look through the windshield side panels.

*F-86E-10 and later airplanes

- If possible, engine rpm should be reduced when the windshield overheat warning light comes on.

CAUTION

- If windshield overheat warning light* comes on, try to extinguish it by reducing power, if possible, or by moving cockpit pressure switch to RAM. Anti-icing system may be left on if necessary, to improve forward vision, even though windshield overheat light comes on.
- If warning light* comes on after landing, leave anti-icing lever ON; reduced power on ground will allow gradual cooling of windshield and prevent cracking of glass by sudden temperature changes.

Turn off windshield anti-icing system as soon after landing as possible, to prevent cracking of windshield.

PITOT HEATER.

The pitot-static head is equipped with a conventional resistance-type electrical heater to prevent ice formation within the unit.

Pitot Heater Switch.

The pitot heater is controlled by primary bus power through an ON-OFF switch (figure 1-16) on the left forward console.

CAUTION

The pitot heater should not be used for extended periods of time on the ground, because lack of sufficient airflow will cause serious overheating of the unit and may cause injury to ground personnel.

*F-86E-10 and later airplanes

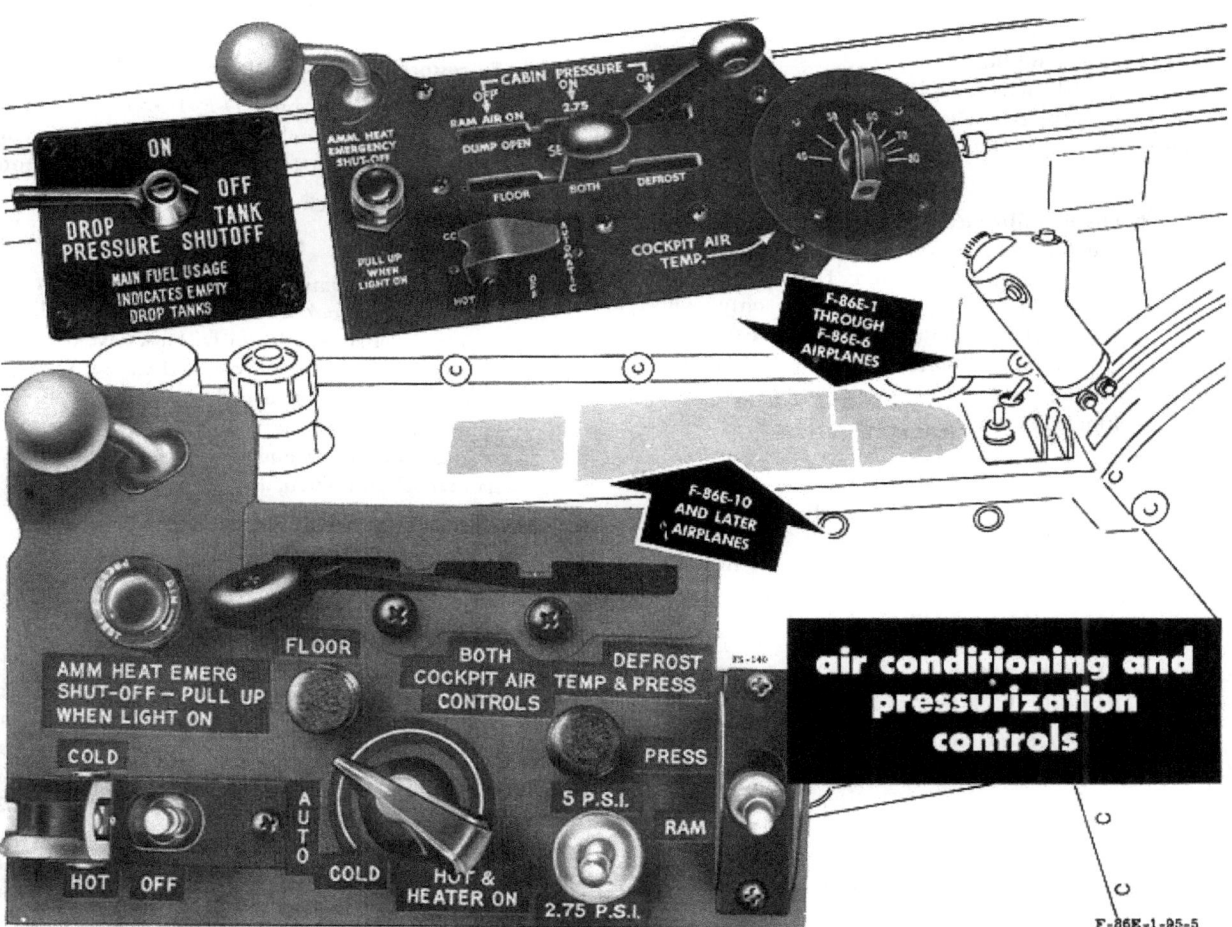

Figure 4-4

Section IV
T. O. 1F-86E-1

FUEL FILTER DEICING SYSTEM.

Alcohol is injected into the fuel filter inlet line to accomplish fuel filter deicing. (See figure 1-13.) Alcohol is pumped from a one-gallon tank to the filter when the fuel filter deicing button is depressed. The alcohol supply will last for approximately one minute of deicing operation. A warning light comes on whenever fuel flow through the filter is restricted by ice formation.

Fuel Filter Deicing Button.

The fuel filter deicing button (33, figure 1-4), on the left side of the instrument panel shroud, is powered by the primary bus. It controls the alcohol system for deicing the fuel filter. When the button is depressed, a shutoff valve is opened, the alcohol pump is started, and alcohol is injected into the fuel filter inlet line. The button should be held in until the ice warning light goes out, indicating that the fuel filter is free of ice.

Fuel Filter Ice Warning Light.

Ice formation within the fuel filter creates a pressure differential across the filter, which in turn illuminates an amber warning light (1, figure 1-4), next to the fuel filter deicing button (on the left side of the instrument panel shroud). The light, powered from the primary bus, goes out when ice has been removed from the filter.

Note

- The fuel filter ice warning light may flicker under certain engine operating conditions, such as rapid acceleration. Therefore, since the alcohol supply will last for only one minute of operation, make certain that light is illuminated steadily before depressing deicing button. Use the deicing system for approximately 15 seconds at a time.
- An accumulation of dirt or other foreign matter in the fuel filter, sufficient to restrict the fuel flow, can also cause illumination of the fuel filter ice warning light. The deicing system will not remove such restrictions, and ground servicing of the filter is required.

COMMUNICATION AND ASSOCIATED ELECTRONIC EQUIPMENT.

TABLE OF COMMUNICATION AND ASSOCIATED ELECTRONIC EQUIPMENT.

See figure 4-5.

VHF COMMAND SET—AN/ARC-3.

The AN/ARC-3 vhf command radio set provides two-way voice and code communication from air-to-air or from air-to-ground within a frequency range of 100 to 156 megacycles. The set, powered from the primary bus, has eight preset channels and a line-of-sight range. Average range is approximately 30 miles at an altitude of 1000 feet and 135 miles at 10,000 feet. Range distances may increase or decrease according to atmospheric conditions. A frequency card for the AN/ARC-3 radio set (17, figure 1-7; 16, figure 1-9) is on the vertical panel, below the right console.

Operation of AN/ARC-3 Command Radio.

1. Move power switch on command radio control panel to ON.

2. Rotate command radio channel selector knob to desired frequency channel, and allow 30 to 45 seconds for equipment to warm up. When tone heard in the headset during the latter portion of the warm-up period stops, the set is tuned and ready for operation.

3. Adjust volume control as desired.

4. To transmit, press microphone button on throttle, and speak into microphone.

5. To restore reception, release microphone button.

6. To transmit code, use "D-F TONE" button on AN/ARC-3 control panel as key. Maximum keying speed is limited to approximately 15 words per minute.

7. Move power switch to OFF to turn off set.

Note

Do not turn off command set immediately after position of channel selector knob is changed, because the channel selector will not have time to complete its change cycle, and the set will be inoperative when turned on again. If this occurs, turn the set on, run through the complete selection of frequencies by means of the channel selector knob, and then select desired frequency. The set will resume normal operation.

UHF COMMAND SET—AN/ARC-33.

Some airplanes have been changed to include the AN/ARC-33 uhf command radio set, in place of the AN/ARC-3 vhf command radio set. The primary-bus-powered AN/ARC-33 equipment provides two-way voice and code communication from air-to-air and from air-to-ground in the ultra-high-frequency region of 225 to 399.9 megacycles. Any of 20 preset frequencies may be selected, and a guard receiver permits monitoring of the guard frequency while operating on any of the other channels. The radio set control, which is a remote control panel, has a "MAIN-BOTH-G" selector switch to

communication and associated electronic equipment

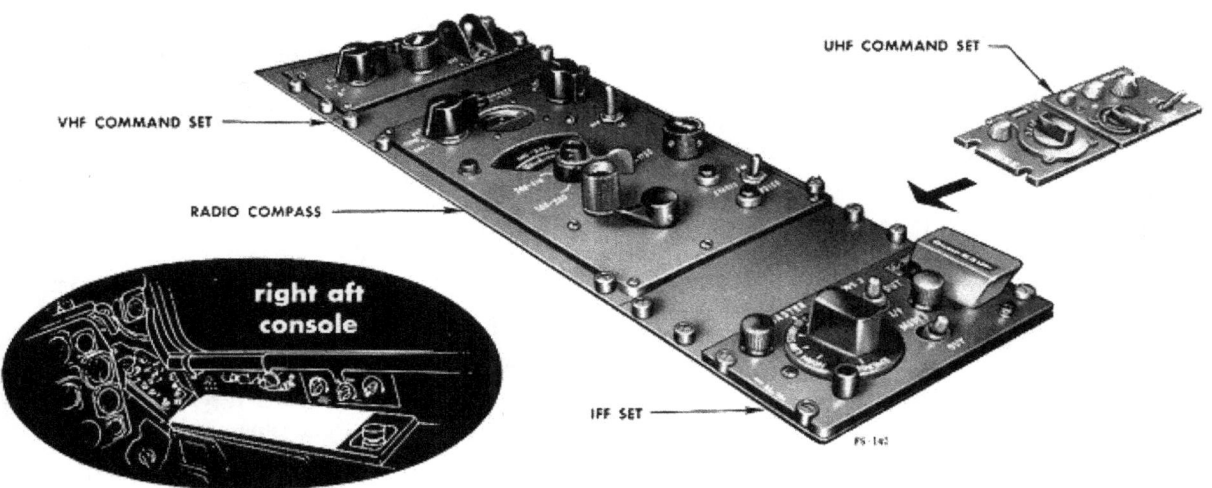

type	designation	function	range
VHF COMMAND SET *	AN/ARC-3	SHORT-RANGE, TWO-WAY VOICE AND CODE COMMUNICATION	LINE OF SIGHT
RADIO COMPASS	AN/ARN-6	RECEPTION OF VOICE AND CODE COMMUNICATION; POSITION FINDING; HOMING	20-200 MILES DEPENDING ON FREQUENCY USED AND TIME OF DAY
IFF	AN/APX-6	AUTOMATIC AIRCRAFT IDENTIFICATION	LINE OF SIGHT
UHF COMMAND SET *	AN/ARC-33	SHORT-RANGE, TWO-WAY VOICE AND CODE COMMUNICATION	LINE OF SIGHT
NAVIGATION COMPASS †	AN/ARN-14	RECEPTION OF VOICE AND CODE COMMUNICATION; POSITION FINDING; HOMING	20-200 MILES DEPENDING ON FREQUENCY USED AND TIME OF DAY

*Some airplanes have been modified to include the AN/ARC-33 uhf command radio set in place of the AN/ARC-3 vhf command radio set.

†Space provisions only.

Figure 4-5

provide a choice of operation on the selected channel (MAIN), on the guard channel (G), or on the selected channel while monitoring on the guard channel (BOTH). During warm-up and while changing frequencies, a tone will be heard in the earphones, reminding the pilot that the radio is inoperative during these functions. Extremely low noise level is a characteristic of the equipment, and absence of the normal background noise in the earphones does not indicate that the receiver is dead.

Operation of AN/ARC-33 Command Radio.

To operate the AN/ARC-33 command radio, proceed as follows:

1. Place power switch at ON. (A warm-up period of 30 seconds is required before the set will be operative.)

2. Move the "MAIN-BOTH-G" selector switch to the desired position.

Do not move the selector switch to the REL position, because this action will release the preset frequency cylinder. This guarded switch position facilitates the presetting of channels, and it is not feasible for the pilot to attempt to change the preset channels in flight.

Note

When the selector switch is placed at the G position, the set will automatically be set up to transmit and receive on the guard frequency.

3. Rotate channel selector to desired main channel.

4. Adjust volume, as necessary, with volume control on panel.

5. To transmit, press microphone button on throttle.

Note

When code transmissions are made, depressing the tone button on the control panel will automatically key the transmitter. The microphone button need not be pressed during code transmission.

6. To turn set off, move power switch to OFF.

RADIO COMPASS—AN/ARN-6.

The AN/ARN-6 radio compass set, powered by the secondary bus, is a navigational aid used in conjunction with the radio compass indicator (31, figure 1-4; 27, figure 1-5), on the instrument panel. Four separate frequency bands are provided: band one, 100 to 200 kilocycles; band two, 200 to 410 kilocycles; band three, 410 to 850 kilocycles; and band four, 850 to 1750 kilocycles. Controls permit selection of automatic or manual direction finding. A tuning meter, on the radio compass control panel, indicates signal strength and accuracy of tuning. The radio compass loop antenna (5, figure 1-3) is installed within the aft portion of the canopy, and the sense antenna (4, figure 1-3) is in the upper arc of the canopy.

Operation of Radio Compass.

1. Turn function selector switch from OFF to COMP. ANT., or LOOP.

2. Rotate band switch to desired frequency band.

3. With function selector switch at ANT., use tuning crank to tune station and obtain maximum swing of tuning meter.

4. Turn volume control to adjust headset volume.

5. With the function switch on COMP. and the station tuned in, place "CW-VOICE" switch to CW and check that 900-cycle continuous tone is heard; then return switch to VOICE.

6. Set "VAR" knob on compass indicator to adjust index.

7. When function selector switch is at LOOP, the "LOOP L-R" switch is used to rotate the loop to obtain aural-null orientation.

8. Return function selector switch to OFF to turn radio compass off.

IDENTIFICATION RADAR—AN/APX-6.

The AN/APX-6 radar identification set, which receives power from the primary bus and single-phase, ac inverter, is used to automatically identify the airplane as friendly whenever it is properly challenged by suitably equipped friendly air or surface forces. The set also has provisions for identifying the airplane in which it is installed by a specific friendly signal while the airplane is within a group of other friendly airplanes and has means for transmitting a special distress code when challenged. The AN/APX-6 set receives challenges and transmits replies to the source of the challengers where the replies are displayed, together with the associated radar targets, on radar indicators. When a radar target is accompanied by a proper reply from the IFF set, the target is considered friendly. Three destructors, in the AN/APX-6 transpondor, may be actuated by the pilot. An impact switch automatically actuates the destructors upon a crash landing.

Operation of Identification Radar.

Before take-off, check that AN/APX-6 frequency counters have been set to the proper frequency channels and that destructors have been inserted in transpondor. (IFF units are accessible through the radio compartment access door on the left side of the fuselage.)

1. To turn equipment on, rotate master control to NORM position (full sensitivity and maximum performance).

2. Rotate master control to STBY to maintain equipment inoperative, but ready for instant use.

3. Do not use LOW position of master control (partial sensitivity), except upon proper authorization.

4. Set three-position "MODE 2" and "MODE 3" switches to their OUT positions unless otherwise directed.

5. For emergency operation, press dial stop and rotate master control to EMERGENCY position, so that set will automatically transmit distress signals when challenged.

6. To manually fire destructors, lift guard and move destructor switch to ON.

7. To turn off IFF set, rotate master control to OFF.

8. If the AN/APX-6 transpondor is destroyed during flight, report this information immediately after landing.

LIGHTING EQUIPMENT.
EXTERIOR LIGHTING.

Exterior lighting consists of two fuselage lights, four position lights, and two landing lights. One fuselage light is within the aft portion of the canopy frame; the other is on the lower surface of the fuselage, below the cockpit. A position light is in each wing tip, and two are faired into the trailing edge of the empennage fillet. These tail lights are mounted side by side; the left light is yellow, and the right light is white. The two retractable landing lights are set side by side in the bottom of the fuselage nose section, forward of the nose wheel. When the weight of the airplane is on the gear, one of the landing lights automatically changes to a different position and is used as a taxi light.

Fuselage Light Switch.*

Illumination of the fuselage lights is controlled by the three-position fuselage light switch (figure 4-6) on the right forward console. Moving the switch from OFF to BRIGHT or DIM illuminates the lights at the selected brilliancy. The light switch operates on power from the primary bus.

Master Code Switch and Code Selector.*

The master code switch (figure 4-6) and code selector (figure 4-6) are on the right forward console. They receive power from the primary bus. This switch and selector make signaling with the fuselage lights possible by increasing the light brilliancy in code. The code selector provides a choice of 12 letters for flashing code. The selected letter is automatically flashed in Morse code when the master code switch is turned ON.

Code Indicator Light.*

The code indicator light (figure 1-16), ahead of the right forward console, is powered by the primary bus and flashes simultaneously with the fuselage lights to indicate that the selected letter is being flashed. The indicator light is of the push-to-test type, permitting check of bulb illumination when the master code switch is OFF.

Position Light Selector Switch.*

The position lights are controlled by the primary-bus-powered, three-position selector switch (figure 4-6), on the right forward console. The lights are illuminated continuously when the switch is moved from OFF to STEADY. When the selector switch is at FLASH, the lights flash at 40 cycles per minute. Brilliancy of the lights is controlled by the position light dimmer switch.

CAUTION
The destructors should be fired only when the AN/APX-6 equipment is in danger of falling into enemy hands. If a forced landing has to be made in an area of doubtful security, fire the destructors.

*F-86E-1 through F-86E-6 Airplanes

Section IV T. O. 1F-86E-1

exterior lighting controls

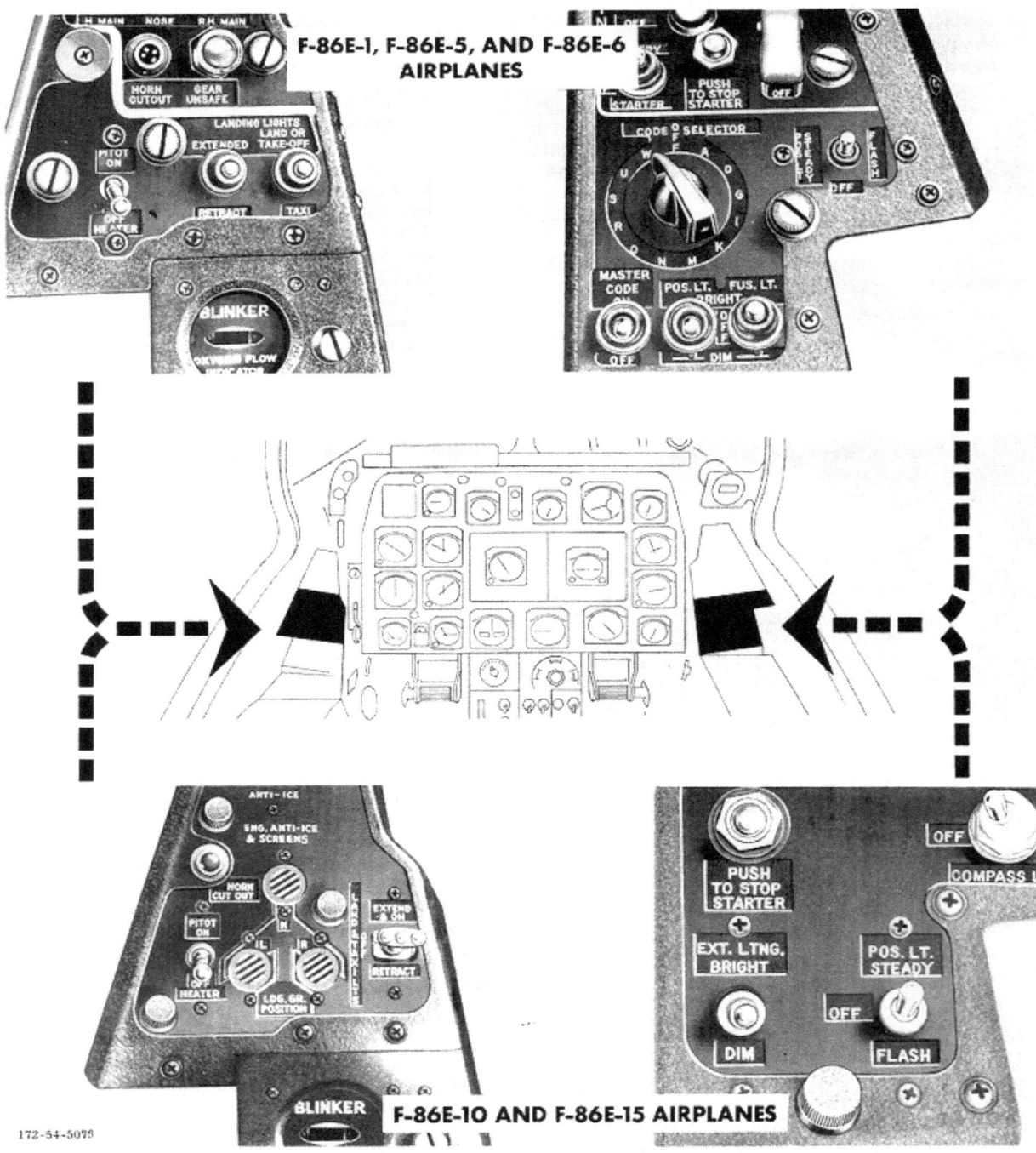

Figure 4-6

4-14

Position Light Dimmer Switch.*

The position light dimmer switch (figure 4-6), on the right forward console and powered by the primary bus, controls the brilliancy of the position lights. Positioning the switch from OFF to BRIGHT or DIM, regulates the brightness of all position lights accordingly.

Position and Fuselage Light Selector Switch.†

The position and fuselage lights are controlled by a selector switch (figures 1-16 and 4-6), on the right forward console, and receive power from the primary bus. When the selector switch is placed at STEADY, the position lights illuminate continuously. Setting the selector switch at FLASH causes the position lights to flash automatically at the rate of 40 cycles per minute. When the selector switch is positioned from OFF to STEADY or FLASH, the fuselage lights illuminate steadily. Brilliancy of the position and fuselage lights is controlled by the exterior lighting dimmer switch.

Exterior Lighting Dimmer Switch.†

The two-position exterior lighting dimmer switch (figures 1-16 and 4-6) is on the right forward console and is powered by the primary bus. Setting the switch at BRIGHT or DIM regulates the brilliancy of the position and fuselage lights accordingly.

Landing Light Position Switch.*

The three-position landing light position switch (figure 4-6), on the left forward console and powered by the primary bus, controls extension and retraction of the landing lights. Setting the switch at either the EXTENDED or RETRACT position moves both lights accordingly. (The landing light extends 69 degrees from its fully retracted position.) Returning the switch to its center (OFF) position during the extension or retraction cycle stops the lights at any desired position. Limit switches automatically cut off power to the light actuation motors when the lights become fully extended or fully retracted. The lights cannot be illuminated when completely retracted. To furnish a properly directed beam for taxiing, one landing light will automatically extend to the taxi position when the weight of the airplane is on the nose gear.

CAUTION

To prevent damage to lights, do not lower landing lights above 185 knots IAS.

Landing Light Selector Switch.*

The three-position landing light selector switch (figure 4-6) is on the left forward console. This switch receives power from the primary bus. With the lights extended from the fully retracted position, moving the switch to LAND or TAKE-OFF turns on both lights when the weight of the airplane is on the nose gear. However, only the landing (right) light will remain on when the weight of the airplane is off the nose gear. Positioning the selector switch at TAXI illuminates the taxi (left) light only when the weight of the airplane is on the nose gear. When retracted, the lights go out automatically and cannot be illuminated while in this position.

Landing and Taxi Light Switch.†

The retractable landing and taxi lights are controlled by a three-position switch (figure 4-6), on the left forward console. The switch is powered by the primary bus. When the switch is moved from the OFF position to EXTEND & ON, both lights are extended to the landing position and illuminated. Upon touchdown, when the weight of the airplane is on the nose gear, the landing light automatically goes out and the illuminated taxi light extends farther, to the taxi position, thus providing a properly directed beam for taxiing. If a touch-and-go landing is made and the switch is left in the EXTEND & ON position, the landing light comes on again and the taxi light returns to the landing position as the weight of the airplane is removed from the nose wheel. Both lights go out and retract when the switch is moved to RETRACT. Limit switches break the retraction circuit when the lights reach the fully retracted position.

INTERIOR LIGHTING.

Interior lighting is furnished by indirect instrument panel lights, console and center pedestal lights, instrument panel auxiliary lights, and a cockpit utility light. A light for the stand-by compass is also provided. The instruments on the panel are individually illuminated by indirect red ring lights. The two console lights (4, figure 1-6; 7, figure 1-7) are above the respective left and right rear consoles. The forward consoles and center pedestals are illuminated indirectly by light beamed edgewise through Lucite panels from bulbs mounted in the face of the units. The bulb covers can be removed to replace bulbs. The left instrument panel auxiliary light (12, figure 1-6; 15, figure 1-8) is just above the control quadrant. The right instrument panel auxiliary light (4, figure 1-7; 3, figure 1-9) is just above the radio compass control panel. Alternate mountings for the instrument panel auxiliary lights are provided on each side of the cockpit. One is at the base of the windshield bow, left of the instrument panel, and the other is just aft of the normal instrument panel auxiliary light mounting, above the radio compass control panel. The

*F-86E-1 through F-86E-6 Airplanes
†F-86E-10 and later airplanes

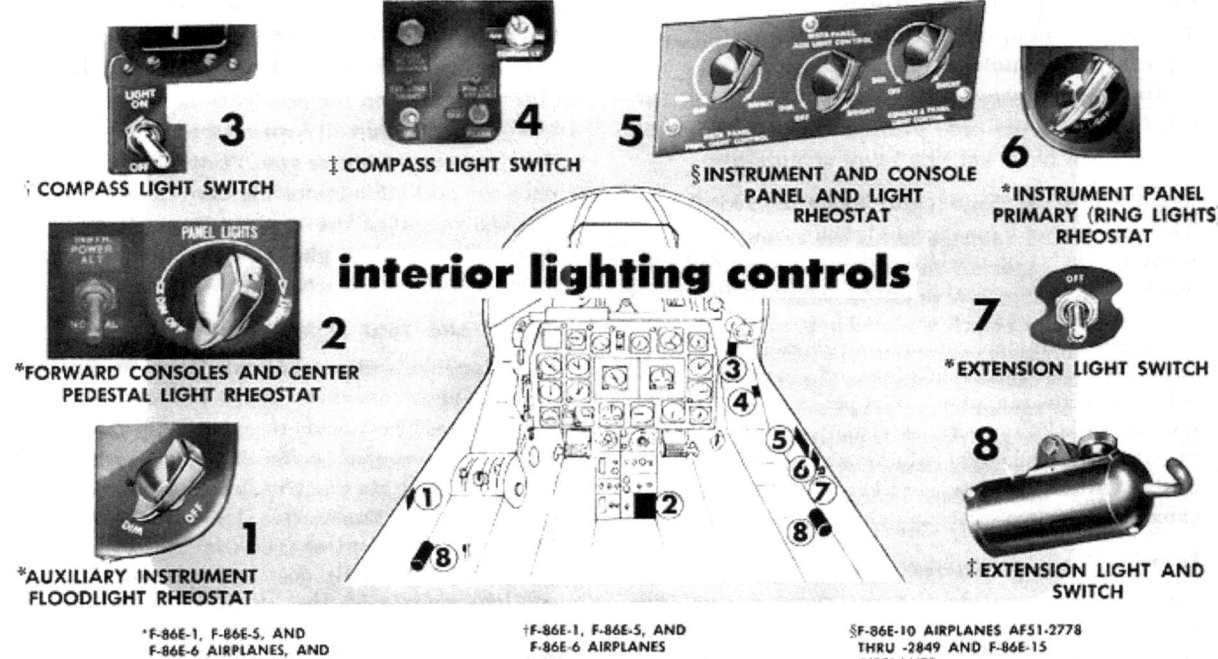

Figure 4-7

cockpit extension light (10, figure 1-7; 8, figure 1-9) on most airplanes* is on the right side of the cockpit, just forward of the right circuit-breaker panel. On late airplanes,✧ the cockpit utility light is just forward of the anti-G suit valve. Spare bulbs (2, figure 1-9) are stowed in a rack on the right side of the cockpit.

Instrument Panel Primary Light Rheostat.

The illumination and brilliancy of the instrument ring lights are controlled by a rheostat (9, figure 1-7; 7, figure 1-9; figure 4-7) above the right aft console. The rheostat is powered by the primary bus.

Instrument Panel Auxiliary Light Rheostat.

On early airplanes,‡ the instrument panel auxiliary lights are illuminated and brilliancy is controlled by a rheostat (7, figure 1-6; 8, figure 1-8; figure 4-7), just above the throttle quadrant. On later airplanes,§ the lights are controlled by a rheostat (6, figure 1-9; figure 4-7) on a panel above the right rear console. The auxiliary lights receive power from the battery bus and, therefore, are operable regardless of battery-starter switch setting.

Console and Center Pedestal Light Rheostat.

The illumination and brilliancy of the console lights on early airplanes‡ are controlled by a rheostat (14, figure 4-12), on the center pedestal. On late airplanes,§ the lighting is controlled by a rheostat (6, figure 1-9; figure 4-7) on a panel above the right rear console. Both of these rheostats operate on primary bus power.

Cockpit Extension (Utility) Light Control.

On F-86E-1 through F-86E-6 Airplanes, the cockpit extension light is controlled by a primary-bus-powered, two-position switch (10, figure 1-7; figure 4-7), just forward of, and adjacent to, the extension light. On F-86E-10 and later airplanes, the utility light is controlled by a rheostat (figure 4-7) on the light reflector. The rheostat is powered by the primary bus.

*F-86E-1 through F-86E-10 Airplanes
✧F-86E-15 Airplanes
‡F-86E-1 through F-86E-6 Airplanes and F-86E-10 Airplane AF51-2718 through -2777
§F-86E-10 Airplane AF51-2778 and all later airplanes

4-16

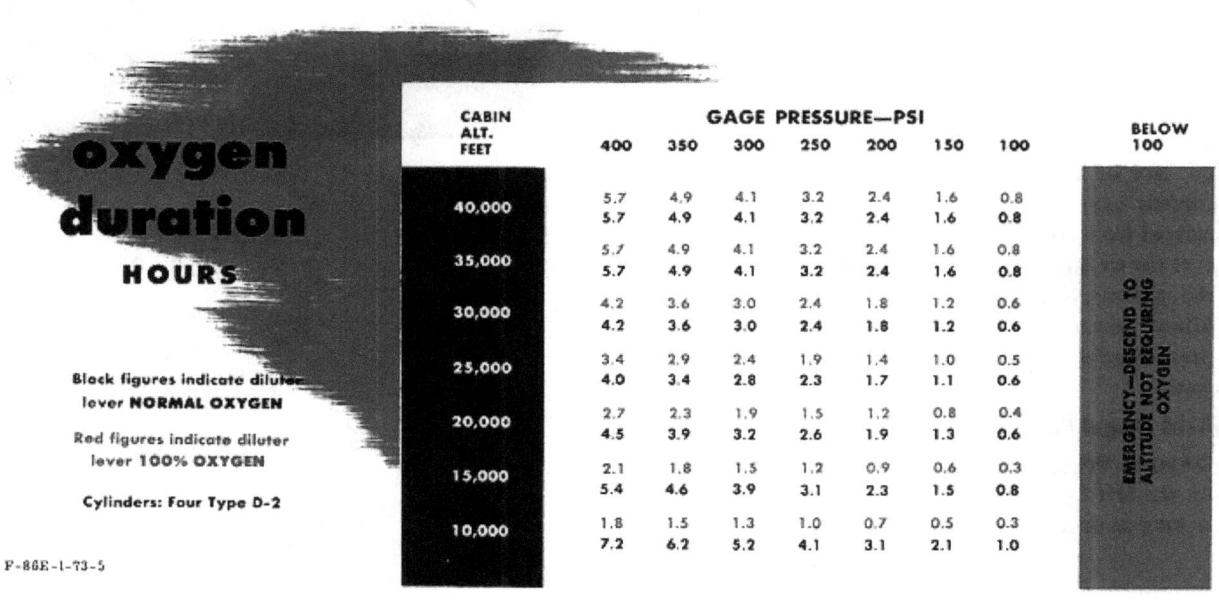

Figure 4-8

Stand-by Compass Light Switch.

On F-86E-1 through F-86E-6 Airplanes, the stand-by compass light switch (figure 4-7) is just below the compass. On F-86E-10 and later airplanes, the switch (figure 4-7) is on the right forward console. The face of the compass illuminates when the switch, which is powered from the primary bus, is placed in the ON position. The console light rheostat must be turned ON for the compass light switch to be operative.

OXYGEN SYSTEM.

The gaseous oxygen system is supplied from four Type D-2 cylinders in the nose section, two on each side, outboard of the intake duct. Included in the system is a pressure-demand regulator, a flow indicator, and a pressure gage. For combat safety, check valves are incorporated in the system to prevent total loss of oxygen in the event of system failure or cylinder punctures. If a cylinder is punctured, it will be isolated by the check valves and the pressure gage indication will remain relatively the same, although the available oxygen supply will be reduced. The oxygen system is serviced by means of a single-point refilling valve. On F-86E-1 through F-86E-6 Airplanes, the valve (12, figure 1-35) is within an access door on the left side of the fuselage, forward of the ammunition compartment door. On F-86E-10 and later airplanes, the valve (7, figure 1-35) is within an access door on the right side of the fuselage, just aft of the gun blast panel. Normal minimum system pressure for take-off is 400 psi. An oxygen duration table is shown in figure 4-8. See figure 1-35 for oxygen specification.

PRESSURE-DEMAND OXYGEN REGULATOR.

A few unmodified airplanes have a Type A-14 pressure-demand regulator (figure 4-10) recessed in the inboard face of the left forward console. This regulator automatically mixes air with oxygen in varying amounts, according to the altitude, and delivers a quantity of this mixture each time the pilot inhales. The percentage of oxygen furnished by the regulator increases with an increase in altitude and becomes 100 percent at approximately 34,000 feet. For operation above 30,000 feet, oxygen may be delivered under pressure.

Use only a pressure-demand oxygen mask with the pressure-demand oxygen regulator.

A-14 Regulator Controls.

Regulator Diluter Handle. The oxygen regulator diluter handle (figure 4-10), on the face of the pressure-demand regulator, is a manual control for selecting the oxygen-air mixture ratio. If the oxygen regulator diluter lever is at NORMAL OXYGEN, the regulator automatically maintains the proper oxygen-air ratio for changes in altitude. When the control lever is moved to the 100% OXYGEN position, the regulator delivers 100 percent oxygen regardless of the altitude.

Regulator Pressure-Breathing Knob. Clockwise rotation of the pressure-breathing knob (figure 4-10), on the face of the regulator, from NORMAL delivers 100 percent oxygen under pressure. The knob should be rotated from NORMAL only above 30,000 feet or whenever the oxygen supply becomes inadequate. Whenever the pressure-breathing knob is not at NORMAL, the diluter mechanism is inoperative, and the resultant pressurized oxygen flow is uneconomical below 30,000 feet.

A-14 Regulator Indicators.

Oxygen Pressure Gage. The oxygen pressure gage, on the left forward console, indicates system pressure as long as the oxygen supply lines are intact.

Note

Since the oxygen cylinders grow colder as the airplane reaches high altitudes, oxygen pressure is reduced. Sometimes, a rather rapid drop in oxygen pressure gage reading is noted. A 100°F decrease in temperature of the oxygen cylinders causes approximately a 20 percent drop in cylinder gage pressure. The drop in pressure is not generally cause for alarm. As the airplane descends to warmer altitudes, the cylinder pressure will tend to rise again, so that the rate of oxygen usage may appear to be slower than normal. A rapid drop in oxygen pressure during level flight or while descending may indicate oxygen leakage.

Oxygen Flow Indicator. A blinker-type flow indicator, on the left forward console, provides a visual indication that oxygen is being supplied. A shutter on the face of the instrument opens and closes with each breath to show that oxygen is flowing through the regulator.

Oxygen System Preflight Check (A-14 Regulator).

1. Check mask unit properly connected (figure 4-9), and note oxygen pressure gage (400 psi minimum).

2. Set oxygen regulator diluter handle at 100% OXYGEN and pressure-breathing knob at NORMAL.

3. Blow *gently* back into the mask-to-regulator hose. Any indication of free flow through the regulator indicates a leak or faulty operation.

4. Set oxygen regulator diluter handle at NORMAL OXYGEN and repeat step 3.

Attach oxygen mask hose (male connector) to parachute harness chest strap by wrapping mask connector tie-down strap underneath and up behind chest strap harness twice, then snapping.

WARNING
Failure to double-loop tie-down strap around chest strap may permit tie-down strap to slip into and open the chest strap snap during ejection.

Attach seat oxygen hose to oxygen mask hose. Listen for click and visually check (or feel) that sealing gasket is only half exposed.

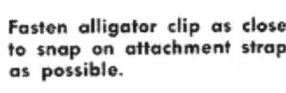

Fasten alligator clip as close to snap on attachment strap as possible.

Figure 4-9

Figure 4-10

A-14 Regulator Normal Operation.

For normal operation, the oxygen regulator diluter handle should be set at NORMAL OXYGEN, and the pressure-breathing knob should be set as follows:

1. For cockpit altitudes below 30,000 feet, leave knob at NORMAL.

2. For cockpit altitudes between 30,000 and 40,000 feet, set knob at SAFETY.

3. For cockpit altitudes above 40,000 feet, set knob at cockpit altitude.

A-14 Regulator Emergency Operation.

Oxygen system controls should be set for various emergency conditions as follows:

1. With symptoms of the onset of anoxia, or if smoke or fuel fumes enter the cockpit, set oxygen regulator diluter handle to 100% OXYGEN.

2. In event of accidental loss of cockpit pressure, turn pressure-breathing knob to the ABOVE 45 M position immediately, and tighten mask to hold pressure.

3. If the oxygen regulator becomes inoperative, pull cord of H-2 bail-out bottle and descend to a cockpit altitude where oxygen is not required.

Note

When emergency is over, set oxygen regulator diluter handle to NORMAL OXYGEN, and set pressure-breathing knob in accordance with procedures in "A-14 Regulator Normal Operation."

DILUTER-DEMAND OXYGEN REGULATOR.

Most airplanes have been changed to include a Type D-2 automatic pressure-breathing, diluter-demand oxygen regulator (20, figure 1-6; 18, figure 1-8; figure 4-10). Mounted on the inboard face of the left forward console, this regulator automatically supplies the proper mixture of oxygen and air at all times for positive pressure-breathing at high altitudes. Regardless of how

4-19

much oxygen is being used, the pressure will always be correct for any specific altitude. A red warning light, mounted in the left forward console, is provided to warn the pilot when the regulator is not operating normally. A pressure relief valve is provided on the outside of the regulator to relieve excess mask pressure. A pressure gage and flow indicator is incorporated in the regulator. The approximate duration of the oxygen supply is shown in figure 4-8.

D-2 Regulator Controls.

Regulator Diluter Lever. A diluter lever (figure 4-10) is in the top right corner of the regulator panel. It is used for selecting either NORMAL OXYGEN for normal usage or 100% OXYGEN for emergency conditions.

Regulator Supply Lever. The regulator supply lever (figure 4-10), on the bottom of the panel, should be safetied in the ON position at all times.

Regulator Emergency Toggle Lever. The emergency toggle lever (figure 4-10), above the supply lever on the oxygen regulator panel, should be at center at all times, unless an unscheduled pressure increase is desired. Moving the toggle lever either way from center provides continuous positive pressure to the oxygen mask. When the toggle lever is at center, it may be depressed momentarily to provide positive pressure to test the mask for leaks.

Regulator Warning Light Switch. The warning light switch (figure 4-10), in the top left corner of the oxygen regulator panel, turns on the red warning light circuit by means of primary bus power. The switch should be ON at all times when the regulator is being used.

D-2 Regulator Indicators.

Pressure Gage and Flow Indicator. The pressure gage and flow indicator (figure 4-10), on the oxygen regulator panel, combines the oxygen pressure gage and the flow indicator in a single instrument. The pressure gage shows the oxygen system pressure. The flow indicator, consisting of four small slots grouped in the lower half of the dial face, shows alternately black and white with each breath.

Note

Since the oxygen cylinders grow colder as the airplane reaches high altitudes, oxygen pressure is reduced. Sometimes, a rather rapid drop in oxygen pressure gage reading is noted. A 100°F decrease in temperature of the oxygen cylinders causes approximately a 20 percent drop in cylinder gage pressure. The drop in pressure is not generally cause for alarm. As the airplane descends to warmer altitudes, the cylinder pressure will tend to rise again, so that the rate of oxygen usage may appear to be slower than normal. A rapid drop in oxygen pressure during level flight, or while descending may indicate oxygen leakage.

Oxygen Regulator Warning Light. The oxygen regulator warning light, on the left forward console (figure 1-16), is illuminated by power from the primary bus. When the warning light switch is moved to ON, the light will come on immediately and then become bright or blinking bright within 15 seconds. It will remain bright if there is no oxygen flow; however, the light may dim within 10 seconds and then return to bright within 60 seconds and remain bright, if there is a continuous flow through the regulator. If the pilot has the mask on, the warning light will become dim within 10 seconds when normal breathing causes proper oxygen flow through the regulator. With the intermittent flow induced by a normal breathing cycle, the warning light will continue to glow dimly. However, any departure from proper operation, that subsequently causes oxygen flow to cease or to flow from the regulator in a continuous stream, will provide a constant or blinking bright light.

Note

The action of the warning light system is based on a normal breathing rate. Too fast or too slow a breathing rate may result in erratic warning light indications.

Oxygen System Preflight Check (D-2 Regulator).

1. Check mask unit properly connected (figure 4-9), and note oxygen pressure gage indication (400 psi minimum).

CAUTION

If mask assembly is not connected, oxygen regulator may be damaged by full, unrestricted flow during test of regulator warning system.

2. Check oxygen regulator with diluter valve first at NORMAL OXYGEN position and then at 100% OXYGEN position as follows: Remove mask and blow gently into end of oxygen regulator hose, as during normal exhalation. There should be resistance to blowing. Little or no resistance to blowing indicates a leak or faulty operation.

3. Place oxygen regulator warning system switch in ON position. Warning light should emit a bright (steady or blinking bright) light. Move emergency toggle lever from center to left or right position. The warning light should change from a bright light to a dim glow and back to bright. Return emergency toggle lever to center.

4. With regulator supply valve ON, oxygen mask connected to regulator, and diluter lever in 100% OXYGEN position, breathe normally into mask and conduct the following checks:

    a. Observe blinker for proper operation. Warning light should change from a bright to a dim glow.

    b. Deflect emergency toggle lever to right or left. A positive pressure should be supplied to mask. Return emergency toggle lever to center.

    c. Depress emergency toggle lever straight in. A positive pressure should result within the mask. Hold breath to determine if there is leakage around mask. Release emergency toggle lever. Positive pressure should cease.

5. Return diluter lever to NORMAL OXYGEN.

D-2 Regulator Normal Operation.

1. Before each flight, be sure oxygen pressure gage reads at least 400 psi. If pressure is below this minimum, have the oxygen system charged to capacity before take-off.

2. Supply lever turned ON.

3. Diluter lever at NORMAL OXYGEN.

4. Warning light switch ON.

Note

Above 30,000 feet, you may sometimes notice a vibration or a wheezing sound in the mask. This noise is a normal characteristic of the regulator operation and should be overlooked.

D-2 Regulator Emergency Operation.

Oxygen system controls should be set as follows for various emergency conditions:

1. With symptoms of the onset of anoxia, or if smoke or fuel fumes enter the cockpit, set oxygen regulator diluter lever to 100% OXYGEN.

2. Push emergency toggle lever either way from center.

3. If the oxygen regulator becomes inoperative, pull the ball handle on the H-2 emergency oxygen bail-out bottle, and descend to a cockpit altitude below 10,000 feet as soon as possible.

NAVIGATION EQUIPMENT.

STAND-BY COMPASS.

Refer to "Stand-by Compass" in Section I.

RADIO COMPASS.

Refer to "Communication and Associated Electronic Equipment" in this section.

DIRECTIONAL INDICATOR (SLAVED).

The directional indicator (slaved), (29, figure 1-4; 17, figure 1-5), on the instrument panel, indicates magnetic headings without oscillation, swinging, or northerly turning error. The directional indicator automatically indicates the magnetic heading of the airplane by means of a transmitter in the left wing, just inboard of the tip. This transmitter "senses" the south-north flow of the earth's magnetic flux. Electrical power for the directional indicator is provided when dc power from the primary bus and 400-cycle, three-phase ac power is available. The gyro is energized when the battery-starter switch is moved to BATTERY and is on a fast-slaving cycle for the first 3 to 4 minutes of operation. During this time it should align with the magnetic heading. The gyro then begins a slow slaving cycle. On most airplanes,* a fast slaving cycle permits faster magnetic heading recovery. The fast slaving cycle is selected through a push-button type switch.

Note

After the gyro reaches operating speed, the indicator should be checked against the stand-by compass indication to make sure that the indicator does not show a 180-degree ambiguity. The directional indicator is not operating properly if such ambiguity exists.

A knob at the lower left of the indicator permits the indicator course index to be rotated to a preselected heading. Indicator readings will be incorrect if the airplane exceeds 85 degrees of climb or dive, or banks left or right more than 85 degrees. Error in heading indication when the airplane is in an extreme bank or roll movement is an inherent characteristic of the gyro; however, it disappears when the airplane returns to straight-and-level flight. An additional error, however, will build up in the indication during turns. This is caused by centrifugal force, which tends to swing the transmitter flux valve into the vertical component of the earth's magnetic field. The amount of error is proportional to time and duration of the turn. Therefore, errors will result in the indicator during turns, banks, or rolls. The fast slaving switch may be actuated after the maneuvers are completed to correct the heading indication at the fastest possible rate.

Fast Slaving Switch.

The fast slaving cycle of the directional indicator can be selected by means of primary bus power through a

---

*F-86E-1 through F-86E-5 Airplanes and F-86E-10 and later airplanes

Section IV

T. O. 1F-86E-1

possible armament and drop tank installation

TWO 120 GAL DROP TANKS
TWO 200 GAL DROP TANKS*

SIXTEEN 5 IN. ROCKETS

TWO 1000 LB BOMBS
TWO 500 LB BOMBS
TWO 100 LB BOMBS
TWO 250 LB BOMBS
TWO CHEMICAL TANKS

TWO FRAGMENTATION CLUSTERS
500 LB EA
TWO FRAGMENTATION CLUSTERS
100 LB EA

EACH ARMAMENT INSTALLATION
INCLUDES SIX .50 CAL GUNS
WITH 300 ROUNDS PER GUN

*F-86E-15 AIRPLANES

F-86E-1-60-2

Figure 4-11

push-button type switch on the right forward console (figure 1-16) or on the instrument panel (6, figure 1-5). Momentarily depressing the switch de-energizes the slow slaving cycle. When the switch is released, the fast slaving cycle is engaged to permit faster gyro recovery to the magnetic heading of the airplane.

CAUTION

Excessive use of the fast slaving switch can damage the slaving torque motor. A minimum of 10 minutes should elapse between each successive use of the fast slaving switch.

ARMAMENT EQUIPMENT.

The basic armament installation consists of six .50-caliber machine guns mounted in the nose of the fuselage. In various external armament loadings, demolition bombs, fragmentation bombs, napalm bombs, rockets, or chemical tanks may be carried. (See figure 4-11.) To record the gunnery or rocket run, provisions are made for a camera to be installed in the nose of the airplane or on the sight head. A gun-bomb-rocket sight is provided for sighting and is coupled with a radar ranging set.

A-1CM AND A-4 GUN-BOMB-ROCKET SIGHTS.

The airplane is equipped with either of two type sights mounted above the instrument panel shroud. The A-1CM sight (figure 4-12) is installed on F-86E-1 through F-86E-10 Airplanes, and the A-4 sight (figure 4-13) is installed on F-86E-15 Airplanes. Both sights operate on the same principle and are basically similar. The A-4 sight is a redesign of the A-1CM sight. The sight reticle image varies between the two sights. On the A-1CM sight, the image is a center dot and a circle;

the A-4 sight has the same center dot, but the outer circle is composed of 10 equally spaced, diamond-shaped dots. The image is projected on the windshield armor glass or on the reflector glass aft of the windshield. The image compensates for the required lead for gun and rocket firing. Range data for gunnery operation may be supplied to the sight by the AN/APG-30 radar equipment, or it may be inserted by the pilot using the manual range control. The radar system, which has an automatic sweep range of approximately 450 to 9000 feet, automatically locks on and tracks a target and provides an indication when the lock-on has been accomplished. On overland targets at altitudes of 6000 feet or less above the terrain, radar ranging is usually erratic because of ground effects. During such conditions, radar ranging distances can be reduced by use of the radar range sweep rheostat, or manual ranging can be employed. When the sight is used as a bombsight, the sight reticle is depressed approximately 10 degrees, requiring the approach to be made so that the flight path becomes tangent to the proper bomb release point, which is indicated when the sight reticle image circle automatically goes out. At this point, bomb release may be accomplished manually or by a mechanism within the sight. (On the A-1CM sight, a flashing red light reflected on the reflector glass indicates when the bomb release circuit is energized.) Electrical power (ac and dc) to the sight is controlled by the gun safety switch. Loss of ac power will eliminate the computing features of the sight; however, each sight can be operated as a fixed-reticle sight as long as dc power is available. (Mechanically caging the sight produces a 100-mil diameter reticle.)

Sight Controls.

Gun Safety Switch. Refer to "Gunnery Equipment Controls and Indicator" in this section.

Reticle Dimmer Control. The sight reticle dimmer control (8, figure 4-12; 7, figure 4-13), to the right of the sight head, is used to regulate the intensity of sight reticle illumination from full bright to off. The dimmer control should be set at DIM when the sight is not in use to prevent damage to the reticle bulb in the event of voltage surges.

Filament Selector Switches (A-1CM Sight).* Either the primary or secondary filaments in the bulbs that illuminate the reticle image is selected by means of the two filament selector switches (11, figure 4-12), on the center pedestal. One switch controls the filaments in the reticle circle bulb; the other is for the reticle dot bulb. Both switches should normally be set at PRIM. The switches should be moved to SEC. if the primary filament in the respective bulb fails.

*F-86E-1 through F-86E-10 Airplanes
†F-86E-15 Airplanes

Filament Selector Switch (A-4 Sight).†
Selection of either the primary or secondary filaments within the lamp that illuminates the sight reticle image is controlled by the filament selector switch (19, figure 4-13) on the center pedestal. The switch should normally be set at PRIM. It should be moved to SEC. if the filament in the bulb fails.

Sight Mechanical Caging Lever. The sight is caged mechanically by means of the caging lever (7, figure 4-12; 6, figure 4-13) on the sight head. The lever is set at the UNCAGE (UNCAGED) position for normal automatic operation of the sight. For ground attacks, or if the sight fails, the lever should be moved to CAGE (CAGED) to provide a 100-mil, fixed-reticle image circle. The sight should be caged mechanically for landing and take-off.

CAUTION

Sight should be mechanically caged during taxiing, take-off, and landing, to prevent damage to the sight.

Sight Electrical Caging Button. The sight is caged electrically (by primary bus power) when the caging button (figure 1-12), on the throttle grip, is held depressed. Before an attack, the sight should be caged in this manner to stabilize the sight reticle image. Image stabilization is necessary to prevent false data from being supplied to the sight as a result of maneuvering on the initial approach to the target.

Manual Ranging Control. A twist-grip control is in the throttle (figure 1-12). This control is used to manually supply range data to the sight system during gunnery operations when radar ranging is erratic (below 6000 feet on overland targets) or inoperative. The range control covers a span of 1500 feet, from approximately 1200 feet to 2700 feet, as indicated on the sight range dial. Clockwise rotation of the twist grip decreases the range (increases reticle diameter); counterclockwise rotation increases range (decreases reticle diameter). The control is spring-loaded to the full counterclockwise position, where it must be for normal operation of radar ranging.

Wing Span Adjustment Wheel (A-1CM Sight)—Wing Span Adjustment Knob (A-4 Sight). The wing span adjustment wheel on the A-1CM sight* (3, figure 4-12) or the wing span adjustment knob on the A-4 sight† (4, figure 4-13), mounted vertically in the sight head, is used for gunnery operations only when ranging is done manually. Graduated markings (from 30 to 120) represent the wing span of the target airplane in

Section IV T. O. 1F-86E-1

A·1CM sight and center pedestal

1. Radar Range Sweep Rheostat
2. Sight Range Dial
3. Wing Span Adjustment Wheel
4. Reflector Glass
5. Radar Target Indicator Light Dimmer Control
6. Radar Target Indicator
7. Sight Mechanical Caging Lever
8. Sight Reticle Dimmer Control
9. Rudder Gust Lock
10. Rocket Setting Unit
11. Filament Selector Switches
12. Chemical Tank Selector Switch

13. Fragmentation Bomb Selector Switch
14. Console and Pedestal Light Control Rheostat*
15. Rocket Fuse (Arming) Switch
16. Rocket Jettison Switch
17. Rocket Release Selector Switch
18. Demolition Bomb Release Selector Switch
19. Demolition Bomb Single-All Selector Switch
20. Demolition Bomb Arming Switch
21. Gun Safety Switch
22. Gun Heater Switch
23. Bomb-Target Wind Control

*Some airplanes. (Refer to applicable text.)

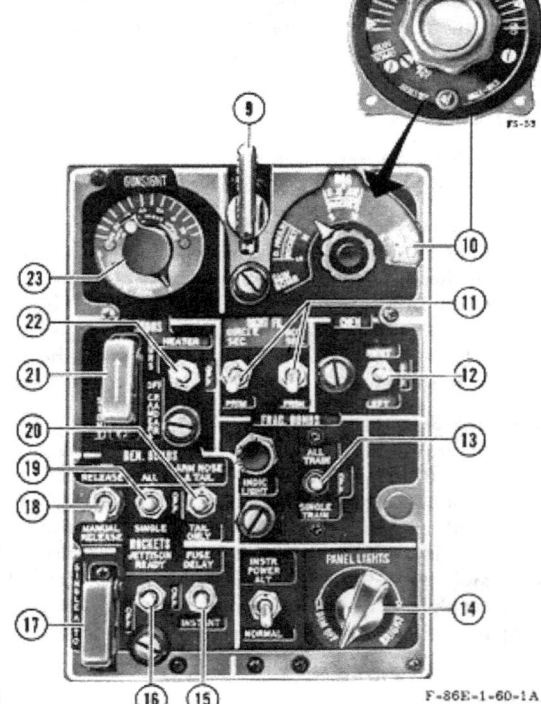

Figure 4-12

T. O. 1F-86E-1 Section IV

1. Radar Range Sweep Rheostat
2. Radar Target Indicator Light
3. Sight Range Dial
4. Wing Span Adjustment Knob
5. Reflector Glass
6. Sight Mechanical Caging Lever
7. Sight Reticle Dimmer Control
8. Bomb-Target Wind Control
9. Sight Selector Unit
10. Rudder Gust Lock
11. Gun Heater Switch
12. Gun Safety Switch
13. Rocket Release Selector Switch
14. Rocket Jettison Switch
15. Rocket Fuse (Arming) Switch

SIGHT WITHOUT CAMERA

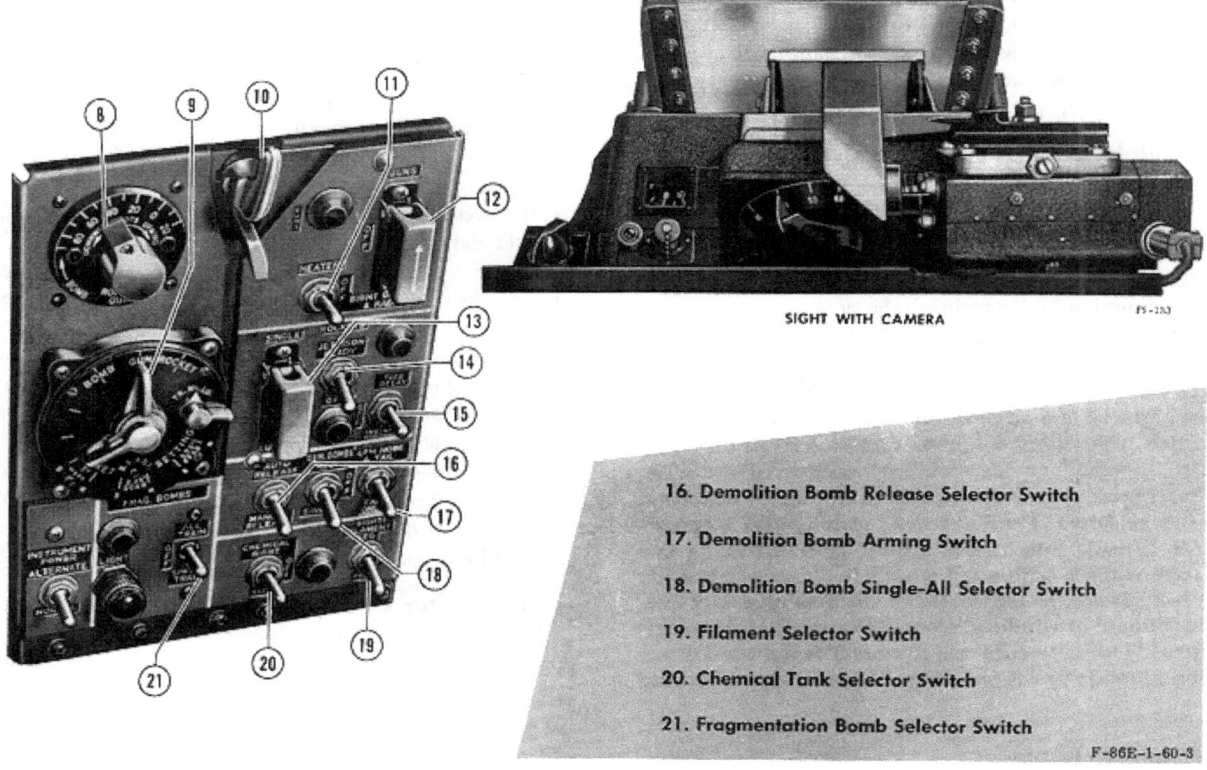

SIGHT WITH CAMERA

16. Demolition Bomb Release Selector Switch
17. Demolition Bomb Arming Switch
18. Demolition Bomb Single-All Selector Switch
19. Filament Selector Switch
20. Chemical Tank Selector Switch
21. Fragmentation Bomb Selector Switch

Figure 4-13

feet. The span adjustment wheel or knob should be rotated until the applicable target span marking (equivalent to the known or estimated span of the target) is aligned with the index mark. Positioning the wheel or knob inserts target size data into the sight, varying the reticle image circle diameter in proportion to target size. The reticle size thus formed serves as a reference dimension to aid in obtaining proper range with the manual range control.

Radar Target Selector Button. After detecting a target, the radar locks on it and measures the range. To override the radar lock-on and shift the radar to another target, it is necessary to actuate the target selector button (figure 1-20) on the control stick grip. To reject the target, the selector button should be depressed momentarily. The radar can then lock on targets at ranges greater than the one rejected, until the maximum sweep range of the radar is reached. It then automatically recycles, commencing to sweep from the minimum sweep range. On airplanes equipped with the A-4 sight,* depressing the radar target selector button automatically moves the sight function selector lever to GUN.

Radar Range Sweep Rheostat. The radar range sweep rheostat (1, figures 4-12 and 4-13), to the left of the sight head on the instrument panel shroud, controls radar ranging distances. Use of the rheostat will prevent the radar from locking on the ground or ground objects during low-altitude attacks. Rotating the rheostat toward MINIMUM decreases range distance; toward MAXIMUM increases range distance. Radar ranging distance is normal with the rheostat at MAXIMUM.

Bomb-target Wind Control. The bomb-target wind control (23, figure 4-12; 8, figure 4-13), on the center pedestal, adjusts the sight system for dive-bombing operations. Clockwise rotation of the control knob from the ROCKET GUN position depresses the sight reticle image on the A-1CM sight and prepares it for the bombing function in determining the proper approach to the target. If, during the attack, the path of the airplane is parallel to the wind or to the direction of a moving target, the bomb-target wind control is used to compensate the sight system accordingly. For attack on stationary targets, corrections for wind speed are made on either the "UPWIND" or "DOWNWIND" portion of the scale. Corrections should correspond to known or estimated wind velocity. (The "UPWIND" scale is used when attack is made into a head wind; "DOWNWIND," when attack is made with a tail wind.) If the wind direction is not parallel to the course of the attacking airplane, the amount of wind correction adjustment must be estimated. This correction approaches 0 as the wind direction becomes 90 degrees to the airplane course. During attack on moving targets, additional corrections must be made in consideration of target velocity. For approaching targets, the correction is "DOWNWIND;" for receding targets, "UPWIND." No correction is necessary when the target is moving at right angles to the path of attack. On airplanes with the A-1CM sight,† the bomb-target wind control knob must be set at the ROCKET GUN position when the sight is to be used for gun or rocket firing. (This is not necessary on the A-4 sight, because the ROCKET GUN position is not operative.)

Rocket Setting Unit (A-1CM Sight). For rocket firing on early unchanged airplanes,† the rocket setting unit (10, figure 4-12), on the center pedestal, is used to provide a depression angle correction for the type of rocket to be fired and the intended dive angle of the attack. Settings are provided for three types of rockets: 5-inch HVAR, 3.5-inch AR, and 5-inch AR. At each of the three positions, there are two detents, marked "S" and "N," for setting the intended dive angle into the sight system. For attack angles between 0 and 40 degrees, the control should be set on N (normal); for attacks between 40 and 60 degrees, the control should be set at S (steep). When the sight is used for firing guns or dropping bombs, the control should be placed at the GUN BOMB position. For rocket firing on early changed airplanes,† the rocket setting unit (10, figure 4-12) has a single control with variable sight capabilities. The rocket setting unit acts as a rocket depression angle selector for sight reticle image depression, with the scale calibrated in mils on the upper segment of the unit. There are no specific rocket settings. Movement of the control knob depresses the sight reticle image in increasing amounts through the full range of the mil scale, according to the position chosen. The nominal rocket depression setting for the 5-inch HVAR at a normal dive angle (0 to 40 degrees) is 17 mils. Through test-firing runs, the pilot should determine the settings for various dive angles most suitable to his own technique. The data obtained should be set on the mil scale variable index markers provided. The index markers, numbered from 1 through 4, are for reference only and have no function on the sight system. When turned, a slotted screw on the lower segment of the unit face unlocks the index markers for adjustment. When the sight is used for firing guns or dropping bombs, the control should be placed at the GUN BOMB position.

Sight Selector Unit (A-4 Sight). Airplanes equipped with the A-4 sight have a fixed sight selector unit. The fixed sight selector unit (9, figure 4-13), on the center pedestal, incorporates three independent sight controls: the rocket setting lever, the sight function selector lever, and the target speed switch. The rocket setting lever has the same function in the A-4 sight system as the

*F-86E-15 Airplanes
†F-86E-1 through F-86E-10 Airplanes

rocket setting unit on the A-1CM sight. The sight function selector lever, on the upper arc of the fixed unit, is set at either BOMB, GUN, or ROCKET to adjust the sight system for the desired operation. When the selector lever is moved to BOMB, the sight reticle image is depressed to approximate the bomb trajectory. Moving the selector lever to ROCKET permits subsequent operation of the rocket setting lever to adjust the sight reticle image for the type of rocket to be fired. The selector lever will automatically return to the GUN position, if set at either BOMB or ROCKET position, when the radar target selector button on the stick grip is depressed. The target speed switch, on the right side of the selector unit, is used during gunnery missions to control lead angle data in accordance with speed ratio between the attacking airplane and its target. When the speed of the attacking airplane is greater than that of the target, the target speed switch is set at LO. The switch is moved to HI when the speeds of the attacking airplane and the target are approximately the same. The TR. position is used when firing on a drogue or other training targets at low speeds.

Sight Indicators.

Radar Target Indicator Light. The radar target indicator light comes on when the radar ranging equipment has locked on the target during tracking. On airplanes equipped with the A-1CM sight,* the radar target indicator (6, figure 4-12) is on the center of the instrument panel shroud. On airplanes equipped with the A-4 sight,† the radar target indicator light (2, figure 4-13) is on the sight head just below the range dial. Both indicator lights can be dimmed. A lever on top of the light housing controls the intensity of the light on the A-1CM sight, while the A-4 indicator light is dimmed when the light housing is rotated.

Sight Range Dial. The target range, as determined by range data supplied to the sight by the radar or manual ranging, is indicated by the range dial (2, figure 4-12; 3, figure 4-13) in hundreds of feet. The dial, which is located on the left side of the sight head, indicates graduations in 100-foot intervals and covers a span of 600 to 6000 feet.

GUNNERY EQUIPMENT.

The six Type M-3 .50-caliber machine guns are arranged in a vertical bank of three in each of the two gun compartments. One compartment is on each side of the fuselage, outboard of the cockpit. Three removable ammunition containers are located below each gun

---

*F-86E-1 through F-86E-10 Airplanes
†F-86E-15 Airplanes

compartment, and containers are provided in the lower portion of the fuselage for retaining ejected cases and links. A maximum of 300 rounds of ammunition is provided for each gun. The guns must be charged on the ground before take-off, by means of the manual charger in each gun compartment. Gun stoppages cannot be cleared in the air. They must be cleared manually on the ground. The guns are normally bore sighted parallel to both the fuselage reference line and the fuselage centerline. For gun firing, the gun sight line is bore sighted down to intersect the mean gun bore at 750 yards. The bore-sighting configuration considers an airplane gross weight of 12,258 pounds (full ammunition load, half fuel, and no external load) during a 1 G flight condition. The open-type gun muzzle openings are capped with plastic plugs that are blown off without damage to the airplane when the guns are fired. A gun camera is operated automatically when guns or rockets are fired.

Gun Camera.

To record the gunnery or rocket run, a gun camera is mounted in the lower portion of the intake duct on some airplanes or on the sight head on other airplanes. When the primary-bus-powered camera is mounted on the sight head, it facilitates analysis of the pilot's aiming technique and accuracy. This camera is equipped with an erector assembly that permits mounting the camera below the pilot's line of vision, yet still maintains full camera view of the sight reticle image during gunnery or rocket operation. The nose camera, if installed, is electrically connected in parallel with the camera mounted on the sight, so that when both cameras are installed they operate together. The camera is operated automatically when the guns or rockets are fired, or it may be operated independently.

Gunnery Equipment Controls and Indicator.

Gun Safety Switch. Electrical power (ac and dc) for operation of the guns, sight, camera, and radar is controlled by the guarded, three-position gun safety switch (21, figure 4-12; 12, figure 4-13), on the center pedestal. Power is supplied to the sight, camera, and radar when the switch is at either GUNS or SIGHT CAMERA RADAR. For the gun-firing circuit to receive power, the switch must be at GUNS and the trigger must be fully depressed. When the switch guard is down, the switch is OFF, and related equipment is inoperative.

Trigger. The gun-firing and camera circuits are actuated when the trigger (figure 1-20), on the control stick, is completely depressed. The trigger has two definite positions, and it is powered by the primary bus. With the gun safety switch at GUNS, the first position closes the camera circuit and directs power to the ammunition boosters. The second, or fully depressed, position continues camera operation and fires the guns. With the

4-27

gun safety switch at SIGHT CAMERA RADAR, both positions close the camera circuit only.

Gun Heater Switch. Two Type AN-J4 electric gun heaters, one on each gun, are controlled by the gun heater switch (22, figure 4-12; 11, figure 4-13) on the center pedestal. The heater switch is powered by the primary bus, and the gun heaters operate on secondary bus power. Turning the switch to ON also turns on ammunition compartment heat by permitting heated air from the engine compressor to enter the compartment. To maintain the proper ammunition temperature range, this air is automatically controlled by thermostats.

Ammunition Compartment Heat Emergency Shut-off Control. An ammunition compartment heat emergency shutoff control (2, figures 1-6 and 1-8), on the left aft console, is provided to manually close a valve in the heating system, thereby stopping the flow of heated air to the compartment. An ammunition compartment overheat warning light will come on when temperatures in the compartment become excessive; however, since the emergency shutoff cannot be reset in flight, it should not be used until it is certain that the warning light will remain on. A momentary illumination of the warning light does not necessarily indicate system malfunction.

Ammunition Compartment Overheat Warning Light. A red overheat warning light (3, figure 1-6; 31, figure 1-8) will come on to warn the pilot if the ammunition compartment temperature exceeds 127°C (260°F). This warning light is on the left aft console. It operates on primary bus power.

Note

Momentary illumination of the ammunition compartment overheat warning light does not necessarily indicate a malfunction of the heat control system.

Firing Guns.

Radar Ranging. To fire the guns using radar ranging, proceed as follows:

Note

- Before take-off, check that all guns are charged.
- Ensure that cockpit pressure schedule is set for 2.75 psi before firing guns on F-86E-1 through F-86E-6 Airplanes, because a higher pressure will cause movement of the windshield armor glass and resultant sight line deflection.
- When firing at stationary ground targets, or in case of sight failure, move caging lever to CAGE and use sight as conventional 100-mil, fixed-reticle sight.

1. Move mechanical caging lever to CAGE (CAGED).
2. Check instrument power switch at NORMAL and inverter warning light off for early airplanes* not changed by T. O. 1F-86E-47 or T. O. 1F-86E-507. Check main radar inverter light off for late airplanes† and early airplanes* changed by T. O. 1F-86E-47 or T. O. 1F-86E-507.
3. Before using sight, place gun safety switch at SIGHT CAMERA RADAR to allow a 5- to 15-minute warm-up period (depending on outside air temperature) for sight and radar.
4. Move mechanical caging lever to UNCAGE. (UNCAGED).
5. Set sight filament selector switches (switch‡) at PRIM, or move to SEC. if primary filaments are inoperative.
6. Make sure throttle twist grip is at the full counterclockwise position (radar ranging engaged).
7. Set gun heater switch at HEATER if outside air temperature is 1.7°C (35°F) or below.
8. Set bomb-target wind control knob at ROCKET GUN; rocket-dive angle knob at GUN BOMB (A-1CM sight). Set sight function selector lever at GUN; target speed switch at TR., HI., or LO., depending on rate of closure (A-4 sight).
9. Move gun safety switch to GUNS.
10. Set wing span adjustment to wing span of target airplane, so that manual ranging can be set up in a minimum of time if radar ranging fails.
11. Adjust sight reticle dimmer control for desired reticle image brilliance.
12. Depress electrical caging button to stabilize reticle image, and begin tracking, estimating the lead.
13. After radar target indicator light comes on (at target range of approximately 1800 yards), release electrical caging button.

Note

If more than one target along the airplane flight path is within range, make sure radar is tracking the desired target. As range decreases, the reticle should grow larger to span target continuously. Check range dial indication against estimated range of target. If radar has locked on undesired target, reject it by depressing radar target selector button on stick grip.

14. Continue to track target smoothly, without slipping or skidding, for approximately one second after releasing caging button; then fire.

Manual Ranging. To fire the guns if radar ranging fails (as indicated by the radar target indicator light

---

*F-86E-1 through F-86E-6 Airplanes and F-86E-10 Airplanes AF51-2718 through -2747
†F-86E-10 Airplane AF51-2748 and all later airplanes
‡F-86E-15 Airplanes

going out or by improper range indications) or at any other time it is necessary or desirable to employ manual ranging:

1. Check wing span adjustment at correct setting.

2. Rotate throttle grip clockwise to engage manual ranging. Continue to rotate grip until reticle image circle is reduced to minimum diameter.

3. Depress electrical caging button to stabilize the reticle image and frame target within reticle circle.

4. Continue to rotate throttle grip so that reticle circle continuously frames target, and begin tracking.

5. When target is within range, release gyro caging button.

6. After releasing caging button, continue tracking target smoothly for about one second; then fire.

BOMBING EQUIPMENT.

A removable bomb rack may be attached to the lower surface of each wing outer panel. Each rack can carry single bombs of various types, ranging from 100 to 1000 pounds, bomb clusters from 100- to 500-pound sizes, or an M-10 smoke tank. The gun-bomb-rocket sight is used for bomb sighting and may be used to release the bombs automatically. Separate controls are provided for normal or emergency bomb release. During normal release, bombs may be dropped singly or simultaneously. The arming condition of the bomb fuzes is selectively controlled upon a normal release. Bomb aiming and automatic release are done with the gun-bomb-rocket sight. In case of electrical failure, most airplanes have a mechanical emergency release system, actuated by the emergency jettison handle. Bombing system controls are also used to release the drop tanks, which may be installed instead of the bomb racks.

WARNING

- Parafragmentation bombs must not be carried at any time, because of the danger of the parachutes opening in the bomb rack.

- To avoid damage to the airplane, do not release bombs weighing 500 pounds or more when using the automatic function of the gun-bomb-rocket sight, or while negative G is being applied to the airplane, because these bombs tend to strike portions of the airplane under such release conditions.

Bombing Equipment Controls.

Bomb-Rocket Release Button. Bomb and rocket release circuits are energized from the primary bus (after the applicable selector switches have been positioned for the desired release condition) when the release button (figure 1-20), on the control stick grip, is depressed. Used primarily for the normal release of bombs and rockets, the release button can also release drop tanks and chemical tanks, as well as discharge chemical tank contents, depending on selector switch positioning. If the rocket release selector switch is at SINGLE or AUTO, the gun camera will operate when the bomb-rocket release button is depressed. If necessary, all external loads can be released simultaneously by means of the bomb-rocket release button when bomb and rocket selector switches have been set accordingly.

WARNING

Before actuating the bomb-rocket release button, make sure that bomb and rocket release selector switches and the rocket jettison switch are positioned correctly for the desired release condition. Failure to check switch positioning may cause accidental bomb or rocket release.

Demolition Bomb Single-All Selector Switch. The three-position, single-all selector switch (19, figure 4-12; 18, figure 4-13), on the center pedestal and powered by the primary bus, can be positioned for single or simultaneous release of bombs (except fragmentation and 3-pound practice bombs) when the bomb-rocket release button on the control stick is depressed. With the selector switch set at the SINGLE position, the left bomb rack is tripped when the release button is depressed. A transfer circuit within the racks permits the right bomb rack to be tripped when the release button is actuated again. With the switch set at the ALL position, both bomb racks release simultaneously when the release button is depressed. The demolition bomb single-all selector switch can also be used to release the drop (or chemical) tanks.

CAUTION

Only the left drop tank can be released when the selector switch is at SINGLE, because there is no transfer circuit to the right tank. Therefore, the selector switch *must* be moved to ALL for simultaneous release of both tanks.

When fragmentation or 3-pound practice bomb racks are installed, the demolition bomb single-all selector switch should be OFF to prevent release of the entire bomb containers.

Note

The demolition bomb single-all selector switch is inoperative if the fragmentation bomb selector switch is not OFF.

Demolition Bomb Release Selector Switch. The two-position release selector switch (18, figure 4-12; 16, figure 4-13), on the center pedestal and powered by the primary bus, permits selection of either manual or automatic bomb release. When the release selector switch is set at MANUAL RELEASE, bomb release occurs when the release button is depressed (provided the demolition bomb single-all selector switch is at SINGLE or ALL). When the release selector switch is at AUTO RELEASE and the release button is held closed, the mechanism within the sight automatically accomplishes bomb release when the path of the airplane, during the bombing run, becomes tangent to a bomb trajectory. (If the demolition bomb single-all selector switch is in the SINGLE position, only one bomb will be dropped during each bomb run.) During either manual or automatic release, the correct bomb release point is indicated when the sight reticle image circle automatically goes out. When bombs are released from airplanes equipped with an A-1CM sight, a red flashing light is reflected on the windshield armor glass. The release selector must be at MANUAL RELEASE when fragmentation or 3-pound practice bomb racks are installed.

Note

The demolition bomb single-all selector switch must be at SINGLE or ALL for the demolition bomb release selector switch to be operative.

Bomb Arming Switch. The arming condition of bombs, except fragmentation and 3-pound practice bombs, is controlled by the arming switch (20, figure 4-12; 17, figure 4-13), powered by the battery bus and located on the center pedestal. The bombs are armed to explode upon impact when the arming switch is set at the ARM NOSE & TAIL position. Setting the arming switch at TAIL ONLY arms the bombs for delayed detonation. The bombs will be released unarmed if the switch is in the OFF position.

Fragmentation Bomb Selector Switch. The fragmentation bomb selector switch (13, figure 4-12; 21, figure 4-13), on the center pedestal and powered by the primary bus, is used only for release of fragmentation or 3-pound practice bombs. Placing the switch at SINGLE TRAIN results in release of fragmentation bombs in a train, from the left rack and then from the right, as long as the release button is held depressed. Placing the switch at ALL TRAIN results in release of the bombs in a train from the left and right racks simultaneously when the release button is depressed. The arming condition of fragmentation bombs cannot be controlled during a normal release, because the bombs are automatically armed upon leaving the racks. Whenever fragmentation bombs are to be released, the demolition bomb release selector switch must be at MANUAL RELEASE.

Bomb-Rocket-Tank Salvo Button. When the bomb-rocket-tank salvo button (figure 1-16), inset in the left forward console, is depressed, all external loads (including all types of bombs, rockets, and tanks) are jettisoned simultaneously from left and right racks. Regardless of the position of bomb or rocket arming switches, bombs and rockets are dropped unarmed when the salvo button is depressed. The salvo button is operable whenever battery power is available, because the salvo circuit receives power from the battery bus.

Note

Rockets cannot be salvoed when the airplane is on the ground, because the salvo circuit is broken when the weight of the airplane is on the landing gear.

Emergency Jettison Handle. Bombs, rockets, chemical tanks, or drop tanks are released simultaneously when the guarded emergency jettison handle (19, figure 1-6; 17, figure 1-8), recessed in the inboard face of the left forward console, is pulled out approximately 6 inches. If electrical release fails, the handle is used to jettison any external load mechanically, independently of the electrical release systems. When the emergency jettison handle is pulled, the bomb arming circuit is interrupted automatically and bombs are dropped unarmed, regardless of the bomb arming switch position. On F-86E-6 Airplanes, the rockets cannot be jettisoned by use of the emergency jettison handle.

Bombing Equipment Indicators.

Sight Bomb Release Indicators. When the sight controls are set for bombing, the sight will indicate bomb release. During the bombing run, the proper bomb release point (the point at which the path of the airplane becomes tangent to the bomb trajectory) is indicated when the reticle image circle automatically goes out. This indication occurs whether the bomb release system is set for automatic or manual release. Upon release of the bomb from airplanes equipped with the A-1CM sight, a red flashing bombs-away light is reflected onto the windshield armor glass from within the sight.

Fragmentation Bomb Indicator Light.

Located on the center pedestal adjacent to the fragmentation bomb selector switch, the fragmentation bomb indicator light (figures 4-12 and 4-13) is illuminated when the fragmentation bombs are installed and goes out automatically as the last fragmentation bomb is released. The indicator light receives power from the primary bus.

Releasing Bombs.

Releasing Demolition Bombs. To release demolition bombs using the Type A-1CM or A-4 sight, proceed as follows:

WARNING

To avoid damage to the airplane, do not release bombs weighing 500 pounds or more when using the automatic function of the gun sight, or while negative G is being applied to the airplane, because these bombs tend to strike portions of the airplane under such release conditions.

1. Move mechanical caging lever to CAGE (CAGED).

2. Check instrument power switch at NORMAL; inverter warning light off for early airplanes* not changed by T. O. 1F-86E-47 or T. O. 1F-86E-507; main radar inverter light off for late airplanes† and those changed by T. O. 1F-86E-47 or T. O. 1F-86E-507.

3. Gun safety switch at SIGHT CAMERA RADAR; allow 10- to 15-minute warm-up period for sight.

4. Move mechanical caging lever to UNCAGE (UNCAGED).

5. Move sight filament selector switches (switch‡) at PRIM, or move to SEC. if primary filaments are inoperative.

6. Adjust sight reticle dimmer control for desired brilliance of reticle image.

7. Set demolition bomb release selector switch at AUTO release for automatic release by means of the sight, or at MANUAL RELEASE for selective manual release.

8. Set demolition bomb single-all selector switch to ALL or SINGLE. Check fragmentation bomb selector switch OFF.

9. Set rocket-dive angle knob at GUN BOMB (A-1CM sight); sight function selector lever at BOMB (A-4 sight).

10. After sighting target and before starting approach, set bomb arming switch at ARM NOSE & TAIL or TAIL ONLY.

11. Turn bomb-target wind control knob from ROCKET GUN to known or estimated target and wind velocities.

12. Make approach to target that will give desired dive angle during bombing run.

13. Depress electrical caging button to stabilize reticle image before pushing over into dive.

14. Place reticle image dot on target.

15. After establishing dive, keep dot on target and release electrical caging button. If automatic release has been selected, depress bomb-rocket release button at this point.

16. Track smoothly, keeping dot on target.

17. On an automatic release, bomb release will occur automatically at the correct release point as indicated by disappearance of reticle circle image. If release is manual, depress bomb-rocket release button as circle image goes out. (On A-1CM sight, bomb release is indicated by a flashing red light reflected from the sight onto the windshield armor glass.)

Releasing Fragmentation Bombs. Fragmentation bombs are released as follows:

Note

The gun-bomb-rocket sight is used for dive-bombing only and therefore is not applicable for release of fragmentation or 3-pound practice bombs.

CAUTION

To prevent excessive damage to the racks, fin-stabilized fragmentation bombs must not be released above 480 knots IAS.

1. Check demolition bomb release selector switch at MANUAL RELEASE.

2. Set fragmentation bomb selector switch at SINGLE TRAIN or ALL TRAIN for type of release desired. Check fragmentation bomb indicator light on.

3. Depress bomb-rocket release button to release bombs.

Note

All bombs within the fragmentation bomb rack are released when the release button is held depressed for approximately 3½ seconds.

4. When last bomb is released, check fragmentation bomb indicator light out.

---

*F-86E-1 through F-86E-6 Airplanes and F-86E-10 Airplanes AF51-2718 through -2747
†F-86E-10 Airplane AF51-2748 and all later airplanes
‡F-86E-15 Airplanes

Section IV

Bomb Emergency Release. The bomb-rocket-tank salvo button or the emergency jettison handle is used to jettison demolition bombs unarmed. Demolition bombs can also be dropped safe simultaneously when the demolition bomb single-all selector switch is set at ALL, the bomb arming switch is positioned to OFF, and the bomb-rocket release button is pressed.

Note

Emergency or simultaneous release of drop tanks is accomplished in the same manner.

Fragmentation bombs are automatically armed as they are released from the racks, so that unarmed release of individual fragmentation bombs is impossible. However, if the fragmentation bomb rack is released with bombs installed, the bombs will be dropped in a safe condition. This unarmed release of fragmentation bombs can be accomplished in any of three ways: the bomb-rocket-tank salvo button may be depressed; the bomb-rocket-release button on the control stick grip may be depressed after the fragmentation bomb selector switch has been set at OFF and the demolition bomb single-all selector switch has been set at ALL; or the emergency jettison handle may be pulled.

ROCKET EQUIPMENT.

Eight removable, zero-rail rocket launcher assemblies may be installed to permit mounting 16 rockets. The launchers are fitted to the lower surface of the wing outer panels, four on each side. Two rockets, one mounted directly below the other, are hung from each launcher assembly. The gun-bomb-rocket sight is used for rocket aiming, and controls permit normal or emergency rocket release. During normal release conditions, rocket arming can be selectively controlled. The gun camera operates automatically when the rockets are fired. Rocket firing order is illustrated in figure 4-14.

Rocket Equipment Controls.

Bomb-Rocket Release Button. Refer to "Bombing Equipment Controls" in this section.

Rocket Release Selector Switch. The guarded, three-position rocket release selector switch (17, figure 4-12; 13, figure 4-13) is on the center pedestal. It is powered by the primary bus. When the selector is at SINGLE, one rocket is fired each time the bomb-rocket-tank release button is depressed. When the selector is at AUTO, all rockets are released in train with the release button held in the depressed position. Automatic firing stops when the button is released. The rocket release sequence is normally applicable during single or automatic release conditions. The rocket-firing circuit is inoperative when the switch is OFF.

Note

The rocket release selector switch is inoperative unless the rocket jettison switch is OFF.

Rocket Fuze (Arming) Switch. The arming condition of the rocket nose fuzes is controlled by primary bus power during normal release conditions by the battery-bus-powered rocket fuze switch (15, figures 4-12 and 4-13), on the center pedestal. With the switch set at INSTANT, the nose fuze is armed upon release to provide detonation on impact. The nose fuze is unarmed if the switch is at DELAY or OFF; however, an internal fuze will cause delayed detonation after impact following a normal release. The rockets are automatically unarmed

Figure 4-14

during jettison release and salvo release. If the rockets are jettisoned or salvoed, the internal fuze is inoperative.

Rocket Setting Unit (A-1CM Sight) and Sight Selector Controls (A-4 Sight).

Refer to "A-1CM and A-4 Gun-Bomb-Rocket Sights" in this section.

Rocket Intervalometer (Projector Release) Control Knob. Rocket-firing sequence during manual and automatic release is controlled by the rocket intervalometer control knob (8, figure 1-6; 9, figure 1-8), on the left side of the cockpit, above the left aft console. When the rocket release selector switch is set at SINGLE, one rocket is released each time the bomb-rocket release button is depressed, and the intervalometer automatically maintains the correct firing sequence for each successive release. When the selector switch is positioned at AUTO, the intervalometer causes the rockets to be fired in proper sequence at approximately 1/10-second intervals as long as the release button is held depressed. A numbered dial, visible through a window in the intervalometer housing, indicates the rocket to be fired. The dial is set at the time of rocket loading and should be at 1 when a normal load of rockets is carried. The reset knob on the intervalometer is used to select release of any particular rocket in case of misfire or other malfunction during a "single" release.

Note

If a lower rocket fails to fire during a normal release, the upper rocket on the same mount cannot be fired.

Rocket Jettison Switch. The rocket jettison switch (16, figure 4-12; 14, figure 4-13), on the center pedestal, permits all rockets to be dropped unarmed from the mounts simultaneously by means of the bomb-rocket release button. For rocket jettison release, the jettison switch is moved to JETTISON READY and the release button is depressed. The internal fuze is inoperative during a jettison release. The jettison switch, powered by the battery bus, must be OFF for the rocket release selector switch to be operative.

Note

Rockets cannot be jettisoned when the airplane is on the ground, because the jettison circuit is interrupted when the weight of the airplane is on the landing gear.

Emergency Jettison Handle. Refer to "Bombing Equipment Controls" in this section.

Bomb-Rocket-Tank Salvo Button. Refer to "Bombing Equipment Controls" in this section.

Firing Rockets.

Sight and armament controls should be set for rocket firing as follows:

1. Move mechanical caging lever to CAGE (CAGED).

2. Check instrument power switch at NORMAL; inverter warning light off for early airplanes* not changed by T. O. 1F-86E-47 or T. O. 1F-86E-507; main radar inverter light off for late airplanes† and those changed by T. O. 1F-86E-47 or T. O. 1F-86E-507.

3. Gun safety switch at SIGHT CAMERA RADAR to supply power to the sight; allow 5- to 15-minute warm-up period (depending on outside air temperature) for sight.

4. Move mechanical caging lever to UNCAGE (UNCAGED).

5. Sight filament selector switches (switch‡) at PRIM, or at SEC. if primary filaments are inoperative.

6. Before initial rocket firing, make sure projector release control dial is at position 1 to ensure proper release of all rockets carried.

7. Bomb-target wind control knob at ROCKET GUN (A1CM sight); sight function selector lever at ROCKET (A-4 sight).

8. Rocket-dive angle knob (levers‡) set for type of rocket to be fired and the intended dive angle.

9. Rocket release selector switch at SINGLE or AUTO.

10. Rocket jettison switch OFF.

11. Rocket fuze (arming) switch at INSTANT or DELAY.

12. Sight reticle dimmer control adjusted to obtain desired reticle image brilliancy.

13. Make approach to target that will give desired dive angle during firing.

14. Before pushing over into dive, press electrical caging button to stabilize reticle image.

15. Put reticle image dot on target.

16. After establishing dive, keep dot on target and release electrical caging button when range is between 700 and 1000 yards.

17. Track smoothly, without skidding or slipping, keeping dot on target for approximately 3 seconds; then depress bomb-rocket release button to fire rockets.

To prevent damage to units within rocket release circuit, do not keep bomb-rocket release button depressed more than 5 seconds when rocket release selector switch is at SINGLE.

---

*F-86E-1 through F-86E-6 Airplanes and F-86E-10 Airplanes AF51-2718 through -2747
†F-86E-10 Airplane AF51-2748 and all later airplanes
‡F-86E-15 Airplanes

Rocket Emergency Release.

> **Note**
>
> Rockets cannot be jettisoned or salvoed electrically when the weight of airplane is on the landing gear.

Rockets can be jettisoned by either of the following methods:

- Momentarily depress bomb-rocket-tank salvo button.
- Pull emergency jettison handle out approximately 6 inches.
- Position rocket jettison switch at JETTISON READY; then depress bomb-rocket release button on control stick.

CHEMICAL TANK EQUIPMENT.

A chemical tank (Type AN-M10) may be carried on each bomb rack in place of bombs. A switch on the center pedestal provides for left and right tank selection and, after discharge of chemicals (by means of the bomb-rocket release button), the tanks may be jettisoned. If the electrical system fails, and it is desired to drop the chemical tanks, the emergency jettison handle may be pulled to simultaneously release both tanks.

> **CAUTION**
>
> When discharging chemicals, the demolition bomb single-all selector switch must be OFF to prevent dropping the tanks.

Chemical Tank Selector Switch.

Located on the center pedestal, the chemical tank selector switch (12, figure 4-12; 20, figure 4-13), powered by the primary bus, controls selection of the tank whose contents are to be discharged. Moving the switch to its RIGHT or LEFT position sets up the circuit to the corresponding tank. After selection, tank contents are discharged when the bomb-rocket release button is depressed.

Bomb-Rocket Release Button.

Refer to "Bombing Equipment Controls" in this section.

Emergency Jettison Handle.

Refer to "Bombing Equipment Controls" in this section.

MISCELLANEOUS EQUIPMENT.

ANTI-G SUIT PROVISIONS.

Air pressure for the anti-G suit bladders is taken from the final stage of the engine compressor and is then routed through a pressure-regulating valve to the suit attachment fitting. The line from the regulating valve to the attachment fitting passes through the quick-disconnect fitting on the front of the seat (figures 1-29, 1-30, and 1-31), so that the line will sever automatically upon ejection. The Type M-4 pressure-regulating valve (32, figure 1-6; 34, figure 1-8), on the left aft console, regulates air pressure to the suit and permits inflation of the suit only when positive G is encountered. The valve operates automatically and begins to function at approximately 1.75 G, whether the cap has been rotated to the HI (clockwise) or LO (counterclockwise) detent. When the valve is at LO, 1 psi of air pressure is exerted in the suit for each additional 1G increase; when the valve is at HI, 1.5 psi is exerted per G increase. Depressing the button on top of the valve permits valve operation to be checked manually and also allows the suit to be inflated momentarily when desired. Use of the suit in this manner will lessen fatigue during prolonged flights.

DATA CASE.

The data case (3, figure 1-3) is located within the aft fuselage below the engine. The data case can be reached through a hinged door on the left side of the fuselage, just forward of the turbine wheel warning stripe. The door is secured by two push-button type latches.

MAP CASE.

The map case (12, figure 1-7; 10, figure 1-9) is recessed in the right aft console, directly below the right circuit-breaker panel.

CHECK LIST.

The pilot's check list, mounted horizontally below the right side of the instrument panel, can be pulled out for reference.

MOORING EQUIPMENT.

Mooring rings are furnished in the mooring and jacking kit, and equipment for anchoring the mooring eyes into the ground is included in the airplane mooring kit. On nontactical missions, the mooring kits are stowed in the left rear ammunition container. Two fuselage fittings and two wing fittings are provided for attaching the mooring eyes. Both fuselage fittings are on the lower surface of the fuselage on the airplane centerline. The forward mooring ring is screwed into the jack-pad fitting, just aft of the nose wheel door; the aft mooring

ring is screwed into a fitting forward of the tail-pipe aperture. The wing mooring rings screw into the attaching holes for the forward rocket mounts. All mooring-ring fittings are identified by markings on the adjacent skin. When the airplane is tied down for extreme weather, it should be headed into the wind, with the surface controls locked and wheel chocks installed. A ¼-inch cable or ¾-inch rope should be used for tie-down.

PROTECTIVE COVERS.

The removable covers, furnished for protecting the airplane while it is on the ground, include wing walkway covers, a cockpit canopy and intake duct cover, an air intake duct plug, a tail-pipe cover, and a pitot head cover.

CAUTION

To prevent formation of excessive moisture, intake duct plug and tail-pipe covers should not be installed until the engine has cooled.

REAR-VISION MIRROR.

An adjustable rear-vision mirror (8, figure 1-3) is suspended from the inner upper surface of the canopy, just aft of the canopy bow.

Section III T. O. 1F-86E-1

4-36

SECTION V
OPERATING LIMITATIONS

TABLE OF CONTENTS	PAGE
Instrument Markings	5-1
Engine Limitations	5-1
Airspeed Limitations	5-1
Prohibited Maneuvers	5-4

	PAGE
Acceleration Limitations	5-4
Asymmetrical Store Limitations	5-4
Center-of-gravity Limitations	5-6
Weight Limitations	5-6

INSTRUMENT MARKINGS.

Careful attention must be given to the instrument markings (figure 5-1), as the limitations shown on these instruments and noted in the captions are not necessarily repeated in the text of this or any other section.

ENGINE LIMITATIONS.

All normal engine limitations are shown in figure 5-1.

ENGINE OVERSPEED.

Maximum permissible rpm is 104%. Should this figure be exceeded under any condition, a notation must be made on DD Form 781 and the engine must be removed for overhaul.

ENGINE OVERTEMPERATURE.

The following conditions constitute overtemperature operation.

- During engine starts up to idle rpm (within 2 minutes):

  950°C or above for 2 seconds or more

- All engine operation except starting:
  690°C to 750°C for 40 seconds or more
  750°C to 800°C for 10 seconds or more
  Above 800°C for 2 seconds or more

The temperature and duration of all overtemperature operation should be entered on DD Form 781.

AIRSPEED LIMITATIONS.

LANDING GEAR AND WING FLAP LOWERING SPEEDS.

The maximum airspeed for landing gear extended or wing flaps down is marked on the airspeed indicator by a yellow radial line. (See figure 5-1.) If the gear or flaps are down at greater speeds, damage to the operating mechanism or fairings is likely to result.

LANDING LIGHT EXTENSION SPEED.

Since the landing lights are not designed to withstand air loads encountered above final approach speed, they must not be extended at speeds above 185 knots IAS.

Section V   T. O. 1F-86E-1

AIRSPEED INDICATOR

▬▬ Clean: 600 knots IAS or airspeed where wing roll becomes excessive.

▬ ▬ With NAA Type I and III 120-gallon drop tanks (15,000 feet and below): Mach .9 or 555 knots IAS, whichever is less. Avoid buffet regions if encountered.*

With NAA Type I and III 200-gallon drop tanks (15,000 feet and below): Mach .95 or 555 knots IAS, whichever is less. Avoid buffet regions if encountered.

With NAA Type I and III 120-gallon drop tanks and all types of 200-gallon drop tanks (above 15,000 feet): Same as clean airplane.*

▬ Maximum airspeed for landing gear extended or wing flaps down (185 knots IAS).

instrument

EXHAUST TEMPERATURE GAGE

▬ 200°C   Minimum
▬ 200°C to 655°C   Continuous
▬ 690°C   Maximum (Take-off and Military Power, 30 min max)
▬ 950°C†   Max during start up to idle rpm within 2 minutes

FUEL PRESSURE GAGE

▬ 40 psi   Minimum
▬ 40-400 psi   Continuous
▬ 600 psi   Maximum

TACHOMETER

▬ 78% rpm   Minimum cruise
▬ 78% - 93% rpm   Continuous
▬ 93% rpm   Max Continuous (Operation above this point limited to 30 minutes max)
▬ 100% rpm   Take-off and Military Power (30 minutes max)

(Fuel pressure gage with expanded scale)

F-86E-1-51-1A

Figure 5-1

ACCELEROMETER

F-86E-15 AIRPLANES CHANGED BY T. O. 1F-86-511

- ▬ 7 G maximum
- ▬ 5 G maximum with 200-gallon drop tanks‡
- ▬ ▬ -2 G maximum negative with external load
- ▬ ▬ -3 G maximum negative
- ▬ NOTE: On F-86E-15 Airplanes not changed by T. O. 1F-86-511, maximum is 5 G.

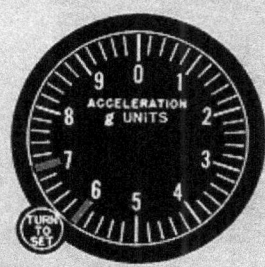

F-86E-1 THROUGH F-86E-10 AIRPLANES CHANGED BY T. O. 1F-86-511

- ▬ 7 G maximum (sea level to 15,000 ft)
- ▬ 6 G maximum (above 15,000 ft)
- ▬ 6 G maximum with external load (all altitudes)

NOTE: On F-86E-1 through F-86E-10 airplanes not changed by T.O. 1F-86-511, maximum is 5 G.

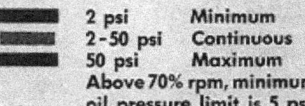

markings
based on all fuel grades

HYDRAULIC PRESSURE GAGE

	UTILITY HYDRAULIC AND FLIGHT CONTROL NORMAL HYDRAULIC SYSTEMS	FLIGHT CONTROL ALTERNATE HYDRAULIC SYSTEM
▬ 650-2700 psi	Malfunction within system—unit operation sluggish	Normal only if system is engaged and controls are operating
▬ 2700-3000 psi	Normal	Normal when controls are not in use
▬ 3400 psi	Maximum	
▬ 650-2550 psi	Malfunction within system—unit operation sluggish	Normal only if system is engaged and controls are operating
▬ 3200-4000 psi	Engine-driven pump compensator failure	Normal only if emergency override handle is pulled
▬ 2550-3200 psi	Normal—when systems are in operation §	Normal when controls are not in use
▬ 3200 psi	Maximum	Maximum when NOT using emergency override handle for alternate system operation

F-86E-1, THROUGH F-86E-6 AIRPLANES

F-86E-10 AND LATER AIRPLANES

OIL PRESSURE GAGE

- ▬ 2 psi Minimum
- ▬ 2-50 psi Continuous
- ▬ 50 psi Maximum

Above 70% rpm, minimum oil pressure limit is 5 psi

*For airspeed limitations with Type II and IV 120-gallon drop tanks installed, refer to ACCELERATION LIMITATIONS in this section.
†Refer to "Starting Engine" in section II.
‡For G-limits with other external loads, refer to ACCELERATION LIMITATIONS in this section.
§For static (no-flow) conditions, gage pressure should indicate 2900 to 3200 psi.

Section V

CANOPY OPERATING SPEED.

Limit airspeed for opening the canopy is 215 knots IAS. At speeds in excess of this value, air loads tend to hold the canopy in the closed position.

MAXIMUM ALLOWABLE AIRSPEEDS.

Maximum allowable indicated airspeeds or Mach numbers are shown in figures 5-1 and 5-2. High-speed flight, when external loads are carried, may be further restricted by general airplane buffet. This buffet may be experienced in the higher speed ranges and will, consequently, impose an airspeed limit. When no external loads are carried, high-speed flight in the transonic region is limited only by airplane rolling tendencies. Above 15,000 feet, wing heaviness in the high-speed range will still be evident but can be checked more readily. Airspeed limitations of the airplane with no external load at these higher altitudes are set only by the controllability of the wing heaviness and general flight characteristics. However, Mach number limits for flight with external loads must still be observed.

DROP TANK RELEASE SPEEDS.

The limit airspeeds for drop tank release are shown in figure 5-5.

PROHIBITED MANEUVERS.

The airplane is restricted from performing the following maneuvers:

1. Snap rolls or any snap maneuver.
2. All aerobatics when bombs or rockets are installed.
3. Spins with bombs, rockets, or 200-gallon drop tanks installed.

Note

Inverted flight, or any maneuver resulting in negative acceleration, must be limited to 10 seconds duration, as there is no means of ensuring a continuous flow of fuel while in this attitude.

4. Continuous rolls when certain external loads are carried. (See figure 5-2.)

ACCELERATION LIMITATIONS.

AIRPLANE.

The G-limitations of the airplane in all configurations are given in figure 5-2. The operating flight limits for the airplane with no external load are graphically shown in figures 5-3 and 5-4. The limit load factors presented are for straight pull-outs. Since rolling pull-outs impose considerably more stress on the airplane, the maximum allowable positive load factor during these maneuvers is correspondingly reduced to two-thirds the values shown. The maximum negative load factor during rolling pull-outs is —1 G.

CAUTION

If the accelerometer indicates over 7.0 G during flight, you should have the airplane inspected, after landing, for signs of structural damage.

ENGINE.

If the airplane has been subjected to a load factor in excess of 10 G, the engine must be removed and a special inspection must be performed.

ASYMMETRICAL STORE LIMITATIONS.

Under normal conditions, take-offs with asymmetrical stores should not be attempted. If the tactical situation requires take-off or flight with asymmetrical stores, the following limitations should be observed.

Take-off and landing: 150 knots IAS.

Level flight: None

Diving flight: Unlimited above 15,000 feet; Mach .92 or 555 knots IAS, whichever is less, below 15,000 feet altitude

Note

Any airspeed limitations for asymmetrical configurations, which are lower than those shown above, should also prevail for asymmetrical stores.

airspeed and acceleration limitations

NOTE
Positive g-limits for rolling pull-outs are two thirds of limits shown. Negative G-limit for rolling push-downs is —1.0 G.

CONFIGURATION	AIRSPEED LIMITATIONS	G-LIMITATIONS MAX POS	MAX NEG
 NO EXTERNAL LOAD	600 knots IAS or airspeed where wing roll is excessive.	7.0 (6.0 above 15,000 feet*)	-3.0
 TWO 120 GAL DROP TANKS	**TYPE I AND III TANKS** Above 15,000 feet—Unlimited except by wing roll. Below 15,000 feet—Mach .9 or 555 knots IAS, whichever is less. Avoid buffet regions.	6.0* 5.5	-2.0
	TYPE II AND IV TANKS 500 knots IAS or Mach .9, whichever is less. No abrupt maneuvers, no continuous rolls, rate of roll limited to 90 degrees per second.	4.0	-2.0
 TWO I OR III 200 GAL DROP TANKS (F-86E-15 AIRPLANES ONLY)	Above 15,000 feet—Unlimited except by wing roll. Below 15,000 feet—Mach .95 or 555 knots IAS, whichever is less. Avoid buffet regions. NO CONTINUOUS ROLLS	5.0	-2.0
 SIXTEEN 5 IN. HVAR	Maximum attainable. Avoid buffet regions. NO CONTINUOUS ROLLS	6.0	-2.0
 TWO 500 LB GP BOMBS OR TWO 500 LB FRAGMENTATION CLUSTERS	Mach .7. Avoid buffet regions. NO CONTINUOUS ROLLS	6.0*	-2.0
	500 LB GP BOMBS WITH T-127 (M-128) FIN Above 15,000 feet—Mach .9. Below 15,000 feet—Mach .85 or 500 knots IAS. NO CONTINUOUS ROLLS	5.5	
 TWO 1000 LB GP BOMBS	Mach .85. Avoid buffet regions. NO CONTINUOUS ROLLS	6.0* 5.5	-2.0
 TWO 250 LB GP BOMBS OR TWO 100 LB FRAGMENTATION CLUSTERS	Above 15,000 feet—Unlimited except by wing roll. Below 15,000 feet—Mach .9 or 555 knots IAS, whichever is less. Avoid buffet regions.	6.0	-2.0

NOTE
Positive G-limits for airplanes not changed by T. O. 1F-86-511 are 5 G for straight pull-outs and 3.3 G for rolling pull-outs. Any positive G-limit listed above which is already lower will prevail.

*F-86E-1 through F-86E-10 Airplanes

F-86E-1-93-4C

Figure 5-2

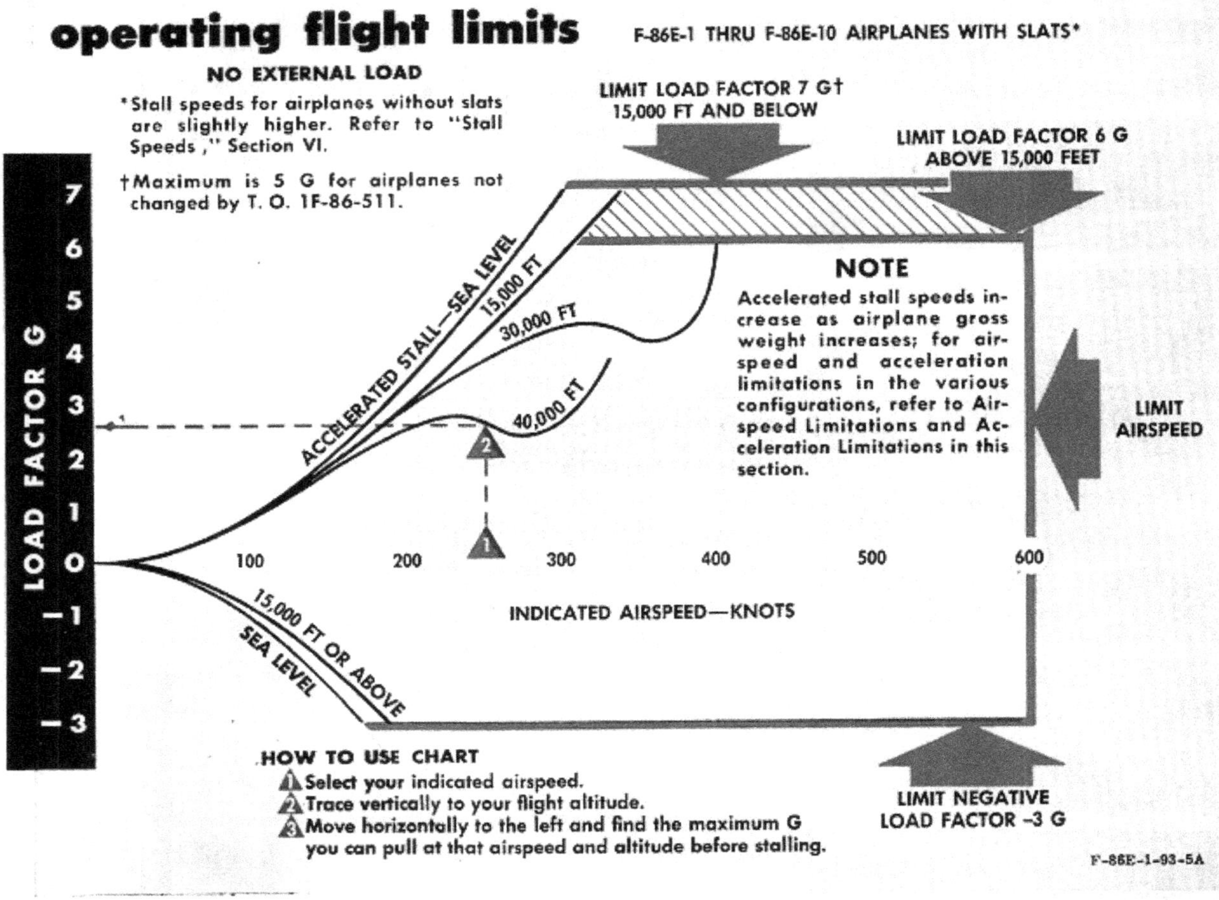
operating flight limits
F-86E-1 THRU F-86E-10 AIRPLANES WITH SLATS*
NO EXTERNAL LOAD
*Stall speeds for airplanes without slats are slightly higher. Refer to "Stall Speeds," Section VI.
†Maximum is 5 G for airplanes not changed by T. O. 1F-86-511.
LIMIT LOAD FACTOR 7 G†
15,000 FT AND BELOW
LIMIT LOAD FACTOR 6 G
ABOVE 15,000 FEET
LOAD FACTOR G
7
6
5
4
3
2
1
0
-1
-2
-3
ACCELERATED STALL—SEA LEVEL
15,000 FT
30,000 FT
40,000 FT
NOTE
Accelerated stall speeds increase as airplane gross weight increases; for airspeed and acceleration limitations in the various configurations, refer to Airspeed Limitations and Acceleration Limitations in this section.
LIMIT AIRSPEED
100
200
300
400
500
600
INDICATED AIRSPEED—KNOTS
15,000 FT OR ABOVE
SEA LEVEL
HOW TO USE CHART
1 Select your indicated airspeed.
2 Trace vertically to your flight altitude.
3 Move horizontally to the left and find the maximum G you can pull at that airspeed and altitude before stalling.
LIMIT NEGATIVE
LOAD FACTOR -3 G
F-86E-1-93-5A

Figure 5-3

CENTER-OF-GRAVITY LIMITATIONS.

Since there is no in-flight control of CG position other than the normal expenditure of ammunition and release of external loads, major factors affecting CG position must be checked before flight, for example, the installation of guns and ammunition. If any guns and/or ammunition are removed from the airplane, the ammunition boxes must be ballasted with an equivalent weight to maintain the CG within limits. Refer to Handbook of Weight and Balance Data T. O. 1-1B-40.

WEIGHT LIMITATIONS.

The design of the airplane precludes the possibility of overloading. Consequently, there are no weight limitations to be observed, provided standard drop tanks and external armament as described in Section IV are carried.

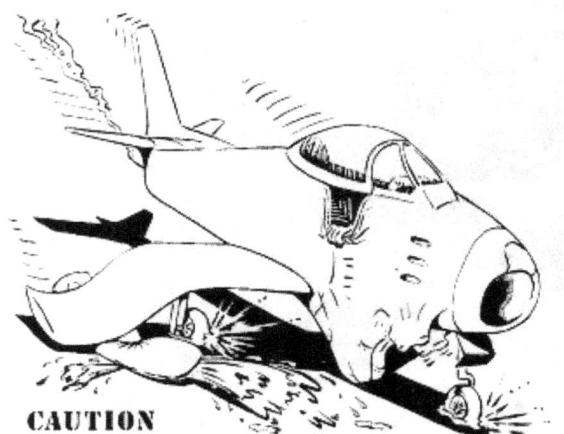

CAUTION

If a hard landing is made while external loads are carried, the airplane should be inspected prior to the next flight for signs of structural damage.

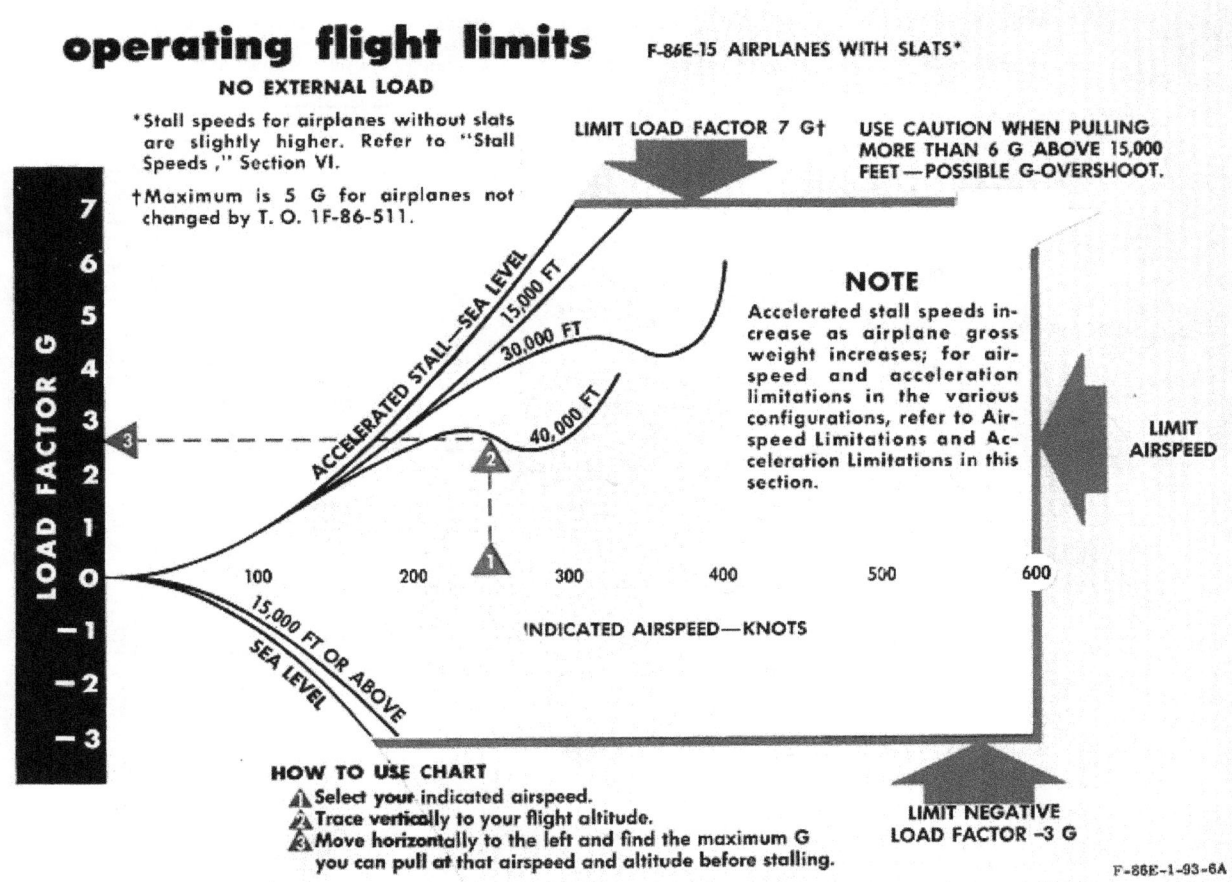

Figure 5-4

Section V
T. O. 1F-86E-1

drop tank release limits

NOTE: For asymmetrical release limits, refer to "Asymmetrical Stores Limitations" in this section.

DROP TANKS	RELEASE LIMITS	
	ORIGINAL FIN	STUKA FIN (Fin with end plates)
TYPES I, II, III, OR IV 200-GALLON (F-86E-15 Airplanes only)	Full tanks.............Drop at any speed in symmetrical (no-roll) flight at 1.0 G. Empty or partially full tanks.............Not recommended for drop; however, in emergency, drop as near cruising speed as practicable.	Full tanks.............Drop at any speed in symmetrical (no-roll) flight at 1.0 G. Empty or partially full tanks.............Drop at any speed above 220 knots IAS in symmetrical (no-roll) flight at 1.0 G.
TYPES I, II, III, OR IV 120-GALLON	Full tanks...Drop at any speed in symmetrical (no-roll) flight at 1.0 G. Empty or partially full tanks........................Drop at any speed above 220 knots IAS in symmetrical (no-roll) flight at 1.0 G.	

F-86E-1-93-40

Figure 5-5

5-8

FLIGHT CHARACTERISTICS

TABLE OF CONTENTS

	PAGE
Mach Number	6-1
Stalls	6-2
Spins	6-4
Flight Control Effectiveness	6-6
Level-flight Characteristics	6-8
Maneuvering Flight	6-9
Dives	6-13
Flight With External Loads	6-16

INTRODUCTION.

The airplane represents an advanced version of its predecessor, retaining many of the same flight characteristics throughout its speed and altitude range. However, because of the adoption of a full-power hydraulic flight control system and the use of the horizontal tail as the primary longitudinal control, handling qualities have been noticeably improved, particularly at high Mach numbers. Use of this type system also provides a more consistent and comfortable stick force level over the entire speed range. Two completely independent hydraulic flight control systems are provided as a safety feature in case of combat damage to one of the systems. Some airplanes have wing slats which reduce stalling speeds and improve lateral control at or near a stall. Modified airplanes have wing extended leading edges (non-slatted) to improve performance and maneuverability, especially at low altitude, but at some sacrifice to the low-speed advantages of the slat configuration. It is important to know that airplanes without slats have higher stalling speeds under certain conditions (principally on take-off and landing).

MACH NUMBER.

For easier association, the speeds in this section are given in terms of Mach number rather than indicated airspeed. In order to relate a flight characteristic to an indicated airspeed, it would be necessary for you to know the different airspeed for every altitude at which that characteristic occurred. However, if a flight characteristic is related to Mach number, you will notice that this flight characteristic occurs at the same Mach number at any altitude and varies only in intensity, depending upon the altitude at which you are flying. The lower the altitude, the higher the indicated airspeed will be for a given Mach number. This higher indicated airspeed is a result of the greater pressure forces that air exerts at lower altitudes. Consequently, you will notice that, although a specific handling quality occurs at the same Mach number at all altitudes, the effect on the airplane and on control is more pronounced, and possibly even dangerous, at low altitudes. In addition to being very useful in high-speed and maneuvering flight, the Machmeter provides an excellent means of obtaining maximum range. Maximum

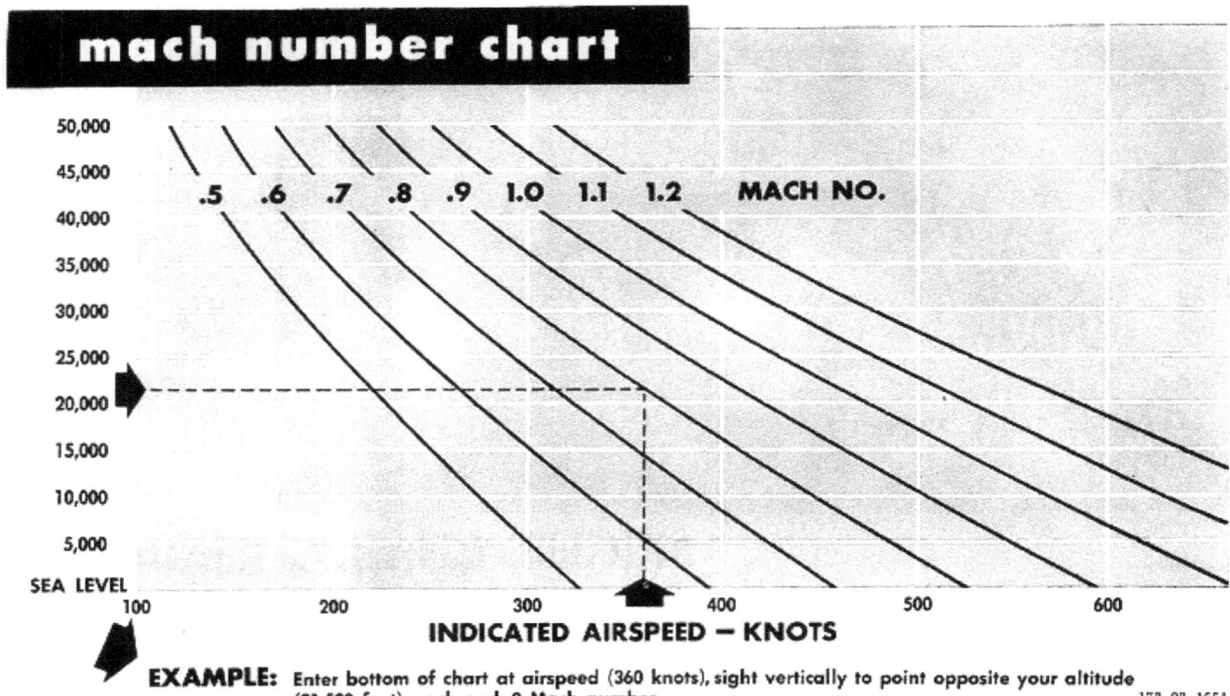

Figure 6-1

range is obtained by flying at high altitude and holding a constant Mach number and constant throttle setting. (Exact power setting and Mach number depend upon airplane gross weight at the start of cruising flight. Refer to maximum range summary chart, figure A-14.) Constant Mach number cruising is economical, because, as fuel is consumed and gross weight is reduced, you will climb slightly as long as you fly at the same Mach number and throttle setting. This means that at a constant Mach number, the airplane will automatically seek the optimum cruising altitude for the particular gross weight, and maximum range will result. To obtain maximum range using the airspeed indicator, you would have to know a different airspeed for every slight change in gross weight. Since the airplane is designed specifically for high-speed, high-altitude operation, you should be very familiar with the Machmeter and know how to use it in order to obtain maximum performance from the airplane. A Mach number chart (figure 6-1) illustrates the variation of indicated airspeed with altitude for given Mach numbers.

STALLS.

Stall characteristics of the airplane are typical for a fighter-type airplane. The swept wing has no unusual effect on the stall other than the higher angle of attack at the stalling point. There is no severe rolling or yawing tendency, and positive aileron control is obtainable up to the stall and during recovery. All stalls are preceded by rudder and general airplane buffet, which begin well in advance of the actual stall. The wing slats become fully open 20 to 25 knots above the stall. On airplanes without slats, the stall characteristics are definitely inferior to those of airplanes with slats because of an abrupt yaw and roll occurring at the stall point. However, general buffet warning is encountered before the actual stall. Landing pattern speeds shown in figure 2-6 should be strictly followed during approach and landing. See figure 6-2 for stall speeds in various configurations.

UNACCELERATED STALLS.

Unaccelerated stalls (stalls at 1 G) *with gear and flaps down* are preceded by a light, general airplane buffet about 10 knots above the stall and a rudder buffet of medium intensity just before the stall. Without power, the stall point will be evidenced by a slight pitching motion, and the nose will drop straight through without appreciable roll. In the power-on stall, there will

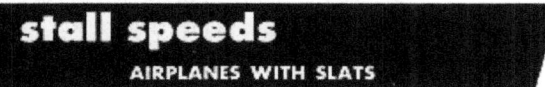

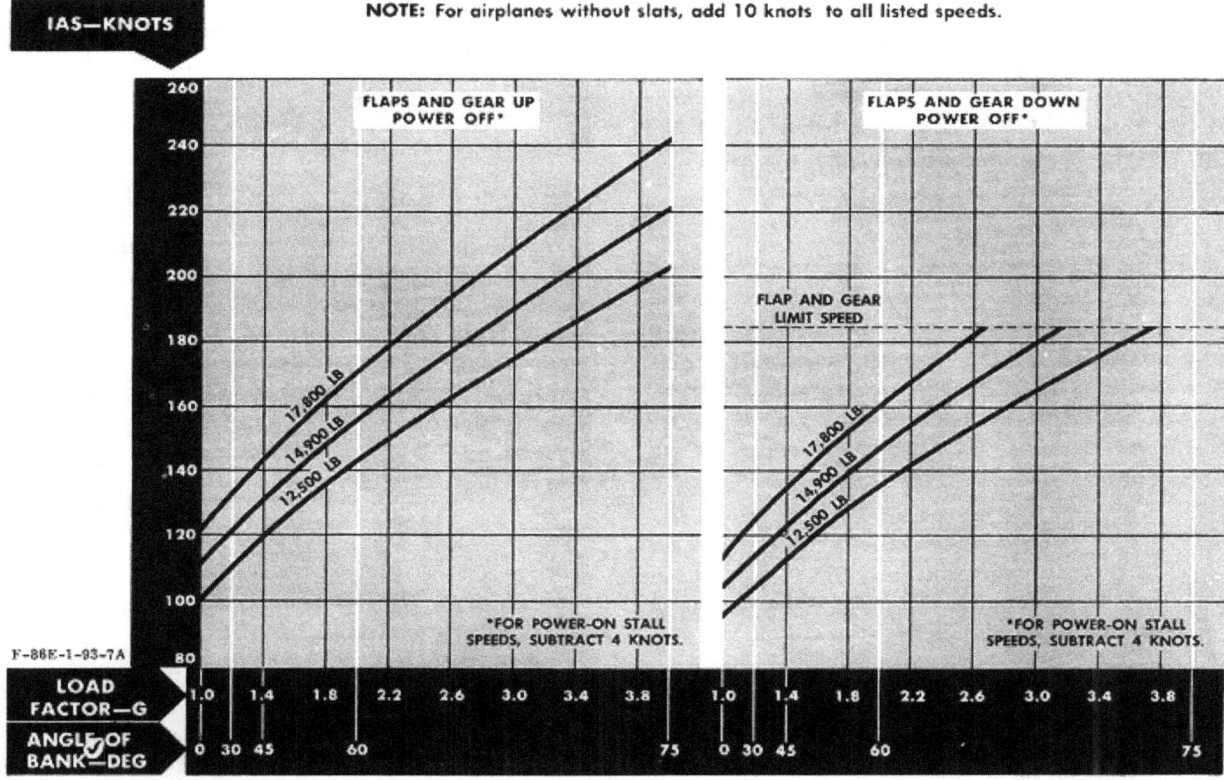

Figure 6-2

be a mild roll as the nose drops. Unaccelerated stalls *with gear and flaps up* (with or without power) are preceded by a light rudder and airplane buffet about 10 to 20 knots above the stall. The buffeting becomes heavy just before the stall. The stall itself is characterized by a slight pitching, with the nose dropping as the airplane rolls about 10 degrees at the stall point. On airplanes without slats, all unaccelerated stalls are preceded by a buffet warning that begins about 20 to 30 knots above the stall. The stall is characterized by an abrupt yaw and roll and is accompanied by an increase in general airplane buffet. At the same gross weight, stall speeds during power-on stalls (with gear and flaps up or down) will be slightly lower than stall speeds during power-off stalls. This is caused by additional lift derived from engine thrust at high angles of attack. If the airplane is trimmed into a stall longitudinally, the push forces required during recovery will be rather high but not uncomfortable.

ACCELERATED STALLS.

An accelerated stall (sometimes referred to as a "high-speed stall") is primarily a stall that occurs while pulling more than 1 G. It is the result of pulling into a tight turn and rapidly increasing G through the buffet region to the stall point. On airplanes without slats, buffet begins at a higher G than on airplanes with slats. Be alert for the buffet warning that precedes the stall.

Low-speed Accelerated Stalls.

Low-speed accelerated stalls, with the airplane in any configuration, are always preceded by a heavy rudder buffet and a medium-to-heavy airplane buffet. This buffeting gives you adequate warning to avoid the stall by reducing back pressure or using push force on the stick, if necessary. The nose will drop out of the turn during the stall.

High-speed Accelerated Stalls.

A high-speed stall is preceded by a distinct warning. As the stall is approached, you will notice considerable airplane buffet.

WARNING

A high-speed accelerated stall below 25,000 feet can damage the airplane, or it can cause you to black out and possibly lose control of the airplane.

Whenever you are pulling G, be alert for any signs of general airplane buffet; be prepared to relax stick back-pressure and, if necessary, apply forward stick pressure to avoid the stall. It is also advantageous to apply power, if available, to avoid the approaching stall. However, it is permissible to fly in the buffet region if you do not exceed the limit load factor. Although use of the horizontal tail as the primary control provides more positive control than can be obtained by use of the conventional elevator control, caution should still be used. To prevent inadvertent high-speed stalls, do not pull stick back abruptly, especially while the speed brakes are opening; also do not trim out all feel during pull-ups.

STALL RECOVERY.

Stall recovery is made in the normal manner by applying forward stick and increasing power. If the gear or flaps are down, you must be careful to avoid exceeding the maximum gear- and flaps-down airspeed during the recovery.

PRACTICE STALLS.

The normal altitude loss during stall and recovery is 1000 feet. However, because of the ever-present possibility of entering a spin during these maneuvers, stalls should be practiced at a minimum altitude of 25,000 feet.

SPINS.

NORMAL SPINS.

Spin characteristics of the airplane are normal. The airplane has been spin-tested both with and without drop tanks, with flaps and gear up and down, with speed brakes open and closed, power on and power off, and in and out of accelerated stalls from low speeds to Mach .9. It has also been spin-tested inverted in all configurations. With proper recovery technique and enough altitude, recovery has been made from every type spin condition encountered. Entry into a spin is either intentional, as practiced during training, or inadvertent. Either may result from a stalled condition obtainable throughout the entire speed range of the airplane. The latter-type spin entry is difficult to define because of the numerous conditions from which a spin can develop. The suddenness of the spin entry can cause an inexperienced pilot to become confused and unaware of what is happening, and may result in control movement that will aggravate the spin. Since a spin is the result of a stalled condition, it is essential that you have a thorough knowledge of the stalling speed at any weight and configuration, as well as the added effects of angle of bank and G-load. Once the spin has developed, the rotational speed is characterized by periodic increases similar to those obtained in a snap roll, which might further confuse the pilot, especially after recovery is started.

WARNING

Practice spins should always be started at more than 30,000 feet above the terrain.

A spin recovery can be made by neutralizing the controls, although it may take an extra turn to recover in this manner. As the airplane enters a spin, the nose drops down through the horizon to a nearly vertical attitude, reaching a dive angle of 50 to 75 degrees about halfway through the first turn of the spin. During the first half of this turn, the airplane begins its spin rotation gradually, but as the nose drops steeply, the rotation rate increases to a point where the pilot senses the airplane suddenly whipping down to almost a vertical attitude. As the first turn of the spin nears completion, the rate of rotation decreases almost as suddenly as it began. As the second half of the turn progresses, the nose pitches up and the spin rotation slows to a point where it appears to stop. At this point, the nose will come up almost to the horizon with the wings level, and the first turn of the spin is complete. On the average, 8 seconds will be required to complete the first turn, with a loss in altitude of 500 to 600 feet. As the airplane rolls into the second turn of the spin, it follows the same pattern of an increasing rate of rotation during the pitch-down and a slowing rotation rate during the pitch-up to the horizon as the second turn is completed. However, the second and any subsequent turns are characterized by the airplane pitching down steeper to the 80- to 90-degree dive angle at the half-turn point and by a smaller amount of pitch-up of the nose toward the horizon as each turn is completed. By the completion of the third or fourth turn, the nose only comes up to within 50 to 60 degrees of the horizon, in contrast to the return of within 10 to 15 degrees during the first turn. Each turn of the spin is completed about one second quicker than the preceding turn, until a minimum of about 3 seconds is reached. The rate of altitude loss increases as the spin progresses, with the second turn requiring 1000 feet on the average, the third turn 1500 feet. Each subsequent turn normally will not exceed a 2000-foot loss in altitude. The airplane spins faster to the right than to the left, but right-hand spins require less altitude to complete. In addition to the greater altitude loss in left-hand spins, the airplane has a tendency to pitch down steeper while rotating in this direction. Use of ailerons during spin recovery is not recommended. Ailerons against the spin increases buffet and slightly increases the pitch-down angles. The outstanding characteristic of using ailerons against the spin is that it slows recovery time by doubling the ordinary 3 seconds required to stop rotation. Use of ailerons with the spin does not delay recovery, but it may cause the airplane to spin slightly faster, with some increase in altitude loss. Speed brakes have no noticeable effect upon spin characteristics. Therefore, if the speed brakes are open when a spin is entered, complete the recovery with them open, if desired, being sure to hold forward stick to allow airspeed to build up above stall speed to about 135 knots IAS (gear and flaps up). Spinning with power on (from a 2 G turn with 80% rpm) is characterized by lesser pitch-down angles and by a 45-degree nose-down attitude after spin rotation has stopped, in contrast to 90-degree dive during power-off recovery. However, the advantage of having a much shallower angle with power on to complete recovery is offset by the fact that speed increases so rapidly that just as much or more altitude is lost in comparison to the 90-degree, power-off recovery completion. If you inadvertently spin with landing gear and flaps down, the airspeed during recovery will exceed placard limits. Retract the landing gear and wing flaps immediately on entering a spin, to avoid structural damage. Spins in the landing configuration are characterized by slightly less altitude loss during the first turn. Spin entry from an accelerated turn with drop tanks installed is different from that with the airplane in the clean configuration. With drop tanks installed, the airplane momentarily rolls into a spin in the direction opposite to the original turn. The airplane spins one or two turns in this direction and then sharply reverses itself and spins in the original direction (direction of accelerated turn). Recovery is made, as during a normal spin, by applying full opposite rudder followed immediately by neutralizing the stick. The only difference between spins with or without drop tanks installed is the initial spin entry, the first one or two turns with drop tanks installed being opposite to the original accelerated turn direction.

If a spin is inadvertently entered when drop tanks are installed, use normal recovery procedure. If the spin does not stop within 1½ turns, jettison drop tanks and repeat normal recovery procedure.

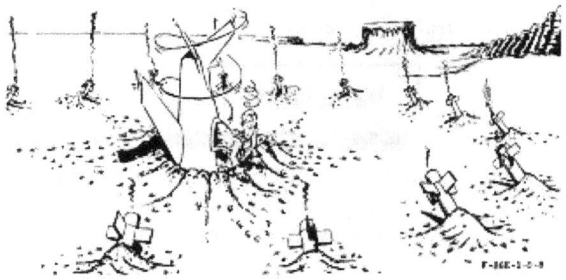

Spins with bombs, rockets, or 200-gallon drop tanks installed are prohibited.

NONOSCILLATORY SPINS.

You may encounter a different kind of spin, a nonoscillatory type, in which the normal rise and fall of the nose of the airplane through each turn does not occur. Instead, the airplane will spin rapidly with a steady pitch angle. The nonoscillatory spin can be encountered on airplanes with slats, and is caused when the outboard or inboard ends of the slats stick closed while the other ends rack open. These spins usually require more turns for recovery after recovery controls are applied.

INVERTED SPINS.

Inverted spins may occur if the airplane stalls during aerobatic maneuvers. The inverted spin is characterized by a roll upright into a 45-degree dive attitude approximately every three-fourths of a turn, followed by a roll into the inverted-spin position, repeating the initial spin. The turning times are similar to the normal spin.

You can start recovery at any time by neutralizing the controls and dropping the nose as the airplane rolls upright.

Flame-outs could occur during an inverted spin, because of interrupted flow of fuel to the engine while the airplane is in the inverted position.

SPIN RECOVERY.

Normal and rapid spin recovery is characteristic of the airplane. Spin recovery technique for the airplane is similar to that for conventional airplanes. To recover from a spin, regardless of the configuration, proceed as follows:

1. Retard throttle to IDLE upon spin entry, to prevent excessive loss of altitude.

2. Apply full opposite rudder and follow immediately by neutralizing the stick.

WARNING

- Do not hold the stick *back* during recovery, because this may cause a spin in the opposite direction when the turn has stopped.
- Hold ailerons neutral during all spin recoveries, since recovery may be prolonged by improper use of ailerons.

3. If the spin is nonoscillatory (as indicated by failure of the nose of the airplane to rise and fall through each turn), maintain standard recovery control for a minimum of three turns, if necessary, and make sure that the ailerons are neutral and that you have neutral or slightly forward stick by orienting the stick to the cockpit visually. Do not depend on stick force for this orientation. If the airplane still does not respond properly, continue to hold recovery controls and apply power.

4. After spin is stopped, neutralize rudder and regain flying speed before opening speed brakes or starting pull-out.

Failure to hold nose down to regain flying speed before opening speed brakes or before beginning pull-out may cause the airplane to stall and snap into another spin. However, full-forward stick is not recommended, because of recovery attitude.

Spin recovery is completed within about one-half turn after recovery control is started. *As recovery control is applied, the spin speeds up momentarily just before the airplane stops rotating. Therefore, do not be misled into thinking your recovery technique is ineffective.*

Note

If altitude permits, you can recover from a normal or inverted spin merely by releasing the controls. Spin rotation should cease within three turns.

WARNING

- If the airplane snaps out of a turn at any speed, enters a spin from a low-speed straight-ahead stall, or enters any form of spinning-type maneuver, apply opposite rudder and simultaneously move the stick abruptly forward to effect immediate recovery.
- Do not trim into a turn, since the stick may not return to neutral if the controls are released for recovery from a spin so entered.

Minimum Altitude For Spin Recovery.

Flight test data indicates that 7000 feet is the terrain clearance required to complete a recovery from normal and inverted spins. To recover from a one-turn spin (plus a one-turn recovery and a 4 G pull-out), the altitude loss will be about 6500 feet. Therefore, if you get into a spin with less than the required 7000-foot terrain clearance, eject, since the margin of safety is too small to attempt recovery. Practice spins should be entered at about 30,000 to 35,000 feet.

FLIGHT CONTROL EFFECTIVENESS.

AILERON CONTROL.

In the low-speed ranges, the ailerons provide control power quite similar to that of airplanes with conventional controls. However, in the cruise Mach number region, the ailerons provide considerably greater roll ability. Until you are familiar with aileron effectiveness at these high speeds, be careful not to overcontrol in making abrupt or consecutive rolls. However, below 5000 feet and at speeds in excess of 570 knots, aileron control naturally becomes sluggish and may require a reduction in speed for satisfactory roll performance. Because of the irreversible feature and the utilization of both a normal and an alternate flight control hydraulic system, no "boost-out" provisions are necessary. Therefore, in this airplane, particular care is not necessary in maintaining lateral trim. Should failure of the normal flight control system occur, automatic changeover to the alternate system is provided instantly, with no reduction in aileron control power or increase in pilot effort. However, excessive use of controls should be avoided when operating on the alternate system. If controls become heavy or sluggish, allow alternate pressure to build up.

HORIZONTAL TAIL CONTROL.

Controllability with the all-movable, hydraulically powered horizontal tail is comparable to that of a conventional control system at the lower airspeeds. However, it is definitely superior at high Mach numbers, since control effectiveness is not lost because of compressibility. This more positive and effective action enables you to recover more readily when G-overshoot or stall is encountered. However, until you have become familiar with the effectiveness of this type of control system, care must be taken to avoid overcontrolling.

RUDDER CONTROL.

The conventional cable-operated rudder provides directional control during take-off and landing and at lower airspeeds. At higher airspeeds, the inherent stability of the airplane is such that coordinated maneuvers can be made with minimum use of the rudder. However, if an extraordinary condition of unbalanced drag occurs, such as when external loads are carried on one wing only, coordinated use of the rudder is required to maintain the desired heading.

TRIM TAB CONTROL.

Aileron and Horizontal Tail.

Because of the type of control system used, trim tabs are unnecessary on either the ailerons or the horizontal tail. The hydraulic actuators at these surfaces do not transmit air loads to the pilot; therefore, control stick feel is provided artificially by spring bungees. Actuating the related trim control merely relocates the stick neutral (no-load) position so that stick (or spring) forces are "zeroed" for a particular flight speed and attitude.

To the pilot, this stick neutral (no-load) position relocation is identical to reactions obtained from trim tab operation on a conventional control system.

CAUTION

Trim should not be used to reduce stick forces during aerobatic maneuvers, since such action may induce a spin condition and, if a spin is entered, the stick will not return to neutral if a hands-off recovery is attempted.

Rudder.

An electrically controlled and actuated trim tab is provided to "zero" rudder pedal forces for a particular airspeed or flight attitude.

SPEED BRAKES.

Any time that deceleration is desired, and especially in high-speed turns or formation flying, speed brakes may be used without objectionable buffeting or uncontrollable changes in trim. Figure 6-3 illustrates an additional advantage of the speed brakes, i.e., their use enables a steeper approach on a target at a given airspeed. In a pull-out, recovery may be made with minimum altitude loss by first opening the speed brakes and then pulling the maximum permissible G. Opening the speed brakes at high speed, without pulling on the stick at all, results in an automatic increase of about 2 G.

WARNING

Remember to allow for the automatic 2 G increase when simultaneously opening the speed brakes at high speed and pulling back on the stick; otherwise, you may exceed the maximum allowable G.

WING SLATS.

Leading-edge wing slats are installed on some airplanes. They reduce the stalling speeds in both accelerated and unaccelerated flight. However, whether open or closed, they do not appreciably change the action of the airplane at the stall or during normal flight. The slats are fully automatic in operation and, depending upon the angle of attack, float to either closed, partially open, or full open positions. Reduction in airspeed extends the slats; conversely, increase in airspeed retracts the

Section VI T. O. 1F-86E-1

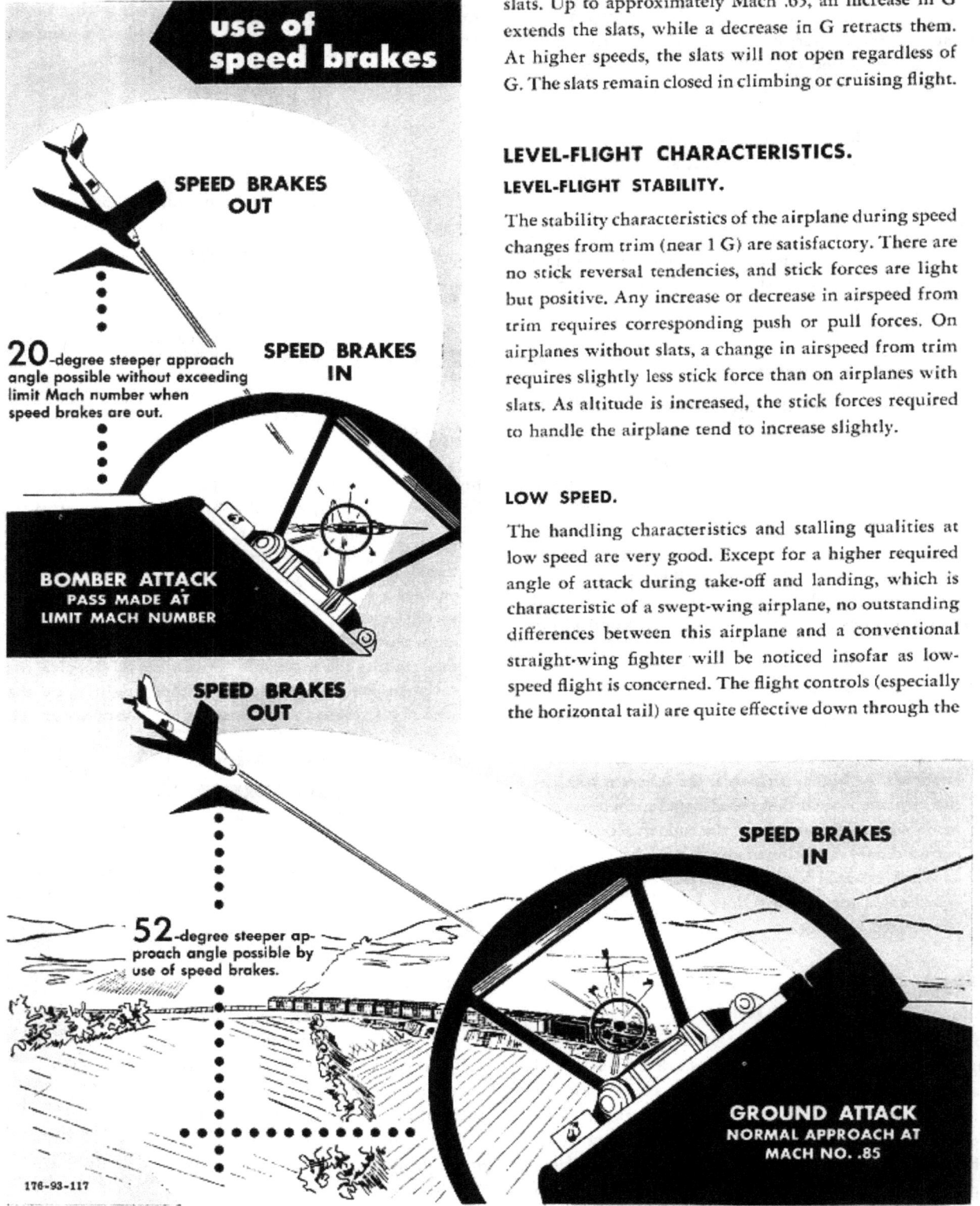

slats. Up to approximately Mach .65, an increase in G extends the slats, while a decrease in G retracts them. At higher speeds, the slats will not open regardless of G. The slats remain closed in climbing or cruising flight.

LEVEL-FLIGHT CHARACTERISTICS.
LEVEL-FLIGHT STABILITY.

The stability characteristics of the airplane during speed changes from trim (near 1 G) are satisfactory. There are no stick reversal tendencies, and stick forces are light but positive. Any increase or decrease in airspeed from trim requires corresponding push or pull forces. On airplanes without slats, a change in airspeed from trim requires slightly less stick force than on airplanes with slats. As altitude is increased, the stick forces required to handle the airplane tend to increase slightly.

LOW SPEED.

The handling characteristics and stalling qualities at low speed are very good. Except for a higher required angle of attack during take-off and landing, which is characteristic of a swept-wing airplane, no outstanding differences between this airplane and a conventional straight-wing fighter will be noticed insofar as low-speed flight is concerned. The flight controls (especially the horizontal tail) are quite effective down through the

Figure 6-3

6-8

stall. On airplanes without slats, low-speed flight handling characteristics are more critical than on those with slats, particularly during landings and take-offs. Special attention should be given to take-off speeds given in Section II under "Take-off" and in figure 2-5, and to landing speeds given in figure 2-6. The effect on the stall speed of varying the angle of bank and G-loading is shown in figure 6-2. This relationship is especially important during the turn onto final approach when external stores are carried or when landing with a heavy fuel load.

CRUISE SPEED.

In the medium- to high-speed range, handling characteristics are considered good about all three axes—roll, pitch, and yaw. In comparison to the conventional elevator control, the more effective horizontal tail is considerably more sensitive because of the faster airplane reaction to small stick motions. It is advisable, therefore, not to attempt close-in formation flight until you are accustomed to the control. You will probably notice that the airplane is most sensitive to small fore-and-aft stick motion between Mach .8 and Mach .9 at low altitudes. This is more noticeable in airplanes without slats.

HIGH SPEED.

Stability and control in high-speed flight are unaffected by compressibility up to approximately Mach .95, with the exception of a slight flattening tendency in the stick force gradient for 1 G flight between Mach .85 and Mach .9. At speeds above Mach .95, the normal nose-up tendency becomes more pronounced and requires steadily increasing push forces and forward stick movement to increase the speed of the airplane. As in other speed ranges, use of the stabilizer results in positive and immediate airplane reaction. The power of the controllable horizontal tail is particularly noticeable above 500 knots, especially in turbulent air. Caution should be used until you become accustomed to the longitudinal control power available in this airplane. Wing heaviness, which may begin above Mach .9, is controllable at medium and high altitudes. However, at low altitudes, where high indicated airspeeds are encountered, this wing heaviness may become a limiting condition.

WING ROLL.

All F-86 Airplanes are subject to a wing roll condition. However, this characteristic is not of much consequence except on certain airplanes which exhibit a strong tendency toward wing roll at high indicated airspeeds.

This so-called wing roll or wing heaviness can be caused by two different flight influences. One is an influence induced by increasing the indicated airspeeds. The other results from a reduction in aileron control at high Mach numbers. The effect of increasing indicated airspeed works as follows: Slight variations in the angle of incidence between left and right wing panels may cause you to use a little aileron to hold a wings-level attitude at low speeds. This aileron displacement causes an aerodynamic twisting moment to be applied to the wing. As the airspeed increases, so does the twisting moment, and in such a direction that more aileron angle must be used to regain wings-level trim. More aileron angle, in turn, means more wing twist, and so on. It can be seen that if incidence variations between left and right wing panels on certain airplanes are large enough, it is possible to reach maximum aileron control before obtaining maximum level-flight speed near sea-level. It is possible to alleviate this tendency, on those airplanes which require an excessive amount of aileron for trim, by rigging the wing flaps to counteract the basic roll tendency. High Mach number wing heaviness is caused as follows: The aileron effectiveness is substantially reduced at a speed beginning around Mach .95. If, for example, the effectiveness fell to one-fourth of its value at low Mach numbers, and the amount of aileron required to hold the wings level at low Mach numbers was about one degree, then the amount of aileron required at high Mach numbers would have to be increased to 4 degrees. In addition to this, standing shock waves will gradually form over each wing panel and may be at a slightly different chordwise location. Since the standing shock waves can disturb the airflow behind them, they may induce a difference in lift between wing panels. This condition may add to the effect caused by the reduction in aileron control. Flap rigging to alleviate wing roll due to high indicated airspeeds will not help wing roll caused by high Mach numbers. It can be seen that, as the airplane altitude changes, the separate effects of indicated airspeed and Mach number on wing roll will combine in varying proportions. Generally, you should be aware of this wing heaviness characteristic of the particular airplane you are flying, so as to anticipate wing roll during combat at altitude, and also to make the required allowance during high-indicated-airspeed, low-level passes.

MANEUVERING FLIGHT.

MANEUVERING-FLIGHT STABILITY.

Stick forces during maneuvering flight are relatively uniform over the entire speed and altitude range of the airplane. The amount of stick force required to obtain

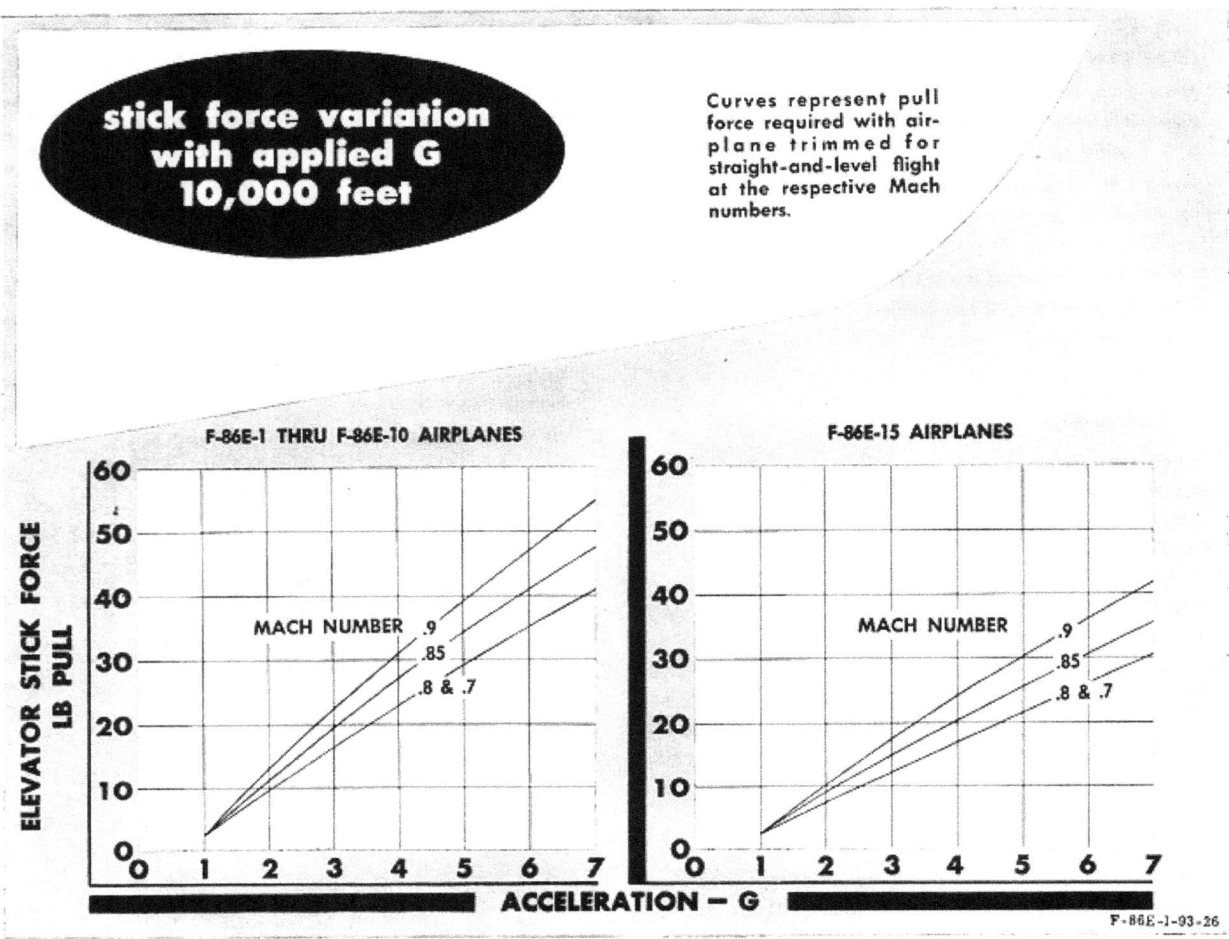

Figure 6-4

a given G does not increase noticeably at high Mach number nor decrease at high altitudes or normal aft CG positions, because of the spring bungee and bob-weight which provide pilot feel. (See figure 6-4.) However, at Mach numbers greater than .9 and also at low airspeeds, you will notice that stick forces are slightly higher for a corresponding G. Although this increase in stick forces at the lower airspeeds may appear somewhat unusual to you during your first few hours in the airplane, *remember that the absolute maximum stick force required at all airspeeds, since it is supplied artificially, will always be within your normal control capabilities.* Flight test experience on this type control system has indicated that pilots readily adapt themselves to this change from normal experience.

MANEUVERABILITY.

At all Mach numbers and airspeeds, maneuvers can be accomplished with relative ease. However, below 5000 feet at speeds in excess of 570 knots, aileron control becomes sluggish. Very little rudder action is necessary in performing all maneuvers. In the climb and cruise speed range, you will find that the airplane is near its peak efficiency in maneuvering, ensuring excellent handling qualities and combat performance. The maximum rate of roll at any one altitude occurs near the best climb speed for that altitude, and the peak airplane G response for the pull force you exert will occur in this speed range. The full flight capabilities of the airplane, through use of the horizontal tail as the direct longitudinal control, will be especially noticeable at high Mach numbers. The swept wings and smooth lines of the airplane present a minimum-drag profile to make possible increased rates of climb and near-sonic, level-flight airspeeds. Although speed is of primary importance, several other factors enter into any discussion on the subject of maneuverability: climb potential, radius

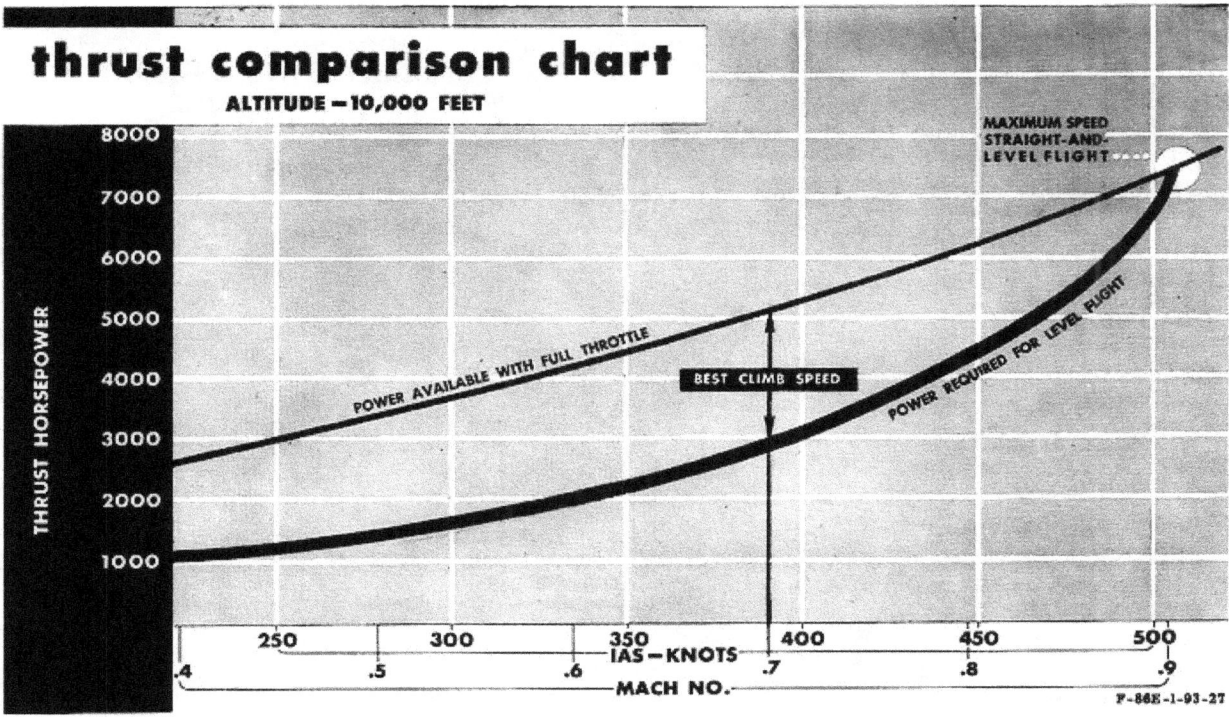

Figure 6-5

of turn, and time to turn. Climb potential, which is graphically illustrated in figure 6-5, is the difference between the curves of power available and power required for straight-and-level flight. The distance between the two curves represents the excess thrust or power available for maneuvering flight, i.e., the extra power available to increase speed or rate of climb or to pull more G. The point of greatest difference between the curves is the best climb speed, which increases from about Mach .61 at sea level to about Mach .8 at 40,000 feet for the airplane with no external load. The best Mach number range at any given altitude is from best climb speed to maximum speed. Therefore, always fly at or above best climb speed in combat, to retain the maximum possible speed advantage. Below best climb speed, the rate of climb falls off rapidly and it takes much longer to accelerate to high speed.

TURNING-RADIUS CONTROL.

Radius of turn or time to turn is important because it determines whether you can bring your guns to bear on a target or cease being a target yourself. At any constant Mach number, the radius will increase as altitude increases. Also, radius of turn will increase as speed increases. These two factors are of primary importance in the control of turn radius. The increase in turning radius with speed at any one altitude is gradual up to approximately Mach .85 and then begins to rise quite rapidly; this is a direct result of the fact that at these speeds, almost all of the engine thrust is being used to maintain speed, and very little is left to maintain altitude during the turn. Above Mach .85, you may obtain a considerably shorter turn radius by diving into a turn, because of the higher effective thrust (engine thrust plus airplane weight). Since loss of altitude is sometimes a disadvantage in combat, a reduction in speed is the more important factor in turning-radius control. One method of slowing down is exchanging excess speed for altitude, as in a sharp climbing turn or an Immelmann. Another is by pulling into a level turn and opening the speed brakes, remembering to ease off on the stick while the brakes are opening, to maintain the same G. However, in either case, be careful to prevent the speed from falling below best climb speed. On airplanes without slats, you will be able to turn in a smaller radius without losing speed rapidly at higher altitudes. This is because the turn can be tightened considerably before buffet is encountered. For example: at maximum speed in level flight at 30,000 feet, you can

Section VI
T. O. 1F-86E-1

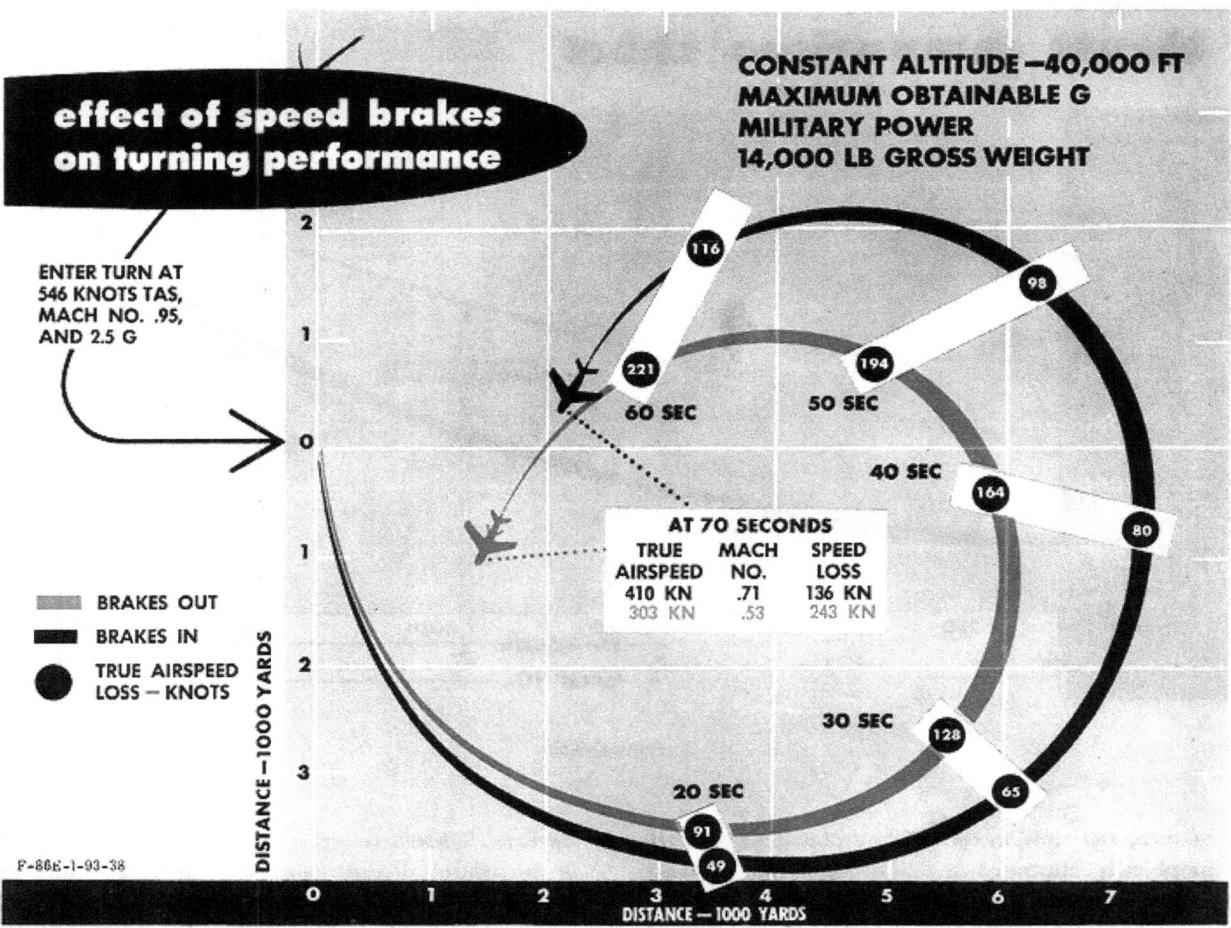

Figure 6-6

pull an additional 1½ G before buffet; and at 40,000 feet, you can pull an additional 1 G. Figure 6-6 compares performance of the airplane with speed brakes open to that of the clean airplane in a high-speed turn at 40,000 feet. Speeds are given as true airspeed and Mach numbers, since you are conscious of closure speed on a target (true speed changes) rather than of changes in indicated airspeed. Note how much tighter a turn can be made by opening the speed brakes. However, note also that speed is lost rapidly with the brakes open. Therefore, use the brakes only to tighten the turn; then close them again before you fall below best climb speed.

RECOMMENDED SPEED FOR MINIMUM-RADIUS TURNS.

The recommended speed for minimum-radius turns is the best climb speed at any altitude. Therefore, in combat, you should not turn with a slower airplane (which generally has a lower best climb speed), because it would outturn your airplane every time. You would gain a distinct advantage by inducing a faster airplane (which generally has a higher best climb speed) to turn with you. Therefore, if operating above best climb speed, open the speed brakes or lose speed by gaining altitude to make the fastest practical turn, but do not allow the speed to drop below that for best climb. If operating at or very near best climb speed, use full throttle to make the fastest practical turn, pulling only enough G to allow best climb speed to be maintained. These, of course, are only general rules of procedure; in actual practice, situations may arise in which further loss of speed, or even a loss of altitude to maintain speed, is desirable.

DIVES.

DIVES AND ACCELERATED FLIGHT.

In high Mach number dives and maneuvers, airplane stability is good. Stick forces are relatively light, and the airplane is easily controlled up to the limit Mach numbers and load factors that may be applied. However, below 5000 feet at speeds in excess of 570 knots, aileron control becomes sluggish. The non-slatted leading edge results in a slightly better dive acceleration.

G-OVERSHOOT.

A characteristic of the airplane with which you must become completely familiar is its response to rapid pull-outs at high Mach numbers. Because of basic airplane pitch characteristics at these Mach numbers, flight conditions can possibly be encountered in which the G-limit may be inadvertently exceeded. This tendency is not predominant in these late airplanes, and it is more rapidly and positively controlled. However, because the basic airplane design remains unchanged, this pitch characteristic still exists. The conditions under which this overshoot or "dig-in" may occur vary with Mach number, altitude, gross weight, and G. However, it is not necessary to remember various combinations of these factors in order to safeguard both yourself and the airplane. Sufficient data has been obtained through flight testing to indicate that overshoot is likely to begin at the "buffet boundary," i.e., the G at which you will notice a distinct increase in the vibration or buffet of the airplane. This buffet increase, or "boundary," is your warning of impending overshoot. *To avoid overshoot and possible damage to the airplane, observe the airplane G-limits and be prepared to immediately decrease your rate of pull-up when encountering buffet.* This does not mean that you cannot fly in the buffet region, but it does mean that pulling up very rapidly into it is dangerous. Because of the higher available load factor before buffet initiation on airplanes without slats, familiarization with airplane response during rapid pull-outs is recommended, particularly in the medium altitude range (15,000 to 30,000 feet). Remember, although the controllable horizontal tail permits a more effective and positive corrective action, it does not prevent the initiation of overshoot.

DIVE RECOVERY.

Because of airplane trim changes which occur during pull-ups at high Mach numbers, the following procedure is recommended for recovering from high Mach number dives or maneuvers:

1. Open speed brakes. Do not pull back on stick rapidly until after speed brakes are open and nose-up pitch due to brake extension has occurred.

2. Pull stick back as necessary to effect desired pull-out.

Altitude Loss in Dive Recovery.

The altitude lost during dive recovery is determined by four interdependent factors: (1) angle of dive, (2) altitude at start of pull-out, (3) airspeed at start of pull-out, and (4) the G maintained during pull-out. Because these factors must be considered collectively in estimating altitude required for recovery from any dive, their relationship is best presented in chart form as shown in figure 6-7. Note that one of the charts is based on a 4 G pull-out, and the other on a 6 G pull-out. Compare the altitude lost during recovery from a 4 G pull-out with that lost during recovery from a 6 G pull-out; also compare the effects of variations in the other three factors. Remember that a value obtained from either chart is the altitude lost during recovery—not the altitude at which recovery is completed. Therefore, in planning maneuvers that involve dives, consider first the altitude of the terrain and then use the charts to determine the altitude at which recovery must be started for pull-out with adequate terrain clearance. In using the charts, you should allow for the fact that, without considerable experience in this airplane, you cannot determine exactly what your dive angle and speed are going to be at the start of the pull-out. If you come out of a split S or another high-speed maneuver in a near-vertical dive, speed builds up rapidly. Consequently, until you know the airplane well, go into the chart at the highest speed and dive angle you might expect to reach after completing your maneuvers. If, for instance, you are in a 90-degree dive at an airspeed above Mach .8 and you wait until 10,000 feet to start your pull-out, you will have to make a 6 G pull-out; a 4 G pull-out will not clear the terrain. (See figure 6-8.) Maneuvers should be planned so that if they terminate in a near-vertical dive, the airplane may be pulled on through to a shallower dive angle before the speed becomes excessive or too low an altitude is reached.

Note

It is a good idea to memorize a few specific conditions from the dive charts so that you have a basis for judgments on pull-outs.

LETDOWN.

Normally, the most economical letdown with the clean airplane is at Mach .8, with the throttle at IDLE. For emergency letdown, descent can be made in minimum time by a vertical dive (power on, if available).

Section VI   T. O. 1F-86E-1

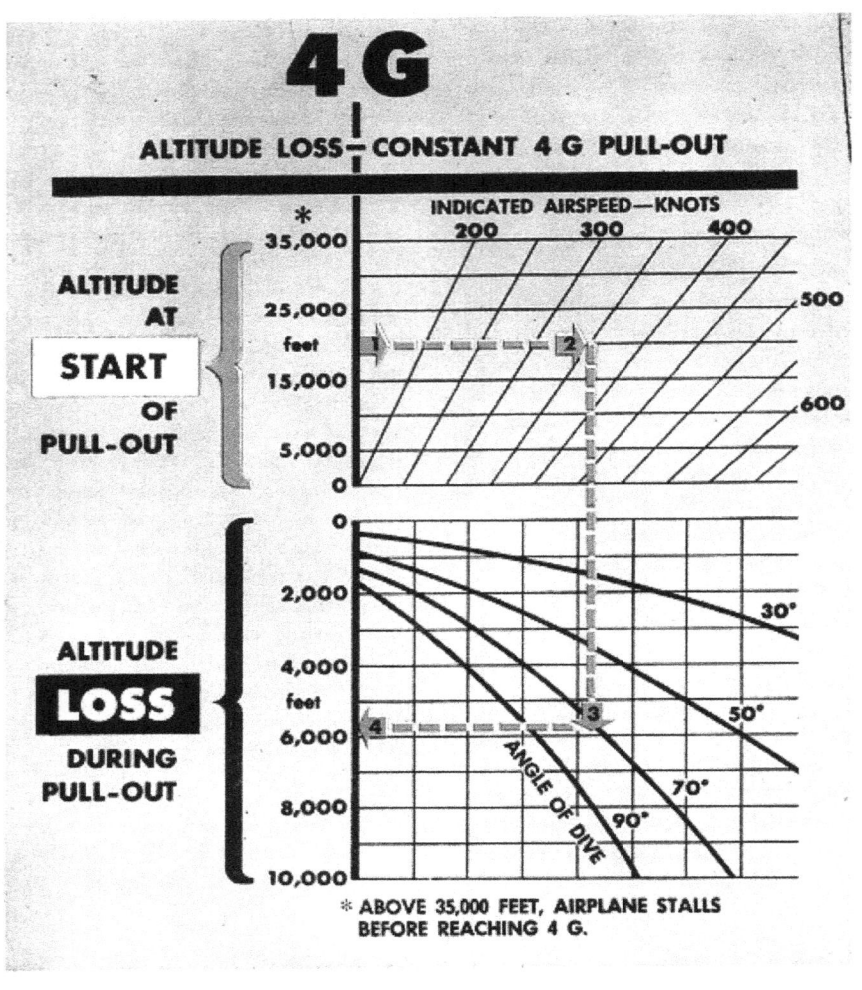

Figure 6-7

6-14

T. O. 1F-86E-1 — Section VI

how to use charts

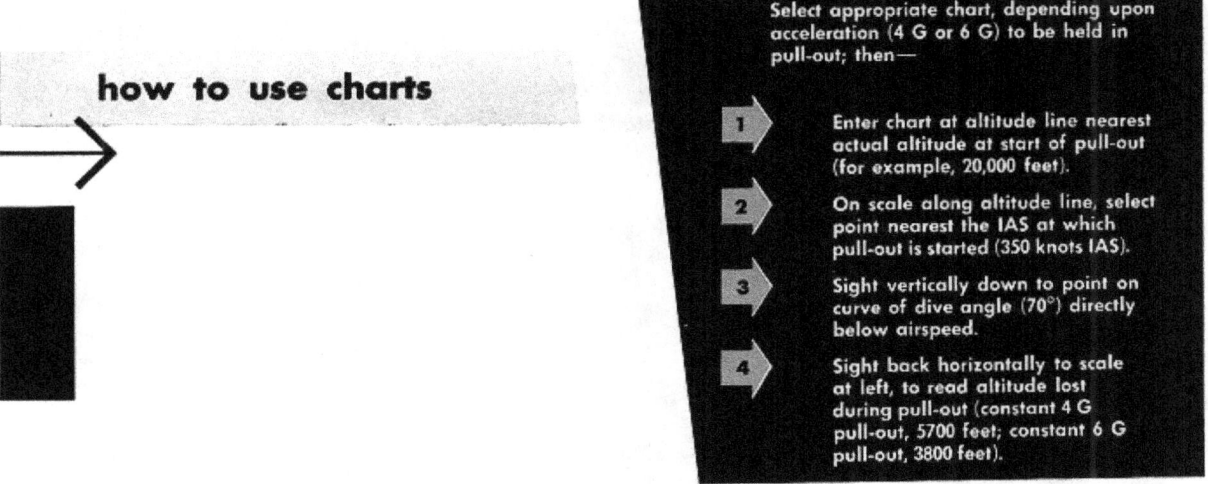

Select appropriate chart, depending upon acceleration (4 G or 6 G) to be held in pull-out; then—

1. Enter chart at altitude line nearest actual altitude at start of pull-out (for example, 20,000 feet).
2. On scale along altitude line, select point nearest the IAS at which pull-out is started (350 knots IAS).
3. Sight vertically down to point on curve of dive angle (70°) directly below airspeed.
4. Sight back horizontally to scale at left, to read altitude lost during pull-out (constant 4 G pull-out, 5700 feet; constant 6 G pull-out, 3800 feet).

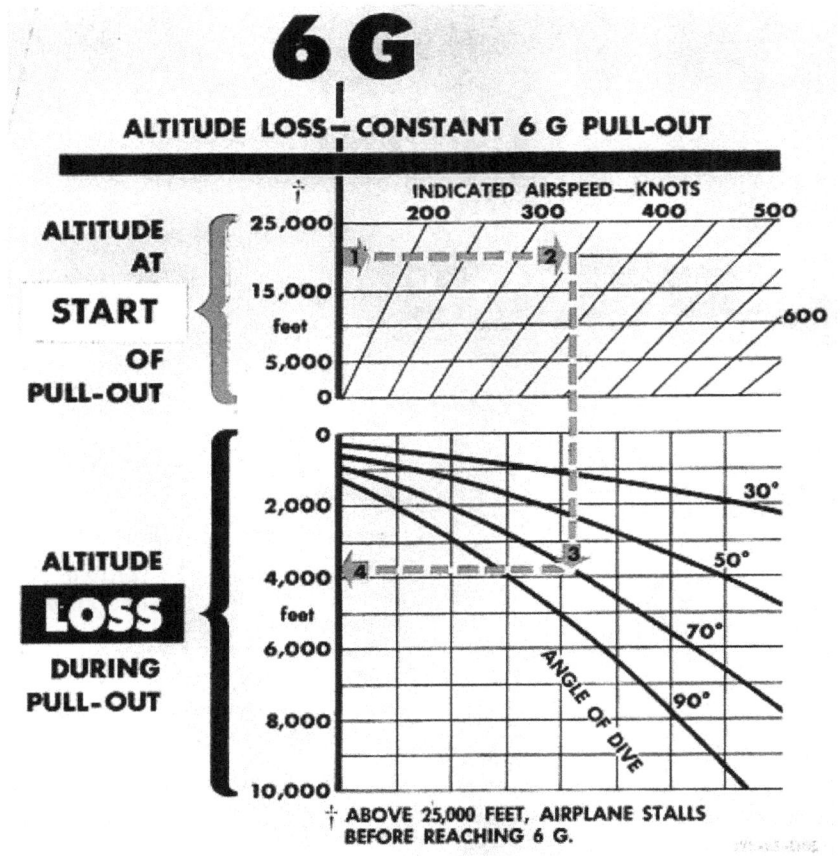

† ABOVE 25,000 FEET, AIRPLANE STALLS BEFORE REACHING 6 G.

6-15

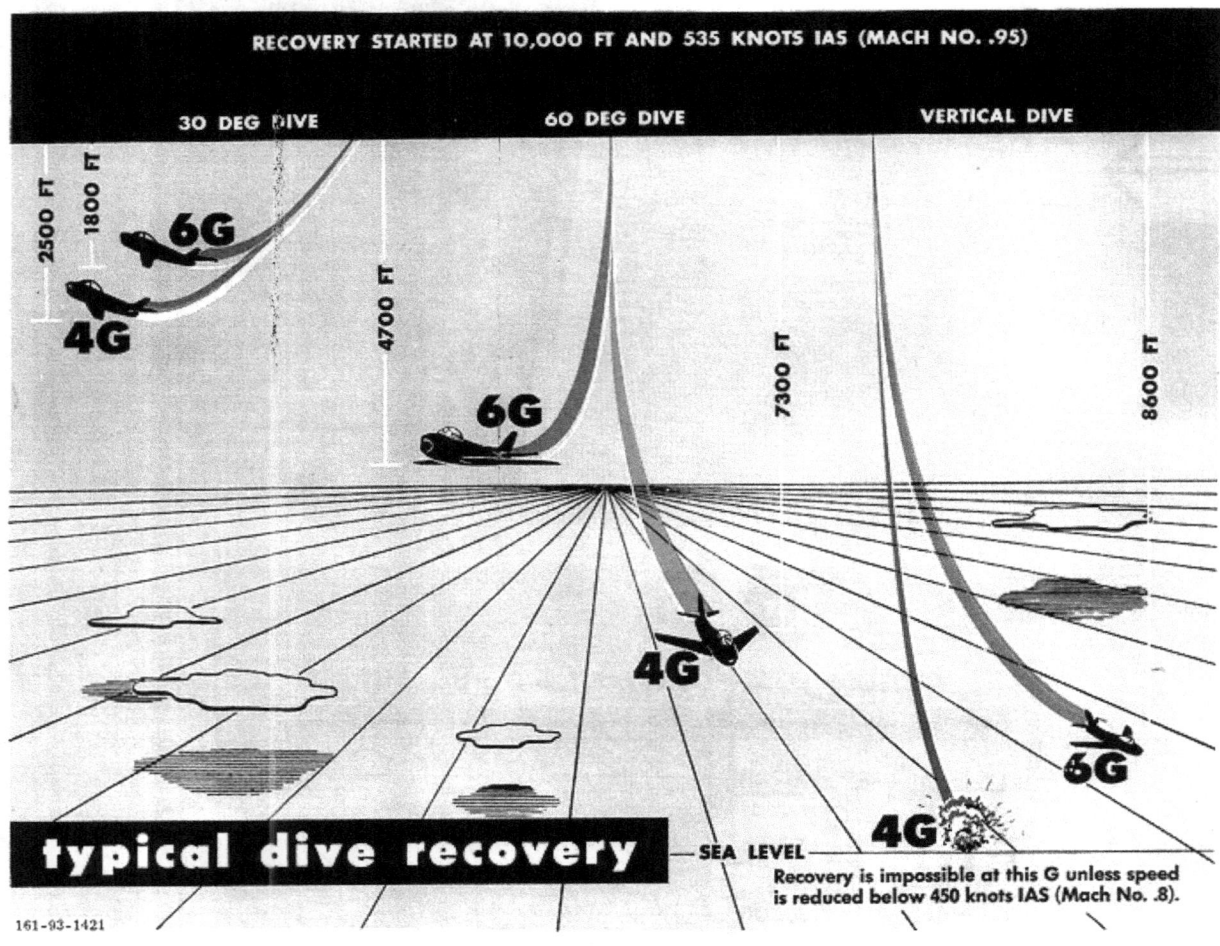

Figure 6-8

FLIGHT WITH EXTERNAL LOADS.

DROP TANKS.

Flying qualities of the airplane are essentially unaffected by the drop tanks. However, because of the increased drag and weight when drop tanks are carried, naturally the take-off distances will be greater and the rate of climb and acceleration will be reduced. The deviation from normal feel and control when flying with one full 200-gallon drop tank and one empty 200-gallon drop tank is hardly noticeable. When landing in cross winds of 25 knots with the full tank away from the wind, full opposite aileron is required to maintain directional control; therefore, when practicable, landings should be made with the heavy tank into the wind in cross winds of 25 knots or more. Refer to "Crosswind Landing" in Section II.

BOMBS.

Excessive buffeting of the wing flaps will occur at high speeds when bombs are carried. Aileron vibration and/or lateral oscillation of the airplane will be present at high speeds, depending upon the type of bomb load. (Refer to Section V.) Vibration or oscillation increases as Mach number increases, and, at slightly higher Mach numbers, the buffeting becomes so pronounced that it can be felt in the control stick. Bomb dropping is evidenced by a momentary pitch-up of the airplane; however, the pitch-up is not objectionable, because the airplane immediately returns to trim.

ROCKETS.

Airplane stability and control are unaffected by the presence of rockets, and dives up to the maximum speed obtainable can be performed without difficulty.

SECTION VII
SYSTEMS OPERATION

TABLE OF CONTENTS	PAGE		PAGE
Engine Acceleration	7-1	Engine Performance With Air Intake Screens	7-5
Main Fuel Regulator Characteristics	7-1	Turbine Noise During Shutdown	7-5
Engine Surge	7-2	Smoke From Turbine During Shutdown	7-6
Compressor Stall	7-3	Tail-pipe Segments	7-6
Flame-out	7-4	Fuel System	7-7
Engine Noise and Roughness	7-4	Hydraulic Systems	7-7
Exhaust Temperature Variation	7-4	Landing Gear	7-8

ENGINE ACCELERATION.

At all altitudes up to 40,000 feet, very rapid accelerations are possible during operation on the main fuel regulator. However, for accelerations at altitudes above 40,000 feet, slower throttle movement must be used to avoid flame-out. When power is added, the throttle should be moved slowly at first and then advanced more rapidly as rpm increases. On airplanes with the three-position emergency fuel switch, the switch should not be ON during operation on the main fuel system, because the emergency system probably would take over during rapid advancement of the throttle and cause compressor stall or flame-out, resulting in complete loss of power. On airplanes with the two-position emergency fuel switch, the switch should not be ON (except in case of main fuel system failure), because the emergency system would be in control of fuel flow to the engine and rapid advancement of the throttle would cause compressor stall or flame-out, resulting in complete loss of power.

MAIN FUEL REGULATOR CHARACTERISTICS.

The main fuel regulator determines the amount of fuel delivered to the combustion chambers by controlling the fuel control valve in accordance with throttle setting, flight conditions, and allowable limits of the engine. When the throttle is at IDLE, it holds a fixed minimum fuel pressure sufficient to maintain combustion at all altitudes. While the minimum fuel pressure remains constant, the resultant minimum rpm increases with altitude. (See figure 7-1.) Overspeed protection is provided through a governor incorporated in the main fuel regulator and is effective from 30% to 100% rpm at sea level. Although the governor control is designed to produce constant engine rpm for a given throttle setting, minimum idle rpm will increase with altitude. This characteristic causes the first portion of throttle travel to be less effective at high altitudes. (See figure 7-1.) The main fuel regulator is designed so that during acceleration (by enriching fuel mixture) and deceleration (by leaning

7-1

Section VII
T.O. 1F-86E-1

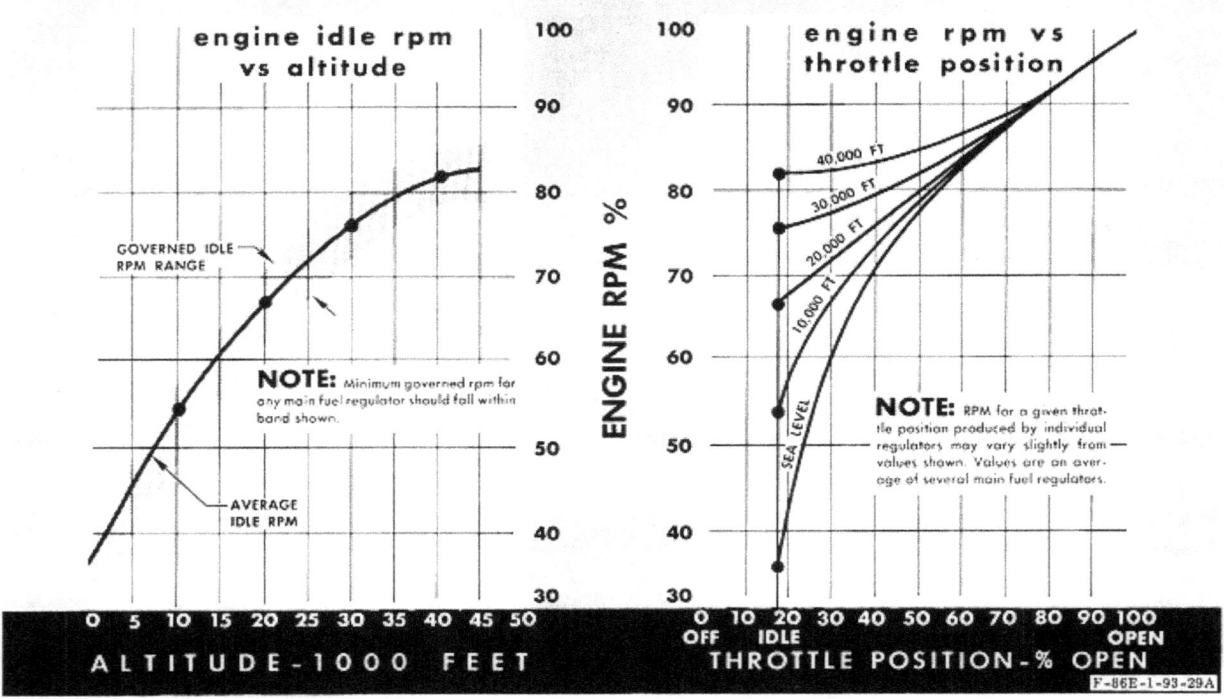

Figure 7-1

fuel mixture), it normally holds the fuel schedule within a certain range of fuel-air ratios where combustion can be maintained. However, it is very difficult for the fuel regulator to maintain the proper fuel-air ratio when operating at very high altitudes. If the fuel schedule cannot be held within the combustion range, the resultant improper fuel-air mixture will not support combustion and a flame-out will result. An increased possibility of flame-out at high altitudes exists because the fuel regulator schedule is a compromise between rapid engine acceleration at low altitudes and slow engine acceleration at high altitudes. Because of this characteristic, flame-out may result at altitudes above 40,000 feet whenever the throttle is advanced rapidly from IDLE to full OPEN at a low airspeed. Under these conditions, the possibility of flame-out is minimized by slow, careful movement of the throttle.

WARNING

When outside air temperature is less than 50°F, rapid throttle movement during operation on the main fuel system below 10,000 feet when engine speed is below 70% may produce compressor stall or total loss of power.

ENGINE SURGE.

ENGINE SURGE DUE TO MAIN FUEL REGULATOR CONTROL OIL STARVATION.

When an extremely high nose-up attitude is maintained during extended climbs to high altitude, you may experience engine surge caused by interruption of the control oil supply to the main fuel regulator. Flight tests, as well as reports from the field, show a very definite relationship between oil system malfunctions and airplane flight attitude. For instance, oil pressure loss and/or power loss resulting from fuel regulator malfunctions due to interruption of oil supply to the regulator occurs most frequently during prolonged climbs, especially in the extreme nose-up attitude common to climbs from sea level to 20,000 feet. This is believed to be due to failure of the aft scavenge pump to properly scavenge the No. 4 bearing sump. To minimize loss of oil and prevent engine surging during climbs to altitude from take-off, you should level off for at least one minute between 18,000 and 20,000 feet. This will permit the aft scavenge pump to return all excess oil in the aft frame to the engine oil tank.

ENGINE SURGE DUE TO MAIN FUEL REGULATOR MALFUNCTION.

Thrust surge accompanied by large synchronized fluctuation in fuel flow, exhaust gas temperature, and engine rpm during stabilized level flight indicates malfunction and impending failure of the main fuel system. Normally, fuel flow fluctuations less than 600 pounds per hour are acceptable; however, synchronized surge of any magnitude is considered undesirable. If synchronized surge is observed during level-flight operation, proceed as follows:

1. Retard throttle until surge is eliminated.

WARNING

On airplanes with the three-position emergency fuel switch, you must not move the switch to ON in an attempt to eliminate the surge condition. With the switch at ON, the emergency fuel system is in stand-by condition and not in full control of fuel flow to the engine; therefore, surges resulting from main fuel regulator malfunction could be greatly aggravated, resulting in serious damage to the engine. On these airplanes, if retarding the throttle will not eliminate surge, land as soon as possible.

2. On airplanes with the two-position emergency fuel switch, if the surge persists or if there is not enough power available at the resulting throttle setting to maintain level flight, retard throttle to IDLE and move emergency fuel switch to ON. (Emergency fuel system will be in full control of fuel flow to the engine.)

3. Gradually advance throttle to obtain desired exhaust gas temperature and rpm.

No automatic engine overspeed protection is provided when the emergency fuel control system is being used; therefore, throttle movement must be smooth and gradual to avoid flame-out or engine overspeed, particularly at high altitude.

COMPRESSOR STALL.

Compressor stall can occur at any altitude as a result of rapid advancement of the throttle while operating on either the main or the emergency fuel system. Although the possibility of such compressor stall is considerably reduced during operation on the main fuel system, it can occur in case of main fuel regulator malfunction or improper fuel scheduling, or at low airspeeds even though the regulator is functioning normally. Compressor stall is likely to occur during any rapid throttle advancement while operating on the emergency fuel system or with the emergency fuel system in stand-by (emergency fuel switch at ON on airplanes with the three-position emergency fuel switch). This is because the emergency fuel regulator schedules fuel as a function of the compressor inlet pressure (altitude and airspeed) and throttle position, thus affording no acceleration fuel schedule for stall protection such as that provided by the main fuel regulator. Stall occurs when rapid throttle advancement injects more fuel into the combustion chamber than the engine can use for acceleration at the existing rpm. The burning of this additional fuel increases the combustion pressures. As these pressures increase, they create a corresponding increase in the pressures against the compressor discharge air. This increase of pressure against the compressor discharge air results in a breakdown of the airflow through the last stages of the compressor, which is the condition known as compressor stall. As a result of the stall, the mass airflow through the compressor is reduced, causing a reduction in airflow through the turbine; thus the energy available to the turbine wheel is decreased. A roaring, pulsating noise and heavy vibration usually accompany compressor stall and may precede any engine instrument indication of changing engine conditions. In addition to the pulsating noise and vibration, the following signs of compressor stall may be present, depending upon the severity of the stall: rapidly rising exhaust gas temperature, failure of the engine to accelerate, a long flame from the tail pipe, and loss of thrust. If the engine is allowed to continue operating in this stalled condition, the increased temperature of the burning gases will cause serious damage to the hot section (combustion, turbine, and exhaust sections) of the engine, resulting in possible engine failure. If stall is encountered during a rapid engine acceleration, action should be taken to eliminate it as follows:

1. Immediately retard throttle to IDLE.

2. If exhaust temperature stabilizes at a normal value, readvance throttle slowly while carefully monitoring exhaust gas temperature. If exhaust temperature continues to drop after the throttle is retarded, flame-out has occurred and an air start should be tried. On rare occasions, a stall condition that may be described as a "cold" or "partial" stall will be encountered during rapid engine acceleration while operating on the main fuel system at low airspeeds. The main distinguishing characteristics of this stall condition are inability of the engine to exceed a maximum rpm of about 70%, an exhaust temperature of from 500°C to 700°C, and little or no vibration or pulsating. No immediate damage will normally result from this condition, but stall recovery should be started as soon as the condition is recognized in order to clear the stall and to increase power. Occasionally, retarding the throttle to IDLE will not eliminate this partial stall, and if the condition persists when the throttle is slowly readvanced, as shown by inability of engine rpm to advance above about 70%, proceed as follows:

1. Retard throttle to IDLE.

2. Increase airspeed by lowering the nose of the airplane, to increase ram-air pressure at the compressor inlet. An exhaust gas temperature drop to normal stabilized values (200°C to 300°C) at IDLE will show that the stall has been cleared.

3. Advance throttle slowly to the desired power setting.

WARNING

Since switching to the emergency fuel system with the engine stalled may result in serious overtemperature, *do not switch to the emergency system, even at idle, when there is a possibility that a compressor stall still is present.*

FLAME-OUT.

Flame-out is just what the name implies. It can happen during acceleration or deceleration of the engine.

Acceleration flame-out, like compressor stall, occurs when more fuel is injected into the combustion chambers than the engine can utilize for acceleration at the existing rpm. But, unlike the fuel-air mixture that causes compressor stall, this mixture is so excessively rich that it cannot burn, so the flame goes out. Flame-out during rapid engine deceleration will result whenever the amount of fuel injected into the combustion chambers is reduced to too low a level to sustain combustion at the existing rpm. Flame-outs are indicated by loss in thrust, drop in exhaust temperature, and possibly by loud noise similar to engine backfire. During a partial flame-out, some of the combustion chambers may still be lighted if the exhaust temperature does not drop below 260°C. The throttle should be retarded to IDLE and readvanced slowly in an attempt to relight the other chambers. If exhaust temperature continues to decrease below 260°C, the flame-out is complete and an air start is necessary. During any rapid throttle movement above 25,000 feet, flame-out may occur because of malfunction or improper scheduling of the fuel regulator, or if the emergency fuel switch is inadvertently left ON. Flame-outs may occur above 40,000 feet during a rapid engine acceleration at low airspeed.

ENGINE NOISE AND ROUGHNESS.

In flight, any unusual noise or roughness that can be attributed to the engine and cannot be eliminated when the engine speed or altitude is varied indicates some mechanical failure, and an immediate landing should be made. The most probable source of noise in flight is the pressurization system; when cabin pressure is dumped for a few minutes, noise should stop. If noise continues, the engine should be checked during shutdown after landing. On some airplanes, roughness may develop in the engine during operation at high power above 15,000 feet. Engine roughness, attributable to irregular combustion, can usually be eliminated if the rpm is changed; however, if the roughness continues, the pilot should land as soon as possible.

EXHAUST TEMPERATURE VARIATION.

Since exhaust temperature is not directly controlled during operation of a turbojet engine equipped with fixed-area exhaust nozzles, it is essential, if maximum airplane performance is to be obtained, that the pilot be familiar with, and understand, some exhaust temperature characteristics of the J47-GE-13 engine. Since the exhaust nozzle area cannot be changed in flight, exhaust temperature is maintained by changing engine rpm. Refer to Section V for limit exhaust temperatures. Exhaust temperature varies with changes in shroud-ring-to-turbine-bucket clearance, as well as with changes in engine inlet air temperature and density. Exhaust temperature can also vary with airspeed changes. Because all of these factors can change singly or simultaneously, the effect on exhaust temperature will be inconsistent for any given rpm. Normal exhaust temperature varies directly with outside air temperature. At outside air temperatures above 60°F, exhaust temperature varies approximately 3°C for each 10°F change in outside air temperature. Below 60°F outside air temperature, exhaust temperature variation is approximately 2°C for each 10°F change in outside air temperature. Maximum exhaust temperature variation occurs during initial ground run-up as the engine attains 100% rpm. The exhaust temperature varies approximately from 650°C to 700°C during the first 2 minutes of engine operation at 100% rpm. This large variation of exhaust temperature is due to engine temperatures not being stabilized. The shroud-ring-to-turbine-bucket clearance is believed to be the main cause for this variation in exhaust temperature. When the engine is first started, the shroud ring, being of lighter metal than the turbine wheel and buckets, expands at a faster rate. The uneven expansion between shroud ring and turbine wheel and buckets results in a larger clearance between the two than occurs after temperature stabilization. This increased clearance permits hotter gases to reach the exhaust temperature thermocouples, in the tail pipe, causing larger variations in exhaust temperature, indications. During approximately the next 3 minutes of operation, the temperature normally drops off to approximately 675°C to 690°C, provided that the rpm is maintained at 100%. As the engine is operated over a period of time, thermal expansion of the shroud ring and turbine wheel and buckets approaches a balance, decreasing the shroud-ring and turbine-bucket clearance and restricting the hot exhaust gases which pass between the shroud ring and turbine buckets; therefore, there is a smaller variation of exhaust temperature. During the period when exhaust temperatures are changing, an engine is said to be "unstabilized;" when temperatures become relatively even, the engine is said to be "stabilized." If take-off is made before the 2-minute 100% rpm run-up is completed, the exhaust temperature may exceed 700°C to 720°C during the take-off roll unless rpm is reduced slightly. If engine temperatures are allowed to stabilize 3 to 5 minutes before take-off, exhaust temperature during take-off and climb will rise slowly and tend to exceed 690°C unless rpm is reduced. The exhaust temperature will continue to rise until approximately 5000 feet is reached. Above 5000 feet, the exhaust temperature will gradually drop with an increase in altitude until about 35,000 feet is reached; then exhaust temperature will again begin to rise as altitude is increased, and may exceed the limit of 690°C unless rpm is reduced. If the engine has been shut down for 8 hours or more before flight, the exhaust temperature on take-off will exceed the limit of 690°C unless rpm is reduced.

Note

On take-offs made within 2 hours after a previous flight, the exhaust temperature will be 5°C to 10°C lower than on the initial take-off.

When rpm is reduced as low as 93% and exhaust temperature is maintained at 690°C, the thrust produced will approximate that obtained at 100% rpm with 690°C exhaust temperature. At engine speeds above approximately 93% rpm, the thrust produced is a function of exhaust temperature and not of engine rpm. At 100% rpm, each degree centigrade drop in exhaust temperature results in a loss of approximately 7 pounds in static thrust; thus, a 25°C reduction in exhaust temperature reduces engine thrust about 175 pounds.

ENGINE PERFORMANCE WITH AIR INTAKE SCREENS.

Static thrust loss for engines changed to include fixed air intake screens is between 5% and 6% of rated Military Power thrust for engines without intake screens. This thrust loss has no appreciable effect on take-off distances, maximum level-flight speed, or cruise performance. However, during Military Power climb, intake screens cause a noticeable loss in the rate of climb and a corresponding increase in the minimum time to climb to any altitude. (See climb charts in Appendix I.) The increased time to climb is naturally accompanied by a correspondingly higher fuel consumption, as well as an increase in ground distance covered. Although maximum level-flight speed is not noticeably reduced when intake screens are installed, time to accelerate to that speed is increased slightly.

TURBINE NOISE DURING SHUTDOWN.

The light scraping or rasping noise sometimes heard during engine shutdown results from interference between the turbine buckets and turbine shroud. Contact of the two parts is due to the tendency of the shroud to shift and distort under varying temperature conditions, as induced by engine shutdown. The scraping, while undesirable, does not damage either part. To minimize the scraping, it is necessary to operate the engine at 65% to 70% rpm for approximately 2 minutes before shutdown after any high-power operation (either flight or ground). If, despite this precaution, heavy scraping does occur on shutdown, no attempt to restart engine should be made until turbine temperature has dropped enough to provide adequate clearance between the buckets and shroud, because a starting attempt might result in destruction of the starter. If a start must be made when interference is suspected, an audible check should be made that engine begins to turn as starter is engaged, or tachometer indication should be noted. If engine does not begin turning at starter engagement, the stop-starter button must be depressed immediately.

SMOKE FROM TURBINE DURING SHUTDOWN.

WHITE SMOKE.

During engine shutdown, fuel may accumulate in the turbine housing, where heat of the turbine section causes the fuel to boil. (Although a turbine-housing drain is provided, it may not prevent accumulation of some fuel.) Presence of this residual fuel in the engine will be indicated by emission of fuel vapor or smoke from the tail pipe or intake duct, depending on ground wind conditions. Boiling fuel, indicated by the appearance of white fuel vapor, is not injurious to the engine but does create a hazard to personnel, since the vapor may ignite with explosive violence if allowed to accumulate in the engine and fuselage. Therefore, all personnel should keep clear of the tail pipe for at least 10 minutes after shutdown and at all times when fuel vapor or smoke comes from the tail pipe.

BLACK SMOKE.

The appearance of black smoke out of the tail pipe after shutdown indicates burning fuel. This burning fuel will damage the engine and should be cleared immediately as follows:

1. External power source connected.
2. Throttle OFF.
3. Hold battery-starter switch at STARTER.
4. Engine master switch ON until starter locks in, then OFF, to close main fuel shutoff valve.

Note

Once starter has engaged, moving engine master switch to OFF will not cause starter to disengage.

5. Listen to confirm that engine begins to turn as starter is engaged, or note tachometer indication.
6. Allow engine to crank to approximately 6% rpm (20 seconds maximum); then depress stop-starter button. Turn battery-starter switch OFF.

TAIL-PIPE SEGMENTS.

On turbojet engines equipped with fixed-area nozzles, the exhaust temperature is a direct indication of thrust output, or power, at a given engine speed. As the exhaust temperature is increased, the velocity of the exhaust jet, and hence the thrust, is increased. It is apparent that, although exhaust temperature should be kept below the maximum operating limit to prevent excessive engine wear, it must be held near the limit to obtain maximum thrust output. In order to obtain maximum operating exhaust temperature, exhaust temperature adjusting segments (figure 7-2) are added to, or removed from, the aft end of the tail pipe. These segments correctly adjust the exhaust nozzle area to produce, as near as possible, a stabilized exhaust temperature of 690°C at 100% rpm during ground run-up.

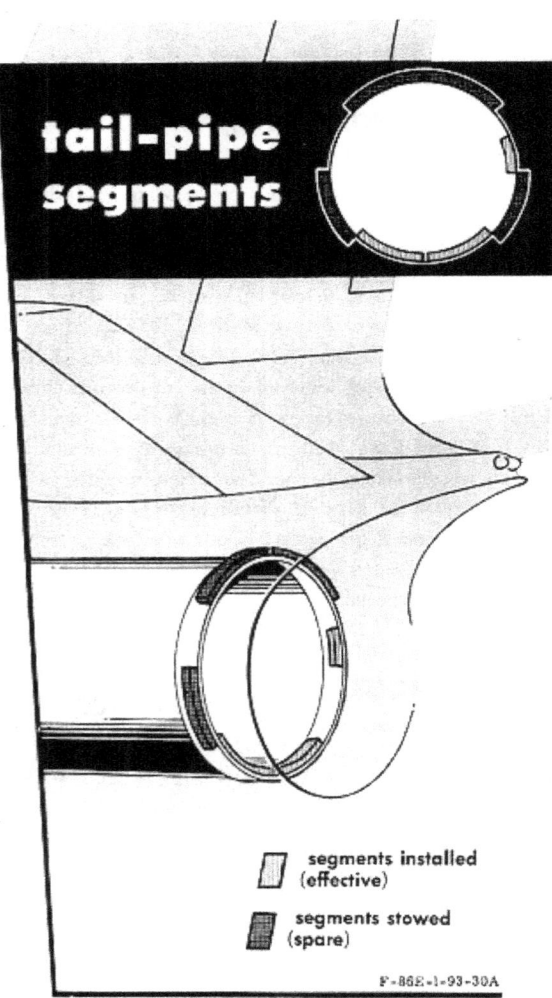

Figure 7-2

Fixed-area nozzles can be adjusted for only one set of operating conditions; thus, for a majority of operating conditions, the exhaust nozzle will usually be too large or too small, resulting in low or high exhaust temperatures, respectively. When tail-pipe segments are added, increased thrust will be evidenced on an engine previously operating with low exhaust temperature. The segments are first installed at the bottom of the tail pipe. As additional segments are needed, they are installed as symmetrically as possible, starting from the bottom of the tail pipe. Initial segment installation beginning at the top of the tail pipe is not recommended, because it will reduce the down-tail load. Down-tail loading aids nose-wheel lift-off and is a reaction caused from the tendency of the jet exhaust stream to cling to the upper fairing shelf, aft of the tail pipe. Whenever this tendency to cling is spoiled, the normal down-tail load is lost. When this down-tail loading is reduced or lost, nose-wheel lift-off speed will increase substantially. Efficient minimum-run take-offs depend upon early nose-wheel lift-offs; thus, if the tail-pipe segments are improperly located, an excessive ground run will be required during take-off.

FUEL SYSTEM.

Operation of the fuel system is essentially automatic, requiring no action from the pilot during flight. However, it is essential that the pilot keep the following precautions in mind.

    1. Keep emergency fuel switch OFF for all operation, except in case of main fuel system failure.

    2. Check drop tank pressure shutoff valve ON at all times when drop tanks are installed, to ensure that all drop tank fuel is consumed. This will also prevent collapsing of the 120-gallon drop tanks during rapid descent from altitude.

    3. Before depressing fuel filter deicer button, be sure fuel filter ice warning light burns steadily. Because the deicer alcohol supply is of one-minute duration, deice no longer than 15 seconds at a time.

HYDRAULIC SYSTEMS.

Hydraulic system pressure should be checked periodically during flight. The utility hydraulic system pressure can be checked by placing the pressure gage selector switch at UTILITY and reading the gage for proper system pressure. To check flight control hydraulic system pressure, fly straight and level for 30 seconds; then, with gage selector switch positioned at NORMAL, read flight control normal system pressure on pressure gage. Continue holding control stick steady, and position gage selector switch at ALTERNATE to read pressure in flight control alternate hydraulic system.

The flight control alternate hydraulic system pump operates continuously as long as the manual emergency change-over handle is actuated. Decreased pump life may result from excessive periods of operation; also, drain on the battery in case of generator failure would appreciably shorten battery life. Therefore, do not actuate the manual emergency change-over handle in flight, except when the normal system fails and automatic (electrical) change-over does not occur, or just before entering the landing pattern when flying on the alternate system after normal system failure.

With conventional flight control systems, intermediate and maximum rate of control movements are both directly proportional to pilot effort. In constant-pressure irreversible hydraulic systems, such as on this airplane, the rate of control movement will vary with pilot effort only until the actuator valve is completely open. Any additional effort by the pilot will not result in further increase in rate of movement. Thus, the maximum rate obtainable is not determined so much by pilot effort as by the hydraulics and kinematics of the system. With a conventional system, almost any malfunction which could occur that would limit maximum rate of control movement would also be readily apparent at some lesser rate. It would be difficult for it to continue undetected. The same is not true of irreversible systems. If there is some restriction in rate of flow of hydraulic fluid in the irreversible system, it will not be apparent until an attempt is made to move the controls faster than the restriction will permit. Also, the rate of movement imposed by the restriction will be maximum, regardless of pilot effort. Inability to lift the nose wheel during take-off can result from the fact that the stabilizer actuator control valves of the normal and alternate systems were not properly synchronized. If the valves are not synchronized, available control valve displacement is reduced, resulting in a corresponding reduction in maximum rate of control movement. This reduced rate would obviously restrict airplane response. The same effect would occur if restriction in hydraulic flow were caused, for example, by improper attachment of quick-disconnect fittings. Experience shows that this reduction in rate of control movement can mislead the pilot and at the same time escape detection by maintenance personnel. Whether the pilot encounters or notices the malfunction depends upon individual technique and whether the pilot desires to move the controls at a rate faster than the malfunction would permit. It is during take-off and landing that full stick deflection is most often necessary. If the stick fails to move at the normal rate, the pilot may apply greater than normal pressure and gain the impression that he has full stick deflection. Because of the short time involved and the surprise element, the pilot may have an erroneous impression of how far the stick moved. Since a ground check will show that full stick deflection occurs (ignoring the fact that it can be moved only at a slower-than-normal rate), the nature of the malfunction remains undetected. Another pilot using a slower technique and not having occasion to move the stick at rapid rates will not encounter the malfunction. During nose wheel lift-off on take-off, during misjudged and consequently late flare-out on landing, and in the technique of "feeling for the runway," a pilot may assume he is getting the desired stick deflection, whereas restriction of hydraulic fluid flow for any of the reasons mentioned may actually be limiting the rate and consequently the amount of immediate stick deflection. These examples are based on use of the horizontal tail but other difficulties could also result from similar malfunctions affecting aileron control. It is important to check rate of control movement before flight. If the rate is slower than normal, based on experience in other F-86E Airplanes, malfunction of the flight control system, as previously described, should be suspected.

LANDING GEAR.

If the landing gear unsafe warning light should come on during flight, indicating an unsafe landing gear condition, reduce airspeed to below gear-down limit speed before attempting to correct the unsafe condition. This is necessary to prevent the air loads from damaging the landing gear doors. When airspeed is below gear-down limit speed, cycle landing gear down and up. If the warning light remains on after cycling the gear several times, land as soon as practicable.

Section VIII
CREW DUTIES

Not applicable to this airplane.

ALL-WEATHER OPERATION

TABLE OF CONTENTS

	PAGE		PAGE
Instrument Flight Procedures	9-1	Night Flying	9-14
Ice and Rain	9-11	Cold-weather Procedures	9-15
Turbulence and Thunderstorms	9-13	Hot-weather and Desert Procedures	9-18

Except for some repetition necessary for emphasis or continuity of thought, this section contains only those procedures that differ from, or are in addition to, the normal operating procedures in Section II.

INSTRUMENT FLIGHT PROCEDURES

Instrument flight should not be undertaken unless you are a qualified instrument pilot and a holder of AF Form 8A (green) or AF Form 8 (white) instrument certificate. You should be thoroughly familiar with existing Air Force regulations, Technical Orders, and other publications applicable to all-weather operation. Special attention should be given to the fuel planning phase of the preflight planning of IFR flights. Because certain phases of instrument flying may require delays in departure and additional time for letdown procedures, which are often made at low altitudes, the endurance factor is critical. Therefore, it is necessary to plan your flight accurately, with special attention to the traffic density and the types of approaches available at your destination. The effect of a go-around on fuel reserve (because of missed-approach or traffic control emergencies) must also be considered. This airplane has satisfactory stability while being flown on instruments, and its flight handling characteristics during all-weather operation are excellent. Flight instruments provided for basic instrument flying and radio navigation equipment will enable the pilot to make low-frequency range, automatic direction finding (ADF), manual direction finding (MDF), and ground controlled approach (GCA) type instrument approaches.

ON ENTERING AIRPLANE.

1. Map case—Flight Handbook, Radio Facility Charts, Pilot's Handbooks—Jet, and other necessary publications and charts available in the cockpit.

2. Command radio—check the tower, and check approach control, ground controlled intercept (GCI), GCA, and CAA channels.

CAUTION

Make radio check after external power is connected to prevent depleting battery power.

AFTER STARTING ENGINE.

1. IFF to STANDBY; then check after warm-up, if radar coverage is available while on the ground.

TAXIING.

1. Turn-and-slip indicator—check deflection of turn needle during turns.

2. Radio compass—check relative bearing to selected station during various taxi operations.

3. Directional indicator—check actual changes of headings on the taxiways against the instrument indications.

4. Pitot heater switch—ON.

Warm-up time for the pitot heater is approximately one minute at 32°F. Allow sufficient heating time if taking off into freezing rain or other visible moisture with surface temperature at or near freezing.

BEFORE INSTRUMENT TAKE-OFF.

1. Line up visually with centerline of runway.

2. Directional indicator—rotate course index until runway heading is aligned with top of dial.

3. Attitude indicator—adjust reference airplane for level indication by aligning it with indices on each side of instrument face.

4. Windshield anti-icing lever—ON if icing is anticipated.

5. Air outlet selector lever—DEFROST if needed.

6. Hold brakes and advance power.

INSTRUMENT TAKE-OFF.

1. Recheck all instruments and release brakes.

2. Maintain runway heading with nose wheel steering until rudder becomes effective (approximately 50 knots IAS).

3. Take off at normal VFR speed.

4. As airplane breaks ground, immediately establish an initial climb attitude on attitude indicator at a rate of 500 fpm.

5. Landing gear handle—UP as soon as altimeter indicates a gain of altitude.

INSTRUMENT CLIMB.

1. Flap lever—UP at 160 knots IAS with a 1500 fpm climb established.

Note

The airplane will sink during flap retraction if sufficient airspeed is not attained. Use nose-down trim after flap retraction, because speed increases rapidly and necessitates increased stick push forces to maintain level flight.

2. Holding a 1500 fpm rate of climb, accelerate to best VFR climbing speed.

3. Do not turn until 500 feet altitude above the terrain is reached.

4. Limit angle of bank to 30 degrees.

5. While flying in visible moisture, maintain a careful watch on tail-pipe temperature for indications of intake duct icing.

INSTRUMENT CRUISING FLIGHT.

The airplane has excellent handling characteristics at cruising speeds and can be flown with ease if properly trimmed and controlled primarily by reference to the attitude indicator. At higher speeds, it becomes more difficult to maintain longitudinal (pitch) control and gains and losses in altitude may result. During maneuvers at these speeds, use of the horizontal tail for nose-up or nose-down corrections should be kept at a minimum, or overcontrolling will result with subsequent altitude changes of 800 to 1000 feet.

RADIO-NAVIGATION EQUIPMENT.

The AN/ARN-6 radio compass is the only radio equipment provided for en route radio navigation. Because this equipment is highly susceptible to precipitation and electrical static, its reliability at high altitudes is considerably reduced by thin overcasts, haze, and dust. For this reason, the automatic operation of the radio compass should not be relied upon entirely to establish fixes. The signals of the station should be monitored at all times to check station passage and to check that the station is still transmitting. With the function selector switch turned to the ANT. position, the radio compass serves as a normal low-frequency receiver. Use of the loop provides better reception during extreme static conditions. Flights should be thoroughly planned, and elapsed flight time between compulsory check points should be plotted against the estimated times, to maintain constant watch on the progress of the flight.

DESCENT.

Descent can be made without difficulty at speeds up to the limiting Mach number and/or airspeed of the airplane. It is not recommended that descents at high Mach number be continued below 10,000 feet because of the very steep angle and high rate of descent. To limit the airspeed and distance covered at high rates of descent, use of speed brakes is recommended.

Note

The windshield and canopy defrosting system provides sufficient heating of the transparent surfaces to effectively eliminate frost or fog during descent.

In medium to heavy rain, forward visibility will be almost completely obscured. By moving the windshield anti-icing lever to ON on late airplanes,* the anti-icing airflow over the windshield is sufficient to improve forward visibility under moderate rain conditions if a minimum engine rpm of 75% is maintained. If rain is still encountered as power is reduced for landing, it may be necessary to look through the windshield side panels during touchdown and roll-out.

CAUTION

- If windshield overheat warning light comes on, try to extinguish it by reducing power if possible or by moving cockpit pressure switch to RAM. Anti-icing system may be left on if necessary to improve forward visibility, even though windshield overheat light comes on.
- If warning light is on after landing, leave anti-icing lever at ON; reduced power on ground will allow gradual cooling of windshield and prevent cracking of glass by sudden temperature changes.
- On early airplanes,† windshield anti-icing airflow will not help remove rain from the windshield.

---

*F-86E-10 and later airplanes
†F-86E-1 through F-86E-6 Airplanes

WARNING

During descents, it is imperative that the altimeter be accurately read, with particular attention given to the 1000- and 10,000-foot pointers.

Recommended Procedure.

For typical descents, proceed as follows:

1. Speed brake switch OUT. (Return switch to neutral (HOLD) position after speed brakes are fully extended.)
2. Throttle IDLE.

Note

In steep dives during high rates of descent with idle power and speed brakes out, the horizon bar of the attitude indicator rises to a very high position, making accurate determination of pitch angle very difficult. The airspeed indicator becomes very important in limiting the pitch angle under these conditions.

3. Limit angle of bank to 30 degrees.

CAUTION

A descending turn at a high rate of descent becomes progressively more difficult to control as bank angle is increased, and there is danger of falling into an uncontrolled spiral unless you use caution.

INSTRUMENT LETDOWNS.

Jet Penetrations.

Jet penetrations have been set up to provide a high-speed and a high-rate-of-descent letdown from cruising altitude to a point where a VFR approach or an instrument approach (such as GCA, low-frequency range, or ADF) can be made. Penetration procedures for specific fields are given on JAL (jet approach and landing) charts. The Pilot's Handbook—Jet, in two parts for the eastern and western United States, has the JAL charts for all fields where jet penetration procedures have been established. Figure 9-1 shows a typical jet penetration and low approach, using radio range, which is made by beginning a letdown at the penetration cone (cruising altitude) on the heading specified in the JAL chart.

Section IX
T. O. 1F-86E-1

jet penetration and low approach
USING RADIO RANGE (TYPICAL)

NOTE
IF ICING IS ANTICIPATED OR IT IS RAINING, MAINTAIN A MINIMUM OF 75% ENGINE RPM TO ENSURE THAT SUFFICIENT AIRFLOW IS AVAILABLE FOR DEICING AND, ON F-86E-10 AND LATER AIRPLANES, RAIN REMOVAL FROM THE WINDSHIELD.

LOSE ONE-HALF ALTITUDE OUTBOUND.

250 KN IAS

PENETRATION TURN
(ONE NEEDLE WIDTH, 90-270 DEG OR 45-180 DEG, AS DESIRED)
LOSE ONE-THIRD ALTITUDE.

250 KN IAS

LOSE REMAINING ALTITUDE INBOUND TO HIGH CONE.

SPEED BRAKES—IN

LOWER FLAPS WHEN VFR.

CAUTION:
Consult the Pilot's Handbook—Jet for the current approach to your destination.

F-86E-1-00-45

Figure 9-1

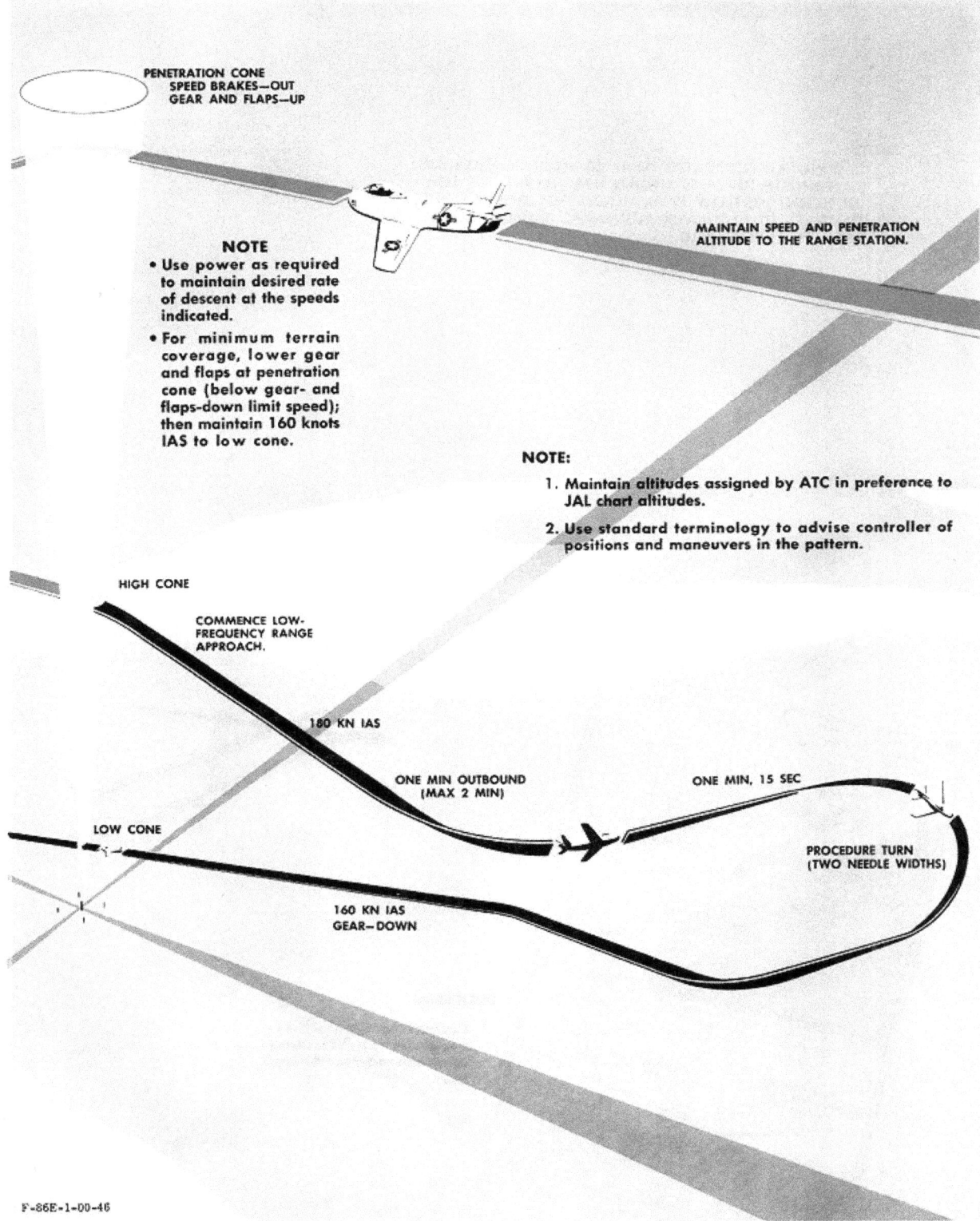

Section IX T. O. 1F-86E-1

jet penetration and low approach
USING ADF (TYPICAL)

NOTE:
IF ICING IS ANTICIPATED OR IT IS RAINING, MAINTAIN A MINIMUM OF 75% ENGINE RPM TO ENSURE THAT SUFFICIENT AIRFLOW IS AVAILABLE FOR DEICING AND, ON F-86E-10 AND LATER AIRPLANES, RAIN REMOVAL FROM THE WINDSHIELD.

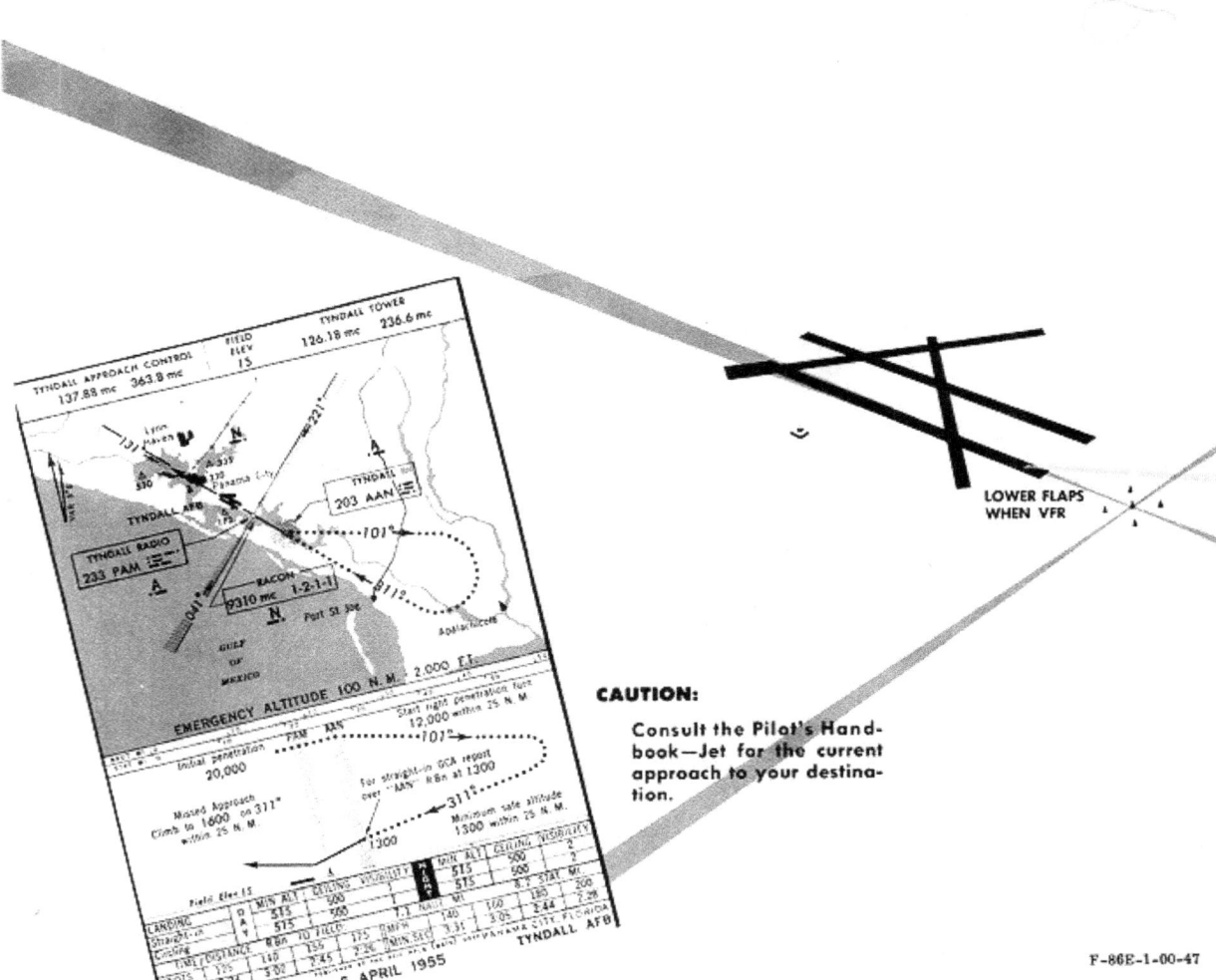

MAINTAIN SPEED AND PENETRATION ALTITUDE TO THE RANGE STATION.

LOWER FLAPS WHEN VFR

CAUTION:
Consult the Pilot's Handbook—Jet for the current approach to your destination.

Figure 9-2

9-6

PENETRATION CONE
SPEED BRAKES—OUT
GEAR AND FLAPS—UP

NOTE:
1. Maintain altitudes assigned by ATC in preference to JAL chart altitudes.
2. Use standard terminology to advise controller of positions and maneuvers in the approach.

NOTE
- Use power as required to maintain desired rate of descent at the speeds indicated.
- For minimum terrain coverage, lower gear and flaps at penetration cone (below gear- and flaps-down limit speed); then maintain 160 knots IAS to low cone.

250 KN IAS

PENETRATION TURN

LOW CONE

160 KN IAS
GEAR—DOWN
SPEED BRAKES—IN

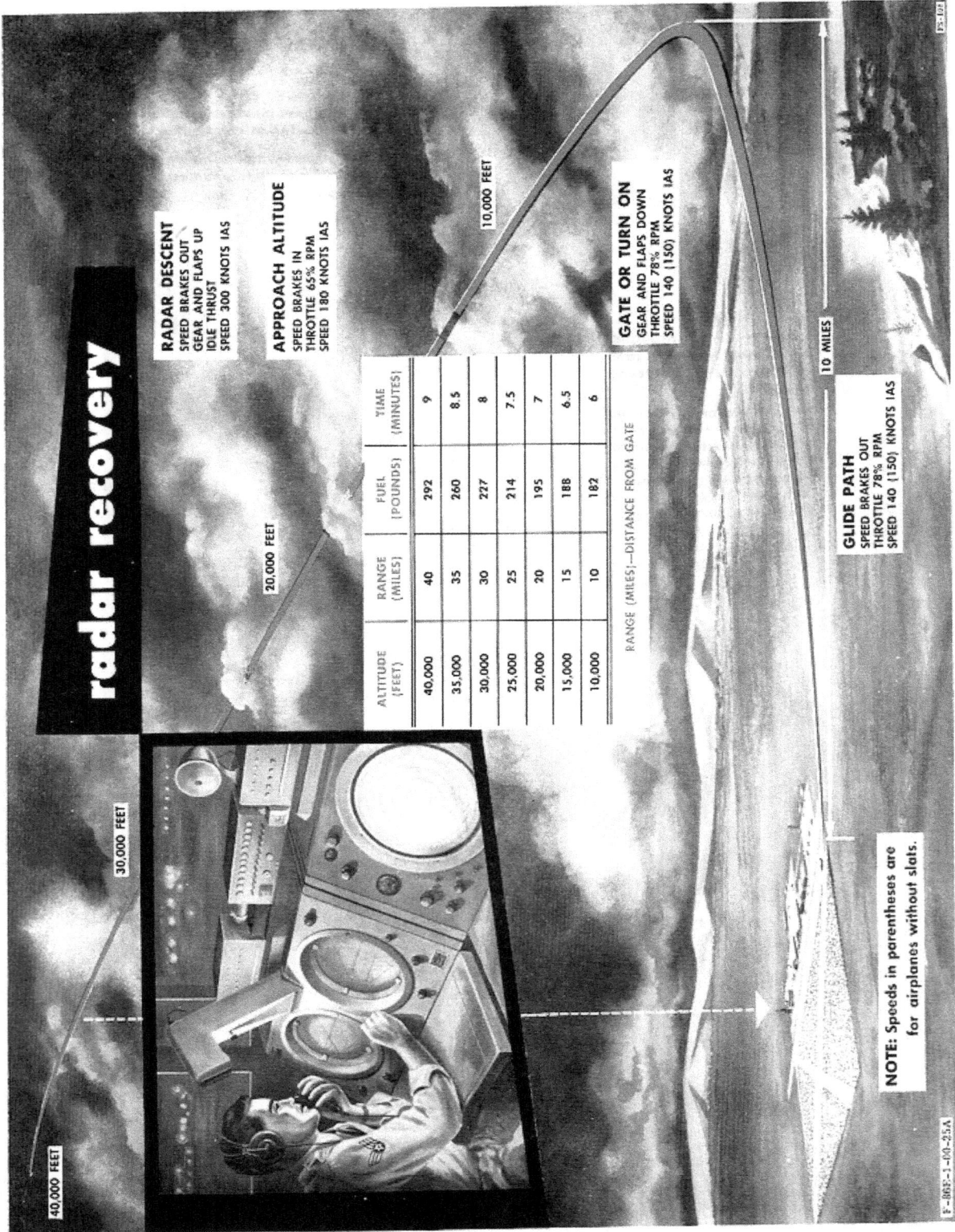

Figure 9-3

The initial phase of the penetration is set up to avoid interference with altitudes occupied by other airplanes. After the high cone is crossed, a conventional instrument approach is begun. A typical penetration and low approach using ADF is shown in figure 9-2.

Note

- Flight paths illustrated in figures 9-1 and 9-2 can be used on both types of penetrations and low approaches. Check the current JAL chart for your destination.
- The conditions set up in the JAL charts should be given careful consideration during flight planning. Availability of GCA, alternates, and operational problems in high-density traffic areas should be analyzed.

Low-frequency Range Approach.

Low-frequency range approach procedures may be used in conjunction with jet penetration procedures, as shown in figure 9-1. JAL charts specify where combined procedures are necessary. A close inspection of the JAL charts shows that though the altitudes for range approaches are usually the same as those shown in the regular Pilot's Handbook, the pattern is often abbreviated or altered in some way for jet airplanes.

ADF Approach.

A great many of the JAL charts in the Pilot's Handbook —Jet call for ADF (automatic direction finding) procedures to be used during the letdown. This approach is preferred to that of the low-frequency range because it is easier to do and can be made on homers.

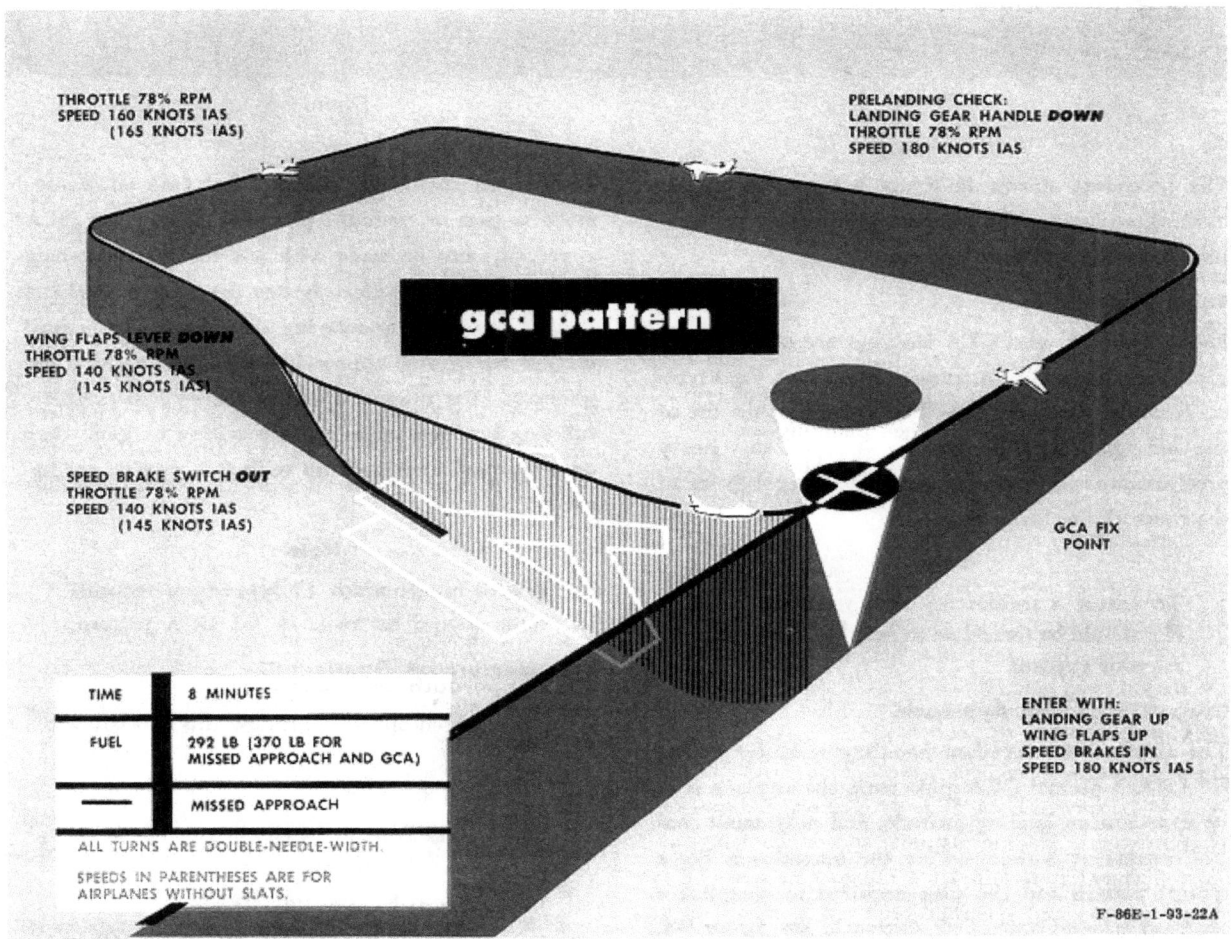

Figure 9-4

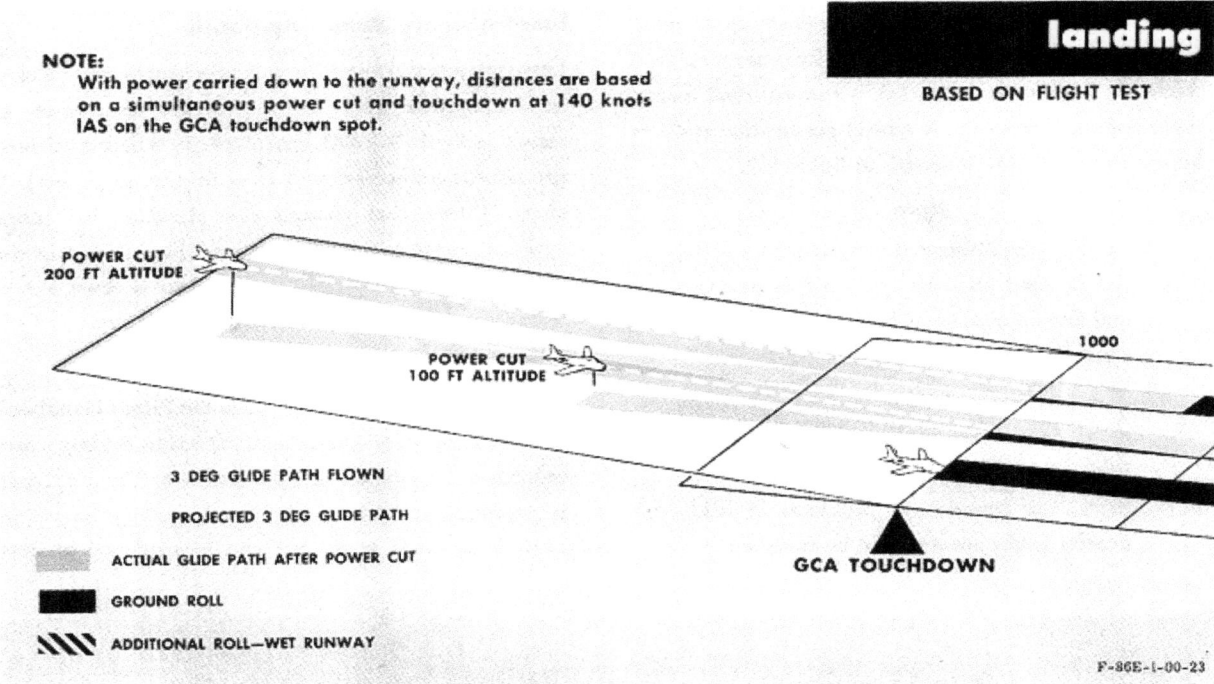

Figure 9-5

The procedure shown in figure 9-2 permits simple tracking with the radio compass, eliminating the need for bracketing and cone passage.

Radar Recovery.

Radar letdowns with GCA landings are optimum for conserving fuel under instrument conditions. For a typical letdown, see figure 9-3. When planning the use of this aid upon an IFR arrival, remember that heavy precipitation can seriously reduce the capabilities of the controller to bring you in.

Note

To ensure a satisfactory radar recovery, the IFF should be turned on to help the controller see your airplane.

Ground-controlled Approach.

The airplane has excellent handling qualities during GCA. On a normal GCA glide path, the airplane is in its approximate landing attitude, and only small control movement is required for the touchdown. For a typical pattern and the time required to complete a standard ground-controlled approach, see figure 9-4. On IFR cross-country flights, the GCA procedure at the destinations should be checked and fuel allowances made as part of preflight planning. Emergency GCA approaches can be made with less fuel by requesting that the GCA controllers shorten the pattern. Fuel can also be conserved by delaying the cockpit check until on base leg of final approach, but before reaching the glidepath. For runway distances required to complete full-stop landings under various ceiling heights when on glide path and lined up with the runway, see figure 9-5.

Note

Double-needle-width (3-degree-per-second) turns should be made in the GCA pattern.

Missed-approach Go-around.

In case of missed approach, follow this procedure for go-around:

1. Throttle 100% rpm.

2. Speed brake switch—IN. [Return switch to neutral (HOLD) position after speed brakes are fully retracted.]

3. Landing gear handle—UP.

4. Wing flap lever—UP (after reaching 160 knots IAS).

roll distances from gca touchdown

FLIGHT CONDITIONS

AIRPLANE: CLEAN AIRPLANE; GROSS WEIGHT 13,000 POUNDS
WEATHER: WIND CALM, TEMPERATURE 59°F
FIELD ELEVATION: SEA LEVEL
RUNWAY CONDITION: DRY OR WET
RUNWAY CONSTRUCTION: CONCRETE
TECHNIQUE: MAXIMUM PRACTICAL BRAKING
APPROACH SPEED: 140 KNOTS IAS
TOUCHDOWN SPEED: 105 KNOTS IAS

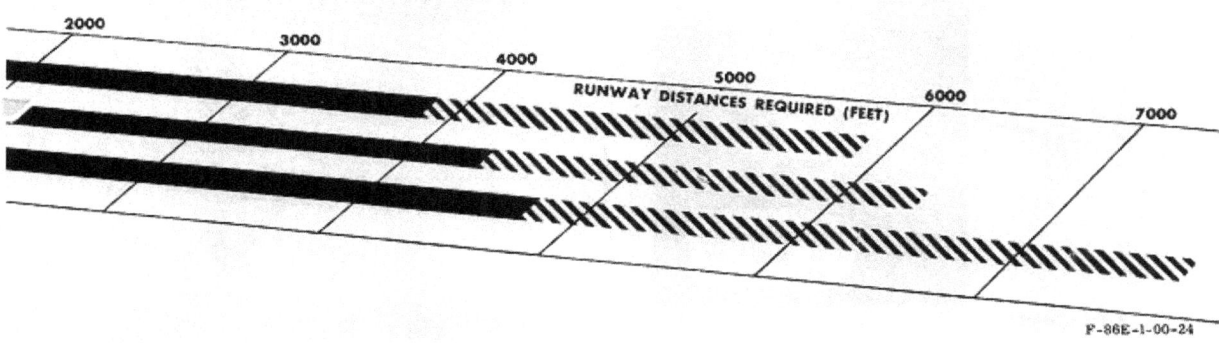

ICE AND RAIN

Ice will normally form on the windshield, wing leading edge, empennage, and the forward portion of the drop tanks. Altitude should be changed immediately upon the first sign of ice accumulation. The resultant drag and weight increase associated with airplane icing reduces the airspeed and increases the power requirements, with consequent reduction in range.

Heavy ice accumulation will greatly increase the stalling speed; therefore, extreme caution must be used when landing under such conditions.

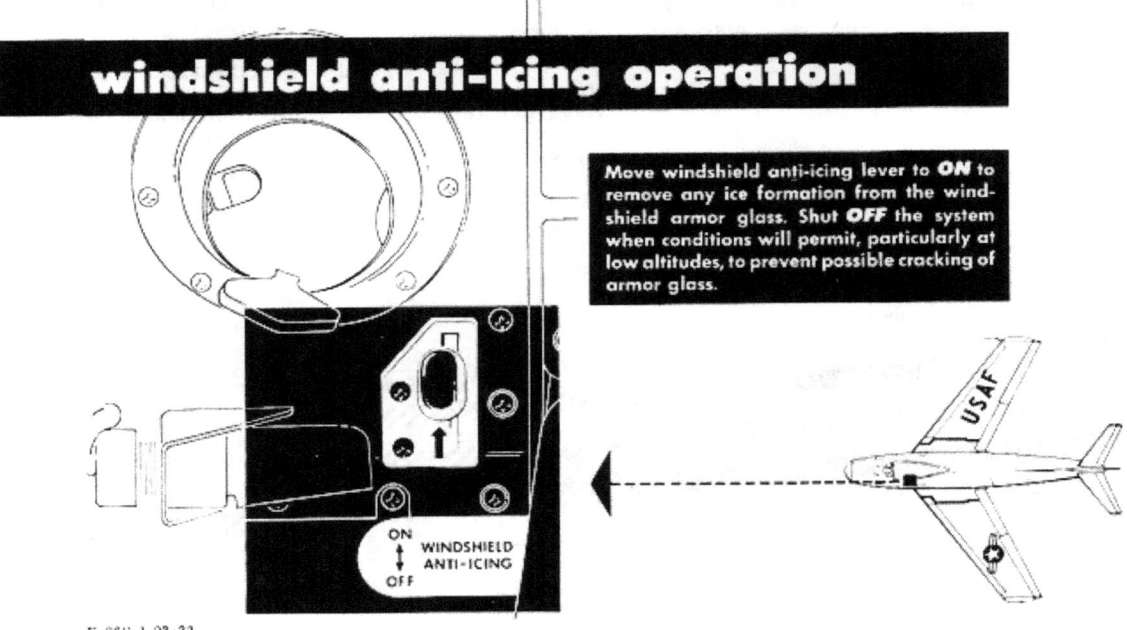

Figure 9-6

Icing of the engine air intake area is possible during operation in weather with temperatures near the freezing point. An increase in fuel flow and a decrease in rpm with a loss of thrust (no mechanical difficulties present) can indicate engine icing. A major rise in tail-pipe temperature with a decrease in thrust is one of the normal indications of engine icing on this type of engine.

WARNING

If icing conditions are encountered and tail-pipe temperature increases, the throttle should be retarded immediately and an effort made to leave the icing area. Low airspeed and high engine rpm are most conducive to engine icing.

During take-off into fog or low clouds, when temperature is at or near freezing, the engine will be subject to icing. Climb should be made at higher than normal indicated airspeeds as a precaution against engine icing. The most proficient weather service cannot always predict accurately just when or where icing may be encountered. However, many areas of probable icing conditions can be avoided by careful flight planning that uses available weather information. If possible, avoid take-offs when the temperature is between $-10°C$ ($14°F$) and $5°C$ ($41°F$) if fog is present or if the dew point is within $4°C$ or $7°F$ of the outside air temperature. These are conditions under which engine icing can occur without wing icing. If the outside air temperature is in the range of $0°C$ ($32°F$) to $5°C$ ($41°F$), the speed of the airplane should be maintained below 250 knots IAS to help prevent intake duct icing. If icing is encountered at freezing atmospheric temperatures, immediate action should be taken as follows:

1. Change altitude rapidly by climb or descent in layer clouds, or vary course as appropriate to avoid cloud formations.

2. Reduce airspeed to minimize rate of ice build-up.

3. Maintain close watch of exhaust temperature, and reduce engine rpm as necessary to prevent excessive exhaust temperature.

4. If ice forms on the windshield, move windshield anti-icing lever to ON.

LANDING IN RAIN.

The windshield anti-icing system on F-86E-10 and later airplanes will provide limited rain removal under moderate rain conditions, provided that engine rpm is maintained at 75% or higher. If the windshield overheat light comes on, reduce engine power setting to decrease anti-icing airflow over the windshield, or place the cockpit pressure switch at RAM position. If these things cannot be done and it is necessary to improve forward visibility, the anti-icing system should be left on. For detailed procedures on removal of ice and rain from the windshield, refer to "Canopy and Windshield Defrosting and Anti-icing System" in Section IV.

TURBULENCE AND THUNDERSTORMS

Flight through a thunderstorm should be avoided if possible. Thunderstorm flying demands considerable instrument experience and should be intentionally undertaken only by well-qualified pilots. However, many routine flight operations require a certain amount of thunderstorm flying, because it is not always possible to avoid storm areas. At night, it is often impossible to detect individual storms and find the in-between clear areas. A pilot using modern equipment and possessing a combination of proper experience, common sense, and instrument flying proficiency can safely fly thunderstorms.

Throttle setting and pitch attitude are the keys to proper flight technique in turbulent air. The throttle and pitch attitude required for desired penetration airspeed should be established before you enter the storm. This throttle setting and pitch attitude, if maintained throughout the storm, must result in a constant airspeed, regardless of any false readings of the airspeed indicator. Specific instructions for preparing to enter a storm and flying in it are given in the following paragraphs.

BEFORE TAKE-OFF.

Note the following precautions:

1. Make a thorough analysis of the general weather situation to determine where thunderstorm areas are, and prepare a flight plan which will avoid thunderstorm areas whenever possible.

2. Check proper operation of all flight instruments, navigation equipment, pitot heater, instrument panel lights, and anti-icing equipment before undertaking instrument flight and also before attempting flight into thunderstorm areas.

APPROACHING THE STORM.

It is imperative that you prepare the airplane before entering a zone of turbulent air. Even if the storm cannot be seen, its proximity will be evidenced by radio crash static. Prepare the airplane as follows:

1. Adjust throttle as necessary to obtain a comfortable penetration speed.

Note

275 knots IAS is a comfortable speed for penetrating a storm or an area of turbulence.

9-13

2. Pitot heater switch—ON.

3. Safety belt tightened. Shoulder harness lock handle—LOCKED.

4. Turn off any radio equipment made useless by static.

5. At night, turn cockpit lights full bright to minimize blinding effect of lightning.

Do not lower landing gear or wing flaps, because they decrease the aerodynamic efficiency of the airplane.

IN THE STORM.

When in the thunderstorm, follow these procedures:

1. Maintain throttle setting and pitch attitude (established before entering) throughout the storm. Hold these constant, and your airspeed will be constant, regardless of the airspeed indications.

2. Give all attention to flying the airplane.

3. Expect turbulence, precipitation, and lightning. Don't allow these conditions to cause undue concern.

4. Maintain attitude. Concentrate principally on remaining level by reference to the attitude indicator.

5. Maintain original heading. Do not make turns unless absolutely necessary.

6. Don't chase the airspeed indicator, because doing so will result in extreme airplane attitudes. If a sudden gust is encountered while airplane is in a nose-high attitude, a stall may result.

7. To minimize the stresses imposed on the airplane, use as little longitudinal control as possible to maintain your attitude.

8. The altimeter may be unreliable in thunderstorms because of differential barometric pressure within the storm. A gain or loss of several thousand feet may be expected. Make allowance for this error in determining the minimum safe altitude.

NIGHT FLYING

There are no specific techniques for flying this airplane at night which differ from those required for daylight operation.

COLD-WEATHER PROCEDURES

While still a factor in successful cold-weather operation, cold-weather postflight preparations are considerably reduced with jet engines because of the lack of oil dilution requirements and other difficulties associated with reciprocating engines. Icing conditions are not covered here. For information about icing problems, refer to "Ice and Rain" in this section. In order to expedite preflight inspection and ensure satisfactory operation for the next flight, normal operating procedures outlined in Section II should be followed, with the following additions and exceptions.

BEFORE ENTERING AIRPLANE.

1. Check that all protective covers and dust plugs have been removed.

2. Check that the airplane—including surfaces, controls, ducts, shock struts, drains, etc—has been cleared of all snow, frost, and ice.

3. Inspect lower portion of engine compressor section for evidence of ice formation on forward stator and rotor blades. If accumulation of ice is present or suspected, check engine for freedom of rotation.

CAUTION

Any attempt to start engine, if engine is not free, will cause starter failure. External heat must be applied to forward section of engine to remove ice. To prevent moisture from refreezing, the engine should be started as soon as possible after heating.

4. Check that oil system has been serviced with proper lubricant.

5. Check that fuel system has been serviced with proper fuel.

Note

JP-4 fuel (Specification MIL-F-5624), or gasoline (Specification MIL-F-5572) if JP-4 fuel is not available, should be used at all temperatures below −18°C (0°F), to ensure satisfactory low-temperature engine starts.

6. Check that fuel filter deicing system alcohol tank has been filled.

7. Be sure that an external dc power source of 28.25 volts (nominal) capable of supplying a minimum of 500 amperes continuous power and 1200 amperes surge power is available for starting.

ON ENTERING AIRPLANE.

1. External dc power source connected.

2. Check flight controls for proper operation.

3. Make sure that canopy can be fully closed.

4. Check electrical and radio equipment.

STARTING ENGINE.

1. JP-4 fuel has good starting characteristics for low-temperature engine starts and permits normal starting procedure.

2. When starting at very low temperatures, best results can be achieved by first obtaining 6% cranking rpm, then advancing throttle to IDLE position until ignition occurs, and immediately retarding throttle to a near-closed position to maintain exhaust temperature below the limit.

9-15

3. If there is no indication of oil pressure after 30 seconds of engine operation at idle, or if oil pressure drops to zero after a few minutes of ground operation, stop engine and investigate.

CAUTION

During cold-weather operation, do not operate engine above 70% rpm until oil temperature is at least −18°C (0°F).

WARM-UP AND GROUND CHECK.

WARNING

Use firmly anchored wheel chocks for engine run-ups. The airplane should be tied down securely before a full-power run-up is attempted. Because of low outside air temperatures, the thrust developed at all engine speeds is noticeably greater than normal.

1. Turn on cockpit heat and windshield defrosting system as required, immediately after engine start.

2. Check flight controls, speed brakes, rudder trim tab, ailerons, and controllable horizontal tail for proper operation.

Note

Cycle flight controls four to six times on both the normal and alternate systems. Check hydraulic pressure and control reaction.

3. Check wing flap operation. Sluggish operation can usually be corrected by cycling flaps three or four times.

CAUTION

Make sure all instruments have warmed up enough to ensure normal operation. Check for sluggishness in the flight instruments during taxiing.

TAXIING.

1. Avoid taxiing in deep snow, because taxiing and steering are extremely difficult and the brakes may freeze.

2. To preserve battery life while taxiing at low engine speeds, use only essential electrical equipment.

3. While taxiing at subfreezing temperatures, increase interval between airplanes to ensure safe stopping distance and to prevent icing of airplane surfaces by melted snow and ice in the jet blast of a preceding airplane.

4. Minimize taxi time to conserve fuel and reduce amount of ice fog generated by the engine.

5. Pitot heater switch—ON.

WARNING

Warm-up time for the pitot heater is approximately one minute at 32°F. Allow enough heating time if taking off into freezing rain or other visible moisture with surface temperature at or near freezing.

BEFORE TAKE-OFF.

Warning

A take-off should not be attempted with snow and ice on the airplane surfaces. Snow and ice on the airplane surfaces constitute a major flight hazard and result in the loss of lift and dangerous stalling characteristics.

1. Make normal full-power check if on a dry, clear runway; however, if take-off is started on ice or snow, make check during the initial part of the take-off roll.

Do not attempt to hold the brakes while the engine is accelerating and the take-off roll is beginning, because you may lose control of the airplane if one wheel begins to slide before the other.

TAKE-OFF.

At low temperatures, excessive tail-pipe temperatures may result from high engine speeds and zero or low ram-air pressures. Therefore, exhaust temperatures may be a limiting factor for take-off rpm during the first part of the take-off roll. Any reduction in engine speed necessary to reduce exhaust temperature to permissible limit will be more than compensated for by the thrust augmentation resulting from increased air density; e.g., 100% rated thrust is reached at 94% rpm at −18°C (0°F) and at 88% rpm at −54°C (−65°F). See figures A-3 and A-4 for take-off distance data.

Note

This airplane may be safely taken off with light frost on the lifting surfaces.

AFTER TAKE-OFF.

1. After take-off from a wet snow- or slush-covered field, operate the landing gear and flaps through several complete cycles to prevent their freezing in the retracted position. (Expect considerably slower operation of the landing gear and wing flaps in cold weather due to stiffening of all lubricants.)

2. Turn on gun heaters immediately after take-off.

3. Check instruments. Many flight instruments may be unreliable at extremely low temperatures.

DURING FLIGHT.

1. Use cockpit heat and canopy and windshield defrosting system as required.

2. Operate fuel filter deicing system as required.

Note

The filter deicer warning light sometimes flickers under certain engine operating conditions, such as rapid acceleration. Therefore, since the deicing alcohol supply will last for only one minute of deicing operation, make sure the light burns steadily before depressing the deicer button. Use the deicer system for 15 seconds at a time.

DESCENT.

Note

The windshield and canopy defrosting system heats the transparent surfaces enough to effectively eliminate frost or fog during descent.

Check engine operating temperatures during descents and in the traffic pattern, since low temperatures are common at low altitudes because of temperature inversions.

APPROACH.

WARNING

Heavy ice accumulation will greatly increase stalling speed; therefore, extreme caution must be used when landing under such conditions.

1. Make normal pattern and landing, but allow for flatter glide due to thrust augmentation caused by extremely low outside air temperatures.

2. Turn off all unnecessary electrical equipment at least one minute before final approach, to reduce battery load when rpm is lowered and generator cuts out.

3. Pump brake pedals several times.

AFTER LANDING.

1. If snow and ice tires are on airplane, apply brakes smoothly and steadily to the point just short of locking the wheels; then release and apply brakes intermittently and carefully to keep treads from filling and glazing over.

CAUTION

Do not use brakes above 100 knots IAS.

Note

- The best technique for obtaining minimum ground roll on slippery runways is to maintain a high angle of attack for as long as possible, keep the flaps full down, and apply brakes only after the nose wheel touches the runway.

- Opening the canopy will help in decreasing the roll, especially with a landing speed of 120 knots.

2. If conditions permit, taxi with sufficient rpm to cut in generator, because low temperatures decrease battery output.

3. Pitot heater switch—OFF.

BEFORE LEAVING AIRPLANE.

1. Leave canopy partly open, if it is not snowing or raining, to allow circulation within the cockpit, to prevent canopy cracking from differential contraction, and to decrease windshield and canopy frosting.

2. Whenever possible, leave airplane parked with full fuel tanks. During servicing, do everything possible to prevent moisture from entering the fuel system.

3. Check that battery is removed when airplane is parked outside at temperatures below −29°C (−20°F) for more than 4 hours.

HOT-WEATHER AND DESERT PROCEDURES

In general, hot-weather and desert procedures differ from normal procedures mainly in that additional precautions must be taken to protect the airplane from damage due to high temperatures and dust. Particular care should be taken to prevent the entrance of sand into the various airplane components and systems (engine, fuel system, pitot-static system, etc). All filters should be checked more often than under normal conditions. Units which have plastic and rubber parts should be protected as much as possible from excessive temperatures. Tires should be checked frequently for signs of blistering, etc.

BEFORE TAKE-OFF.

The emergency fuel regulator is set to give a maximum of 99% rpm on a 100°F day. It does not compensate for temperature changes. If the emergency fuel system is turned on at maximum rpm when temperature is above 100°F, the engine will overspeed. The following procedure is recommended for testing the emergency fuel system at excessively high outside air temperatures before take-off.

1. Run up engine to 80% rpm.

2. Hold emergency fuel switch at ON (two-position switch, or at TEST (three-position switch) and advance throttle until 100% rpm is obtained. If 100% rpm is obtained at less than the full open position and the main fuel regulator fails during take-off, necessitating a switch to the emergency fuel system (emergency fuel switch ON), be prepared to retard throttle immediately to prevent engine overspeeding. Take-off normally will be made on the main fuel system (emergency fuel switch at OFF), and the throttle will be full OPEN.

Note

- If airplane is based at a field where normal temperature range is above 100°F, the emergency regulator should be reset to give a maximum of 99% rpm at the maximum outside air temperature.

- At high outside air temperatures, it may be necessary to have exhaust nozzle segments reset to avoid excessive exhaust temperatures at maximum rpm.

TAKE-OFF.

Note
Do not attempt a take-off in a sand or dust storm. Park the airplane cross-wind and shut down the engine.

The increase in required take-off distances commonly associated with hot-weather operation of any airplane is even greater for jet airplanes. See figures A-3 and A-4 for take-off distance data.

AFTER TAKE-OFF.

Follow normal flight procedures, being particularly careful to maintain a power setting that will keep the tail-pipe exhaust temperature within limits.

BEFORE LEAVING AIRPLANE.

1. Leave canopy slightly open if sand or dust is not blowing, to permit air circulation within the cockpit.
2. Make sure that protective covers are installed on pitot head, canopy, and intake and exhaust ducts.

APPENDIX I

PERFORMANCE DATA

TABLE OF CONTENTS

	PAGE
Discussion of Charts	A-1
Compressibility Correction Table	A-2
Airspeed Conversion	A-2
Take-off Distances	A-6
Climb	A-8
Descent	A-13
Landing Distances	A-14
Combat Allowance	A-15
Maximum Endurance	A-16
Maximum Continuous Power	A-18
Maximum Range Summary	A-20
Flight Operation Instruction Charts	A-22

INTRODUCTION.

To promote efficient operation of the airplane and facilitate flight planning, the charts on the following pages present performance data. All charts are based on NACA Standard Day conditions, except the take-off distances charts, which have columns for various temperatures. The flight operation instruction charts are also applicable in nonstandard atmosphere if the recommended CAS values are maintained. The cruise control charts are easy to interpret and enable you to fly a greater distance at better cruising speed and to arrive at your destination with more reserve fuel. Fuel quantities are given in pounds so that the charts can be used with standard jet fuels or gasoline.

AIRSPEED INSTALLATION CORRECTION.

Airspeed installation error is very minor and may be considered negligible with the airplane in any configuration. Therefore, calibrated airspeed (CAS) is considered equal to indicated airspeed (IAS).

AIRSPEED COMPRESSIBILITY CORRECTION.

A compressibility correction table (figure A-1) is provided for computing equivalent airspeed (EAS) from calibrated airspeed (CAS). For direct conversion of calibrated airspeed to true airspeed on an NACA Standard Day, an airspeed conversion graph (figure A-2) is provided.

EXAMPLE—USE OF CORRECTION TABLE.

An airplane is flying at 20,000 feet, with a true free air temperature of −29°C and an airspeed indicator reading of 393 knots. The value of 393 knots is also the calibrated airspeed (CAS), because installation error is negligible in any configuration. Use CAS and true air temperature with a Type D-4 or Type G-1 airspeed computer to determine true airspeed (TAS) of 512 knots. When the dead-reckoning computer (AN5835-1) is used, the CAS (393 knots) must be corrected for compressibility error. The compressibility correction table

Appendix I T. O. 1F-86E-1

compressibility correction table

SUBTRACT CORRECTION FROM CALIBRATED AIRSPEED TO OBTAIN EQUIVALENT AIRSPEED

PRESSURE ALTITUDE	CAS — KNOTS									
	150	200	250	300	350	400	450	500	550	600
5,000	0	0	1	2	2	3	5	6	8	10
10,000	0	1	2	3	5	7	10	13	17	21
15,000	1	2	3	5	8	12	16	21	27	
20,000	1	3	5	8	12	17	23	31		
25,000	2	4	7	11	17	24	32			
30,000	2	5	9	15	23	32				
35,000	3	7	12	20	29					
40,000	4	9	16	25						

172-93-1560

Figure A-1

airspeed conversion

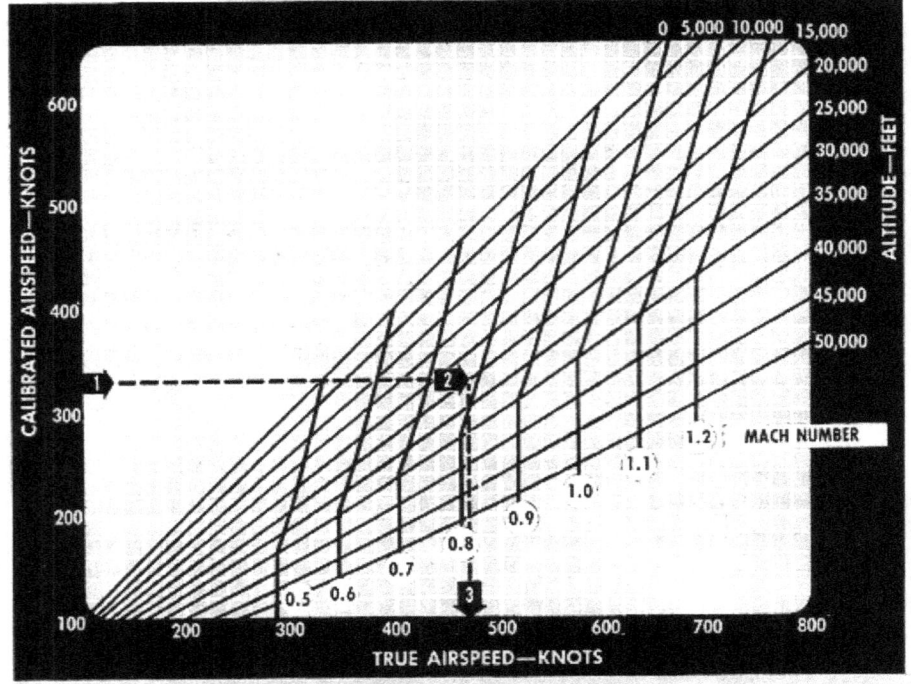

TO USE CHART:
Enter with CAS 1 ; move horizontally to altitude 2 to find Mach number.
Drop vertically to find TAS 3
TAS values from the graph are correct only on an NACA standard day. Otherwise, TAS values will tend to be conservative when true free air temperature is higher than standard, and optimistic when true free air temperature is lower than standard.

EXAMPLE:
On an NACA Standard Day, 330 knots CAS at 25,000 feet is Mach .78 and 470 knots TAS.

F-86E-1-93-41

Figure A-2

(figure A-1) shows that 17 knots must be subtracted from CAS (393 knots) to obtain equivalent airspeed (376 knots). Use the dead-reckoning computer and the values of 376 knots and −29°C to determine the true airspeed of 512 knots.

Note

Indicated airspeed (IAS) is the airspeed indicator reading. Calibrated airspeed (CAS) is indicated airspeed corrected for installation error. Equivalent airspeed (EAS) is calibrated airspeed corrected for compressibility error. True airspeed (TAS) is equivalent airspeed corrected for atmospheric density.

TAKE-OFF DISTANCES.

Ground-run distances and total distance to clear a 50-foot obstacle are tabulated in figures A-3 and A-4. A dry, hard-surfaced runway, zero wind and 30-knot wind, and varying temperatures are considered. The charted distances are based on estimated and actual flight test data, assuming the use of normal take-off technique.

CLIMB.

From the normal power climb and military power climb charts (figures A-5 and A-6), the best climb speed, fuel consumed, time to climb, distance covered, and rate of climb for either Normal Rated or Military Power can be determined. A fuel allowance for warm-up and take-off is listed at sea level. Fuel requirements at other altitudes include this allowance plus the fuel needed to climb from sea level. Fuel required for an in-flight climb from one altitude to another is the difference of the tabulated fuel required to climb to each altitude from sea level. Time and distance covered during an in-flight climb may be obtained in the same manner.

DESCENT.

The descent chart (figure A-8) is based on airspeed corresponding to approximately Mach .5 for descents with speed brakes in and approximately Mach .6 to Mach .8 with speed brakes out. To minimize fuel consumption, the lowest allowable fuel pressure is used.

LANDING DISTANCES.

Figures A-9 and A-10 show landing distances, both ground-run and total, to clear a 50-foot obstacle, for landings with speed brakes out. A percentage increase noted on the charts may be applied to estimate the additional distance required for landings with speed brakes in. A dry, hard-surfaced runway and no wind are the only landing conditions considered.

COMBAT ALLOWANCE.

The combat allowance chart (figure A-11) presents fuel flow at Military Power and at Maximum Continuous Power (Normal Rated Power).

MAXIMUM ENDURANCE.

The maximum endurance chart (figure A-12) gives the best rpm and airspeed to use in obtaining the lowest possible fuel consumption in level flight.

MAXIMUM CONTINUOUS POWER.

Airspeeds and fuel flow rates in level flight at Maximum Continuous Power (Normal Rated Power) are shown for different gross weights and altitudes in the maximum continuous power chart (figure A-13).

MAXIMUM RANGE SUMMARY.

The maximum range summary chart (figure A-14) summarizes the cruising operating procedures for no-wind condition entered on the flight operation instruction charts.

FLIGHT OPERATION INSTRUCTION CHARTS.

The flight operation instruction charts (figures A-15 through A-20) are provided to facilitate flight planning. They show the range of the airplane at maximum-range airspeeds and the procedure required to obtain this range. The charts contain columns for each 5000-foot increase in altitude up to the maximum altitude at which 93% rpm operation is possible. On the line opposite available fuel in the upper half of the chart, ranges are shown for each initial altitude. In general, two range values are quoted for each altitude and fuel quantity. One is for continued flight at the initial altitude, and the other is for the maximum range obtainable by climbing to a high altitude. The charted ranges do not include fuel consumed and distance covered during warm-up, take-off, and initial climb at the start of a flight. However, fuel used and distance covered during letdown or during in-flight climb to a optimum altitude are taken into account. The lower half of each chart presents operating procedure necessary to obtain the ranges quoted in the upper half. When altitude is changed, operating instructions in the column according to the new altitude must be used if the ranges listed are to be obtained. Under different wind conditions, ranges (in ground miles) are varied by the effect of wind on ground speed. Letdown distances are affected for the same reason. Recommended CAS also may change in order to maintain the most favorable ground miles per pound. To facilitate range computation under wind conditions, the operating procedure in the lower half of each chart contains instructions for various winds at each altitude listed. Ground miles in a wind are obtained by multiplying chart air miles by the range factor found opposite the effective wind at the cruising altitude. Thus, range factors may be used to determine the best altitude for cruising when there is a known wind difference at different altitudes. Although a wind may be from any direction with respect to the airplane course, it may be expressed as an effective wind. An effective wind has the same effect on the airplane ground speed as if it were a straight head wind or tail wind. In other words, the wind component in the direction of the airplane heading is the effective wind. For example, a 100-knot wind at 30 degrees to the course is an effective head wind of approximately 85 knots. If the true airspeed is 485 knots, the true ground speed is approximately 400 knots. The approximate rpm values quoted on any one chart are based on the gross weight equal to the high limit of the chart weight band. If the recommended CAS values are maintained, the rpm values will decrease slightly as the gross weight decreases. No allowances are made for navigational errors, combat, formation flight, landing, or other contingencies. Such allowances must be made as required.

USE OF CHARTS.

PREFLIGHT RANGE PLANNING.

Select the applicable flight operation instruction chart. Determine the amount of fuel available for flight planning. Available fuel is equal to the total amount in the airplane before the engine is started, minus the amount needed for warm-up, taxi, take-off, initial climb, and necessary reserves. Select a figure in the fuel column equal to, or less than, the amount available for flight planning. Interpolate if necessary. To determine maximum range at a given altitude, move horizontally right or left to the desired altitude column. Multiply the range value thus obtained by the correct range factor, and add the distance covered in initial climb to obtain total range with a given wind at altitude. Fly according to the instructions in the lower half of the chart. To fly a given distance, determine range factors for the effective winds and altitudes to be considered. From the desired distance, subtract the miles covered in climb. Divide the resultant figure by the range factor to obtain miles to be covered in cruise and descent. Select a figure in the fuel column equal to, or less than, the amount available for flight; then move horizontally right or left to a range figure which exceeds the calculated air distance to be covered in cruise and descent. Fly according to the instructions for the altitude so obtained. If altitude, wind, or external load does not remain reasonably constant, break the flight up into several sections and plan each section separately.

IN-FLIGHT RANGE PLANNING.

To use the charts in flight, determine altitude, available fuel, and effective wind. Available fuel is equal to fuel on board minus necessary reserves. Enter the appropriate flight operation instruction chart at a fuel quantity equal to, or less than, the available fuel. Move horizontally right or left to the applicable altitude column. From the ranges and wind factors listed, determine the altitude at which the flight will be continued. For continued cruising at the present altitude, refer to the instructions directly below. When changing charts, refer to cruising instructions on the new chart at the altitude of flight. To obtain the range shown at optimum altitude when flying at a given altitude, climb immediately according to the recommended climb procedure. For cruising instructions at the new altitude, refer to the lower half of the chart in the column under the new altitude. When changing charts, refer to cruising instructions on the new chart at the new altitude of flight.

Note

For absolute maximum range, climb (using Military Power) until rate of climb is 500 feet per minute. Then hold Mach .75 and 93% rpm constant, allowing the airplane to seek its own altitude.

SAMPLE PROBLEMS BASED ON JP-4 FUEL.

Problem 1.

To illustrate use of the charts for planning a flight, suppose an airplane must be ferried 500 nautical miles. For unexpected difficulties, a general reserve of 900 pounds (140 gallons JP-4 fuel) is considered necessary. From the flight operation instruction charts, it is apparent that drop tanks must be carried; however, it is desired to retain the empty tanks. Use of 120-gallon drop tanks will give a maximum fuel capacity of 670 gallons x 6.5 (pounds per gallon JP-4 fuel), or 4350 pounds. The initial, known conditions are as follows:

Required range .... 500 nautical miles
Effective winds .... 40-knot head wind at 30,000 feet and below; 80-knot head wind at 35,000 feet

From the military power climb chart (figure A-6) and the flight operation instruction chart for 120-gallon drop tanks (figure A-19), the following data is obtained:

	20,000	25,000	35,000
a. Cruising altitude, feet	20,000	25,000	35,000
b. Fuel capacity, pounds	4350	4350	4350
c. Reserve fuel, pounds	900	900	900
d. Fuel used to altitude (climb at 100% rpm), pounds	740	890	1260
e. Available cruise fuel, pounds (b−c−d)	2710	2560	2190
f. Cruise and descent air distance (interpolate as necessary), nautical miles	485	505	515
g. Range factor	.9	.9	.8
h. Cruise and descent ground distance, nautical miles (f × g)	435	455	410
i. Nautical miles covered in initial climb	35	50	100
j. Nautical ground miles range (h + i)	470	505	510

Therefore, the flight can be made at 25,000 feet or higher. The cruise airspeed at 25,000 feet for a 40-knot head wind, while within the weight limits of 16,400 and 14,600 pounds, is 270 knots CAS. However, when the weight has decreased to 14,600 pounds or less, the cruise airspeed is 260 knots CAS. The letdown would begin 9 nautical miles from destination.

Problem 2.

Suppose that during the descent at the end of this theoretical flight the pilot has reached 5000 feet when he learns that the field is closed, and he must use an alternate airport some 100 nautical miles farther. Fuel remaining is only the 900 pounds originally planned for general reserve. Reference to the flight operation instruction chart for 120-gallon drop tanks (figure A-19) shows that with the existing head wind and with the empty tanks still on, available range with 1000 pounds of fuel is approximately 110 nautical miles at 5000 feet (135 nautical miles at optimum altitude, 20,000 feet), with no reserve for landing. It is evident, therefore, that the empty drop tanks should be jettisoned immediately. Reference to the flight operation instruction chart for no external load (figure A-15) shows that even without the drop tanks, only 125 (.85 × 150) miles can be covered at 5000 feet with 1000 pounds of fuel and a 40-knot head wind. However, by climbing immediately to 25,000 feet (optimum altitude) at 100% rpm, a range of 180 miles with zero wind or 160 (180 × .90) miles with existing 40-knot head wind can be attained. At 25,000 feet, the cruise conditions will be 285 knots CAS, 1700 pounds per hour fuel flow, 370 knots ground speed, and letdown begun 15 miles from destination. Since the required range is only 100 nautical miles, the difference between 160 and 100 miles is the reserve, which (expressed in time) is 9.5 minutes (60 miles ÷ 370 knots ground speed = .16 hour or 9.5 minutes). The corresponding fuel reserve is 270 pounds (.16 hour × 1700 pounds per hour). However, this was figured for 1000 pounds of fuel at 5000 feet and only 900 pounds was available, so the landing reserve will be 100 pounds less, or 170 pounds. Judging from this sample problem, when you must get all you can out of the fuel available, climb immediately to optimum altitude and, if necessary, jettison empty drop tanks. Also, when operating on a limited fuel reserve, it is best to determine the condition of the intended destination before descending from altitude. In this problem, with 1000 pounds of fuel available at the cruising altitude of 25,000 feet, by reference to the flight operation instruction chart, it is seen that the range with 120-gallon drop tanks at existing 40-knot head wind is 190 (210 × .90) nautical miles, and without the drop tanks it is 215 (240 × .90) nautical miles. By staying at altitude, you would have a landing reserve of approximately 400 pounds at the alternate airport.

Appendix I
T. O. 1F-86E-1

TAKE-OFF DISTANCES
(FEET)

HARD-SURFACE RUNWAY
(AIRPLANES WITHOUT SLATS)

ENGINE (S): J47-GE-13

MODEL: F-86E

CONFIGURATION AND GROSS WEIGHT	PRESSURE ALTITUDE	-5 DEGREES CENTIGRADE				+15 DEGREES CENTIGRADE				+35 DEGREES CENTIGRADE				+55 DEGREES CENTIGRADE			
		ZERO WIND		30 KNOT WIND		ZERO WIND		30 KNOT WIND		ZERO WIND		30 KNOT WIND		ZERO WIND		30 KNOT WIND	
		GROUND RUN	TO CLEAR 50 FT OBST	GROUND RUN	TO CLEAR 50 FT OBST	GROUND RUN	TO CLEAR 50 FT OBST	GROUND RUN	TO CLEAR 50 FT OBST	GROUND RUN	TO CLEAR 50 FT OBST	GROUND RUN	TO CLEAR 50 FT OBST	GROUND RUN	TO CLEAR 50 FT OBST	GROUND RUN	TO CLEAR 50 FT OBST
TWO 200 GAL TANKS (4) 17,900 POUNDS	SL	3200	4600	1950	3000	4300	5800	2700	3900	5600	7,500	3600	5100	7,900	10,200	5,200	7,100
	1000	3500	4900	2150	3200	4700	6300	2950	4300	6200	8,200	4000	5600	8,700	11,200	5,900	7,900
	2000	3800	5300	2350	3500	5100	6900	3300	4700	6900	9,000	4500	6200	9,700	12,500	6,700	8,900
	3000	4200	5800	2600	3800	5600	7500	3600	5100	7800	9,800	5000	6800	10,900	14,000	8,100	10,600
	4000	4700	6300	2900	4200	6200	8200	4000	5600	8400	10,900	5700	7600	12,400	15,900	9,600	12,400
	5000	5200	6900	3300	4600	6800	8900	4500	6200	9300	11,900	6400	8500	13,900	17,800	11,030	14,200
16 ROCKETS 16,900 POUNDS	SL	2850	4100	1650	2850	3700	5100	2300	3400	4900	6,600	3100	4400	6,700	8,700	4,300	6,000
	1000	3100	4400	1850	2850	4000	5500	2550	3700	5400	7,100	3400	4800	7,400	9,600	4,800	6,600
	2000	3400	4700	2050	3100	4400	6000	2800	4000	5900	7,800	3800	5300	8,200	10,700	5,500	7,400
	3000	3700	5100	2250	3400	4800	6500	3100	4400	6500	8,500	4200	5800	9,100	11,700	6,300	8,400
	4000	4000	5500	2550	3700	5300	7100	3400	4800	7200	9,400	4800	6500	10,200	13,100	7,300	9,700
	5000	4500	6100	2850	4100	5900	7800	3800	5300	8000	10,300	5400	7300	11,400	14,700	8,500	11,200
TWO 120 GAL TANKS 16,400 POUNDS	SL	2600	3800	1600	2500	3400	4800	2100	3100	4500	6,100	2800	4100	6,200	8,100	3,900	5,400
	1000	2800	4100	1700	2650	3700	5200	2300	3400	4900	6,600	3100	4400	6,800	8,900	4,400	6,000
	2000	3100	4400	1900	2900	4100	5600	2550	3700	5400	7,200	3500	4900	7,400	9,700	4,900	6,600
	3000	3400	4800	2100	3200	4500	6100	2850	4100	6000	7,900	3900	5400	8,300	10,800	5,500	7,400
	4000	3700	5200	2350	3500	4900	6600	3200	4500	6600	8,600	4300	5900	9,400	12,000	6,300	8,400
	5000	4100	5600	2600	3800	5500	7300	3600	5000	7300	9,500	4800	6500	10,400	13,300	7,100	9,400
CLEAN 14,600 POUNDS	SL	1950	2950	1050	1800	2550	3700	1450	2300	3300	4,700	1950	3000	4,500	6,100	2,850	4,100
	1000	2100	3100	1200	2000	2750	4000	1600	2500	3800	5,000	2150	3300	4,900	6,600	3,100	4,400
	2000	2300	3400	1350	2200	3000	4300	1800	2650	4000	5,500	2400	3600	5,400	7,200	3,400	4,800
	3000	2550	3700	1500	2400	3300	4700	2000	3000	4400	6,000	2700	3900	6,000	7,900	3,800	5,300
	4000	2800	4000	1650	2600	3600	5100	2200	3300	4800	6,500	3000	4300	6,600	8,700	4,200	5,900
	5000	3100	4300	1800	2800	4000	5500	2450	3600	5300	7,100	3300	4900	7,300	9,500	4,800	6,600

REMARKS:
1. Take-off distances are aircraft requirements under normal service conditions.
2. Take-off with full flaps and 100% rpm.
3. Chart values are based on normal take-off technique.
4. F-86E-15 Airplanes only.

DATA AS OF 7-1-55
BASED ON FLIGHT TEST

WADC Form 243G (11 Jun 54)

F-86E-1-93-38A

Figure A-3. Take-off Distances—Airplanes Without Slats

T. O. 1F-86E-1 Appendix I

TAKE-OFF DISTANCES
(FEET)

HARD-SURFACE RUNWAY
(AIRPLANES WITH SLATS)

MODEL: F-86E
ENGINE (S): (1) J47-GE-13

CONFIGURATION AND GROSS WEIGHT	PRESSURE ALTITUDE	-5°C (+23°F)						-15°C (+50°F)						-35°C (+95°F)						+55°C (+131°F)					
		ZERO WIND		30-KNOT WIND				ZERO WIND		30-KNOT WIND				ZERO WIND		30-KNOT WIND				ZERO WIND		30-KNOT WIND			
		GROUND RUN	TO CLEAR 50 FT OBST	GROUND RUN	TO CLEAR 50 FT OBST			GROUND RUN	TO CLEAR 50 FT OBST	GROUND RUN	TO CLEAR 50 FT OBST			GROUND RUN	TO CLEAR 50 FT OBST	GROUND RUN	TO CLEAR 50 FT OBST			GROUND RUN	TO CLEAR 50 FT OBST	GROUND RUN	TO CLEAR 50 FT OBST		
TWO 200 GAL TANKS 17,700 POUNDS	SL	2500	3900	1450	2400			3200	4700	1850	2950			4200	5900	2550	3800			5600	7700	3500	5100		
	1000	2750	4200	1600	2600			3500	5100	2050	3200			4600	6400	2850	4200			6100	8400	3900	5700		
	2000	3000	4500	1750	2800			3800	5500	2300	3600			5000	7000	3200	4600			6700	9300	4300	6300		
	3000	3300	4800	1950	3000			4200	5900	2550	3900			5500	7600	3500	5100			7300	10,200	4700	7100		
	4000	3600	5100	2150	3300			4600	6400	2850	4200			6000	8300	3800	5600			8000	11,400	5200	8000		
	5000	3900	5600	2400	3700			5000	7000	3200	4600			6800	9100	4200	6200			8800	12,700	5800	8900		
16 ROCKETS 16,900 POUNDS	SL	2300	3600	1300	2200			2850	4300	1650	2650			3800	5400	2250	3500			5000	6800	3100	4500		
	1000	2500	3800	1450	2400			3200	4600	1850	2900			4200	5900	2500	3800			5400	7100	3400	5000		
	2000	2700	4100	1550	2550			3500	5000	2100	3200			4600	6400	2800	4200			5900	8200	3800	5500		
	3000	2900	4400	1700	2750			3800	5400	2300	3500			5000	6900	3100	4500			6500	9000	4200	6000		
	4000	3200	4700	1900	3000			4200	5900	2550	3800			5500	7500	3500	5000			7100	9900	4600	6700		
	5000	3500	5100	2150	3300			4500	6300	2800	4100			6000	8200	3900	5500			7900	11,200	5200	7700		
TWO 120 GAL TANKS 16,400 POUNDS	SL	2150	3400	1200	2100			2750	4100	1600	2550			3600	5100	2100	3300			4700	6500	2800	4200		
	1000	2350	3700	1350	2250			2950	4400	1700	2700			3900	5600	2450	3600			5100	7100	3300	4700		
	2000	2550	3900	1450	2400			3200	4700	1900	2950			4300	6000	2600	3900			5600	7700	3500	5200		
	3000	2750	4200	1600	2600			3500	5100	2100	3200			4700	6500	2900	4200			6100	8500	3900	5600		
	4000	3000	4500	1750	2800			3900	5500	2450	3600			5100	7100	3200	4600			6800	9300	4400	6300		
	5000	3300	4800	1900	3000			4300	6000	2650	3900			5700	7700	3400	5000			7500	10,300	4800	7000		
CLEAN 14,600 POUNDS	SL	1650	2750	900	1650			2100	3300	1150	2000			2650	4000	1500	2450			3500	5000	2100	3200		
	1000	1800	2950	1000	1800			2250	3500	1300	2150			2900	4300	1700	2650			3800	5400	2250	3400		
	2000	1950	3100	1100	1950			2450	3800	1400	2300			3300	4700	1900	3000			4200	5900	2450	3700		
	3000	2100	3400	1200	2050			2650	4000	1500	2450			3500	5000	2050	3200			4600	6400	2700	4100		
	4000	2300	3600	1300	2200			2850	4300	1700	2700			3800	5400	2300	3500			5000	6900	3000	4500		
	5000	2600	4000	1400	2350			3200	4700	2000	2950			4200	5900	2550	3800			5500	7600	3400	5000		

REMARKS: Take-off distances are aircraft requirements under normal service conditions.
1. Take-off with full flaps and 100% rpm.
2. Chart values based on normal take-off technique.

DATA AS OF 2-1-53
BASED ON FLIGHT TEST

Figure A-4. Take-off Distances—Airplanes With Slats

Appendix I T. O. 1F-86E-1

NORMAL POWER CLIMB CHART
STANDARD DAY

WADC Form 241J (11 Jun 51)

MODEL: F-86E ENGINE(S): (1) J47-GE-13

CONFIGURATION: TWO 200-GALLON DROP TANKS [5] CONFIGURATION: TWO 200-Gallon DROP TANKS [5]

GROSS WEIGHT: 17,900 POUNDS GROSS WEIGHT: 15,300 POUNDS

RATE OF CLIMB	APPROXIMATE FROM SEA LEVEL			CAS (KNOTS)	PRESSURE ALTITUDE (FEET)	CAS (KNOTS)	APPROXIMATE FROM SEA LEVEL			RATE OF CLIMB
	DISTANCE	TIME	FUEL				FUEL	TIME	DISTANCE	
2100	0	0	200 [3]	335	SEA LEVEL	335	200 [3]	0	0	2600
1800	15	2.5	420	320	5,000	320	380	2.0	10	2200
1400	35	5.5	670	305	10,000	305	570	4.5	25	1800
1000	55	10.0	950	285	15,000	285	780	7.5	45	1400
700	95	16.0	1320	270	20,000	270	1040	12.0	70	1000
300	155	26.5	1890	250	25,000	250	1370	18.0	105	600
					30,000	230	1980	29.0	160	300
					35,000					
					40,000					
					45,000					

CONFIGURATION: TWO 120-GALLON DROP TANKS CONFIGURATION: TWO 120-GALLON DROP TANKS

GROSS WEIGHT: 16,400 POUNDS GROSS WEIGHT: 14,600 POUNDS

RATE OF CLIMB	APPROXIMATE FROM SEA LEVEL			CAS (KNOTS)	PRESSURE ALTITUDE (FEET)	CAS (KNOTS)	APPROXIMATE FROM SEA LEVEL			RATE OF CLIMB
	DISTANCE	TIME	FUEL				FUEL	TIME	DISTANCE	
3000	0	0	200 [3]	330	SEA LEVEL	325	200 [3]	0	0	3500
2600	10	2.0	360	310	5,000	305	340	1.5	10	3000
2100	20	4.0	530	295	10,000	295	480	3.5	20	2500
1600	35	6.5	720	280	15,000	275	630	5.5	30	2000
1200	60	10.0	940	260	20,000	260	810	8.5	50	1500
800	85	15.0	1220	245	25,000	245	1020	12.0	70	1100
400	140	24.0	1630	225	30,000	225	1290	18.0	105	600
					35,000	210	1750	30.0	175	200
					40,000					
					45,000					

REMARKS:
1. Divide pounds by 6.5 to obtain gallons of MIL-F-5624A, JP-4 fuel.
2. Divide pounds by 6.0 to obtain gallons of MIL-F-5572 fuel (gasoline).
3. Warm-up and take-off allowance.
4. Multiply nautical units by 1.15 to obtain statute units.
5. Data is for F-86E-15 Airplanes only.

LEGEND
RATE OF CLIMB - FEET PER MINUTE
DISTANCE - NAUTICAL MILES
TIME - MINUTES
FUEL - POUNDS
CAS - CALIBRATED AIRSPEED IN KNOTS

DATA AS OF 7-1-54
BASED ON FLIGHT TEST
F-86E-1-93-10

BASED ON ANY FUEL LISTED IN REMARKS

Figure A-5. Normal Power Climb (Sheet 1 of 2)

T.O. 1F-86E-1　　　　　　　　　　　　　　　　　　　　　　　　　　　　　　　　Appendix I

WADC Form 2413 (11 Jun 51)

NORMAL POWER CLIMB CHART

STANDARD DAY
93% RPM

MODEL: F-86E　　　　　　　　　　　　　　　　　　　　　　　ENGINE(S): (1) J47-GE-13

CONFIGURATION: 16 ROCKETS　　　　　　　　　　　　　　　CONFIGURATION: CLEAN

GROSS WEIGHT: 16,900 POUNDS　　　　　　　　　　　　　GROSS WEIGHT: 14,600 POUNDS

RATE OF CLIMB	APPROXIMATE FROM SEA LEVEL			CAS (KNOTS)	PRESSURE ALTITUDE (FEET)	CAS (KNOTS)	APPROXIMATE FROM SEA LEVEL			RATE OF CLIMB
	DISTANCE	TIME	FUEL				FUEL	TIME	DISTANCE	
2200	0	0	200[3]	280	SEA LEVEL	355	200[3]	0	0	4200
1800	10	2.5	420	265	5,000	340	320	1.5	5	3600
1400	25	5.5	660	250	10,000	325	440	3.5	15	3100
1100	45	9.5	940	240	15,000	310	570	4.5	30	2500
700	75	15.0	1300	225	20,000	295	700	7.0	40	2000
300	130	26.0	1850	215	25,000	280	870	10.0	60	1600
					30,000	265	1050	14.0	90	1100
					35,000	245	1290	20.0	130	600
					40,000	225	1770	35.0	235	100
					45,000					

CONFIGURATION:　　　　　　　　　　　　　　　　　　　　　　　CONFIGURATION:

GROSS WEIGHT:　　　　　　　　　　　　　　　　　　　　　　　　GROSS WEIGHT:

RATE OF CLIMB	APPROXIMATE FROM SEA LEVEL			CAS (KNOTS)	PRESSURE ALTITUDE (FEET)	CAS (KNOTS)	APPROXIMATE FROM SEA LEVEL			RATE OF CLIMB
	DISTANCE	TIME	FUEL				FUEL	TIME	DISTANCE	
					SEA LEVEL					
					5,000					
					10,000					
					15,000					
					20,000					
					25,000					
					30,000					
					35,000					
					40,000					
					45,000					

REMARKS:
1. Divide pounds by 6.5 to obtain gallons of MIL-F-5624A, JP-4 fuel.
2. Divide pounds by 6.0 to obtain gallons of MIL-F-5572 fuel (gasoline).
3. Warm-up and take-off allowance.
4. Multiply nautical units by 1.15 to obtain statute units.

LEGEND
RATE OF CLIMB - FEET PER MINUTE
DISTANCE - NAUTICAL MILES
TIME - MINUTES
FUEL - POUNDS
CAS - CALIBRATED AIRSPEED IN KNOTS

DATA AS OF 8-23-51
BASED ON FLIGHT TEST　　　F-86E-1-93-23　　　　　　　　BASED ON ANY FUEL LISTED IN REMARKS

Figure A-5. Normal Power Climb (Sheet 2 of 2)

Appendix I T.O. 1F-86E-1

MILITARY POWER CLIMB CHART
STANDARD DAY

WADC Form 241J (11 Jun 51)

MODEL: F-86E ENGINE(S): (1) J47-GE-13

CONFIGURATION: TWO 200-GALLON DROP TANKS [5]
GROSS WEIGHT: 17,900 POUNDS

CONFIGURATION: TWO 200-GALLON DROP TANKS [5]
GROSS WEIGHT: 15,300 POUNDS

RATE OF CLIMB	APPROXIMATE FROM SEA LEVEL			CAS (KNOTS)	PRESSURE ALTITUDE (FEET)	CAS (KNOTS)	APPROXIMATE FROM SEA LEVEL			RATE OF CLIMB
	DISTANCE	TIME	FUEL				FUEL	TIME	DISTANCE	
3900	0	0	200 [3]	400	SEA LEVEL	400	200 [3]	0	0	4600
3400	10	1.5	380	375	5,000	375	350	1.0	10	4200
3000	20	3.0	550	350	10,000	350	490	2.5	15	3700
2500	30	5.0	830	325	15,000	325	640	4.0	25	3100
2000	45	7.0	1010	300	20,000	300	760	5.5	40	2600
1500	65	10.0	1110	275	25,000	275	940	8.0	55	2000
1000	90	13.5	1350	255	30,000	255	1100	11.0	70	1500
					35,000	230	1310	15.0	100	900
					40,000					
					45,000					

CONFIGURATION: TWO 120-GALLON DROP TANKS
GROSS WEIGHT: 16,400 POUNDS

CONFIGURATION: TWO 120-GALLON DROP TANKS
GROSS WEIGHT: 14,600 POUNDS

RATE OF CLIMB	APPROXIMATE FROM SEA LEVEL			CAS (KNOTS)	PRESSURE ALTITUDE (FEET)	CAS (KNOTS)	APPROXIMATE FROM SEA LEVEL			RATE OF CLIMB
	DISTANCE	TIME	FUEL				FUEL	TIME	DISTANCE	
5200	0	0	200 [3]	400	SEA LEVEL	400	200 [3]	0	0	5900
4600	5	1.0	330	375	5,000	375	320	1.0	5	5200
4000	15	2.0	470	350	10,000	350	430	2.0	15	4600
3400	25	3.5	600	330	15,000	330	550	3.0	20	3900
2700	35	5.0	740	310	20,000	310	670	4.5	30	3300
2100	50	7.5	890	290	25,000	290	790	6.0	40	2600
1500	70	10.0	1050	275	30,000	270	920	8.5	55	1900
900	100	14.0	1260	255	35,000	250	1080	12.0	80	1200
200	165	23.0	1630	230	40,000	230	1320	18.0	120	500
					45,000					

REMARKS:
1. Divide pounds by 6.5 to obtain gallons of MIL-F-5624A, JP-4 fuel.
2. Divide pounds by 6.0 to obtain gallons of MIL-F-5572 fuel (gasoline).
3. Warm-up and take-off allowance.
4. Multiply nautical units by 1.15 to obtain statute units.
5. Data is for F-86E-15 Airplanes only.
6. When engine inlet screens are installed and two 200-gallon drop tanks are carried:
   Increase values under DISTANCE, TIME, and FUEL by 30%.
   Decrease values under RATE OF CLIMB by 500 feet per minute.
7. When engine inlet screens are installed and two 120-gallon drop tanks are carried:
   Increase values under DISTANCE, TIME, and FUEL by 15%.
   Decrease values under RATE OF CLIMB by 350 feet per minute.

LEGEND
RATE OF CLIMB - FEET PER MINUTE
DISTANCE - NAUTICAL MILES
TIME - MINUTES
FUEL - POUNDS
CAS - CALIBRATED AIRSPEED IN KNOTS

DATA AS OF 7-1-54
BASED ON FLIGHT TEST
BASED ON ANY FUEL LISTED IN REMARKS

F-86E-1-93-11

Figure A-6. Military Power Climb (Sheet 1 of 2)

T. O. 1F-86E-1 — Appendix I

WADC Form 241J (11 Jun 51)

MILITARY POWER CLIMB CHART

STANDARD DAY
100% RPM

MODEL: F-86E
ENGINE(S): (1) J47-GE-13

CONFIGURATION: 16 ROCKETS
CONFIGURATION: CLEAN

GROSS WEIGHT: 16,900 POUNDS
GROSS WEIGHT: 14,600 POUNDS

RATE OF CLIMB	APPROXIMATE FROM SEA LEVEL			CAS (KNOTS)	PRESSURE ALTITUDE (FEET)	CAS (KNOTS)	APPROXIMATE FROM SEA LEVEL			RATE OF CLIMB
	DISTANCE	TIME	FUEL				FUEL	TIME	DISTANCE	
4400	0	0	200 (3)	330	SEA LEVEL	430	200 (3)	0	0	7100
3800	5	1.0	360	315	5,000	410	300	1.0	5	6200
3200	15	2.5	510	295	10,000	390	390	1.5	10	5400
2700	25	4.5	680	275	15,000	365	490	2.5	20	4700
2100	35	6.5	850	255	20,000	340	590	3.5	30	3900
1600	50	9.0	1050	240	25,000	320	690	5.0	40	3200
1000	75	13.0	1290	220	30,000	295	790	7.0	50	2500
400	115	21.0	1650	205	35,000	270	910	9.0	70	1800
					40,000	240	1070	13.0	100	900
					45,000					

CONFIGURATION:
CONFIGURATION:

GROSS WEIGHT:
GROSS WEIGHT:

RATE OF CLIMB	APPROXIMATE FROM SEA LEVEL			CAS (KNOTS)	PRESSURE ALTITUDE (FEET)	CAS (KNOTS)	APPROXIMATE FROM SEA LEVEL			RATE OF CLIMB
	DISTANCE	TIME	FUEL				FUEL	TIME	DISTANCE	
					SEA LEVEL					
					5,000					
					10,000					
					15,000					
					20,000					
					25,000					
					30,000					
					35,000					
					40,000					
					45,000					

REMARKS:
1. Divide pounds by 6.5 to obtain gallons of MIL-F-5624A, JP-4 fuel.
2. Divide pounds by 6.0 to obtain gallons of MIL-F-5572 fuel (gasoline).
3. Warm-up and take-off allowance.
4. Multiply nautical units by 1.15 to obtain statute units.
5. When engine inlet screens are installed and 16 rockets are carried:
    Increase values under DISTANCE, TIME, and FUEL by 25%.
    Decrease values under RATE OF CLIMB by 400 feet per minute.
6. When engine inlet screens are installed and no external load is carried:
    Increase values under DISTANCE by 15%.
    Increase values under TIME and FUEL by 10%.
    Decrease values under RATE OF CLIMB by 350 feet per minute.

LEGEND
RATE OF CLIMB — FEET PER MINUTE
DISTANCE — NAUTICAL MILES
TIME — MINUTES
FUEL — POUNDS
CAS — CALIBRATED AIRSPEED IN KNOTS

DATA AS OF 8-23-51
BASED ON FLIGHT TEST
F-86E-1-93-24
BASED ON ANY FUEL LISTED IN REMARKS

Figure A-6. Military Power Climb (Sheet 2 of 2)

Appendix I T. O. 1F-86E-1

WADC Form 2413 (11 Jun 51)

FORMATION POWER CLIMB CHART

STANDARD DAY

97% RPM

MODEL: F-86E ENGINE(S): (1) J47-GE-13

CONFIGURATION: NO EXTERNAL LOAD							CONFIGURATION: TWO 120-GALLON DROP TANKS			
GROSS WEIGHT: 14,600 LB							GROSS WEIGHT: 16,400 LB			
RATE OF CLIMB	APPROXIMATE FROM SEA LEVEL			CAS (KNOTS)	PRESSURE ALTITUDE (FEET)	CAS (KNOTS)	APPROXIMATE FROM SEA LEVEL			RATE OF CLIMB
	DISTANCE	TIME	FUEL				FUEL	TIME	DISTANCE	
5500	0	0	200(3)	430	SEA LEVEL	375	200(3)	0	0	4200
5000	5	1	310	405	5,000	350	340	1.5	5	3700
4400	15	2	410	380	10,000	330	480	3	15	3300
3800	25	3.5	520	360	15,000	310	620	4.5	25	2800
3300	35	4.5	620	335	20,000	290	760	6	40	2400
2800	45	6.5	720	315	25,000	270	910	9	55	1900
2200	60	8.5	830	295	30,000	250	1070	12	75	1300
1600	80	11	960	270	35,000	230	1290	17	110	700
550	115	16	1130	240	40,000					
					45,000					

CONFIGURATION:							CONFIGURATION:			
GROSS WEIGHT:							GROSS WEIGHT:			
RATE OF CLIMB	APPROXIMATE FROM SEA LEVEL			CAS (KNOTS)	PRESSURE ALTITUDE (FEET)	CAS (KNOTS)	APPROXIMATE FROM SEA LEVEL			RATE OF CLIMB
	DISTANCE	TIME	FUEL				FUEL	TIME	DISTANCE	
					SEA LEVEL					
					5,000					
					10,000					
					15,000					
					20,000					
					25,000					
					30,000					
					35,000					
					40,000					
					45,000					

REMARKS:
1. Divide pounds by 6.5 to obtain gallons of MIL-F-5624A, JP-4 fuel.
2. Divide pounds by 6.0 to obtain gallons of MIL-F-5572 fuel (gasoline).
3. Warm-up and take-off allowance.
4. Multiply nautical units by 1.15 to obtain statute units.

LEGEND
RATE OF CLIMB - FEET PER MINUTE
DISTANCE - NAUTICAL MILES
TIME - MINUTES
FUEL - POUNDS
CAS - CALIBRATED AIRSPEED

DATA AS OF 8-23-51
BASED ON FLIGHT TEST

F-86E-1-93-25 BASED ON ANY FUEL LISTED IN REMARKS

Figure A-7. Formation Power Climb

T. O. 1F-86E-1   Appendix I

DESCENT CHART
STANDARD DAY

WADC Form 2410 (11 Jun 51)

MODEL: F-86E   ENGINE(S): (1) J47-GE-13

CONFIGURATION: WITH OR WITHOUT DROP TANKS, SPEED BRAKES CLOSED
GROSS WEIGHT: 12,000 POUNDS

CONFIGURATION: WITH OR WITHOUT DROP TANKS, SPEED BRAKES OPEN
GROSS WEIGHT: 13,000 POUNDS

RATE OF DESCENT	APPROXIMATE TO SEA LEVEL			CAS (KNOTS)	PRESSURE ALTITUDE (FEET)	CAS (KNOTS)	APPROXIMATE TO SEA LEVEL			RATE OF DESCENT
	DISTANCE	TIME	FUEL				FUEL	TIME	DISTANCE	
2,500	45	9.0	160	140	45,000	160	40	3.5	18	13,000
3,000	35	7.0	130	155	40,000	180	35	3.0	16	14,000
3,500	25	5.5	105	175	35,000	210	30	2.5	14	15,000
4,000	20	4.0	80	190	30,000	270	25	2.0	12	16,000
5,000	15	3.0	60	210	25,000	320	25	1.5	10	17,000
6,500	10	2.0	45	225	20,000	370	20	1.0	8	18,000
7,500	10	1.5	35	245	15,000	390	15	1.0	6	19,000
9,000	5	1.0	20	260	10,000	400	10	0.5	4	17,500
10,000	5	0.5	10	280	5,000	410	5	0.5	2	15,000
0	0	0	0	295	SEA LEVEL	420	0	0	0	0

CONFIGURATION:
GROSS WEIGHT:

CONFIGURATION:
GROSS WEIGHT:

RATE OF DESCENT	APPROXIMATE TO SEA LEVEL			CAS (KNOTS)	PRESSURE ALTITUDE (FEET)	CAS (KNOTS)	APPROXIMATE TO SEA LEVEL			RATE OF DESCENT
	DISTANCE	TIME	FUEL				FUEL	TIME	DISTANCE	
					45,000					
					40,000					
					35,000					
					30,000					
					25,000					
					20,000					
					15,000					
					10,000					
					5,000					
					SEA LEVEL					

REMARKS:
1. Speed brakes open - maintain 40 psi fuel pressure.
2. For maximum range without power, descend at 185 knots CAS with speed brakes closed.

LEGEND
RATE OF DESCENT - FEET PER MINUTE
DISTANCE - NAUTICAL MILES
TIME - MINUTES
FUEL - POUNDS
CAS - CALIBRATED AIRSPEED

DATA AS OF
BASED ON FLIGHT TEST

Figure A-8. Descent

Appendix I T. O. 1F-86E-1

LANDING DISTANCES
(FEET)
STANDARD DAY
(AIRPLANES WITHOUT SLATS)

WADC Form 241Q (11 Jun 51)
MODEL: F-86E   ENGINE(S): J47-GE-13

GROSS WEIGHT (LB)	AIRSPEED - KNOTS IAS			HARD SURFACE—NO WIND							
	FINAL APPROACH	OVER 50-FOOT OBSTACLE	TOUCH-DOWN	AT SEA LEVEL		AT 2000 FT		AT 4000 FT		AT 6000 FT	
				GROUND ROLL	TO CLEAR 50 FT OBST.	GROUND ROLL	TO CLEAR 50 FT OBST.	GROUND ROLL	TO CLEAR 50 FT OBST.	GROUND ROLL	TO CLEAR 50 FT OBST.
12,000	135	120	115	2600	3900	2700	4100	2900	4400	3100	4600
14,000	145	130	125	2900	4300	3200	4600	3300	4800	3500	5000
16,000	155	140	135	3300	4800	3500	5000	3700	5200	3900	5400
18,000	165	150	145	3600	5100	3800	5300	4000	5500	4200	5700

REMARKS:
1. Landing distances are airplane requirements under normal service conditions.
2. Speed brakes closed increase distance by 10 percent.

LEGEND
IAS - INDICATED AIRSPEED
OBST. - OBSTACLE

DATA AS OF 30 Sept. 1955
BASED ON FLIGHT TEST

F-86E-1-93-37A

Figure A-9. Landing Distances—Airplanes Without Slats

LANDING DISTANCES
(FEET)
STANDARD DAY
(AIRPLANES WITH SLATS)

WADC Form 241Q (11 Jun 51)
MODEL: F-86E   ENGINE(S): (1) J47-GE-13

GROSS WEIGHT (LB)	AIRSPEED - KNOTS IAS			HARD SURFACE—NO WIND							
	FINAL APPROACH	OVER 50-FOOT OBSTACLE	TOUCH-DOWN	AT SEA LEVEL		AT 2000 FT		AT 4000 FT		AT 6000 FT	
				GROUND ROLL	TO CLEAR 50 FT OBST.	GROUND ROLL	TO CLEAR 50 FT OBST.	GROUND ROLL	TO CLEAR 50 FT OBST.	GROUND ROLL	TO CLEAR 50 FT OBST.
12,000	130	110	105	2100	3200	2200	3300	2400	3400	2500	3600
14,000	140	120	115	2400	3600	2600	3700	2800	3900	3000	4000
16,000	150	130	125	2700	4000	2800	4100	3100	4300	3300	4500
18,000	160	140	135	3000	4400	3200	4600	3400	4800	3600	5000

REMARKS:
1. Landing distances are airplane requirements under normal service conditions.
2. Speed brakes closed increase distance by 20 percent.

LEGEND
IAS - INDICATED AIRSPEED
OBST. - OBSTACLE

DATA AS OF 30 Sept. 1955
BASED ON FLIGHT TEST

F-86E-1-93-34A

Figure A-10. Landing Distances—Airplanes With Slats

A-14

COMBAT ALLOWANCE CHART
STANDARD DAY

MODEL: F-86E   ENGINE(S): (1) J47-GE-13

PRESSURE ALTITUDE (FEET)	FUEL REQUIRED (POUNDS PER MINUTE)	
	MILITARY POWER 100% RPM (30 MIN LIMIT)	NORMAL POWER 93% RPM (NO LIMIT)
SEA LEVEL	140	95
5,000	125	85
10,000	105	80
15,000	90	70
20,000	80	60
25,000	65	50
30,000	55	45
35,000	45	40
40,000	35	30
45,000	30	25
50,000		

REMARKS
1. Military Power exhaust temperature limits 690°C.
2. Normal Power exhaust temperature limit 655°C.
3. Divide pm by 6.5 to obtain gpm of JP-4 fuel.
4. Divide pm by 6.0 to obtain gpm of MIL-F-5572 fuel (gasoline).

DATA AS OF 8-23-51
BASED ON FLIGHT TEST

172-93-1224B

Figure A-11. Combat Allowance

Appendix I
T. O. 1F-86E-1

WADC Form 241R (11 Jun 51)

MAXIMUM ENDURANCE CHART
STANDARD DAY

MODEL: F-86E ENGINE(S): (1) J47-GE-13

CONFIGURATION: TWO 200-GALLON DROP TANKS (3)				CONFIGURATION: TWO 200-GALLON DROP TANKS (3)		
GROSS WEIGHT: 17,900 POUNDS				GROSS WEIGHT: 15,300 POUNDS		
APPROXIMATE		CAS	PRESSURE ALTITUDE	CAS	APPROXIMATE	
LB/HR	% RPM	(KNOTS)	(FEET)	(KNOTS)	% RPM	LB/HR
2000	73	200	SEA LEVEL	190	70	1800
1950	75	195	5,000	185	72	1700
1950	78	200	10,000	185	75	1650
1950	81	200	15,000	190	78	1650
1950	83	205	20,000	190	80	1650
2000	86	210	25,000	200	83	1650
2000	89	220	30,000	200	85	1700
			35,000	210	89	1800
			40,000			
			45,000			
			50,000			

CONFIGURATION: TWO 120-GALLON DROP TANKS				CONFIGURATION: TWO 120-GALLON DROP TANKS		
GROSS WEIGHT: 16,400 POUNDS				GROSS WEIGHT: 14,600 POUNDS		
APPROXIMATE		CAS	PRESSURE ALTITUDE	CAS	APPROXIMATE	
LB/HR	% RPM	(KNOTS)	(FEET)	(KNOTS)	% RPM	LB/HR
1850	70	195	SEA LEVEL	195	67	1750
1750	73	195	5,000	195	69	1600
1700	75	195	10,000	195	71	1450
1650	78	195	15,000	195	74	1400
1650	80	195	20,000	195	76	1350
1650	83	195	25,000	195	78	1300
1700	85	195	30,000	195	81	1300
1800	89	195	35,000	195	83	1300
			40,000	195	88	1400
			45,000			
			50,000			

REMARKS:
1. Divide lb/hr by 6.5 to obtain gph of MIL-F-5624A, JP-4 fuel.
2. Divide lb/hr by 6.0 to obtain gph of MIL-F-5572 fuel (gasoline).
3. Data is for F-86E-15 Airplanes only.

LEGEND
CAS – CALIBRATED AIRSPEED IN KNOTS
LB/HR – FUEL CONSUMPTION – POUNDS PER HOUR

DATA AS OF 7-1-54
BASED ON FLIGHT TEST
F-86E-1-93-12
BASED ON ANY FUEL LISTED IN REMARKS

Figure A-12. Maximum Endurance (Sheet 1 of 2)

T. O. 1F-86E-1 Appendix I

MAXIMUM ENDURANCE CHART
STANDARD DAY

WADC Form Z41B (11 Jan 51)

MODEL: F-86E ENGINE(S): (1) J47-GE-13

CONFIGURATION: 16 ROCKETS				CONFIGURATION: CLEAN		
GROSS WEIGHT: 16,900 POUNDS				GROSS WEIGHT: 14,600 POUNDS		
APPROXIMATE		CAS	PRESSURE ALTITUDE	CAS	APPROXIMATE	
LB/HR	% RPM	(KNOTS)	(FEET)	(KNOTS)	% RPM	LB/HR
1950	73	185	SEA LEVEL	195	67	1750
1950	75	185	5,000	195	69	1600
1950	77	185	10,000	195	71	1450
1950	81	185	15,000	195	74	1400
2000	83	185	20,000	195	76	1350
2050	86	185	25,000	195	78	1300
2200	90	185	30,000	195	81	1300
			35,000	195	83	1300
			40,000	195	88	1400
			45,000	190	91	1350
			50,000			

CONFIGURATION:				CONFIGURATION:		
GROSS WEIGHT:				GROSS WEIGHT:		
APPROXIMATE		CAS	PRESSURE ALTITUDE	CAS	APPROXIMATE	
LB/HR	% RPM	(KNOTS)	(FEET)	(KNOTS)	% RPM	LB/HR
			SEA LEVEL			
			5,000			
			10,000			
			15,000			
			20,000			
			25,000			
			30,000			
			35,000			
			40,000			
			45,000			
			50,000			

REMARKS:

1. Divide lb/hr by 6.5 to obtain gph of MIL-F-5624A, JP-4 fuel.
2. Divide lb/hr by 6.0 to obtain gph of MIL-F-5572 fuel (gasoline).

LEGEND

CAS — CALIBRATED AIRSPEED IN KNOTS
LB/HR — FUEL CONSUMPTION — POUNDS PER HOUR

DATA AS OF 8-23-51
BASED ON FLIGHT TEST
172-93-1569B

FUEL GRADE:
FUEL DENSITY: ANY FUEL LISTED IN REMARKS

Figure A-12. Maximum Endurance (Sheet 2 of 2)

A-17

Appendix I   T. O. 1F-86E-1

WADC Form 241T (11 Jun 51)

MAXIMUM CONTINUOUS POWER CHART
STANDARD DAY

MODEL: F-86E   ENGINE(S): (1) J47-GE-13

CONFIGURATION: TWO 200-GALLON DROP TANKS (4)   CONFIGURATION: TWO 200-GALLON DROP TANKS (4)

GROSS WEIGHT: 17,900 POUNDS   GROSS WEIGHT: 15,300 POUNDS

APPROXIMATE			% RPM	PRESSURE ALTITUDE (FEET)	% RPM	APPROXIMATE		
LB/HR	TAS (KNOTS)	CAS (KNOTS)				CAS (KNOTS)	TAS (KNOTS)	LB/HR
5600	435	435	93	SEA LEVEL	93	435	435	5600
5050	440	410	93	5,000	93	415	445	5050
4500	445	390	93	10,000	93	395	450	4500
4000	450	370	93	15,000	93	370	455	4000
3500	450	340	93	20,000	93	345	460	3550
3000	445	310	93	25,000	93	315	455	3000
2550	435	280	93	30,000	93	290	450	2550
				35,000	93	255	430	2150
				40,000				
				45,000				
				50,000				

CONFIGURATION: TWO 120-GALLON DROP TANKS   CONFIGURATION: TWO 120-GALLON DROP TANKS

GROSS WEIGHT: 16,400 POUNDS   GROSS WEIGHT: 14,600 POUNDS

APPROXIMATE			% RPM	PRESSURE ALTITUDE (FEET)	% RPM	APPROXIMATE		
LB/HR	TAS (KNOTS)	CAS (KNOTS)				CAS (KNOTS)	TAS (KNOTS)	LB/HR
5650	465	465	93	SEA LEVEL	93	465	465	5700
5100	470	440	93	5,000	93	445	475	5100
4550	480	420	93	10,000	93	420	480	4550
4000	480	385	93	15,000	93	395	485	4050
3550	480	365	93	20,000	93	370	490	3600
3050	480	335	93	25,000	93	340	485	3200
2600	470	305	93	30,000	93	305	470	2600
2150	450	265	93	35,000	93	270	450	2200
				40,000	93	220	425	1700
				45,000				
				50,000				

REMARKS:
1. Maximum exhaust temperature 655 C.
2. Divide lb/hr by 6.5 to obtain gph of MIL-F-5624A, JP-4 fuel.
3. Divide lb/hr by 6.0 to obtain gph of MIL-F-5572 fuel (gasoline).
4. Data is for F-86E-15 Airplanes only.

LEGEND
LB/HR - FUEL CONSUMPTION
TAS - TRUE AIRSPEED IN KNOTS
CAS - CALIBRATED AIRSPEED IN KNOTS

DATA AS OF 7-1-54
BASED ON FLIGHT TEST   F-86E-1-93-13   BASED ON ANY FUEL LISTED IN REMARKS

Figure A-13. Maximum Continuous Power (Sheet 1 of 2)

T. O. 1F-86E-1 — Appendix I

| WADC Form 241T (11 Jun 51) | **MAXIMUM CONTINUOUS POWER CHART**
 STANDARD DAY | | | | | | | |

MODEL: F-86E
ENGINE(S): (1) J47-GE-13
CONFIGURATION: 16 ROCKETS
CONFIGURATION: CLEAN
GROSS WEIGHT: 16,900 POUNDS
GROSS WEIGHT: 14,600 POUNDS

APPROXIMATE			% RPM	PRESSURE ALTITUDE (FEET)	% RPM	APPROXIMATE		
LB/HR	TAS (KNOTS)	CAS (KNOTS)				CAS (KNOTS)	TAS (KNOTS)	LB/HR
5600	395	395	93	SEA LEVEL	93	520	520	5750
5000	400	375	93	5,000	93	500	530	5150
4500	405	350	93	10,000	93	470	535	4650
4000	405	320	93	15,000	93	440	535	4100
3500	405	305	93	20,000	93	400	525	3500
3000	395	275	93	25,000	93	370	520	3050
2850	385	245	93	30,000	93	335	510	2550
				35,000	93	300	500	2300
				40,000	93	260	480	1700
				45,000	93	225	480	1450
				50,000				

CONFIGURATION:
CONFIGURATION:
GROSS WEIGHT:
GROSS WEIGHT:

APPROXIMATE			% RPM	PRESSURE ALTITUDE (FEET)	% RPM	APPROXIMATE		
LB/HR	TAS (KNOTS)	CAS (KNOTS)				CAS (KNOTS)	TAS (KNOTS)	LB/HR
				SEA LEVEL				
				5,000				
				10,000				
				15,000				
				20,000				
				25,000				
				30,000				
				35,000				
				40,000				
				45,000				
				50,000				

REMARKS:
1. Maximum exhaust temperature 655°C.
2. Divide lb/hr by 6.5 to obtain gph of MIL-F-5624A, JP-4 fuel.
3. Divide lb/hr by 6.0 to obtain gph of MIL-F-5572 fuel (gasoline).

LEGEND
LB/HR - FUEL CONSUMPTION
TAS - TRUE AIRSPEED
CAS - CALIBRATED AIRSPEED IN KNOTS

DATA AS OF: 8-23-51
BASED ON: FLIGHT TEST
172-93-1570B
FUEL GRADE
FUEL DENSITY: ANY FUEL LISTED IN REMARKS

Figure A-13. Maximum Continuous Power (Sheet 2 of 2)

Appendix I T. O. 1F-86E-1

WADC Form 2415 (11 Jun 51)

MAXIMUM RANGE SUMMARY CHART
STANDARD DAY

MODEL: F-86E ENGINE(S): (1) J47-GE-13

CONFIGURATION: TWO 200-GALLON DROP TANKS [1]   CONFIGURATION: TWO 200-GALLON DROP TANKS [1]

GROSS WEIGHT: 17,900 POUNDS   GROSS WEIGHT: 15,300 POUNDS

APPROXIMATE		MACH NO.	CAS (KNOTS)	PRESSURE ALTITUDE (FEET)	CAS (KNOTS)	MACH NO.	APPROXIMATE	
% RPM	MI/LB						MI/LB	% RPM
79	.105	.42	280	SEA LEVEL	270	.41	.110	77
80	.116	.45	270	5,000	255	.43	.124	78
83	.127	.51	280	10,000	255	.46	.138	80
85	.140	.54	275	15,000	250	.50	.152	82
86	.151	.58	270	20,000	250	.55	.166	84
88	.163	.63	260	25,000	245	.60	.183	86
92	.171	.71	270	30,000	245	.66	.194	88
				35,000	242	.73	.205	92
				40,000				
				45,000				
				50,000				

CONFIGURATION: TWO 120-GALLON DROP TANKS   CONFIGURATION: TWO 120-GALLON DROP TANKS

GROSS WEIGHT: 16,400 POUNDS   GROSS WEIGHT: 14,600 POUNDS

APPROXIMATE		MACH NO.	CAS (KNOTS)	PRESSURE ALTITUDE (FEET)	CAS (KNOTS)	MACH NO.	APPROXIMATE	
% RPM	MI/LB						MI/LB	% RPM
77	.114	.44	290	SEA LEVEL	280	.42	.117	76
78	.129	.46	280	5,000	275	.45	.133	77
80	.145	.50	275	10,000	265	.48	.151	79
82	.160	.54	270	15,000	265	.52	.168	80
83	.175	.58	265	20,000	255	.56	.186	83
86	.191	.64	265	25,000	255	.61	.205	84
88	.203	.69	260	30,000	250	.67	.220	86
91	.213	.76	255	35,000	245	.73	.233	88
				40,000	220	.74	.248	93
				45,000				
				50,000				

REMARKS: 1. Data is for F-86E-15 Airplanes only.

LEGEND
CAS — CALIBRATED AIRSPEED
MI/LB — NAUTICAL MILES PER POUND OF FUEL CONSUMED

DATA AS OF 7-1-54
BASED ON FLIGHT TEST

F-86E-1-93-14

BASED ON ANY FUEL LISTED IN REMARKS

Figure A-14. Maximum Range Summary (Sheet 1 of 2)

T. O. 1F-86E-1   Appendix I

MAXIMUM RANGE SUMMARY CHART
STANDARD DAY

WADC Form 2415 (11 Jun 51)

MODEL: F-86E   ENGINE(S): (1) J47-GE-13

CONFIGURATION: 16 ROCKETS   CONFIGURATION: CLEAN

GROSS WEIGHT: 16,900 POUNDS   GROSS WEIGHT: 14,600 POUNDS

APPROXIMATE		MACH NO.	CAS (KNOTS)	PRESSURE ALTITUDE (FEET)	CAS (KNOTS)	MACH NO.	APPROXIMATE	
% RPM	MI/LB						MI/LB	% RPM
78	.099	.39	265	SEA LEVEL	325	.49	.125	77
80	.109	.41	250	5,000	305	.50	.145	77
82	.119	.45	250	10,000	295	.53	.166	78
84	.128	.50	250	15,000	290	.57	.190	80
86	.136	.54	245	20,000	285	.62	.215	81
90	.143	.59	245	25,000	275	.66	.242	82
92	.148	.63	235	30,000	270	.72	.266	84
				35,000	265	.78	.287	86
				40,000	250	.82	.302	91
				45,000	225	.84	.329	93
				50,000				

CONFIGURATION: CONFIGURATION:

GROSS WEIGHT: GROSS WEIGHT:

APPROXIMATE		MACH NO.	CAS (KNOTS)	PRESSURE ALTITUDE (FEET)	CAS (KNOTS)	MACH NO.	APPROXIMATE	
% RPM	MI/LB						MI/LB	% RPM
				SEA LEVEL				
				5,000				
				10,000				
				15,000				
				20,000				
				25,000				
				30,000				
				35,000				
				40,000				
				45,000				
				50,000				

REMARKS:

LEGEND
CAS   CALIBRATED AIRSPEED
MI/LB   NAUTICAL MILES PER POUND OF FUEL CONSUMED

DATA AS OF 8-23-51
BASED ON FLIGHT TEST

172-93-1568A

Figure A-14. Maximum Range Summary (Sheet 2 of 2)

A-21

Appendix I

T. O. 1F-86E-1

FLIGHT OPERATION INSTRUCTION CHART

EXTERNAL LOAD ITEM: NONE
NUMBER OF ENGINES OPERATING: ONE

WADC Form 241M (11 Jun 51)								
ENGINE(S):	J47-GE-13				MODEL	F-86E		
LIMITS	TIME (MIN)	% RPM	TAIL PIPE TEMP. C	OIL PRESS. (PSI)		CHART WEIGHT LIMITS: 14,600		
MILITARY	30	100	690	50		FUEL PRESS (PSI)		OR LESS
NORMAL	NONE	93	655	50		600		
						400		

INSTRUCTIONS FOR USING CHART: (A) IN FLIGHT - Select figure in fuel column equal to or less than, fuel available for cruise (fuel on board minus allowance for reserve, combat, navigational errors, for-motion flight, etc). Move horizontally right or left to section according to present altitude and read total range available (no wind) by cruising at that altitude or by climbing to another altitude of maximum range for a flight at initial altitude. Operating instructions are given directly below for a flight at higher altitude, climb moved entirely to desired altitude and read cruising instruction in appropriate cruising altitude section.
(B) FLIGHT PLANNING - From initial fuel on board subtract fuel required for take-off and climb to desired cruising altitude and all other necessary allowances. Then use chart as for the FLIGHT above, adding initial climb distance to range values. DATA BELOW CONTAINS NO FUEL RESERVE FOR LANDING.

NOTE: Ranges shown at optimum altitudes are maximum. In order to obtain maximum range on flights requiring more than one chart (because of external configuration or gross weight changes), it is necessary to observe the optimum cruising altitude on each chart, i.e., when changing charts, a climb may be required to attain a maximum range. All range values include allowances for descent distance and fuel. Climb distance and fuel are included where climbs are indicated.

DATA AS OF 8-23-51
BASED ON FLIGHT TEST

122-93-1222

LOW-ALTITUDE CHART

IF YOU ARE AT SEA LEVEL				FUEL (POUNDS)	IF YOU ARE AT 5000 FT				IF YOU ARE AT 10,000 FT				IF YOU ARE AT 15,000 FT				IF YOU ARE AT 20,000 FT			
RANGE IN AIR MILES		OPT ALT (1000 FT)	LET DOWN DIST		RANGE IN AIR MILES		OPT ALT (1000 FT)	LET DOWN DIST	RANGE IN AIR MILES		OPT ALT (1000 FT)	LET DOWN DIST	RANGE IN AIR MILES		OPT ALT (1000 FT)	LET DOWN DIST	RANGE IN AIR MILES		OPT ALT (1000 FT)	LET DOWN DIST
BY CRUISING AT SL	BY CRUISING AT OPT ALT				BY CRUISING AT 5000 FT	BY CRUISING AT OPT ALT			BY CRUISING AT 10,000 FT	BY CRUISING AT OPT ALT			BY CRUISING AT 15,000 FT	BY CRUISING AT OPT ALT			BY CRUISING AT 20,000 FT	BY CRUISING AT OPT ALT		
(370)		45	0	3000	(440)	(810)	45	0	(500)	(810)	45	5	(570)	(640)	45	10	(650)	(660)	45	5
310	(770)	45	0	2500	360	640	45	0	420	640	45	5	480	670	45	10	540	700	45	10
250	600	40	0	2000	290	480	45	0	330	480	40	5	380	500	40	10	430	530	45	10
190	440	30	0	1500	220	310	35	0	250	330	35	5	290	350	35	10	320	380	40	10
120	290	25	0	1000	150	180	25	0	170	200	30	5	190	220	30	10	220	230	30	10
60	160	5	0	500	80				80	90	15	5	100				110			15

	EFFECTIVE WIND (KNOTS)	CRUISING AT SEA LEVEL					CRUISING AT 5000 FT					CRUISING AT 10,000 FT					CRUISING AT 15,000 FT					CRUISING AT 20,000 FT				
		APPROXIMATE					APPROXIMATE					APPROXIMATE					APPROXIMATE					APPROXIMATE				
		CAS	% RPM	LB/HR	G.S. (KN)	RANGE FACTOR	CAS	% RPM	LB/HR	G.S. (KN)	RANGE FACTOR	CAS	% RPM	LB/HR	G.S. (KN)	RANGE FACTOR	CAS	% RPM	LB/HR	G.S. (KN)	RANGE FACTOR	CAS	% RPM	LB/HR	G.S. (KN)	RANGE FACTOR
	120 H.W.											335	81	2400	305	.75	315	82	2100	310	.75	325	84	2100	310	.70
	80 H.W.						325	79	2450	310	.85	315	80	2200	320	.85	300	81	2000	320	.90	315	83	2000	340	.80
	40 H.W.	350	77	2550	310	.85	325	77	2350	325	1.00	295	78	2050	340	1.00	285	80	1850	360	1.00	300	82	1900	360	.90
	0	325	77	2600	325	1.00	305	76	2250	325	1.00	280	77	1950	365	1.15	275	79	1800	380	1.10	285	81	1750	380	1.00
	40 T.W.	300	75	2400	340	1.15	290	76	2150	350	1.15	280	77	1800	365	1.15	265	76	1700	380	1.10	275	80	1700	410	1.10
	80 T.W.											265	76	1800	385	1.25	265	76	1700	410	1.25	265	80	1650	435	1.25
	120 T.W.																					260	79	1600	470	1.35

Figure A-15. Flight Operation Instruction Chart—No External Load—14,600 Pounds or Less (Sheet 1 of 2)

A-22

T. O. 1F-86E-1　　　　　　　　　　　　　　　　　　　　　　　　　　　　　　　Appendix I

HIGH-ALTITUDE CHART

MODEL: F-86E　　**ENG:** (1)J47-GE-13　　**CHART WT LIMITS:** 14,600 OR LESS LB　　**EXT LOAD:** NONE　　**NO. OF ENGINES OPERATING:** ONE

IF YOU ARE AT 25,000 FT — RANGE IN AIR MILES

BY CRUISING AT 25,000 FT	OPT ALT (1000 FT)	BY CRUISING AT OPT ALT
(730)	45	(860)
610	45	720
460	45	550
360	40	400
240	30	250
120		

IF YOU ARE AT 30,000 FT — RANGE IN AIR MILES

BY CRUISING AT 30,000 FT	OPT ALT (1000 FT)	BY CRUISING AT OPT ALT
(800)	45	(900)
(660)	45	(740)
530	45	570
400	40	410
270		
130		

(RANGE FIGURES INCLUDE ALLOWANCES FOR PRESCRIBED CLIMB AND DESCENT TO SEA LEVEL)

IF YOU ARE AT 35,000 FT — RANGE IN AIR MILES

BY CRUISING AT 35,000 FT	OPT ALT (1000 FT)	BY CRUISING AT OPT ALT
(680)	45	(920)
(710)	45	(760)
570	45	600
420	40	430
280		
140		

IF YOU ARE AT 40,000 FT — RANGE IN AIR MILES

BY CRUISING AT 40,000 FT	OPT ALT (1000 FT)	BY CRUISING AT OPT ALT
(900)	45	(950)
(750)	45	(780)
600	45	620
450		
300		
150		

IF YOU ARE AT 45,000 FT — RANGE IN AIR MILES

BY CRUISING AT 45,000 FT	OPT ALT (1000 FT)	BY CRUISING AT OPT ALT
(960)		
(820)		
(650)		
480		
320		
150		

FUEL (POUNDS)

3000
2500
2000
1500
1000
500

CRUISING AT 25,000 FT — APPROXIMATE

CAS	% RPM	LB/HR	G.S. (KN)	RANGE FACTOR	LET. DOWN DIST.
310	85	1950	325	.70	10
295	84	1800	345	.80	10
285	83	1700	370	.90	15
275	82	1650	400	1.00	15
270	82	1600	430	1.10	15
265	82	1600	465	1.20	20
260	81	1550	495	1.30	20

CRUISING AT 30,000 FT — APPROXIMATE

CAS	% RPM	LB/HR	G.S. (KN)	RANGE FACTOR	LET. DOWN DIST.
295	86	1800	340	.70	15
285	85	1700	365	.80	15
275	84	1650	390	.90	15
270	84	1600	425	1.00	20
260	83	1500	450	1.10	20
255	83	1500	480	1.20	25
250	82	1450	515	1.30	25

CRUISING AT 35,000 FT — APPROXIMATE

CAS	% RPM	LB/HR	G.S. (KN)	RANGE FACTOR	LET. DOWN DIST.
275	87	1650	345	.70	20
270	86	1600	380	.80	20
270	86	1600	420	.90	20
265	85	1600	450	1.00	25
260	85	1550	485	1.10	25
260	85	1550	525	1.20	30
255	85	1500	555	1.30	30

CRUISING AT 40,000 FT

CAS	% RPM	LB/HR	G.S. (KN)	RANGE FACTOR	LET. DOWN DIST.
255	91	1600	360	.75	25
255	91	1600	400	.80	30
250	91	1550	435	.90	30
250	91	1550	475	1.00	35
250	91	1550	515	1.10	40
250	91	1550	555	1.15	40
245	90	1500	585	1.25	45

CRUISING AT 45,000 FT

CAS	% RPM	LB/HR	G.S. (KN)	RANGE FACTOR	LET. DOWN DIST.
225	93	1450	360	.75	35
225	93	1450	400	.85	40
225	93	1450	440	.90	40
225	93	1450	480	1.00	45
225	93	1450	520	1.10	50
225	93	1450	560	1.15	50
225	93	1450	600	1.25	55

EFFECTIVE WIND (KNOTS)

120 H.W.
80 H.W.
40 H.W.
0
40 T.W.
80 T.W.
120 T.W.

REMARKS:

1. Climb at 100% rpm.
2. Alt distances and speeds are nautical units.
3. Multiply all nautical units by 1.15 to obtain statute units.
4. Divide lb/hr by 6.5 to obtain gph of MIL-F-5624A, JP-1 fuel.
5. Divide lb/hr by 6.0 to obtain gph of MIL-F-5572 fuel (gasoline).
6. Multiply gallons by factor in Note 4 to obtain pounds.
7. Multiply 430 gallons by factor in Note 4 to obtain maximum available fuel in pounds.
8. Maximum weight at 45,000 feet is 13,600 pounds.

EXAMPLE

If you are flying at 10,000 feet with 2500 pounds of available fuel, you can fly 420 nautical air miles by holding 295 knots CAS. However, you can fly 640 nautical air miles by immediately climbing to 45,000 feet using 100% rpm. At 45,000 feet, cruise at 225 knots CAS and start letdown 45 nautical miles from home. With an 80-knot head wind, the range at 45,000 feet would be .85 x 640, or 545 nautical miles. Cruise at 225 knots CAS with this wind and start letdown 40 nautical miles from destination.

LEGEND

EFFECTIVE WIND — H.W.: HEAD WIND; T.W.: TAIL WIND
RANGE FACTOR — RATIO OF GROUND DISTANCE TO AIR MILES FOR CORRESPONDING WINDS
G.S. — GROUND SPEED IN KNOTS
CAS — CALIBRATED AIRSPEED IN KNOTS
LB/HR — FUEL CONSUMPTION — POUNDS PER HOUR
RANGE — NAUTICAL MILES
KN — KNOTS
OPT. ALT — OPTIMUM ALTITUDE
DISTANCE — NAUTICAL MILES

DATA AS OF 8-23-51　　　BASED ON FLIGHT TEST　　　172-93-1223B

WADC Form 241N (11 Jun 51)

Figure A-15. Flight Operation Instruction Chart—No External Load—14,600 Pounds or Less (Sheet 2 of 2)

Appendix I — T.O. 1F-86E-1

FLIGHT OPERATION INSTRUCTION CHART
STANDARD DAY

MODEL: F-86E-15
EXTERNAL LOAD ITEM: TWO 200 GAL DROP TANKS
NUMBER OF ENGINES OPERATING: ONE
CHART WEIGHT LIMITS: 17,900 TO 15,300 POUNDS
ENGINE(S): (1) J47-GE-13

POWER LIMITS	TIME LIMIT	% RPM	TAIL PIPE TEMP (°C)	OIL PRESS. (PSI)	FUEL PRESS. (PSI)
MILITARY	30	100	690	50	600
NORMAL	NONE	93	655	50	400

NOTES: Ranges shown at optimum altitudes are maximum. In order to obtain maximum range on flights requiring more than one chart (because of external configuration or gross weight changes), it is necessary to observe the optimum cruising altitude on each chart, i.e., when changing charts, an climb may be required to obtain a maximum range. All range values include allowances for descent distance and fuel. Climb distance and fuel are included where climbs are indicated.

INSTRUCTIONS FOR USING CHART. (A) IN FLIGHT—Select figure in fuel column equal to, or less than, fuel available for cruise (fuel on board minus allowance for reserve, combat, navigational errors, formation flights, etc). Move horizontally right or left to section according to present altitude and read total range available (no wind) by cruising at that altitude or by climbing to another altitude of maximum range. For a flight at initial altitude, operating instructions are given directly below. For a flight at higher altitude, climb immediately to desired altitude and read cruising instruction in appropriate cruising altitude section.
(B) FLIGHT PLANNING—From initial fuel on board subtract fuel required for ease of end climb to desired cruising altitude and all other necessary allowances. Then use chart as for IN FLIGHT above, adding initial climb distance to range values. DATA BELOW CONTAINS NO FUEL RESERVE FOR LANDING.

DATA AS OF 6-1-54
BASED ON FLIGHT TEST
F-86E-1-93-15

LOW-ALTITUDE CHART

(RANGE FIGURES INCLUDE ALLOWANCES FOR PRESCRIBED CLIMB AND DESCENT TO SEA LEVEL)

IF YOU ARE AT SEA LEVEL			IF YOU ARE AT 5000 FT			IF YOU ARE AT 10,000 FT			IF YOU ARE AT 15,000 FT			IF YOU ARE AT 20,000 FT			FUEL (POUNDS)
RANGE IN AIR MILES			RANGE IN AIR MILES			RANGE IN AIR MILES			RANGE IN AIR MILES			RANGE IN AIR MILES			
BY CRUISING AT S.L.	OPT ALT (1000 FT)	BY CRUISING AT OPT ALT	BY CRUISING AT 5000 FT	OPT ALT (1000 FT)	BY CRUISING AT OPT ALT	BY CRUISING AT 10,000 FT	OPT ALT (1000 FT)	BY CRUISING AT OPT ALT	BY CRUISING AT 15,000 FT	OPT ALT (1000 FT)	BY CRUISING AT OPT ALT	BY CRUISING AT 20,000 FT	OPT ALT (1000 FT)	BY CRUISING AT OPT ALT	
580	30		660	30		720	30			30			30	(910)	5400
540	30	920	600	30	940	660	30	960	730	30	900	(800)	30	810	5000
480	30	840	540	30	860	590	30	880	650	30	790	710	30		4500
430	30	730	480	30	750	520	30	770	580	30	690	630	30	700	4000
370	30	630	420	30	650	460	30	610	500	30	580	550	30	600	3500
320	30	520	350	30	550	390	30	570	430	30	490	470	30	500	3000
260	30	430	290	30	450	320	30	470	350	30	390	380	30	410	2500
		330			350			370							

	CRUISING AT SEA LEVEL					CRUISING AT 5000 FT					CRUISING AT 10,000 FT					CRUISING AT 15,000 FT					CRUISING AT 20,000 FT					EFFECTIVE WIND (KNOTS)
	APPROXIMATE					APPROXIMATE					APPROXIMATE					APPROXIMATE					APPROXIMATE					
CAS	% RPM	LB/HR	G.S.	RANGE FACTOR	LET. ON DIST	CAS	% RPM	LB/HR	G.S.	RANGE FACTOR	LET. ON DIST	CAS	% RPM	LB/HR	G.S.	RANGE FACTOR	LET. ON DIST	CAS	% RPM	LB/HR	G.S.	RANGE FACTOR	LET. ON DIST	CAS	% RPM	LB/HR	G.S.	RANGE FACTOR	LET. ON DIST	
300	81	2950	260		0	295	82	2800	275		2	315	86	3000	280	.75	3	300	87	2750	290	.75	4	305	89	2900	290	.65	5	120 H.W.
280	79	2650	280	.85	0	270	80	2500	290	.85	2	300	84	2750	305	.85	3	285	86	2550	315	.90	5	290	88	2650	310	.75	6	80 H.W.
260	77	2450	300	1.0	0	255	79	2350	315	1.0	2	280	83	2550	325	1.0	4	275	85	2450	340	1.0	5	280	87	2500	330	.90	7	40 H.W.
				1.15						1.15		260	81	2350	340	1.15	5	265	84	2350	370	1.15	7	270	86	2350	355	1.0	8	0
												245	80	2200	365	1.30	5	255	83	2300	400	1.25	8	260	86	2300	390	1.10	9	40 T.W.
																								255	85	2250	420	1.25	10	80 T.W.
																								250	85	2200	455	1.35	11	120 T.W.

WADC Form 241M (11 Jun 51)

Figure A-16. Flight Operation Instruction Chart—Two 200-gallon Drop Tanks—17,900 to 15,300 Pounds (Sheet 1 of 2)

T. O. 1F-86E-1 Appendix I

HIGH-ALTITUDE CHART

| MODEL: F-86E-15 | ENG: (1) J47-GE-13 | CHART WT LIMITS: 17,900 TO 15,300 LB | EXT LOAD: TWO 200-GALLON DROP TANKS | NO. OF ENGINES OPERATING: ONE |

IF YOU ARE AT 25,000 FT — RANGE IN AIR MILES

BY CRUISING AT 25,000 FT	OPT ALT (1000 FT)	BY CRUISING AT OPT ALT
	30	(930)
	30	820
	30	720
	30	620
	30	520
	30	420

IF YOU ARE AT 30,000 FT — RANGE IN AIR MILES

BY CRUISING AT 30,000 FT	OPT ALT (1000 FT)	BY CRUISING AT OPT ALT
	30	(1940)
	30	840
	30	730
	30	630
	30	530
	30	440

IF YOU ARE AT 35,000 FT — RANGE IN AIR MILES
(RANGE FIGURES INCLUDE ALLOWANCES FOR PRESCRIBED CLIMB AND DESCENT TO SEA LEVEL)

IF YOU ARE AT 40,000 FT — RANGE IN AIR MILES

IF YOU ARE AT 45,000 FT — RANGE IN AIR MILES

FUEL (POUNDS)

5400
5000
4500
4000
3500
3000
2500

CRUISING AT 25,000 FT — APPROXIMATE

% RPM	LB/HR	CAS	G.S.	RANGE FACTOR	LT ON DIST
91	2700	290	300	.70	7
90	2550	280	325	.80	8
89	2400	270	350	.90	9
88	2350	260	380	1.0	10
88	2300	255	410	1.10	11
87	2250	250	440	1.25	12
87	2200	245	480	1.35	13

EFFECTIVE WIND (KNOTS)

120 H.W.
80 H.W.
40 H.W.
0
40 T.W.
80 T.W.
120 T.W.

CRUISING AT 30,000 FT — APPROXIMATE

CAS	% RPM	LB/HR	G.S.	RANGE FACTOR	LT ON DIST
275	93	2550	315	.70	8
275	93	2550	355	.80	10
275	93	2550	390	.90	11
270	92	2450	420	1.0	12
260	91	2350	450	1.10	13
255	91	2350	485	1.20	14
250	90	2300	515	1.30	16

CRUISING AT 35,000 FT — APPROXIMATE

CRUISING AT 40,000 FT — APPROXIMATE

EFFECTIVE WIND (KNOTS)

120 H.W.
80 H.W.
40 H.W.
0
40 T.W.
80 T.W.
120 T.W.

CRUISING AT 45,000 FT — APPROXIMATE

REMARKS

1. Climb at 100% rpm.
2. All distances and speeds are nautical units.
3. Multiply all nautical units by 1.15 to obtain statute units.
4. Divide lb/hr by 6.5 to obtain gph of MIL-F-5624, JP-4 fuel. Divide lb/hr by 6.0 to obtain gph of MIL-F-5512 fuel (gasoline).
5. Multiply gallons by factor in Note 4 to obtain pounds.
6. Multiply 430 gallons by factor in Note 4 to obtain maximum available fuel in pounds.

EXAMPLE

If you are flying at 15,000 feet with 4000 pounds of available fuel, you can fly 580 nautical air miles by holding 275 knots CAS. However, if you climb immediately, using Military Power, to optimum altitude of 30,000 feet and cruise at 270 knots CAS, you can fly 690 nautical air miles by observing the optimum altitude and cruising instructions on succeeding charts, as the gross weight changes. With an 80-knot head wind, this range would be approximately 550 nautical air miles (.80 x 690). Cruise at 275 knots CAS with this wind and observe cruising instructions on succeeding charts.

LEGEND

H.W. — HEAD WIND T.W. TAIL WIND
RANGE FACTOR — RATIO OF GROUND DISTANCE TO AIR MILES FOR CORRESPONDING WINDS
G.S. — GROUND SPEED IN KNOTS
CAS — CALIBRATED AIRSPEED IN KNOTS
LB/HR — FUEL CONSUMPTION, POUNDS PER HOUR
RANGE — NAUTICAL MILES
OPT ALT — OPTIMUM ALTITUDE
DISTANCE — NAUTICAL MILES

FUEL GRADE
FUEL DENSITY

DATA AS OF: 6-1-54
BASED ON: FLIGHT TEST

F-86E-1-93-16

WADC Form 241N (11 Jun 51)

Figure A-16. Flight Operation Instruction Chart—Two 200-gallon Drop Tanks—17,900 to 15,300 Pounds (Sheet 2 of 2)

Appendix I
T. O. 1F-86E-1

FLIGHT OPERATION INSTRUCTION CHART
STANDARD DAY

MODEL: F-86E-15

EXTERNAL LOAD ITEM: TWO 200-GALLON DROP TANKS

NUMBER OF ENGINES OPERATING: ONE

CHART WEIGHT LIMITS: 15,300 POUNDS OR LESS

ENGINE(S): (1) J47-GE-13

POWER LIMITS	TAIL PIPE TEMP °C	RPM	OIL PRESS. PSI	FUEL PRESS. PSI	TIME LIMIT
MILITARY	690	100	50	600	30
NORMAL	655	93	50	400	NONE

NOTES: Ranges shown at optimum altitudes are maximum. In order to obtain maximum range on flights requiring more than one chart (because of external configuration) on gross weight change), it is necessary to observe the optimum cruising altitude on each chart, i.e., when changing charts, a climb may be required to obtain a maximum range. All range values include allowances for descent distance and fuel. Climb distance and fuel are included where climbs are indicated.

DATA AS OF: 6-1-54
BASED ON: FLIGHT TEST

F-86E-1-93-17

LOW-ALTITUDE CHART

	IF YOU ARE AT SEA LEVEL				IF YOU ARE AT 5000 FT				IF YOU ARE AT 10,000 FT				IF YOU ARE AT 15,000 FT				IF YOU ARE AT 20,000 FT				FUEL
	RANGE IN AIR MILES				RANGE IN AIR MILES				RANGE IN AIR MILES (RANGE FIGURES INCLUDE ALLOWANCES FOR PRESCRIBED CLIMB AND DESCENT TO SEA LEVEL)				RANGE IN AIR MILES				RANGE IN AIR MILES				
	BY CRUISING AT SL	OPT ALT (1000 FT)	G.S.	RANGE FACTOR	BY CRUISING AT 5000 FT	OPT ALT (1000 FT)	G.S.	RANGE FACTOR	BY CRUISING AT 10,000 FT	OPT ALT (1000 FT)	G.S.	RANGE FACTOR	BY CRUISING AT 15,000 FT	OPT ALT (1000 FT)	G.S.	RANGE FACTOR	BY CRUISING AT 20,000 FT	OPT ALT (1000 FT)	G.S.	RANGE FACTOR	POUNDS
	330	35	245		370	35	260		420	35	240		460	35	275		500	35	275	.65	3000
	270	35	270	.85	310	35	275		350	35	270	.75	440	35	290	.75	420	35	290	.75	2500
	220	25	285	1.0	250	25	295	.85	280	25	280	.85	340	35	315	.85	340	35	310	.85	2000
	170	15	270	1.0	190	10		1.0	210	15	320	1.0	240	25	340	1.0	250	25	335	1.0	1500
	110	5	285	1.15	130			1.15	140		350	1.15	160	20	370	1.15	170		360	1.10	1000
	60				60				70			1.30	80			1.30	90		395	1.25	500
																			425	1.40	

	CRUISING AT SEA LEVEL				CRUISING AT 5000 FT				CRUISING AT 10,000 FT				CRUISING AT 15,000 FT				CRUISING AT 20,000 FT				EFFECTIVE WIND (KNOTS)	LET DN DIST
	APPROXIMATE				APPROXIMATE				APPROXIMATE				APPROXIMATE				APPROXIMATE					
CAS	% RPM	LB/HR			CAS	% RPM	LB/HR		CAS	% RPM	LB/HR		CAS	% RPM	LB/HR		CAS	% RPM	LB/HR			
285	78	2650			280	80	2500		280	82	2400		285	85	2450		295	87	2550		120 H.W.	
270	76	2450			255	78	2200		270	81	2300		265	83	2200		275	86	2300		80 H.W.	
245	74	2200			235	76	2050		255	80	2150		250	82	2050		260	85	2150		40 H.W.	
									245	79	2050		240	81	1950		250	84	2050		0	4
									235	78	1950		230	80	1900		240	83	1900		40 T.W.	5
																	235	82	1900		80 T.W.	7
																	230	82	1850		120 T.W.	8

WADC Form 241M (11 Jun 51)

Figure A-17. Flight Operation Instruction Chart—Two 200-gallon Drop Tanks—15,300 Pounds or Less (Sheet 1 of 2)

Figure A-17. Flight Operation Instruction Chart—Two 200-gallon Drop Tanks—15,300 Pounds or Less (Sheet 2 of 2)

Appendix I
T. O. 1F-86E-1

Figure A-18. Flight Operation Instruction Chart—16 Rockets—16,900 Pounds or Less (Sheet 1 of 2)

Figure A-18. Flight Operation Instruction Chart—16 Rockets—16,900 Pounds or Less (Sheet 2 of 2)

Appendix I　　　　　　　　　　　　　　　　　　　　　　　　　　　T. O. 1F-86E-1

FLIGHT OPERATION INSTRUCTION CHART

					EXTERNAL LOAD ITEM
WADC Form 241M (11 Jun 51)		MODEL F-86E			TWO 120-GALLON DROP TANKS
ENGINE(S): J47-GE-13					NUMBER OF ENGINES OPERATING: ONE

LIMITS	TIME LIMIT	% RPM	TAIL PIPE TEMP. (°C)	OIL PRESS. (PSI)
MILITARY	30	100	690	50
NORMAL	NONE	93	655	50

CHART WEIGHT LIMITS:	16,400	TO	14,600	FUEL (POUNDS)
FUEL PRESS. (PSI)				
600				
400				

INSTRUCTIONS FOR USING CHART: (A) IN FLIGHT—Select figure in fuel column equal to, or less than, fuel available for cruise (fuel on board minus allowance for reserve, combat, navigational errors, formation flights, etc). Move horizontally right or left to section according to present altitude and read total range available (no wind) by cruising at that altitude or by climbing to another altitude of maximum range for a flight of initial altitude, operating instructions are given directly below. For a flight of higher altitude, climb immediately to desired altitude and read cruising instruction in appropriate cruising altitude section. (B) FLIGHT PLANNING—From initial fuel on board subtract fuel required for take-off and climb to desired cruising altitude and all other necessary allowances. Then use chart as for IN FLIGHT above, adding initial climb distance to range values. DATA BELOW CONTAINS NO FUEL RESERVE FOR LANDING.

NOTES: Ranges shown at optimum altitudes are maximum in order to obtain maximum range on flights requiring more than one chart (because of external configuration or gross weight changes). It is necessary to observe the optimum cruising altitude on each chart; i.e., when changing charts, a climb may be required to obtain a maximum range. All range values include allowances for descent distance and fuel. Climb distance and fuel are included where climbs are indicated.

DATA AS OF 8-23-51
BASED ON FLIGHT TEST

172-93-1220

LOW-ALTITUDE CHART

IF YOU ARE AT SEA LEVEL				IF YOU ARE AT 5000 FT				IF YOU ARE AT 10,000 FT				IF YOU ARE AT 15,000 FT				FUEL (POUNDS)	IF YOU ARE AT 20,000 FT			
RANGE IN AIR MILES			LET. DOWN DIST.	RANGE IN AIR MILES			LET. DOWN DIST.	RANGE IN AIR MILES			LET. DOWN DIST.	RANGE IN AIR MILES			LET. DOWN DIST.		RANGE IN AIR MILES			LET. DOWN DIST.
BY CRUISING AT SL	OPT ALT (1000 FT)	BY CRUISING AT OPT ALT		BY CRUISING AT 5000 FT	OPT ALT (1000 FT)	BY CRUISING AT OPT ALT		BY CRUISING AT 10,000 FT	OPT ALT (1000 FT)	BY CRUISING AT OPT ALT		BY CRUISING AT 15,000 FT	OPT ALT (1000 FT)	BY CRUISING AT OPT ALT			BY CRUISING AT 20,000 FT	OPT ALT (1000 FT)	BY CRUISING AT OPT ALT	
(520)	30	(910)	0	(590)	30	(930)	2	(670)	30	(950)	3	(750)	30	(960)	5	4500	(820)	30	(1000)	5
460	30	760	0	530	30	800	2	590	30	820	4	660	30	860	5	4000	730	30	880	6
400	30	660	0	460	30	680	2	520	30	700	4	580	30	730	5	3500	640	30	750	7
350	30	530	0	390	30	550	2	440	30	570	4	490	30	610	6	3000	540	30	630	8
290	30	420	0	330	30	440	2	370	30	460	5	410	30	500	7	2500	450	30	520	9

(RANGE FIGURES INCLUDE ALLOWANCES FOR PRESCRIBED CLIMB AND DESCENT TO SEA LEVEL)

CRUISING AT SEA LEVEL			APPROXIMATE			CRUISING AT 5000 FT			APPROXIMATE			CRUISING AT 10,000 FT			APPROXIMATE			CRUISING AT 15,000 FT			APPROXIMATE			EFFECTIVE WIND (KNOTS)	CRUISING AT 20,000 FT			APPROXIMATE		
CAS	% RPM	LB/HR	G.S. (KN)	RANGE FACTOR		CAS	% RPM	LB/HR	G.S. (KN)	RANGE FACTOR		CAS	% RPM	LB/HR	G.S. (KN)	RANGE FACTOR		CAS	% RPM	LB/HR	G.S. (KN)	RANGE FACTOR			CAS	% RPM	LB/HR	G.S. (KN)	RANGE FACTOR	
310	79	2550	270	.85		300	80	2550	280	.85		305	83	2500	270	.75		300	84	2400	280	.75		120 H.W.	305	86	2450	285	.65	
290	77	2300	290	1.00		280	78	2300	300	1.00		290	81	2350	295	.85		285	83	2250	315	.85		80 H.W.	290	85	2300	305	.75	
265	75	2300	305	1.15		265	77	2200	325	1.15		275	80	2200	315	1.00		270	82	2100	335	1.00		40 H.W.	275	84	2100	330	.90	
												265	79	2100	345	1.15		265	82	2050	370	1.15		0	265	83	2050	355	1.00	
												255	78	2000	375	1.25		255	81	1950	395	1.25		40 T.W.	260	83	2000	390	1.10	
																								80 T.W.	255	83	1950	420	1.25	
																								120 T.W.	250	82	1900	455	1.35	

Figure A-19. Flight Operation Instruction Chart—Two 120-gallon Drop Tanks—16,400 to 14,600 Pounds
(Sheet 1 of 2)

T. O. 1F-86E-1 Appendix I

HIGH-ALTITUDE CHART

| MODEL: F-86E | ENG: (J)J47-GE-13 | CHART WT LIMITS: 16,400 TO 14,600 LB | EXT LOAD: TWO 120-GALLON DROP TANKS | NO. OF ENGINES OPERATING: ONE |

IF YOU ARE AT 25,000 FT

RANGE IN AIR MILES		FUEL (POUNDS)
BY CRUISING AT 25,000 FT	BY CRUISING AT OPT ALT	
(900)	(1030)	4500
800	890	4000
700	770	3500
600	640	3000
400	530	2500

CRUISING AT 25,000 FT — APPROXIMATE

CAS	% RPM	LB/HR	G.S. (KN)	RANGE FACTOR	LET-DOWN DIST.
290	88	2300	295	.70	7
280	87	2200	325	.80	8
270	86	2050	350	.90	9
265	86	2000	385	1.00	10
260	85	1950	415	1.10	11
255	86	1900	450	1.20	12
250	84	1900	485	1.35	13

IF YOU ARE AT 30,000 FT

RANGE IN AIR MILES		FUEL (POUNDS)
BY CRUISING AT 30,000 FT	BY CRUISING AT OPT ALT	
(970)		4500
(860)		4000
750		3500
640		3000
530		2500

(RANGE FIGURES INCLUDE ALLOWANCES FOR PRESCRIBED CLIMB AND DESCENT TO SEA LEVEL)

EFFEC. TIVE WIND (KNOTS)
120 H.W.
80 H.W.
40 H.W.
0
40 T.W.
80 T.W.
120 T.W.

CRUISING AT 30,000 FT — APPROXIMATE

CAS	% RPM	LB/HR	G.S. (KN)	RANGE FACTOR	LET-DOWN DIST.
280	90	2250	315	.70	8
275	89	2200	350	.80	10
265	88	2050	375	.90	11
260	88	2030	410	1.00	12
255	87	1950	440	1.10	13
255	87	1950	480	1.20	14
250	87	1950	515	1.30	16

IF YOU ARE AT 35,000 FT

RANGE IN AIR MILES		FUEL (POUNDS)
BY CRUISING AT 35,000 FT	BY CRUISING AT OPT ALT	
(1020)	(1050)	4500
(900)	(930)	4000
790	800	3500
670	680	3000
550		2500

CRUISING AT 33,000 FT — APPROXIMATE

CAS	% RPM	LB/HR	G.S. (KN)	RANGE FACTOR	LET-DOWN DIST.
265	93	2150	330	.70	10
265	93	2150	370	.80	11
260	92	2100	405	.90	13
255	91	2050	435	1.00	14
255	91	2050	475	1.10	15
250	91	2000	505	1.20	17
245	90	1950	540	1.30	18

IF YOU ARE AT 40,000 FT

RANGE IN AIR MILES		FUEL (POUNDS)
BY CRUISING AT 40,000 FT	BY CRUISING AT OPT ALT	
		4500
		4000
		3500
		3000
		2500

CRUISING AT 40,000 FT

(empty)

IF YOU ARE AT 45,000 FT

RANGE IN AIR MILES		
BY CRUISING AT 45,000 FT	OPT ALT (1000 FT)	BY CRUISING AT OPT ALT

CRUISING AT 45,000 FT

| CAS | % RPM | LB/HR | G.S. (KN) | RANGE FACTOR | LET-DOWN DIST. |

EFFECTIVE WIND (KNOTS): 120 H.W., 80 H.W., 40 H.W., 0, 40 T.W., 80 T.W., 120 T.W.

REMARKS:
1. Climb at 100% rpm.
2. All distances and speeds are nautical units.
3. Multiply all nautical units by 1.15 to obtain statute units.
4. Divide lb/hr by 6.5 to obtain gph of MIL-F-5624A, JP-4 fuel.
5. Divide lb/hr by 6.0 to obtain gph of MIL-F-5572 fuel (gasoline).
6. Multiply gallons by factor in Note 4 to obtain pounds.
7. Multiply 670 gallons by factor in Note 4 to obtain maximum fuel available in pounds.

EXAMPLE

If you are at 10,000 feet with 4000 pounds of available fuel, you can fly 580 nautical air miles by holding 275 knots CAS. However, you can fly 820 nautical air miles by immediately climbing to 30,000 feet using 100% rpm. At 30,000 feet, cruise at 260 knots CAS and start letdown 12 nautical miles from home. With an 80-knot head wind, the range at 30,000 feet would be .80 x 820, or 660 nautical miles. Cruise at 275 knots CAS with this wind and start letdown 10 nautical miles from destination.

LEGEND

EFFECTIVE WIND - H.W. - HEAD WIND, T.W. - TAIL WIND
RANGE FACTOR - RATIO OF GROUND DISTANCE TO AIR MILES FOR CORRESPONDING WINDS
G.S. - GROUND SPEED IN KNOTS
CAS - CALIBRATED AIRSPEED IN KNOTS
LB/HR - FUEL CONSUMPTION—POUNDS PER HOUR
RANGE - NAUTICAL MILES
KN - KNOTS
OPT ALT - OPTIMUM ALTITUDE
DISTANCE - NAUTICAL MILES

DATA AS OF 8-23-51 BASED ON FLIGHT TEST

WADC Form 241N (11 June 51)

Figure A-19. Flight Operation Instruction Chart—Two 120-gallon Drop Tanks—16,400 to 14,600 Pounds (Sheet 2 of 2)

Appendix I
T. O. 1F-86E-1

FLIGHT OPERATION INSTRUCTION CHART

EXTERNAL LOAD ITEM: TWO 120-GALLON DROP TANKS
NUMBER OF ENGINES OPERATING: ONE

CHART WEIGHT LIMITS: 14,600 OR LESS POUNDS

MODEL: F-86E
ENGINE(S): J47-GE-13

LIMITS	TIME LIMIT	% RPM	TAIL PIPE TEMP (°C)	OIL PRESS. (PSI)	FUEL PRESS. (PSI)
MILITARY	30	100	690	50	600
NORMAL	NONE	93	655	50	400

NOTES: Ranges shown at optimum altitudes are maximum. In order to obtain maximum range on flights requiring more than one chart (because of external configuration or gross weight changes), it is necessary to observe the optimum cruising altitude on each chart, i.e., when changing charts, a climb may be required to obtain a maximum range. All range values include allowances for descent distance and fuel. Climb distance and fuel are included where climbs are indicated.

DATA AS OF 8-23-51
BASED ON FLIGHT TEST
172-93-1218

LOW-ALTITUDE CHART

INSTRUCTIONS FOR USING CHART. (A) IN FLIGHT — Select figure in fuel column equal to, or less than, fuel available for cruise (fuel on board minus allowance for reserve, combat, navigational errors, formation flights, etc). Move horizontally right or left to section according to present altitude and read total range available (no wind) by cruising at that altitude or by climbing to another altitude of maximum range. For a flight at initial altitude, operating instructions are given directly below. For a flight at higher altitude, climb immediately to desired altitude and read cruising instruction in appropriate cruising altitude section. (B) FLIGHT PLANNING — From initial fuel on board subtract fuel required for take-off and climb to desired cruising altitude and all other necessary allowances. Then use chart as for IN FLIGHT above, adding initial climb distance to range values. DATA BELOW CONTAINS NO FUEL RESERVE FOR LANDING.

IF YOU ARE AT SEA LEVEL			IF YOU ARE AT 5000 FT			IF YOU ARE AT 10,000 FT			IF YOU ARE AT 15,000 FT			FUEL (POUNDS)	IF YOU ARE AT 20,000 FT		
RANGE IN AIR MILES			RANGE IN AIR MILES			RANGE IN AIR MILES (RANGE FIGURES INCLUDE ALLOWANCES FOR PRESCRIBED CLIMB AND DESCENT TO SEA LEVEL)			RANGE IN AIR MILES				RANGE IN AIR MILES		
BY CRUISING AT SL	OPT ALT (1000 FT)	BY CRUISING AT OPT ALT	BY CRUISING AT 5000 FT	OPT ALT (1000 FT)	BY CRUISING AT OPT ALT	BY CRUISING AT 10,000 FT	OPT ALT (1000 FT)	BY CRUISING AT OPT ALT	BY CRUISING AT 15,000 FT	OPT ALT (1000 FT)	BY CRUISING AT OPT ALT		BY CRUISING AT 20,000 FT	OPT ALT (1000 FT)	BY CRUISING AT OPT ALT
350	40	600	400	40	620	460	40	640	510	40	660	3000	560	40	680
290	40	470	330	40	490	380	40	520	430	40	540	2500	470	40	560
230	35	350	270	40	370	300	40	390	340	40	410	2000	380	40	430
180	30	240	200	30	260	230	30	270	260	35	290	1500	280	35	310
120	15	130	130	20	150	150	25	170	170	25	180	1000	190	25	200
60			70			80			90			500	100		

CRUISING AT SEA LEVEL					CRUISING AT 5000 FT					CRUISING AT 10,000 FT					EFFECTIVE WIND (KNOTS)	CRUISING AT 15,000 FT					CRUISING AT 20,000 FT				
			APPROXIMATE					APPROXIMATE					APPROXIMATE						APPROXIMATE					APPROXIMATE	
CAS	% RPM	LB/HR	G.S. (KN)	RANGE FACTOR	LET DOWN DIST	CAS	% RPM	LB/HR	G.S. (KN)	RANGE FACTOR	LET DOWN DIST	CAS	% RPM	LB/HR	G.S. (KN)	RANGE FACTOR	LET DOWN DIST		CAS	% RPM	LB/HR	G.S. (KN)	RANGE FACTOR	LET DOWN DIST	CAS	% RPM	LB/HR	G.S. (KN)	RANGE FACTOR	LET DOWN DIST
305	78	2650	285	.85	0	290	79	2350	270	.85	2	300	82	2400	265	.75	3	120 H.W.	290	83	2200	280	.75	5	300	85	2300	280	.65	5
																		80 H.W.							285	84	2100	300	.80	6
290	76	2400	280	1.00	0	275	77	2200	295	1.00	2	280	80	2250	285	.85	4	40 H.W.	275	81	2050	300	.85	5	270	83	1950	320	.90	7
280	74	2200	300	1.15	0	260	76	2050	320	1.15	2	265	79	2050	305	1.00	4	0	265	80	1950	330	1.00	6	255	83	1850	340	1.00	8
												255	78	1950	335	1.15	4	40 T.W.	250	79	1850	350	1.15	7	245	81	1750	370	1.10	9
300												245	77	1850	365	1.30	5	80 T.W.	145	79	1800	365	1.25	8	235	80	1700	400	1.25	10
																		120 T.W.							230	80	1650	430	1.35	11

Figure A-20. Flight Operation Instruction Chart—Two 120-gallon Drop Tanks—14,600 Pounds or Less (Sheet 1 of 2)

W ADC Form 241M (11 Jun 51)

Figure A-20. Flight Operation Instruction Chart—Two 120-gallon Drop Tanks—14,600 Pounds or Less
(Sheet 2 of 2)

ALPHABETICAL INDEX

PAGE NUMBERS IN BOLDFACE DENOTE ILLUSTRATIONS

A

Acceleration Limitations	5-4, **5-5—5-7**
Accelerometer	1-42
After Landing	2-21
cold-weather procedure	9-17
After Take-off	2-15
cold-weather procedure	9-17
hot-weather and desert procedure	9-19
Ailerons	
see Flight Control System	
Air Conditioning and Pressurization	
Systems, Cockpit	4-1, **4-4, 4-6**
altimeter, cabin pressure	4-3
controls	4-2, **4-9**
controls, side air outlet	4-3
lever, air outlet selector	4-3
lever, pressure control	4-3
rheostat, air temperature control	4-2
switch, air temperature control	4-3
switch, pressure control	4-3
switch, pressure selector	4-3
normal operation	4-3
outlets, air	4-2
pressure schedule, cockpit	4-2
pressurization system emergency operation	4-5
refrigeration unit failure	4-7
regulator, air pressure	4-2
Airspeed Compressibility Correction	A-1, A-2
Airspeed Indicator	1-41
Airspeed Installation Correction	A-1
Airspeed Limitations	5-1, 5-2, 5-5
Air Start, Engine	3-3
Altimeter	1-41, **1-42**
Altimeter, Cabin Pressure	4-3
Anti-G Suit Provisions	4-34
Anti-icing System, Windshield	4-7
lever, anti-icing	4-8
lever, cabin pressure control	4-3
light, overheat warning	4-8
operation	4-8, 9-12
switch, cockpit pressure control	4-3
Approach	
ADF approach	9-9
cold-weather procedure	9-17
ground-controlled approach	9-9, 9-10, **9-10**
low-frequency range approaches	9-9
Armament	1-1, 4-22, **4-22**
also see: Bombing Equipment	
Chemical Tank Equipment	
Gunnery Equipment	
Rocket Equipment	
Sights, A-1CM and A-4 Gun-Bomb-Rocket	
Artificial Feel System	1-29
failure	3-21
Asymmetrical Store Limitations	5-4
Attitude Indicator	1-42, **1-43**

B

Battery-Starter Switch	1-17
Before Entering Airplane	
cold-weather procedure	9-15
instrument flight procedure	9-2
Before Leaving Airplane	2-21
cold-weather procedure	9-18
hot-weather and desert procedure	9-19
Before Take-off	2-10
airplane check	2-10
cold-weather procedure	9-16
engine check	2-11, 2-12
hot-weather and desert procedure	9-18
instrument flight procedure	9-2
thunderstorm flying	9-13
Block Number Designations	1-2
Bombing Equipment	4-22, **4-29**
also see Sights, A-1CM and A-4 Gun-Bomb-Rocket	
bombs:	
asymmetrical store limitations	5-4
flight with	6-16
releasing	4-31
demolition bombs	4-31
emergency release	3-23, 4-32
fragmentation bombs	4-31
controls	4-29
button, bomb-rocket release	4-29
button, bomb-rocket-tank salvo	4-30
handle, emergency jettison	4-30
switch, bomb arming	4-30
switch, demolition bomb release selector	4-30
switch, demolition bomb single-all selector	4-29
switch, fragmentation bomb selector	4-30
indicators	4-30
indicators, sight bomb release	4-30
light, fragmentation bomb indicator	4-31

X-1

INDEX
Brake System, Wheel—Electrical Power Supply System

PAGE NUMBERS IN BOLDFACE DENOTE ILLUSTRATIONS

Brake System, Wheel 1-41
    handle, parking brake 1-41
Buttons, Control
    see applicable system

C

Cabin Pressure Altimeter 4-3
Camera, Gun 4-27
Canopy 1-43
    check 2-2
    controls 1-45
        buttons, external control 1-45
        handle, alternate emergency jettison 1-45
        handle, declutch 1-45
        handle, external emergency release 1-46, **1-46**
        handle, manual operating 1-45
        release, emergency jettison 1-45
        switch, canopy 1-45
    cover, protective 4-35
    failure to eject 3-13
    operating speed 5-4
    remover, canopy 1-44
    seal 1-44
Canopy Defrosting System 4-7
    operation 4-8
Center-of-Gravity Limitations 5-6
Charts
    airspeed compressibility correction A-1, **A-2**
    climb .... A-3, A-8—A-12
    combat allowance A-3, **A-15**
    descent A-3, **A-13**
    flight operation instruction .... A-3, A-22—A-33
    fuel quantity data 1-19
    instrument markings 5-2
    landing distances A-3, **A-14**
    Mach number 6-2
    Maximum Continuous Power A-3, **A-18**
    maximum endurance A-3, **A-16**
    maximum range summary A-3, **A-20**
    operating flight limits 5-6, **5-7**
    oxygen duration table 4-17
    stall speeds 6-3
    take-off distances A-3, A-6, **A-7**
    use of A-4
Check List 4-34
Check Lists, Condensed 2-23
Checks
    airplane check, preflight 2-10
    before leaving airplane 2-21
    canopy check 2-2
    engine check, preflight 2-11
    exterior inspection 2-3
        before exterior inspection 2-2
    ground tests 2-9
        cold-weather procedure 9-16
    interior check 2-4
    oxygen system preflight 4-18, **4-18**, 4-20
    pre-traffic-pattern check 2-17
    seat check, ejection 2-2
    traffic-pattern check 2-17, **2-18**
    weight and balance 2-1
Chemical Tank Equipment **4-22**, 4-34
    asymmetrical store limitations 5-4
    button, bomb-rocket release 4-29
    handle, emergency jettison 4-30
    switch, selector 4-34
    tank emergency release 3-23
Circuit Breakers 1-24
Climb 2-16
    climb charts .... A-3, A-8—A-12
    instrument flight procedure 9-2
Cockpit .... 1-6, 1-8—1-11
    emergency entrance 3-11
    entrance 2-2, **2-2**
    smoke or fumes, elimination of 3-9
Cockpit Air Conditioning and Pressurization Systems
    see Air Conditioning and Pressurization Systems, Cockpit
Cockpit Extension (Utility) Light Control 4-16
Code Indicator Light 4-13

Code Switch and Code Selector, Master 4-13
Cold-weather Procedures 9-15
Combat Allowance A-3, **A-15**
Communication and Associated Electronic Equipment .. 4-10, **4-11**
    command set, AN/ARC-3 vhf 4-10, **4-11**
    command set, AN/ARC-33 uhf 4-10, **4-11**
    compass, AN/ARN-6 radio **4-11**, 4-12
    identification radar, AN/APX-6 .... **4-11**, 4-12
Compass, Stand-by 1-42
    switch, light 4-17
Consoles, Forward **1-25**
    rheostat, light 4-16
Controls
    see applicable system
Control Stick 1-29, **1-31**
Control Surfaces
    see Flight Control System
Covers, Protective 4-35
Crash Barrier, Engaging 3-10
Cross-wind Landing 2-19
Cross-wind Take-off 2-15

D

Danger Areas 2-7
Data Case 4-34
Defrosting System, Canopy and Windshield 4-7
    controls 4-7
        controls, side air outlet 4-3
        lever, air outlet selector 4-3
        lever, auxiliary defrost 4-8
        lever, cabin pressure control 4-3
        switch, cockpit pressure control 4-3
    operation 4-8
Deicing System, Fuel Filter 4-10
    button, deicing 4-10
    light, ice warning 4-10
Densitometer Selector Switch 1-20
Descent 2-16
    cold-weather procedure 9-17
    descent chart A-3, **A-13**
    instrument flight procedure 9-3
Desert Procedures 9-18
Dials
    see applicable system
Dimensions 1-1
Directional Indicator (Slaved) 4-21
    switch, fast slaving 4-21
Ditching 3-10
Dives 6-13
    G-overshoot 6-13
    letdown 6-13
    recovery 6-13, 6-14, 6-16
Drop Tanks
    see Fuel System, Airplane

E

Ejection 3-12, 3-14, 3-16
    also see Seat, Ejection
    failure of canopy to jettison 3-13
    failure of seat to eject 3-13
Electrical Power Supply System 1-21, **1-22**
    ac power distribution 1-21
    circuit breakers 1-24
    controls 1-24
        rheostat, generator voltage regulator 1-24
        switch, battery-starter 1-17
        switch, generator 1-24
        switch, instrument power 1-24
    dc power distribution 1-21
    failure 3-18
    fire 3-8
    generator irregularity 3-19
        failure or undervoltage 3-19
        overvoltage 3-19
    indicators 1-26
        light, generator warning 1-26
        light, instrument power warning 1-26
        lights, inverter failure warning 1-26, **1-26**

X-2

PAGE NUMBERS IN BOLDFACE DENOTE ILLUSTRATIONS

loadmeter 1-26
voltmeter 1-26
inverter failure 3-19
receptacles, external power 1-24
Electronic Equipment
   see Communication and Associated Electronic Equipment
Elevator
   see Flight Control System
Emergency Equipment 1-43
  fire detector system, engine 1-43
Emergency Fuel Control System 1-13, **1-14**
  check 2-11, 2-12, **2-12**
  switch, three-position 1-15
  switch, two-position 1-16
Emergency Hydraulic System 1-27, **1-28**
  hand-pump 1-27
  selector 1-27
Emergency Ignition Switch 1-17
Emergency Jettison Handle 4-30
Emergency Jettison Handle, Canopy Alternate ... 1-45
Emergency Jettison Release, Canopy 1-45
Emergency Lever, Speed Brake 1-37
Emergency Override System, Flight Control Manual ... 1-34
  handle, emergency override **1-35**, 1-36
Emergency Procedures 3-1
  artificial feel system failure, flight control 3-21
  bomb emergency release 4-32
  ditching 3-10
  ejection 3-12, **3-14**, 3-16
    failure of canopy to jettison 3-13
    failure of seat to eject 3-13
  electrical power system failure 3-18
    generator irregularity 3-19
      failure or undervoltage 3-19
      overvoltage 3-19
    inverter failure 3-20
  engine failure 3-1
    air start 3-3
    during flight 3-2
    during take-off 3-2
    during take-off run 3-1
    forced landing, simulated 3-5, **3-6**
    landing with engine inoperative 3-5, **3-6**
    maximum glide 3-5, **3-5**
  entrance, emergency 3-11
  external load emergency release 3-23
  fire 3-7
    electrical fire 3-8
    engine fire:
      after shutdown 3-8
      during flight 3-8
      during starting 3-7
      during take-off 3-7
  fuel system failure 3-18
  hydraulic system failure, flight control 3-20
  hydraulic system failure, utility 3-20
  landing emergencies 3-9
    any one gear up or unlocked 3-9
    barrier, engaging runway 3-10
    belly landing 3-9
    landing with flat tire 3-10
    no-flap landing 3-10
  landing gear emergency operation 3-21
    emergency lowering 3-21, **3-22**, 3-23
    emergency retraction 3-21
    in-flight operation 3-21
  oxygen system emergency operation:
    diluter-demand regulator 4-21
    pressure-demand regulator 4-19
  pressurization system emergency operation 4-5
  refrigeration unit failure 4-7
  rocket emergency release 4-34
  smoke or fumes, elimination of 3-9
  speed brake system failure 3-22
  trim failure 3-21
  wing flap emergency operation 3-23
Emergency Release Handle, Canopy External ... 1-46, **1-46**
Emergency Release Handle, Landing Gear 1-38
Emergency Toggle Lever, Oxygen Regulator 4-20
Emergency-up Button, Landing Gear 1-39

Engine 1-2, 1-12
  air intake screens 1-2
  controls 1-15
    switch, emergency fuel 1-15, 1-16
    switch, master 1-15
    throttle 1-15, **1-15**
  covers, protective 4-35
  failure 3-1
    air start 3-3
    during flight 3-2
    during take-off 3-2
    during take-off run 3-1
    forced landing, simulated 3-5, **3-6**
    landing with engine inoperative 3-5, **3-6**
    maximum glide 3-5, **3-5**
  fire 3-7
  fire detector system 1-43
  fuel control systems 1-2, **1-14**
    emergency fuel system test, maximum rpm available ... 2-12
    failure 3-18
    flow divider 1-13
    operation 7-7
    stopcock 1-13
  icing 9-11
  ignition system 1-17
    switch, emergency ignition 1-17
  indicators 1-16
    flowmeter and totalizer, fuel 1-17
    gage, exhaust temperature 1-16
    gage, fuel pressure 1-16
    gage, oil pressure 1-16
    tachometer 1-16
  limitations 5-1, **5-2**
    overspeed 5-1
    overtemperature 5-1
  operation:
    acceleration 7-1
      limitations 5-4
    compressor stall 7-3
    exhaust temperature variation 7-4
    flame-out 7-4
    ground operation 2-8
    main fuel regulator characteristics 7-1, **7-2**
    noise and roughness 7-4
    performance with air intake screens 7-5
    preflight check 2-11, **2-12**
    smoke from turbine during shutdown 7-6
    starting 2-6, **2-7**
      after starting, instrument flight procedure ... 9-2
      cold-weather procedure 9-15
      fire during starting 3-7
    stopping 2-21
      fire after shutdown 3-8
    surge 7-2
    tail-pipe segments 7-6, **7-6**
    turbine noise during shutdown 7-5
  starter-generator 1-17
    button, stop-starter 1-19
    switch, battery-starter 1-17
Entrance 2-2, **2-2**
  emergency 3-11
Exhaust Temperature Gage 1-16
Exterior Inspection 2-3
  before exterior inspection 2-2
Exterior Lighting Dimmer Switch 4-15
External Loads
  asymmetrical store limitations 5-4
  emergency release 3-23
  flight with 6-16
External Power Receptacles 1-24

F

Fire 3-7
  electrical fire 3-8
  engine fire 3-7
    light, aft fire-warning 3-7, 3-8
    light, forward fire-warning 3-7, 3-8
Fire Detector System, Engine 1-43

X-3

INDEX
Flaps, Wing—Knobs, Control

PAGE NUMBERS IN BOLDFACE DENOTE ILLUSTRATIONS

Flaps, Wing
  see Wing Flap System
Flight Characteristics 6-1
Flight Control System 1-27, **1-30**
  aileron control 6-6
  artificial feel system 1-29
    failure 3-21
  controls 1-29
    lock, flight control 1-31
    lock, rudder gust 1-31
    pedals, rudder 1-29
    stick, control 1-29, **1-31**
    switch, lateral alternate trim 1-32
    switch, longitudinal alternate trim 1-31
    switch, normal trim 1-31
    switch, rudder trim 1-31
  horizontal tail 1-29
    control 6-7
  hydraulic systems 1-32, **1-33**
    controls 1-35
      handle, emergency override 1-35, **1-36**
      switch, flight control 1-35
    failure 3-20
    ground tests 2-9
    indicators 1-36
      gage, hydraulic pressure 1-27
        switch, selector 1-27
      indicator, hydraulic fluid level 1-36
      light, alternate-on warning 1-36
    operation 7-7
    override system, manual emergency 1-34, **1-35**
  light, take-off (trim) position indicator 1-32
  rudder control 6-7
  trim failure 3-21
  trim tab control 6-7
Flight Operation Instruction Charts ....A-3, A-22—A-33
Flow Divider, Fuel 1-13
Flowmeter and Totalizer, Fuel 1-17
Forced Landing, Simulated 3-5, **3-6**
Fuel Control Systems, Engine
  see Engine
Fuel Filter Deicing System 4-10
  button, deicing 4-10
  light, ice warning 4-10
Fuel Pressure Gage 1-16
Fuel System, Airplane 1-18, 1-19
  controls 1-20
    release, drop tank 1-20
    switch, densitometer selector 1-20
    valve, drop tank pressure shutoff 1-20
  failure 3-18
  fuel quantity data **1-19**
  fuel specification **1-55**
  gage, fuel quantity 1-20
  operation 7-7
  pumps, booster 1-20
  tanks, drop 1-20, 4-22
    asymmetrical store limitations 5-4
    emergency release 3-23
    flight characteristics 6-16
    icing 9-11
    release speeds **5-8**
  valve, fuel shutoff 1-20
Fumes, Elimination of 3-9
Fuselage Light Switch 4-13, 4-15

G

Gages
  see applicable system
Generator
  see Electrical Power Supply System
Go-around 2-20, 2-21
  missed-approach 9-10
G-overshoot 6-13
Ground-controlled Approach 9-9, 9-10, **9-10**
Ground Operation, Engine 2-8
Ground Tests 2-9
  cold-weather procedure 9-16

Gunnery Equipment 4-22, 4-27
  also see Sights, A-1CM and A-4 Gun-Bomb-Rocket
  camera, gun 4-27
  controls 4-27
    control, ammunition compartment
      heat emergency shutoff 4-28
    switch, gun heater 4-28
    switch, gun safety 4-27
    trigger 4-27
    guns, firing 4-28
  light, ammunition compartment overheat warning 4-28

H

Handgrips 1-50
Handles, Control
  see applicable system
Heater, Pitot 4-9
  switch 4-9
Heavy-weight Landing 2-19
Horizontal Tail
  see Flight Control System
Horn, Landing Gear Warning 1-40
Hot-weather Procedures 9-18
Hydraulic Power Supply Systems 1-26
  flight control systems 1-32, **1-33**
  fluid specification **1-55**
  utility system 1-27, 1-28
    emergency system 1-27
      hand-pump, emergency hydraulic 1-27
      selector, emergency hydraulic 1-27
    failure 3-20
    gage, hydraulic pressure 1-27
    switch, selector 1-27
    ground tests 2-9
    operation 7-7

I

Ice and Rain 9-11
Identification Radar, AN/APX-6 ....4-11, 4-12
Ignition System 1-17
  switch, emergency ignition 1-17
  switch, engine master 1-15
Indicators
  see applicable system
Instrument Flight Procedures 9-1
Instrument Letdowns 9-3
  approach, ADF 9-9
  approaches, low-frequency range 9-9
  approach, ground-controlled 9-9, 9-10, **9-10**
  go-around, missed-approach 9-10
  penetrations, jet 9-3, **9-4**, **9-6**
  recovery, radar **9-8**, 9-10
Instrument Power Switch 1-24
Instrument Power Warning Light 1-26
Instruments 1-41
  also see applicable system
  accelerometer 1-42
  altimeter 1-41, **1-42**
  compass, stand-by 1-42
  indicator, airspeed 1-41
  indicator, attitude 1-42, **1-43**
  indicator (slaved), directional 4-21
    switch, fast slaving 4-21
  indicator, turn-and-slip 1-43
  Machmeter 1-42
  markings **5-2**
  panel 1-6, **1-7**
  rheostats, light 4-16
Interior Check 2-4
Intervalometer Control Knob, Rocket 4-33
Inverted Spins 6-5
Inverter
  see Electrical Power Supply System

K

Knobs, Control
  see applicable system

X-4

PAGE NUMBERS IN BOLDFACE DENOTE ILLUSTRATIONS

L

Landing	2-17
after landing	2-21
cold-weather procedure	9-17
cross-wind	2-19
distances	A-3, **A-14**
emergencies	3-9
any one gear up or unlocked	3-9
barrier, engaging runway	3-10
belly landing	3-9
landing with flat tire	3-10
no-flap landing	3-10
forced landing, simulated	3-5, **3-6**
heavy-weight	2-19
landing in rain	9-12
minimum-run	2-19
normal	2-17, **2-18**
wet-runway landing	2-19
with engine inoperative	3-5, **3-6**
Landing and Taxi Light Switch	4-15
Landing Gear System	1-37
button, emergency-up	1-39
emergency operation	3-21
emergency lowering	3-21, **3-22, 3-23**
emergency retraction	3-21
in-flight operation	3-21
handle	1-38
handle, emergency release	1-38
horn, warning	1-40
indicators, position	1-40
light, handle-up indicator	1-40
light, unsafe warning	1-40
lock, nose gear ground safety	1-38, **1-38**
lowering speeds, landing gear	5-1, **5-2**
operation	7-8
Landing Light Extension Speed	5-1
Landing Light Position and Selector Switches	4-15
Leading Edge, Wing	1-37
Letdown	6-13
also see Instrument Letdowns	
Level-flight Characteristics	6-8
Levers	
see applicable system	
Lighting Equipment	4-13
exterior	4-13, **4-14**
landing light lowering speed	5-1
light, code indicator	4-13
switch and code selector, master code	4-13
switch, exterior lighting dimmer	4-15
switch, fuselage light	4-13
switch, landing and taxi light	4-15
switch, landing light position	4-15
switch, landing light selector	4-15
switch, position and fuselage light selector	4-15
switch, position light dimmer	4-15
switch, position light selector	4-13
interior	4-15, **4-16**
control, cockpit extension (utility) light	4-16
rheostat, console and center pedestal light	4-16
rheostat, instrument panel auxiliary light	4-16
rheostat, instrument panel primary light	4-16
switch, stand-by compass light	4-17
Lights, Indicator	
see applicable system	
Limitations, Operating	5-1, **5-2, 5-5—5-8**
Loadmeter, Electrical	1-26
Locks	
flight control	1-29
nose gear ground safety	1-38, **1-38**
rudder gust lock	1-31
shoulder harness	1-51

M

Machmeter	1-42
Mach Number	6-1, **6-2**
Main Differences	1-3
Maneuvering Flight	6-9, **6-10—6-12**
Maneuvers, Prohibited	5-4
Map Case	4-34
Master Switch, Engine	1-15
Maximum Allowable Airspeeds	5-2, 5-4, **5-5**
Maximum Continuous Power Chart	A-3, **A-18**
Maximum Endurance	A-3, **A-16**
Maximum Glide	3-5, **3-5**
Maximum Range Summary	A-3, **A-20**
Minimum-run Landing	2-19
Minimum-run Take-off	2-14, **2-14**
Mirror, Rear-vision	4-35
Missed-approach Go-around	9-10
Mooring Equipment	4-34

N

Navigation Equipment	4-21
compass, AN/ARN-6 radio	4-11, **4-12**
compass, stand-by	1-42
indicator (slaved), directional	4-21
switch, fast slaving	4-21
instrument flight procedure	9-2
Night Flying	9-14
Nose Gear Ground Safety Lock	1-38, **1-38**
Nose Wheel Steering System	1-40
button, steering	1-41
pin, towing release	1-40

O

Oil Pressure Gage	1-16
Oil System	1-19
oil specification	1-55
On Entering Airplane	
cold-weather procedure	9-15
instrument flight procedure	9-1
Oxygen System	4-17
duration chart	**4-17**
preflight check:	
A-14 regulator	4-18, **4-18**
D-2 regulator	4-20
regulator, A-14 pressure-demand	4-17
controls	4-17, **4-19**
handle, diluter	4-17
knob, pressure-breathing	4-18
emergency operation	4-19
indicators	4-18
gage, pressure	4-18
indicator, flow	4-18
normal operation	4-19
regulator, D-2 diluter-demand	4-19
controls	4-19, **4-20**
lever, diluter	4-20
lever, emergency toggle	4-20
lever, supply	4-20
switch, warning light	4-20
emergency operation	4-21
indicators	4-20
light, warning	4-20
pressure gage and flow indicator	4-20
normal operation	4-21

P

Panels, Control	
see applicable system	
Parking Brake Handle	1-41
Pedestals, Center	1-39, **4-24, 4-25**
Penetrations, Jet	9-3, **9-4, 9-6**
Pitot Heater	4-9
switch	4-9
Position Indicator Light, Take-off (Trim)	1-32
Position Indicators, Landing Gear	1-40
Position Light Switch	4-13, **4-15**
Power Control	1-15
Preflight Checks	
airplane check	2-10
canopy check	2-2
engine check	2-11, **2-12**
exterior inspection	2-2, **2-3**

INDEX
Pressurization System, Cockpit—Voltmeter

PAGE NUMBERS IN BOLDFACE DENOTE ILLUSTRATIONS

ground tests 2-9
interior check 2-4
oxygen system 4-18, **4-18**, 4-20
seat check, ejection 2-2
weight and balance 2-1
Pressurization System, Cockpit
  see Air Conditioning and Pressurization
    Systems, Cockpit
Pre-traffic-pattern Check 2-17
Prohibited Maneuvers 5-4
Pumps, Fuel Booster 1-20

R

Radar, AN/APX-6 Identification 4-11, 4-12
Radio, AN/ARC-3 Command 4-10, **4-11**
Radio, AN/ARC-33 Command 4-10, **4-11**
Radio Compass, AN/ARN-6 .... 4-11, 4-12
  instrument flight procedure 9-2
Rear-vision Mirror 4-35
Receptacles, External Power 1-24
Regulators
  see applicable system
Remover, Canopy **1-44**
Rheostats
  see applicable system
Rocket Equipment 4-22, 4-32
  also see Sights, A-1CM and A-4 Gun-Bomb-Rocket
  controls 4-32
    button, bomb-rocket release 4-29
    button, bomb-rocket-tank salvo 4-30
    handle, emergency jettison 4-30
    knob, rocket intervalometer (projector
      release) control 4-33
    rocket setting unit (A-1CM sight) 4-26
    sight selector unit (A-4 sight) 4-26
    switch, rocket fuze (arming) 4-32
    switch, rocket jettison 4-33
    switch, rocket release selector 4-32
  rockets:
    asymmetrical store limitations 5-4
    emergency release 3-23, 4-34
    firing 4-33
    firing order **4-32**
    flight with 6-16
Rudder
  see Flight Control System

S

Safety Belt 1-51, **1-52–1-54**, 1-56
Seat, Ejection 1-46, **1-47–1-49**
  check 2-2
  controls 1-50
    handgrips 1-50
    handle, shoulder harness lock 1-51
    lever, vertical adjustment 1-50
    pins, headrest adjustment 1-50
    trigger, catapult 1-50
  safety belt 1-51, **1-52–1-54**, 1-56
Selectors
  see applicable system
Servicing Diagram **1-55**
Shoulder Harness Lock Handle 1-51
Sights, A-1CM and A-4
  Gun-Bomb-Rocket 4-22, **4-24**, **4-25**
  controls 4-23
    button, electrical caging 4-23
    button, radar target selector 4-26
    control, bomb-target wind 4-26
    control, manual ranging 4-23
    control, reticle dimmer 4-23
    knob, wing span adjustment (A-4 sight) 4-23
    lever, mechanical caging 4-23
    rheostat, radar range sweep 4-26
    rocket setting unit (A-1CM sight) 4-26
    sight selector unit (A-4 sight) 4-26
    switches, filament selector 4-23
    switch, gun safety 4-27

    wheel, wing span adjustment
      (A-1CM sight) 4-23
  indicators 4-27
    dial, sight range 4-27
    light, radar target indicator 4-27
Smoke or Fumes, Elimination of 3-9
Speed Brake System 1-37
  failure 3-22
  flight characteristics 6-7, **6-8**
  lever, emergency 1-37
  switch 1-37
Spins 6-4
  inverted spins 6-5
  nonoscillatory spins 6-5
  recovery 6-6
Stalls 6-2, **6-3**
  accelerated stalls 6-3
  practice 6-4
  recovery 6-4
  unaccelerated stalls 6-2
Stand-by Compass 1-42
  switch, light 4-17
Starter-Generator 1-17
  button, stop-starter 1-19
  switch, battery-starter 1-17
Starting Engine 2-6, **2-7**
  after starting, instrument flight procedure 9-2
  air start 3-3
  cold-weather procedure 9-15
  fire during starting 3-7
Status of Airplane 2-1
Steering System, Nose Wheel 1-40
  button, steering 1-41
  pin, towing release 1-40
Stick, Control 1-29, **1-31**
Stopcock, Engine Fuel 1-13
Stopping Engine 2-21
  fire after shutdown 3-8
Switches
  see applicable system

T

Tachometer 1-16
Take-off 2-13
  also see: After Take-off
        Before Take-off
  cold-weather procedure 9-17
  cross-wind 2-15
  distances A-3, **A-6**, **A-7**
  engine failure during take-off 3-2
  engine failure during take-off run 3-1
  engine fire during take-off 3-7
  hot-weather and desert procedure 9-19
  instrument flight procedure 9-2
  minimum-run 2-14, **2-14**
  normal 2-13
  with high outside air and runway temperatures .. 2-14
Tanks, Drop
  see Fuel System, Airplane
Taxiing 2-10
  cold-weather procedure 9-16
  instrument flight procedure 9-2
Throttle 1-15
  grip 1-15
Thunderstorm Flying 9-13
Traffic pattern Check 2-17, **2-18**
Trigger, Gun 4-27
Trigger, Seat Catapult 1-50
Trim Failure 3-21
Trim Switches 1-31, 1-32
Trim Tabs
  see Flight Control System
Turn-and-Slip Indicator 1-43

V

Valves
  see applicable system
Voltmeter 1-26

PAGE NUMBERS IN BOLDFACE DENOTE ILLUSTRATIONS

W

Warm-up and Ground Check 9-16
Warning Horn, Landing Gear 1-40
Warning Lights
   flight control hydraulic system alternate-on 1-36
   generator 1-26
   instrument power 1-26
   inverter failure 1-26, **1-26**
   landing gear unsafe 1-40
   oxygen regulator, diluter-demand 4-20
      switch 4-20
Weight 1-1
   limitations 5-6
   weight and balance 2-1
Wheel Brake System 1-41
   handle, parking brake 1-41
Windshield Defrosting and Anti-icing System
   see: Anti-icing System, Windshield
      Defrosting System, Canopy and Windshield
Wing Flap System 1-36
   emergency operation 3-23
   lever 1-36
   lowering speed, wing flap 5-1, **5-2**
Wing Icing 9-11
Wing Leading Edge 1-37
   slats, flight characteristics 6-8

Warships DVD Series

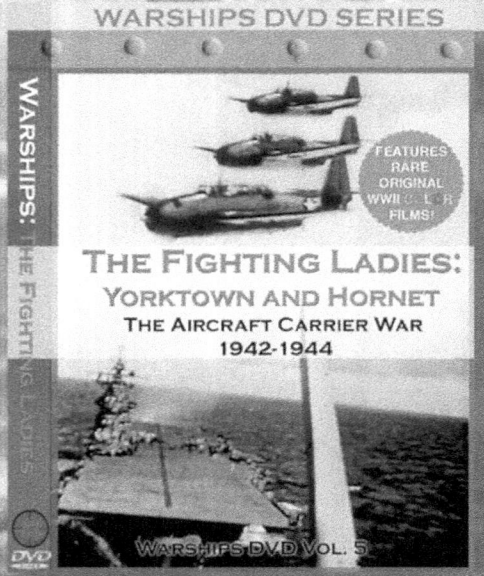

Now Available!

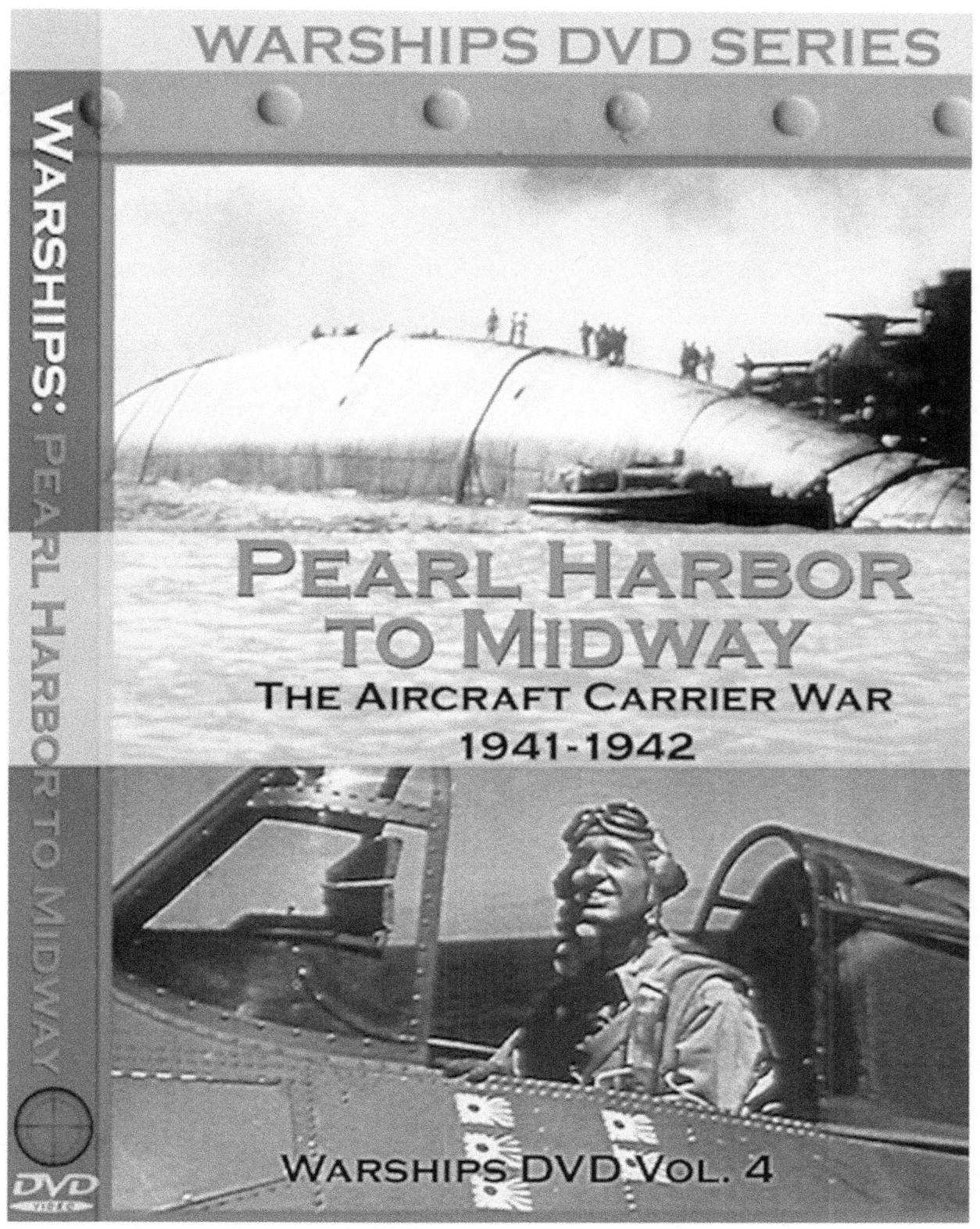

HISTORIC U.S. NAVY FILMS ON DVD!

Aircraft At War DVD Series

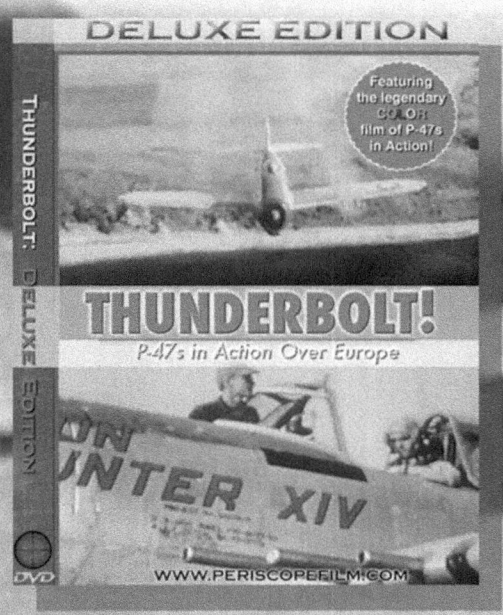
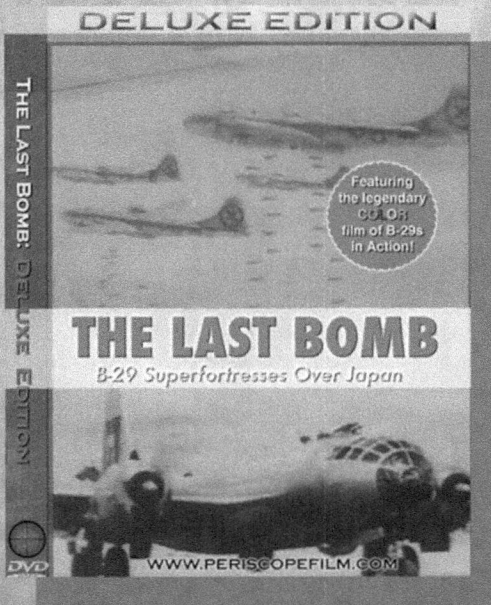
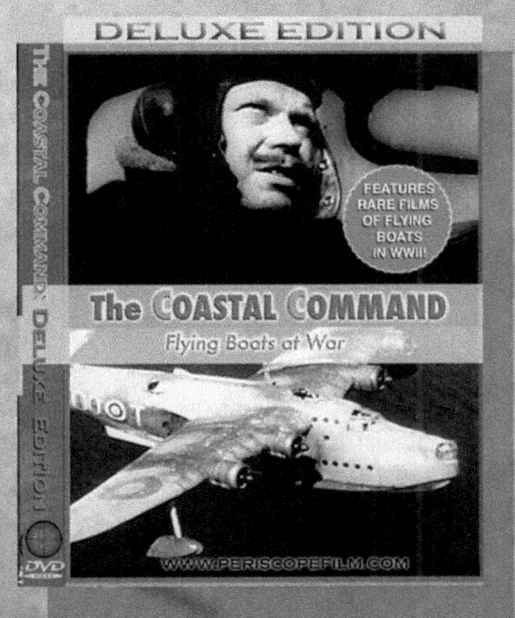

Now Available!

Epic Battles of WWII

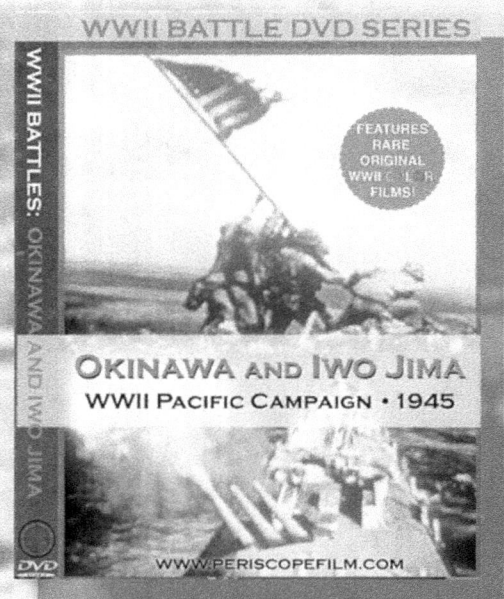

Now Available on DVD!

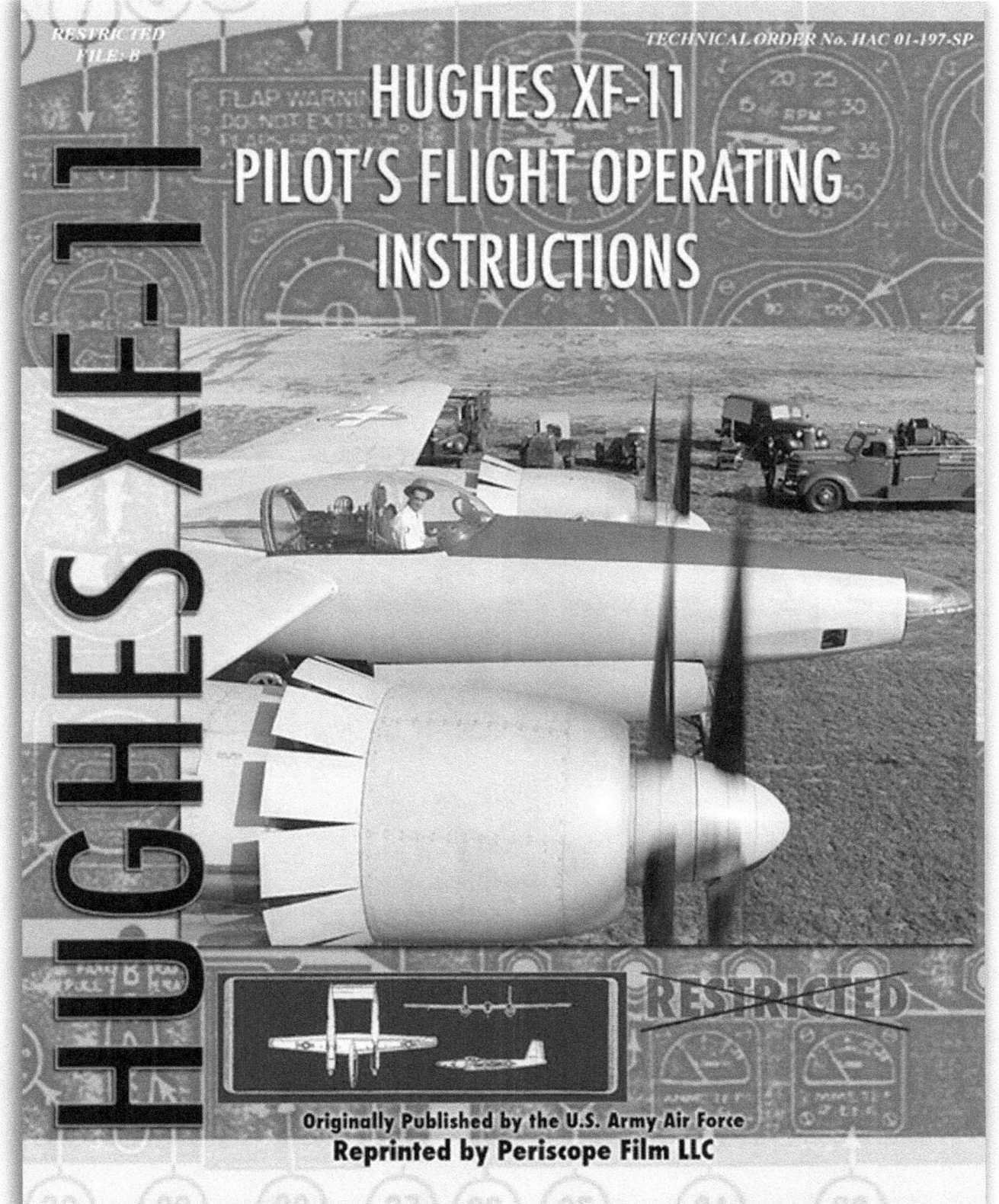

NOW AVAILABLE!

SPRUCE GOOSE
HUGHES FLYING BOAT MANUAL

~~RESTRICTED~~

Originally Published by the War Department
Reprinted by Periscope Film LLC

NOW AVAILABLE!

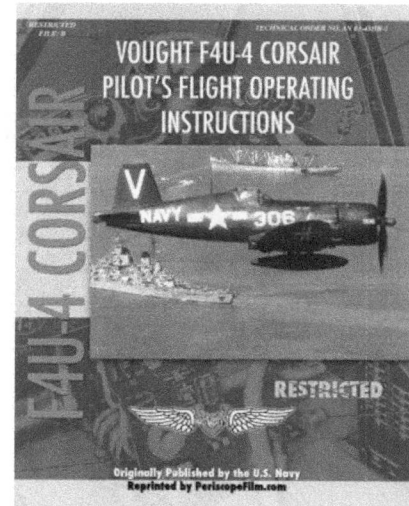
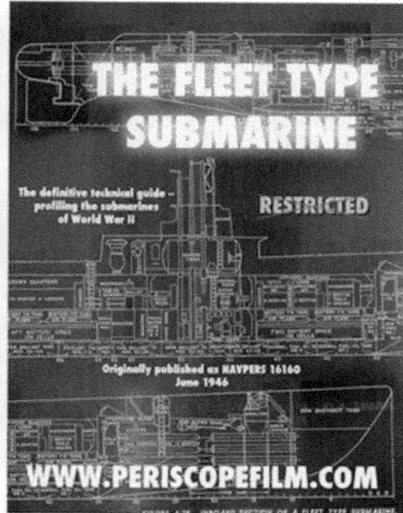
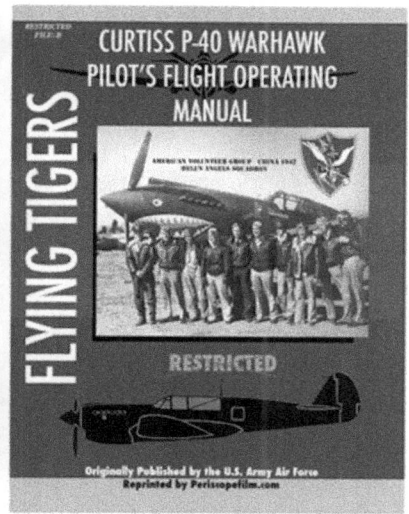

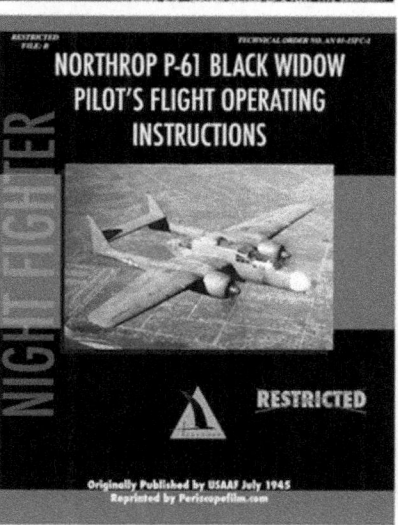

ALSO NOW AVAILABLE FROM PERISCOPEFILM.COM

©2007-2010 Periscope Film LLC
All Rights Reserved
ISBN #978-1-935700-39-5
www.PeriscopeFilm.com

www.ingramcontent.com/pod-product-compliance
Lightning Source LLC
Chambersburg PA
CBHW081832170426
43199CB00017B/2707